Second Edition

FAMILY LIFE
EDUCATION

CH6 (182)(184-186)
11 (201-223)
12(240-244--247-250)
CH5 (all)
6(184-186)
9 (172-185)
4(all)

CH1
ch2(26-35; 41-44,52, 49-52, 38-40)
CH4 (92-95)
Aperdix A+B
NCFR (30-36, 1-16, 17-23)

Second Edition

FAMILY LIFE EDUCATION

Working with Families across the Life Span

Lane H. Powell, PhD, CFLE
Texas Tech University

Dawn Cassidy, MEd, CFLE
National Council on Family Relations

with special contributions from
Carol A. Darling, PhD, CFLE
Florida State University

Nancy Gonzalez, MEd, CFLE
National Council on Family Relations

WAVELAND

PRESS, INC.

Long Grove, Illinois

For information about this book, contact:
Waveland Press, Inc.
4180 IL Route 83, Suite 101
Long Grove, IL 60047-9580
(847) 634-0081
info@waveland.com
www.waveland.com

Photo credits
Pp. 100, 201: courtesy of Lane H. Powell; pp. 171, 183, 219, 237, 241: Skjold Photographs.

Contents

PART III
CONTEXTS FOR FAMILY LIFE EDUCATION 151

Preface

Although this book is written primarily with undergraduate majors in human development and family studies in mind, it can be useful to persons in related fields of study who are preparing for careers in community education and outreach. Such careers require the preparation, presentation, and evaluation of educational programs and workshops for persons at all stages of the life span. It is imperative that practitioners have a working knowledge of how to accomplish these tasks effectively. The text is a realistic blend of theory and praxis (action with reflection) designed to encourage the type of hands-on experience needed to interact comfortably with diverse groups and a variety of topics.

In this second edition, we retain our focus on presenting family life education (FLE) as a profession with a history and an exciting future. Persons seeking certification as family life educators through the certification program of the National Council on Family Relations will find this book greatly helpful in understanding and developing competency in the area of family life education methodology. A new chapter (chapter 6) has been added to more specifically address the steps in designing family life education programs. It walks students through the process with a case study for praxis. A second new chapter, chapter 13, addresses the growing interest and impact of international family life education. Its author, Dr. Carol A. Darling, Distinguished Teaching Professor at Florida State University, reviews global trends across nations. Using a family ecosystem framework, she discusses unique educational challenges that cultural restraints can bring. A cross-continent survey ranks interest in the various content areas of family life education and professional issues, revealing some interesting similarities across continents. Dr. Darling also addresses opportunities for current and future professionals and shares ways to build student awareness and appreciation of diversity through interactive classroom exercises. Other major updates include revision of statistical demographics, using data from the 2000 census and follow-up interpretation, and new trends in parent education and professional development.

Each chapter still includes a series of questions for class discussion, research problems, activities for independent or auxiliary study, and a case-study suggestion. The case-study suggestions are indicative of a problem-based learning focus, which many educational specialists now recommend as preferable to a lecture course based on a body of content. Certainly it is preferable for a class that emphasizes praxis. When students are challenged to figure things out for themselves, they tend to retain information and strengthen their personal skills. An online teacher's guide (http://www.familylifeeducation2E.com) provides an opportunity to share innovative teaching strategies. As a teacher, we trust you also will share successful strategies through the online outlet.

In Part III we address three areas that are most highly developed in the field of FLE and that have received evaluation and certification attention: sexuality education, marriage education, and parent education. Chapter 12 suggests ways to adapt these programs (and others) to religious, work, and school settings and considers future trends. Chapter 13, Dr. Darling's contribution, adds an international focus.

We wish to express our deep appreciation to several persons who have contributed to the success of this endeavor: Genie and Preston Dyer of Baylor University for their assistance on the marriage education chapter; Nancy Gonzalez of the National Council on Family Relations for playing a major role in the revision of the chapters on professionalism, evaluation, and parenting education; Christa Treichel of Cooperative Ventures for her input on the evaluation chapter; Dana Murphy of The Caring Project and Betty Cooke of the University of Minnesota for contributing their insights to the chapter on parenting education; Neil Rowe, Don Rosso, and Waveland Press for their enthusiastic interest in publishing a second edition; and of course our patient and encouraging spouses, Bob Powell and Tom Cassidy. We are also indebted to Margaret Arcus, Jay D. Schvaneveldt, and Joel Moss, editors of a seminal book in our field, the *Handbook of Family Life Education*, Volumes 1 and 2 (1993). Their foundational work provided a starting point for our efforts, and we are eternally grateful.

PART I

THE FIELD OF FAMILY LIFE EDUCATION

Why and What Is Family Life Education?

In a city anywhere in America, a group of couples gathers at the neighborhood library for an evening of couple enrichment. Some are newlyweds, some are engaged or seriously dating, others have been married 20 years or more, a few are in second marriages. All are there with the same goal: to intentionally focus on their own couple growth and understanding of their partner. "Making good marriages better, beginning with our own" is the motto of this particular program design. A facilitator couple shares with the group about how they are learning to handle conflict in their relationship and then poses a few questions for the couples to discuss, first as individuals and then with each other, before returning to the group. Afterwards, the couples go to dinner together, always raising a toast "to marriage." The couples look forward to these monthly meetings where they can give attention to each other rather than jobs, children, deadlines, and all the usual demands on their time and energy.

Down the street, a grandparents' support group is meeting at the New Hope Community Church. A nursery is provided, because some of these elders are raising a second generation of children: a task that has its own unique set of stressors. Others are there because of the recent loss of a spouse—or a child or grandchild—or just as a way to deal with loneliness. The sharing often centers around ways of coping with life crises for which they have no prior experience. Their leader, a grandmother herself, is a family resource coordinator at a church association office in the area. She hopes to develop and train support-group leaders in many neighborhoods around the city. Every week she meets with the group. Although she brings some handouts and suggestions of available resources, she also learns from her group. She opens the floor for sharing, then listens with a practiced ear, responding to every person's concerns and opinions with empathy and appreciation. She takes mental notes and transfers them to paper after the meetings. This proves helpful when training other group leaders and perhaps for writing a manual or a book that would help others to cope.

Not far away, another group meets for study and support, sponsored by the family case managers of Family and Child Services. These are foster parent applicants who responded to a plea for more temporary placement homes for children and teens. They are meeting with the case manager–group leader for the first time. Their faces register their anxiety: What if the child doesn't warm up to us? How do you keep them from running away? What if a teen turns violent?

The group leader has anticipated their questions. He has brought some seasoned foster parents to share their own experiences. "It's not an easy job," they all seem to say, "but the agency will help you, and it's amazing what persistent caring can accomplish." The group leader has planned a six-session orientation for the potential new caregivers. He outlines the plan tonight. The anxiety visibly lessens. He knows that the couples will form a support group of their own by the time the six sessions end. This process involves some minilectures, but the bulk of the time involves doing exercises, sharing case studies, and role-playing. The couples will enter the process with low-level sharing and involvement and gradually increase the interaction level. It will keep them busy, awake, and growing in confidence.

Family . . . life . . . education . . . three words that encompass a multitude of images and expectations. The situations described previously list only a few. All call for a combination of skills and expectations of the leader-educator and of the group. How do we define family life education in a way that encompasses its multifaceted contexts? How do we even define "family"? And what value does family life education have in supporting and educating individuals for family living? How do you, as a professional or future professional who will work with families, develop the skills to respond effectively to so many demands?

This book was written to address the many issues involved in the educational preparation of family life educators, using an approach that promotes the interactive teaching style that is typical of the family life education model. Chapter 1 provides an overview of the definitions, history, and future directions of family life education, setting the context and developing an understanding and appreciation for the profession. Chapter 2 continues the discussion of the family life educator as a professional: what it means and how one gains certification and recognition. Chapters 3 through 7 address the practice of family life education, from theory models and types of methodology to assessing the needs of the audience, understanding group dynamics, and the actual design, implementation, and evaluation of programs. Chapters 8 through 11 become more specific and address three areas of family life education that are the most developed and the most often presented within the profession: sexuality education, premarital and marriage education, and parent education. Chapter 12 discusses how to adapt programs for the workplace, religious settings, and schools. Chapter 13, written by Dr. Carol Darling, discusses the growing field of international family life education. This is truly designed to be a practitioner's handbook. So when you get that call: "Will you help us start a group for . . . ?", you'll be ready!

THE DEFINITION DEBATE

The problem of coming to general agreement on a definition of family life education is fully examined in the *Handbook of Family Life Education*, volume 1 (Arcus, Schvaneveldt & Moss, 1993). Lee (1963) and Kerckhoff (1964) observed that because family life educators differed on what they meant by family life education, there was general confusion and a retarding of growth in the field. Prominent family specialists in the 1970s and 1980s (e.g., Arcus, 1986; Darling, 1987; Fisher & Kerckhoff, 1981; Somerville, 1971) agreed. Yet a definition that is broad enough to gain consensus is also criticized as "too vague, ambiguous, and idealistic" (Arcus et al., 1993, p. 2). For example, in 1964, 90 family specialists representing public education and community and national agencies were asked to comment on the following definition by Avery and Lee (1964):

> Family life education involves any and all school experiences deliberately and consciously used by teachers in helping to develop the personalities of students to their fullest capacities as present and future family members—those capacities which equip the individual to solve most constructively the problems unique to his family role. (p. 27)

Although response to the definition was largely positive—some 75% of the specialists accepted this as a working definition—the reader may have some immediate questions: Is the definition too broad and too vague? Is it too limited in its assumption about families or where family life education takes place? Is it too complex? Arcus et al. (1993) concluded that "in spite of the general agreement among these early family life educators on a working definition, little real consensus was apparently achieved, as family life educators continued their efforts to refine and redefine the term" (p. 4). Box 1.1 summarizes the attempts at further definition.

More success at consensus has been achieved by moving beyond a concise definition to a descriptive discussion of the aims and concepts (i.e., "analytical inquiry") that comprise family life education. Arcus et al. (1993) reduced the aims, or rationale, for family life education to three primary ones: (1) dealing with problems that impinge upon families, (2) preventing problems, and (3) developing potentials for individuals and families. In other words, family life education is a process designed to "strengthen and enrich individual and family well-being" (p. 12). Such a process can incorporate a broad range of topics, from child development and parenting skills to adjusting to divorce or retirement as well as learning communication and time, money, or conflict management skills.

To develop an "operational definition" of family life education, Thomas and Arcus (1992) asked what features something must have in order to be called family life education. After extensive review of the literature and of program designs, Arcus et al. (1993) concluded that family life education generally:

- is relevant to individuals and families across the life span
- is based on the needs of individuals and families
- is multidisciplinary in area of study and multiprofessional in practice
- is offered in many different settings
- is an educational rather than a therapeutic approach
- presents and respects differing family values
- requires qualified educators who are cognizant of the goals of family life education

Although not all of these principles have been fully analyzed or examined from a theoretical perspective, they do provide a foundation for the discipline of family life education that supports the framework for life-span family life education that was developed by the National Council on Family Relations in 1984 and revised in 1997. The framework looks at three major dimensions of family life education: age, topic area, and content. The National Council on Family Relations has developed the framework in tabular poster form and has transparencies for use in the classroom. Also illustrated in the framework poster is the inclusive perspective of the educator, which should be multicultural, gender-fair, and aware of special needs. Appendix A presents the whole framework in age categories.

For example, within the "childhood" age category, the topic area of human sexuality includes content that addresses physical and sexual development, body privacy and protection against sexual abuse, uniqueness of each person, similarities and differences in individual sexual development, aspects of human repro-

Box 1.1　Emerging Definitions of Family Life Education, 1962–1989

Date	Definition and Author
1962, 1963, and 1964	"Family life education involves any and all school experiences deliberately and consciously used by teachers in helping to develop the personalities of students to their fullest capacities as present and future family members—those capacities which equip the individual to solve most constructively the problems unique to his family role" (Avery, 1962, p. 28; Avery & Lee, 1964, p. 27; Lee, 1963, p. 106).
1964	"Family life education included facts, attitudes, and skills related to dating, marriage, and parenthood. . . . Throughout the concept of family life education is woven the idea of relationships—parent-child, husband-wife, boy-girl, and so on" (Kerckhoff, 1964, p. 883).
1967	"Family life education is the study of the behavior of people as family members . . . to broaden the student's understanding of the alternatives from which he can choose in his functioning as a family member in a changing society which brings new responsibilities and opportunities in spousal, parental, filial, sibling, and grandparental roles" (Somerville, 1967, p. 375).
1968	"It is a program of learning experiences planned and guided to develop the potentials of individuals in their present and future roles as family members. Its central concept is that of relationships through which personality develops, about which individuals make decisions, to which they are committed, and in which they gain convictions of self worth" (Smith, 1968, p. 55).
1968	"To help individuals and families learn what is known about human growth, development, and behavior throughout the life cycle is the main purpose of family life education. Learning experiences are provided to develop the potentials of individuals in their present and future family roles. The central concept is that of relationships through which personality develops, about which individuals make decisions, to which they are committed, and in which they develop self-esteem" (National Commission on Family Life Education, 1968, p. 211).
1969	"Family life education . . . deals with people in groups primarily on a cognitive and information exchange level, around issues and problems of family life . . . [and] the cognitive components of behavioral and emotional functioning. Its techniques involve discussions and didactic teaching around ideas, values, and behavioral patterns of the family as a social system and the consequences of these on individual functioning, as well as more behavioristic material concerning interpersonal functioning within the family unit" (Stern, 1969, p. 40).
1971	". . . any activity by any group aimed at imparting information concerning family relationships and providing the opportunity for people to approach their present and future family relationships with greater understanding" (Vanier Institute of the Family, 1971, p. i).
1973	"Programs of family-life education that will help individuals to prove [sic] their understanding of and capacity for forming and maintaining effective human interrelationships . . . [it] has come to center about the many interactions between individuals and within the family, and the characteristics in individuals that influence the quality of interpersonal relationships" (Kirkendall, 1973, p. 696).

1973   ". . . human education in the broadest sense, the essence being human relations . . . concerned with one's total being: physical, mental, and emotional" (Whatley, 1973, p. 193).

1974   "Family life education is the study of individual roles and interpersonal relationships, family patterns and alternative life styles, emotional needs of individuals at all ages, and the physiological, psychological and sociological aspects of sexuality" (Herold, Kopf, & deCarlo, 1974, p. 365).

1975   ". . . an educational program geared to enrich family life and help the individual better understand himself in relation to others" (Levin, 1975, p. 344).

1976   "Family life education promotes the development, coordination and integration of family development resources to individual family units in order to improve family life" (Cromwell & Thomas, 1976, p. 15).

1984   ". . . instruction to develop an understanding of physical, mental, emotional, social, economic, and psychological aspects of interpersonal relationships . . . between persons of varying ages" (Sheek, 1984, p. 1).

1985   "Family life education . . . builds on the strengths of individuals to extend their knowledge of personality development, interpersonal relations, and the influence of environmental factors on behaviors" (Barozzi & Engel, 1985, p. 6).

1985   ". . . as the professional process by which information is offered to individuals of all ages, about various life issues, through the use of the small group setting" (Gross, 1985, p. 6).

1987   ". . . concerned with preserving and improving the quality of human life by the study of individuals and families as they interact with the resources in their multifaceted environments" (Darling, 1987, p. 818).

1989   "Family life education . . . is devoted to enabling adults to increase the effectiveness of their skills in daily living, that is, in relating to others, in coping with life events, and in realizing personal potential" (Tennant, 1989, p. 127).

From Arcus, M. E., Schvaneveldt, J. D., & Moss, J. J. (1993). The nature of family life education. In M. E. Arcus, J. D. Schvaneveldt, & J. J. Moss (Eds.), *Handbook of family life education* (Vol. 1, pp. 5–6). Copyright 1993 by Sage Publications. Reprinted by permission of Sage Publications.

duction (prenatal development, birth, puberty), children's perceptions about sexuality, and social and environmental conditions affecting sexuality. It is easy to see how personal values could also affect content and receptivity to family life education. Certainly the field is not without its points of controversy! This further underscores the need for educators to be carefully chosen, well trained, and informed about the history and future directions of family life education.

THE HISTORY OF FAMILY LIFE EDUCATION

The task of passing on education in family living to the next generation has been part of the human experience since life began. But how and by whom it is done have varied among family groups, tribes, and cultures. It has also changed drastically over time and is still evolving. But at the beginning of the twenty-first century, one thing is agreed upon by all: The family—in all its different forms and circumstances—needs support and education. This is not such a new idea.

Early Concerns

As early as the fourth century BC, the Greek philosopher Aristotle listed among his educational purposes "the education of parents for raising their children" (Dickinson, 1950, p. 5). The famous educator Horace Mann (1796–1859) echoed that observation, calling for "such education as qualifies for the fulfillment of parental duties" (Dickinson, 1950, p. 5). Philosopher Herbert Spencer (1820–1903) listed among his five types of activities that constitute human life those activities involved in the rearing and discipline of children. Spencer urged educators to include courses in public school curricula that would "develop efficiency" in these activities. Yet he observed that formal education was largely ignoring this universal task (Dickinson, 1950). Why was this so?

It is easy to understand how formal education for family living was bypassed in the early years of U.S. history. Pioneer life was hard, and children's lives were often short and tragic. At a survival level, the tasks needed for daily living have always taken precedence over the finer subtleties of excellence in parenting and family life. Youcha (1995) reports that during the seventeenth century, one child in 10 died before his or her first birthday. Today, the infant mortality ratio is less than one in 100 overall (although it is still drastically higher among disadvantaged groups and in developing nations). Recollections from early settlers and Native Americans illustrate the fragility and harsh demands of family life, as well as the enmity that existed between groups who saw their ways of life threatened by one another. The Reverend John Williams (1707) described an Indian attack on a settlement in Deerfield, Massachusetts:

> On the twenty-ninth of February, 1703, not long before the break of day, the enemy came in like a flood upon us. . . . They came to my house in the beginning of the onset, and by their violent endeavors to break open door and windows, with axes and hatchets, awaked me out of sleep. . . . I cannot relate the distressing care I had for my dear wife, who had lain-in but a few weeks before, and for my poor children, family, and Christian neighbors. . . . Some (of the attackers) were so cruel and barbarous as to take and carry to the door two of my children and murder them, as also a Negro woman. (p. 9)

During the forced march of the captive settlers, some persons who could not keep up were killed by the attackers, including Williams's wife. Yet apparently many settlers were spared and eventually returned to their homes.

Life among Indian tribes and settlers on the western frontier also left little time to ponder parenting and life-management skills. Pretty Shield, a Crow Indian, recalled the expectations of the women in her tribe during the late 1800s:

> We women had our children to care for, meat to cook and to dry, robes to dress, skins to tan, clothes, lodges and moccasins to make. Besides these things we not only pitched the lodges, but took them down and packed the horses and the travois when we moved camp, yes, and we gathered the wood for our fires too. We were busy, especially when we were going to move. (As cited in Bartley & Loxton, 1991, p. 7)

The pioneer settler also had her hands full. Mathilda Wagner, a Texas pioneer, recounted a typical day:

> This was a little of my day: When you first get up in the morning, before day-break, you start your fire . . . and put your coffee on. Then, just as it is getting light over the hills, you go after the calves. When you bring back the calves, you milk the cows; then bring the calves to their mother cows. Leaving them for a while, you fix breakfast, which is a big meal. After breakfast, at a time when people are getting up in the cities nowadays, you skim the milk and make the butter, feed the dogs, cats and the hogs . . . and turn the calves in their pasture and the cows in theirs. When the butter is made and the dishes washed, the house spic and span, you go to help in the fields. The woman leaves the little baby at the edge of the field with a quilt put above it so the sun won't harm it. When the baby cries the woman leaves the hoe or the plow and goes to tend it or nurse it. Then she goes back to the plow or her work in the field. There was usually a little baby or several small children at a time. When the sun is in the middle of the sky it is time for dinner. The woman leaves for the house and prepares the food. After eating, the men might lay down for a little while to rest, but there is no rest for the women. There is always work to be done. In the afternoon there may be more work in the fields, or baking, candle making, soap-making, sewing, mending, any of the hundred pressing tasks, and then the calves must again be rounded up and brought home, as the shadows fall the cows milked, the chickens fed, always something, early and late. (As cited in Bartley & Loxton, 1991, p. 24)

Large families were the norm in the days when working the farm called for many hands and before birth-control devices were available and legal. Rebecca Felton (1919) recalled life for her grandmother in rural Georgia:

> When my grandmother's brood of eleven circled around the big open fireplace in the evening, knitting work in hand, she understood without doubt, that she must rise early and work late, start before daylight and endure until after dark to put clothes on them and keep them with changes and well-fed for their health's sake. (p. 41)

The inhumane conditions endured by slave families of the eighteenth and nineteenth centuries are recorded in detail by Youcha (1995). Although conditions varied widely for slave families depending on the size of the plantation and the temperament of the owners, parenting was always an exhausting extra task for the mother who spent all her daylight hours working in the fields. One mother recalled:

> My master would make me leave my child before day to go to the canefield; and he would not allow me to come back till ten o'clock in the morning to nurse my child. When I did go I could hear my poor child crying long before I got to it. And la, me! My poor child would be so hungry! Sometimes I would have to walk more than a mile to get my child, and when I did get there I would be so tired I'd fall asleep while my baby was sucking. (Sterling, 1984, as cited in Youcha, 1995, p. 52)

Children past infancy were usually cared for in large groups, "watched over" by elderly slaves and older children who were not big enough to use a hoe or pick crops. Some spent their entire young lives in this communal living setting, rarely seeing their parents. While no account is typical, Jennie Webb's story of her childhood has elements that appear again and again:

> "De fus things I recollect is living in a slave cabin back of o'marse's big house along wid forty or fifty other slaves. All my childhood life I can never remember seeing my pa or ma gwine to wuk or coming in from wuk in de day light as dey went to de fiel's fo'day an' wuked 'till after dark." Jennie was born someplace between the fields and the cabin as her mother returned from a regular workday. When she was old enough to help, Jennie looked after the younger children, keeping them quiet and getting them to go to sleep. She also helped feed them from the large wooden bowls that held all the food. She and the other bigger children scooped the food out with their hands. The bowls were never washed, and "after we got through eatin' in 'em de flys swarmed over 'em and de dogs licked 'um an' day sho' did smell bad." Finally, the big children virtually stopped eating and "we began to git skinny." One day the master stopped by, saw Jennie hand-feeding a toddler, and asked why she wasn't eating herself. She told him. He scolded the cook (who was Jennie's aunt) with "Adeline, how do you think I can raise de little niggers an' you feedin 'em lak dis?" And after that "we wuz fed right." (Rawick, 1972, as cited in Youcha, 1995, p. 51)

Needless to say, many women and babies died under such harsh conditions. Such intolerable conditions were made somewhat bearable because of a strong *fictive kin* support network of other slave families on larger plantations. This was especially important because many fathers were sold and permanently separated from their families.

Family Education in Nineteenth-Century America

Not all white families of the nineteenth century were wealthy slave owners with servants to help in the house and with the children. Actually, only a very few were. Many more families lived backbreaking existences of demanding work and poverty. It was concern for the physical and mental health of the many women who were not able to bear up under the demands of large families and unending tasks that caused Catherine Beecher to write *A Treatise on Domestic Economy* in 1842. In the preface to the third edition (1858), she stated her concern:

> The number of young women whose health is crushed, ere the first few years of married life are past, would seem incredible to one who has not investigated this subject, and it would be vain to attempt to depict the sorrow, discouragement, and distress experienced in most families where the wife and mother is a perpetual invalid. (p. 5)

The nineteenth century also saw a wave of immigrants arriving in the "promised land," who supplied factories with cheap labor. Youcha (1995) described the life of women living in tenements in the cities:

> Women in the tenements who tried to maintain any semblance of order and cleanliness often had to cart water five flights up. Privies were in the backyards. There was no "outside" as there had been in the small European villages from which most of them had come. Here, all life—birth, eating, sleeping,

dying—took place in three rooms into which were crammed families and boarders and relatives. The only "outside" was the street, or the air space between buildings over which laboriously hand-washed clothes could be hung on lines like flags of defiance against the dehumanizing conditions. (p. 122)

While the poor struggled with basic survival for their families, middle- and upper-class families lived an existence in stark contrast. The new and popular ladies' magazines pictured the ideal home as a refuge for the family. Here the tired husband relaxed from the struggles of the wage-earning day and happy children played under the benevolent eye of a loving mother. Home was no longer the center of work for the whole family, as it had been in colonial days, and motherhood was considered the purpose of life for women. "Of course, some women were beginning to question their confinement to a golden cage and to stand up for women's rights. A small number entered the professions and were economically independent" (Youcha, 1995, p. 123).

Jane Addams (1860–1935) was such a young woman. Born to affluence, she struggled with physical and emotional distress until she discovered a valuable purpose for her life: bettering the lives of poor families by living among them and offering parent education and child-care services. Centered around Hull House in Chicago, Illinois, Addams developed a model of family intervention and education that came to be known as the settlement house model. It was—and is—one of the most successful to be found:

Addams envisioned the settlement as serving two purposes: It would help the poor "Germans and Bohemians and Italians and Poles and Russians and Greeks in Chicago, vainly trying to adjust their peasant habits to the life of a large city," while at the same time giving privileged young women a purpose and a place. (Youcha, 1995, p. 138)

As the women of Hull House cared for the children of desperate mothers who were widowed or abandoned by their husbands and had to work 10- to 12-hour days for pennies, they practiced parent education as well. Using the child as the "bridge" for education, they introduced new habits of hygiene and medical care, new foods and activities. The children's improved health and spirits then demonstrated to their parents the advisability of the education. The parents asked for recipes and explanations of what the teachers did. The teachers asked for daily reports on each child's activities at home, including diet, bedtime, and bowel movements. This interchange called attention to the importance of such factors and routines in children's lives, and the parents made adjustments to carry them out. Weekly mothers' meetings that included instruction on making children's clothes and preparing American foods were also held. Often the meetings were the mothers' only social outlet in a life of burdened toil. They were eagerly attended. Addams noted, "Through this medicine, the faces of the mothers have been noticeably softened" (as cited in Youcha, 1995, p. 145).

Ironically, Addams's highly successful model of family life education, which included home visits, interactive learning, and individualized group learning goals, has been a victim of what Youcha (1995) calls "national amnesia." Addams's programs and her life have been "relegated to the historical dustbin in which this country stores its forgotten past" (p. 140).

Another issue that has been addressed, then ignored, then addressed again for more than 150 years is whether family life education is worthy or appropriate for academic study. Quoting a well-known educator of the day, George B. Emmerson, Catherine Beecher (1858) wrote in her nineteenth-century text:

> It may be objected that such things cannot be taught by books. Why not? Why may not the structure of the human body and the laws of health deduced therefrom, be as well taught as the laws of natural philosophy? Why are not the application of these laws to the management of infants and young children as important . . . as the application of the rules of arithmetic to the extraction of the cube root? (p. 7)

In 1872, the Massachusetts legislature responded affirmatively to that question and became the first state to recognize and support family life education in a public school setting by passing a statute to legalize domestic science for educating young women (Quigley, 1974). Other states soon followed suit, and between 1875 and 1890, domestic science and industrial education courses in public schools proliferated nationwide. In 1884, the first college program to meld subject matter and teaching methodology was offered at Columbia University. By 1895, 16 colleges were offering courses in home economics (East, 1980). Their subject matter and focus varied widely, but recognition of the importance of training for family living skills was certainly increasing. Male as well as female scholars promoted the concern for home and family education as the home economics movement gained credibility. When the New York Board of Regents decided to include household science on college entrance exams, Ellen Richards was invited to construct the questions. Richards, who held degrees in chemistry from Vassar College and the Massachusetts Institute of Technology, was interested in household management and the quality of family life (Quigley, 1974). In 1898, Richards was invited to speak at a conference in Lake Placid, New York, on the topic of applying scientific principles to management of the home.

Nine annual conferences at Lake Placid were instrumental in making the last years of the nineteenth century a time of clarification on expanded views of education for family, home, and household management orientations. "Home economics" was given formal recognition as the title of education for home and family life in the public school system (McConnell, 1970).

The Rise of Professional Organizations

Another outgrowth of the conferences was the official formation of the American Home Economics Association (AHEA) on January 1, 1909, with 830 charter members: 765 women and 65 men. Its stated purpose was "the improvement of life conditions in the home, the institutional household, and the community" (Baldwin, 1949, p. 2). The group started a journal publication the same year, with Benjamin Andrews of Columbia's Teachers College as editor (Parker, 1980). The first White House Conference on Child Welfare was also held in 1909 and resulted in a 1914 publication on infant care for parents (Bridgeman, 1930).

The two decades that followed (1910–1930) were a time of great support and study of the American family. In 1914, the Cooperative Extension Service was established at land-grant universities in each state. Included in their responsibilities was the charge to "aid in diffusing . . . useful and practical information in subjects relating to . . home" (Rasmussen, 1989, p. 153). In the first year, it was reported that home economists visited 5,500 homes and trained 6,000 women to lead in educating others (Rasmussen, 1989).

Research on child development and family organization became a strong interest of sociologists and social psychologists. The first Child Welfare Research Center was established at the University of Iowa in 1917, and other centers, including the Merrill Palmer Institute, rapidly followed at several major universities (Frank, 1962). Parent education became a national interest during the 1920s. The National Congress of Parents and Teachers, organized during this decade, boasted more than 500 study groups comprising both fathers and mothers by 1929. All told, more than 75 major organizations were conducting parent education programs at this time. Many were supported with government grants, which then were seriously curtailed in the 1930s. The reason? The increasing instability of marriages made some professionals question if money spent on parent education was worth the effort when families appeared to be crumbling (Brim, 1959). A curious logic, but perhaps understandable in the years of a depressed economy and the resulting stress on families. Ernest Burgess, who developed the first documented course on the family at the University of Chicago in 1917, described the crisis in contemporary families in a 1926 journal article:

> In a stable, homogeneous society, ideas of family life and the roles of its different members are relatively fixed and constant. In a changing society composed of heterogeneous elements, familiar attitudes are almost inevitably in a state of flux. Instead of a common pattern of family life entrenched in tradition and crushing out all impulse to variation by the sheer weight of universal conformity, our American society presents what at first sight seems to be a chaotic conglomeration of every conceivable pattern of family organization and disorganization, from the patriarchal kinship groups of our Southern Mountain highlands to the free unions of our Greenwich Villages. Hardly a day passes but the public is shocked and outraged by some new form of wild and reckless behavior, particularly of youth in revolt no longer regulated by customary controls. (p. 5)

Burgess was not a pessimist, however, and he challenged the gloomy prediction that the family was disintegrating into chaotic ruin:

> But these random and aimless variations away from the basic pattern of family life are not, as some believe, an indication of the future of family life and sexual relationships. They are only the symptoms in the present, as in similar times in the past, that society is undergoing change. When an equilibrium is re-established a new pattern of family life will emerge, better adapted to the new situation, but only a different variety of the old familiar pattern of personal relationships in the family. (p. 6)

One professional response to the growing family crisis brought together representatives from the American Home Economics Association, the American Social Hygiene Association, the Teachers College of Columbia, and other professionals from the fields of sociology and psychology for the Conference on Education for Marriage and Family Social Relations in 1934. Their concern for collaboration among professionals who study the family resulted in the organization of the National Conference on Family Relations, renamed the National Council on Family Relations in 1938 (NCFR; Kerckhoff, 1964). A combined interest in theory, research, and practice has allowed NCFR to develop a membership base among academicians and practitioners in several disciplines related to family studies—primarily human development, marriage and family therapy, family sociology, and developmental psychology. NCFR has also spearheaded the development of standards and certification for family life educators. The process for approval as a Certified Family Life Educator (CFLE) reviews a practitioner's academic preparation, work experience, and continuing education. Most recently, NCFR has established a program certification process that allows graduates of approved academic programs to participate in an expedited review for provisional CFLE approval.

Canada has also seen great activity in the area of family life education in the last 40 years. In 1964, the first Canadian Conference on the Family brought together leaders in the family area (Gross, 1993). Out of the conference was born a permanent organization, the Vanier Institute of the Family, in order to "encourage research and study in family life as well as serve as a clearing house for information" (Gross, 1993, p. 10). The Vanier Institute also recognized the importance of high qualifications and standards for educators. In 1970, they issued a statement emphasizing that more than academic training was needed among family life educators. The "quality of mind and spirit" was seen as equally important. This concept was further defined as depth of perception, personal integrity, flexibility in teaching methods, sensitive awareness to the human condition, and commitment to growth, both intellectually and emotionally, as a person and a professional (Gross, 1993).

Despite getting a later start than the United States in developing the profession, Canada has moved rapidly to incorporate family studies in a number of colleges and universities and to develop a professional certification program. In 1993, the Canadian Certified Family Educator (CCFE) was established. The National Committee of Family Service of Canada is working to further consolidate family life educators in the country by publishing a newsletter, *Putting Families First*, particularly for the educator. Canadian family life educator Pauline Gross observes:

> Clearly the significance of Family Life Education and its role in prevention have gained acceptance and recognition. More and more families turn to our programs for help in addressing their current needs and interests, solving their problems, supporting their aspirations, and enriching the quality of their lives. (p. 15)

Increased Interest in Family Life Education

Ninety percent of all research and publication about family sociology and related issues has been written since 1940 (Mogey, as cited in Howard, 1981, pp. viii–ix). The first textbook for use in high school and college family living courses was written in 1945 by Evelyn Mills Duvall, executive secretary of NCFR, and

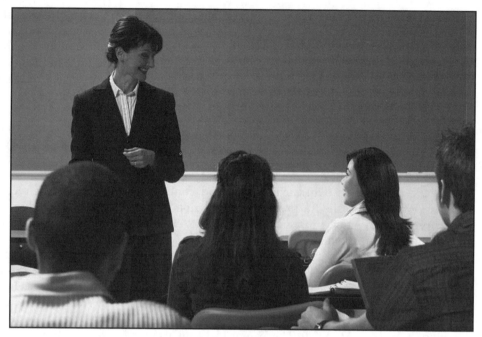

In recent years, family life education has focused more attention on collaboration, definition, academic research and theory, leader training, and certification.

Reuben Hill, a family sociologist at the University of Minnesota. Entitled *When You Marry*, the book had a very readable style, with many examples and cartoon illustrations. Because it was written at the end of World War II, it particularly addressed the problems of war brides' adjustment to couple living after the war (Duvall & Hill, 1945). The book was expanded in 1950 to respond to some 25,000 questions asked by student readers of the first text and was published as *Family Living* (Duvall, 1950).

> Because of home economics' ties to public education delivery systems, Duvall's book helped set the stage for home economics to replace sociology as the preponderant discipline in family life education. Home economics' position of dominance was enhanced nationally through the publication of specific materials related to family life education and enhanced internationally as home economists, supported by such government programs as the Marshall Plan, established family life education programs nationwide. (Lewis-Rowley et al., 1993, p. 39)

The American Home Economics Association has remained a strong force in public school education for family life skills. However, as family roles and responsibilities changed drastically during the last half of the twentieth century, public concern and undergraduate student interest have shifted away from a generalist approach that taught traditional homemaking skills (clothing construction, food preparation), as well as family living (Schultz, 1994). In 1994, members of the national organization voted to change their name to the American Association of Family and Consumer Sciences (AAFCS) in order to more accurately reflect the new emphases of the discipline. Many public schools, under state-legislated mandates to add more "academic" course requirements for their graduates, have squeezed out vocational education programs, which often included the home economics curriculum. Many college and university home economics programs have also been phased out because of low enrollment of majors. At the same time, interest in the area of human development and family studies (HDFS) has expanded rapidly. Students see the HDFS major as a good foundation from which to launch careers in marriage and family counseling, family ministry, social work, and child life and early childhood education. All of these careers carry an expectation of expertise in conducting family life education classes in a variety of community settings and for diverse audiences.

Resources and interest in parent education have also greatly increased in the past four decades, with a number of programs being developed that include leader training and a complete package of promotional and training materials. In the 1980s, some employee assistance programs and health maintenance organizations (HMOs) began to appreciate the value of education and preventive programs as appropriate billable therapeutic services. The number of clinically trained faculty in university departments that prepare family life educators has concurrently increased, and marriage and family enrichment programs with research and therapeutic foundations are emerging in clinics and community centers (Lewis-Rowley et al., 1993).

THE MANY FACES OF TODAY'S FAMILIES

Burgess's 1929 assessment of trends toward diversity and change in the family not only has continued to prove true but also has accelerated. In the past 100 years, from 1900 to 2000, the total U.S. population has more than tripled, from 76 million in 1900 to 281 million in 2000 (U.S. Census Bureau, 2000). Diverse racial and ethnic culture groups now represent a larger percentage of the total U.S. population than ever before. At the beginning of the twentieth century, one in eight persons was classified as "other than white" (U.S. Census Bureau, 2004a). At the beginning of the twenty-first century, that ratio has risen to one in four. As more biracial couples and families are formed, the classification of "race" becomes increasingly blurred. Taylor (1994) also stresses the diversity *within* the major culture groups. Customs and cultural values can vary widely within a general cultural classification. African Americans comprise people of color from Haiti, Jamaica, Trinidad, and many countries in Latin America. Hispanics include an amalgamation of persons from Spanish-speaking countries, including Mexican Americans, or Chicanos (the largest single group in the Hispanic category), but also Cubans, Puerto Ricans, and other persons from Central and South America, as well as Spain. The Asian American category encompasses more than a dozen distinct subgroups and cultures. Among the largest are Chinese, Japanese, Koreans, Filipinos, and Vietnamese. By the year 2020, all minority groups combined are projected to represent 38.7% of the total population, with persons of Hispanic origins comprising the largest minority group: 17.8% (U.S. Census Bureau, 2004a). If current trends continue, Census Bureau projections predict that by the year 2050, persons of nonwhite racial and ethnic origins will comprise 50.1% of the total population.

The term "minority" is also a blurry designation. Taylor (1994), referring to the work of Simpson and Yinger (1985), defines minority families as "those families that have historically experienced social, economic, and political subordination vis-à-vis families of the dominant majority, as a consequence of their race, ancestry, and/or other characteristics the latter holds in low esteem" (p. 1). In other words, from a sociological standpoint, *minority* and *majority* do not refer necessarily to the size of the population but rather to its status. In that sense women, who are actually the gender majority (51%), are often categorized as a minority group (U.S. Census Bureau, 2000).

Marital status, family composition, and economic conditions of families also continue to change. According to the latest census data, two-thirds of all U.S. citizens currently live in family households, although the percentage of married-couple households is declining (from 82% in 1970 to 52% in 2000). Although children under five represented the largest five-year sub-group in 1900 and 1950, they have been overtaken in the twenty-first century by the two groups of middle adults, ages 35–39 and 40–44.

Single Adults

With the number of remarriages declining more than 44% between 1970 and 1988 and with people marrying much later than they did 4 decades ago (now around age 26.8 for males and 25.4 for females), there is a burgeoning population of single adults totaling over 95.7 million (U.S. Census Bureau, 2004b). One-person households have skyrocketed in the past 50 years. In 1950, they represented one in ten households. Today, that ratio is one in four. With increasing life expectancy, the number of older adults has increased 300% in a century: from 4% of the population to 12.1%. Persons over 65 account for about 1/3 of one-person households (U.S. Census Bureau, 2000).

Single Parents

The number of households headed by a single female now totals more than 12.5 million, with 7 million single women parenting children under 18 years old. Between 1983 and 1993, births to unmarried women increased by 70% (Saluter, 1994). Birth rates to unmarried teens aged 18–19 reached an unprecedented high of 65.7 per 1,000 in 1991. Birth rates to unmarried teens aged 15–17 increased by more than 50% during the 1980s. Births to older unmarried women, aged 20–44, also rose rapidly during this time. Although the rate of teen pregnancy has slowed somewhat in the past 10 years, it is still twice as high as in most of Western Europe (Connelly, 2006). Coupled with the rising number of divorces among families with children, these statistics show that the single mother, ages 15–44, is a major constituent in the population of parents today.

Stepfamilies

According to demographer Paul Glick, at least one of every three Americans is part of a stepfamily: either a stepparent, a stepchild, a stepsibling, or some other relation (Ahlburg & DeVita, 1992). A 1996 Census Bureau report found that 4.9 million children in the United States lived with at least one stepparent (Fields, 2001). The difficulty and complexity involved in blending two or more families is considered to be one of the reasons that there is such a high rate of divorce among remarried couples. Some 23% of second marriages end in divorce after five years and 39% have ended after ten years. (NCHS/CDC Public Affairs, 2002).

Mothers in the Workforce

Married or single mothers with young children now make up 58.2% of the workforce, an increase of more than 20% since 1978, when only 30% of married women and 52% of single women with children under six were in the workplace (Cohen & Bianchi, 1999). At every level, women continue to earn less than men with equivalent schooling or experience, making only about 76% of what men earned in 1998 (Bowler, 1999). Because 90% of custodial parents are women, the discrepancy in earnings represents increased stress and economic distress for many single mothers and their children.

Older Americans

By the year 2030, the elderly population in the United States (those aged 65 or older) is expected to climb to 20% of the total population. By age 75, 60% of women are predicted to be living alone, many on a fixed income with declining buying power and increasing medical costs (Zimmerman, 1995). Many older Americans are called upon to raise a second generation of children. The U.S. Census Bureau (Fields, 2001) reports that over 1.2 million children under 18 are currently living in a grandparent-led household with no parent present.

Economic Distress

The general economy experienced a significant upheaval during the last years of the twentieth century. Since 1990, median incomes for minority wage earners have increased significantly, yet most still fall far below the median income of all workers combined ($43,318). Asians now report a higher median income ($45,250) than non-Hispanic White workers ($38,975), Hispanics ($26,630), or African Americans ($25,050) ("Fresh Look," 1998). Although an unprecedented economic boom has moved some segments of the population into higher income brackets and pushed the unemployment rate to an all-time low, wages and job security have declined for many others and brought added pressure to bear on families of all types. The Personal Responsibility and Work Opportunity Reconciliation Act of 1996 (PRWORA), commonly referred to as welfare reform, nudged persons— many of them single mothers—into the workforce and phased out subsidies for cash assistance. Some new workers have received training and education that have positively influenced their self-esteem and their income level. But others have moved into low-paying entry-level jobs with few benefits. Very few families in this wage bracket have access to private health insurance. Between 2002 and 2003, the number of persons in the United States without health insurance coverage increased to more than 45 million. (U.S. Census Bureau News, 2005). A recent

Associated Press release citing Department of Agriculture data estimates that one in 10 American households is unable to afford the food it needs (Briscoe, 2000).

Among female single parents with children under the age of five, 46.4% fall below the poverty line. Unfortunately, even a raise in the minimum wage by $1 per hour will not significantly enhance the ability of many families to cover the basic costs of food, housing, child care, health care, and other necessary expenses. For example, a person working full-time at a minimum-wage job (currently $5.15 per hour) cannot provide enough income to lift a family of two or more above the poverty threshold, which now stands at $13,133 for a family of two and $16,700 for a family of four (HHS Poverty Guidelines, 1999). A raise of $1 per hour would bring yearly earnings for a full-time minimum-wage job to $12,792, still significantly below the poverty threshold for a family of four. A week's food expense for a family of four with two children under the age of six has increased from $87.30 in 1990 to $117 in 2002 (U.S. Census Bureau, 2003).

Homelessness is another fear that becomes reality for an estimated 2 million people a year in the United States as housing costs continue to rise and subsidized housing becomes more scarce (Franklin, 2000). Increasingly the homeless include families and women and children who may be escaping abusive situations.

FUTURE DIRECTIONS OF FAMILY LIFE EDUCATION

"We must think of families differently than scholars have in the past," note family scientists Wesley Burr, Randal Day, and Kathleen Bahr (1993). They propose a new terminology and way of perceiving "the family." Rather than the narrow definition of the traditional family that has been considered the normative standard, that is, "a cultural unit which contains a husband and wife who are the mother and father of their child or children" (Schneider, 1980, p. 33), Burr et al. suggest viewing the family as a sphere of one's life similar to the way one views the spiritual, occupational, or educational aspects of one's life. The *family realm* addresses aspects of the human experience that are uniquely tied to procreation and the generational connections that are created by birth or adoption of children and committed unions of adults. The family realm also includes the spatial and emotional relationships that persons develop with those they call "family," the ability to manage crises together and to show affection and loyalty, and the shared family traditions, rituals, values, and routines that form strong connections.

Burr et al. also strongly caution against imposing one's own cultural and class standards on those we are teaching. An example is the assumption that higher income and social status are automatically "improvements" in family function and are sought by all family groups:

> It is noteworthy that the educators and social workers [through the years] represented the middle and upper classes, while the families who needed to be taught "proper" principles of family economics tended to be poor or ethnic. Their poverty and their adherence to "foreign" or "primitive" values were evidence that they managed inefficiently. The possibility that they cherished values other than income maximization or economic advantage seems to have been entirely lost on the specialists grounded in the economic perspective who,

over much of the twentieth century, devoted their professional lives to foster-ing family choices based on economic maximization. (Burr et al., 1993, p. 10)

The purposes and goals for engaging in family life education with diverse families need to be reevaluated in light of this growing understanding of the unique and varied ways that cultures and ethnic groups "do family." Moreover, the study of diverse families should include more attention to the unique strengths, and not just comparative deficits, of various culture groups. Identifying and affirming a culture's ways of coping and connecting can enhance the lives of "enlightened" middle- and upper-class families and educators. If members of a particular culture group are utilized as the primary resources for designing family life education programs relevant to them, program effectiveness and design will be strengthened.

In predicting future directions for the field, Lewis-Rowley et al. (1993) fore-saw four major trends:

1. Collaborative approaches to family life education will increase between generalists and specialists who value each other's contributions and realize that issues are too complex to be solved by one single organization or pro-fessional group.

2. More refinement of theory and research will strengthen understanding and practice of educational intervention and support. The research is expanding and becoming more discriminating as it is driven by the full force of computer-age technology. Communicating findings to practitioners, legislators, and the general public continues to be a challenge.

3. Intervention in private and public spheres will focus more on prevention and education, appreciating the involvement of the total family as part of the teaching/learning team.

4. Global information gathering and policy making will increase as technol-ogy allows information to flow across oceans and continents and as cross-cultural studies and diversity in families are recognized and appreciated.

Are their predictions coming to pass? Certainly technology has enabled every-one to access information (both good and questionable) with ease. A quick com-puter search with the key words "family life education" yields more than 20 million results! Family life educators have experienced an upsurge of interest in family life education on several continents (see chapter 11). There is progress toward collabo-ration between researchers and practitioners but still much room for growth.

SUMMARY

David Mace was a strong champion of preventive education programs for couples and families for many years until his death in 1990. He often told the story of a little town planted deep in a valley at the end of a twisty and treacher-ous mountain road. The road was dark and narrow, with no caution signs or reflectors to mark the most dangerous curves. Over the years, many cars plunged over the cliff. Scores of people were seriously injured or killed. Finally, the town council decided to do something about the problem. After several weeks of study, the council issued a report. An ambulance would be purchased to park at the bottom of the cliff. Then, when a crash occurred, survivors could be rushed to the hospital, and hopefully a few lives would be saved. The illogical reasoning is obvious: Why wait to do something until after an accident occurs? Why not invest in caution signs and reflectors? Then many accidents would be prevented and it would cost so much less in money and human misery!

We continue to ask the same questions regarding the value of family life education. Why wait until children and families have suffered great emotional anguish when education could prevent many tragedies from occurring, greatly enhance the quality of family interaction, or both? Such solutions have always been an emphasis of visionary educators and social reformers. Unfortunately, society and the government are still more likely to respond to crisis than to preventive correction. In past centuries, family life education also lacked definition. That is changing. In the last 50 years more attention has been focused on collaboration, definition, academic research and theory, and leader training and certification. Family life education is moving to a new level of appreciation among behavioral scientists and program developers.

Furthermore, the crisis in families that Burgess and others observed in the 1930s has come to the forefront of attention in the 1990s. Skeletons long hidden in closets of abuse, exploitation, and violence have seen the light of celebrity confession and high media coverage. Divorce and single parenthood are no longer squelched by social stigma. The sexual revolution has "outed" us all. Courts are mandating anger control and parent education programs. Technology is taking us to new levels of involvement with one another, offering new opportunities for distance education and resources. Around the world, we are interacting with diverse cultures and discovering new ways of being family. And families, struggling to survive and to thrive, are more willing to ask for help. It is time to bring knowledge and families together, and it can best be done face-to-face with person-centered, trained professionals and effective programs. Chapter 2 addresses what it means to be a profession and a professional.

Questions/Problems for Discussion and Review

Class Discussion

1. From the list of definitions in box 1.1, choose the definition you think best describes the range of tasks and settings for family life education described by Thomas and Arcus (1992). Explain why you chose this particular one. In reviewing all the definitions, what do you see that has endured over time? What elements have expanded or contracted?

2. Do you agree with Herbert Spencer that public school curricula should include parenting courses? Why or why not? Spencer observes that formal education has largely ignored this aspect of education. Is this still the case? What do you think is the reason?

3. How do the demands and stresses of family life today differ from those in the past? Consider particularly the dual-career family; the single-parent, low-income family; and the immigrant family.

Research Problems

1. What makes prevention and education programs hard to document in terms of effectiveness? Find examples of research that document the effectiveness of prevention strategies.

2. What do you see as the value of prevention/education programs, in comparison to crisis intervention and remediation programs?

Case Study Design

Using the three examples at the beginning of this chapter and the three other examples in Chapter 12 as cases for study, complete the following tasks through the use of reasoning, research, and interview. (Over a period of several weeks, as you study the succeeding chapters, you will add to your "found" knowledge.)

1. After reading the example, what basic information do you have about

   a. the target population?

   b. the training and task of the family life educator?

2. What additional information would you need in order to design an effective family life education program?

3. What programs have been developed and assessed for this population? Find some examples.

4. Design a short-term and a long-term program for this population.

   a. How can you determine what the learning goals should be for each program?

   b. What format and teaching methodologies will you use?

5. Develop an assessment design to measure program effectiveness.

CHAPTER two

The Developing Profession/Professional

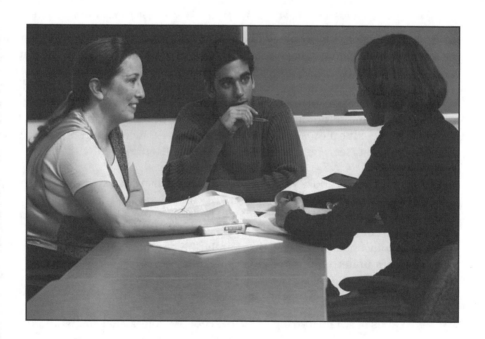

The Developing Profession/Professional

Carl has a baccalaureate degree in art history. He has worked for the past 9 years as a youth coordinator for the YMCA and organizes activities and classes for neighborhood kids identified as high risk. He is a member of the National Association for the Education of Young Children and has served on their board of directors.

Gretchen has a degree in child development. She organizes a parent group in her neighborhood for other stay-at-home moms and dads with kids under two years old. The group meets regularly and discusses a predetermined topic each time. Members rotate responsibility for researching the topic and presenting information. Much of the meeting is spent in casual conversation and support.

Kathleen is the executive director of a neighborhood family resource center. She has a degree in human development and family studies and is a Certified Family Life Educator. Her responsibilities include overseeing the development and implementation of family activities, well-baby classes, parent support groups, and a home visiting program. She has worked in the field of family life education for more than 12 years.

Which of these people would you consider to be professional family life educators? What makes someone a professional? What criteria are needed in order for an occupation to be considered a profession? Is family life education a profession?

Chapter 1 recounted the history of family life education and the gradual appreciation of its importance and role in strengthening society. With this evolution has come recognition of the importance of the individual's role in effective family life education programs and offerings—a recognition of the value of professionalism (see, e.g., Fohlin, 1971; National Commission on Family Life Education, 1968).

This chapter looks at issues of professionalism. How do we define a profession? What is involved in becoming a competent professional? What skills and knowledge are needed to provide quality family life education experiences and to develop effective materials? Are there certain personal characteristics or traits that make someone a more effective family life educator? What ethical practices are necessary underpinnings of the profession?

Defining the Profession

Let us begin by looking at the concept of professionalism. Numerous individuals and organizations have studied professionalism. Some identify certain attributes commonly acquired in the process of professionalization (Weigley, 1976), whereas others focus on the political and sociological aspects of identifying professions (Torstendahl & Burrage, 1990). One approach developed by East (1980) contends that the development of a profession involves eight criteria. According to East's framework, certain criteria must be in place in order for a field or occupation to be considered a profession. Application of these criteria to the field of family life education shows that many criteria have been met, with progress being made toward meeting others.

The Activity Becomes a Full-Time Paid Occupation

Although the title "family life educator" is not always used specifically, family life education is practiced by professionals in various settings throughout the world, including junior and senior high schools; education extension programs; the military, community education, health care, and faith communities; and higher education. Family life education is carried out under such titles as parent education, sex education, health education, coaching, marriage enrichment, youth advocacy, and so forth.

Training Schools and Curricula Are Established

Universities and colleges have been offering family degree programs since the 1960s. However, recognition of the training requirements needed for family life education has come more recently. In 1984 the National Council on Family Relations established standards and criteria for the certification of family life educators, college/university curriculum guidelines, and content guidelines for family life education, including a framework for planning programs over the life span (NCFR, 1994). In 1996, NCFR introduced the Academic Program Review and began to review university and college family degree programs for adherence to the standards and criteria needed for the Certified Family Life Educator program. Numerous programs have sought this "industry" approval, which recognizes a defined and accepted curriculum content for the field.

Those Who Are Trained Establish a Professional Association

A number of related professional organizations exist, including the American Association of Family and Consumer Sciences (formerly the American Home Economics Association, established in 1909), Family Service International (established in 1911), NCFR (established in 1938), and Family Support America (formerly the Family Resource Coalition of America, established in 1980). NCFR is most widely recognized as the professional association for family life educators because of its involvement in the development of standards related to the content of family life education and its sponsorship of the CFLE program.

Development of a professional association recognizes a shared body of knowledge and common interests among a select group of professionals. Professional family associations offer membership at several levels of involvement and provide opportunities for continuing education and networking with others practicing in the family field.

A Name, Standards of Admission, a Core Body of Knowledge, and Competencies for Practice Are Developed

Through a series of task forces and committees beginning in 1968, the National Council on Family Relations developed its college and university curriculum guidelines (NCFR, 1994). Published in 1994, they provided content guidelines for university and college programs. The same committee developed standards and criteria for the certification of family life educators (NCFR, 1994), which provided minimum standards and criteria for professional practice. The first Certified Family Life Educators were approved in 1985.

The CFLE Standards and Criteria originally included nine family life content areas considered to represent the core of family life education. They were families in society, internal dynamics of families, human growth and development, human sexuality, interpersonal relationships, family resource management, parent education and guidance, family law and public policy, and ethics (see appendix B, this volume). Family life education methodology was added as a tenth content area in 1991. Professionals seeking certification provide documentation of academic preparation, professional development, and work experience in each of these 10 areas as part of the application process. In 1996, the National Council on Family Relations began approving university and college family degree programs for adherence to the criteria needed for the Certified Family Life Educator designation. The NCFR review process recognizes the preceding as a defined and accepted curriculum for the field.

Internal Conflict within the Group and External Conflict from Other Professions with Similar Concerns Lead to a Unique Role Definition

There is ongoing debate among many organizations regarding the nature of the field and the appropriate "home" for family life educators. The National Council on Family Relations has been active in defining and developing family life education curriculum and certification criteria since the early 1960s. The American Home Economics Association identified competencies and criteria for home economics in 1974 and established the Certified Home Economist (CHE) designation in 1987. In 1995, the AHEA changed its name to the American Association of Family and Consumer Sciences, reflecting increased emphasis on the family. Subsequently, the name of the certification credential awarded by AAFCS was changed to Certified in Family and Consumer Sciences (CFCS). There are some similarities between the NCFR and AAFCS certification programs. Both require a minimum level of education and knowledge in the areas of human growth and development, family systems, and family resource management. The redesign and expansion of the AAFCS credentialing program in 2004 resulted in three separate credentials with a competency-based qualifying exam for each. AAFCS maintained the original broad CFCS credential, but also created separate credentials focused on human development and family studies (CFCS-HDFS) and hospitality, nutrition, and food science (CFCS-HNFS). The new Human Development and Family Studies credential more closely resembles the Certified Family Life Educator credential than did the original composite CFCS credential because of the separation of topics related to nutrition and design, but there are still sufficient differences to warrant separate credentials.

Numerous other organizations exist with interests relevant to family life education. For example, professionals involved directly in sex education might join the American Association of Sexuality Educators, Counselors, and Therapists

(AASECT), and parent educators might be members of the National Parenting Education Network (NPEN). Couples or educators active in couples and marriage education may wish to join the Association for Couples in Marriage Enrichment (ACME) or the Coalition for Marriage, Family and Couples Education (CMFCE). These organizations have formed to provide a professional forum for discussion of the many issues inherent in family life education. The number of related organizations reflects the multidisciplinary nature of the field.

The recent proliferation of life and parent "coaches" has provided an opportunity to clarify the knowledge and skills needed to be a family life educator. As of 2006 no national academic standards have been established in order to call oneself a "coach." The less-defined criteria create opportunities for those without sufficient education or training to offer coaching services. While there are an increasing number of training programs, certifications, and organizations focused on coaching, it is still a relatively undefined and emerging field. The popularity of coaching speaks to the need of individuals to seek guidance in dealing with daily life issues from a strengths-based perspective. Family life educators can benefit from this interest by promoting their unique qualifications to provide information derived from evidence-based research.

The Public Served Expresses Some Acceptance of the Expertise of Those Practicing the Occupation

As society increasingly faces crises and challenges related to family (e.g., divorce, single parenting, blended families, delinquency, youth violence), the interest in prevention and education for families is growing. There has been an increased recognition of the value of prevention and education in the past decade. Health maintenance organizations more frequently offer classes dealing with parenting, stress management, and balancing work and family because they recognize the relationship between stress and health. More businesses recognize that personal and family problems account for decreased productivity and attendance. More companies offer lunchtime brown-bag seminars and other educational opportunities to employees in the hope of increasing employee productivity.

When groups or organizations decide to offer a family life education program, they tend to seek someone to lead the experience who has expertise in an academic discipline or profession related to families. Certification and experience can enhance one's credibility as an expert in the area of family relationships.

The marriage enrichment movement has for more than 40 years offered opportunities for enhancing couple-relationship skills and intentional-growth activities (Mace, 1982). Acceptance and recognition from therapists and academicians, as well as from couples who have participated in the weekend or ongoing experiences over the years, is growing. The well-attended national conferences of the CMFCE, formed in 1996, attest to this burgeoning interest. The value of trained leadership has always been emphasized by such international marriage enrichment organizations as the Association for Couples in Marriage Enrichment, founded by David and Vera Mace in 1973, and Marriage Encounter, founded by Father Gabriel Calvo in 1962. Both groups offer rigorous and well-developed leader-training programs, which require leader couples to have experience as well as academic preparation. Leaders in training must also work under the supervision of an experienced leader couple and receive positive evaluations of their skills by participants before receiving full certification.

But the increased interest in marriage education over the past years has also led to a proliferation of marriage education programs that can be taught "out of the box." These programs are designed to be taught by lay leaders and do not require specific academic training in marriage and family techniques. This approach has created some tension between those who have specific education and training in family education and those who do not. While some feel it is possible to be an effective marriage educator by following prescribed guidelines provided through specific curricula or approaches, others feel the most effective educators are those with formal training in addition to proven skills in program development and implementation. They argue that formally trained family life educators are better able to draw from a variety of approaches and techniques that are more specifically adapted to the audience and situation rather than applying a "one size fits all" approach. Persons trained in a specific approach or curriculum may, in fact, be very effective, but they would not be considered "professionals" in that their expertise is limited to just one curriculum or setting.

Family life education professionals, as well as program participants, recognize that it takes more than being a "good parent" or a "happy couple" to facilitate effective learning experiences and the skill building that enhances interpersonal relationships. Adequate training and experience are imperative.

Certification and Licensure Are the Legal Signs That a Group Is Sanctioned for a Particular Service to Society and That It Is Self-Regulated

The CFLE program was developed by the NCFR for the purpose of regulating the qualifications of family life education providers and, indirectly, the quality of the materials presented. Since 1989 Minnesota has required early childhood and parent educators to be licensed in order to provide family education through the Early Childhood Family Education (ECFE) program. In 2002 the North Carolina Parenting Education Network developed a certification for parenting educators and the National Parenting Education Network (NPEN) is continuing to pursue the option of a national parent education credential. These efforts reflect recognition of the importance of establishing some form of formal recognition of minimum standards for effective practice.

A Code of Ethics Is Developed to Eliminate Unethical Practice and to Protect the Public

In 1995, the Family Science Section of the National Council on Family Relations approved *Ethical Principles and Guidelines* (NCFR, 1995a) for use by family scientists. These guidelines deal primarily with ethical issues inherent in teaching and research in academic settings. In 1997, the Minnesota Council on Family Relations published *Ethical Thinking and Practice for Parent and Family Educators* (MCFR, 1997) for family life education practitioners. This publication provides information and guidelines useful in making ethical decisions and is discussed in more detail later in this chapter. The fact that a need was perceived for these ethical guidelines and codes provides further evidence of the recognition of family life education as a profession within itself.

This step-by-step discussion of East's (1980) criteria for defining a profession shows that family life education is indeed a profession but growing through its adolescence towards maturity. Through the efforts of family life education pioneers and those currently working in the field, the profession continues to move toward recognition; the goal is to be as understood and accepted as the fields of marriage and family therapy, counseling, social work, and teaching.

Table 2.1 Family Life Education: Defining the Profession

East's Criteria (1980)	Progress Made	Room to Grow	Criterion 1= No Progress 5= Criterion Has Been Fully Met
1. The activity becomes a full-time occupation	Though rarely called family life education, many professionals practice family life education on a full-time basis under such descriptions as parent education, sex education, marriage enrichment, etc.	Family life education is often only a part of a family life educator's job responsibilities or employment specifically in family life education may only be available on a part-time basis.	4
2. Training schools and curricula are established	Family-related degrees have been offered since the 1960's. NCFR began recognizing academic programs that meet the criteria needed for the CFLE designation beginning in 1996. To date there are 94 NCFR-approved programs.	Few degrees are called family life education but rather, child and family studies, human development and family studies, human services, family studies, etc.	4
3. Those who are trained establish a professional association	Numerous family-related associations have been in existence since the early 1900s including NCFR, AAFCS, FSA, etc.	There are numerous other family-related associations and organizations, which can cause a fragmented identity.	4
4. A name, standards of admission, a core body of knowledge, and competencies for practice are developed	NCFR developed university and college curriculum guidelines and standards and criteria for the certification of family life educators in 1984.		5

(continued)

Table 2.1   *(continued)*

East's Criteria (1980)	Progress Made	Room to Grow	Criterion 1= No Progress 5= Criterion Has Been Fully Met
5. Internal conflict within the group and external conflict from other professions with similar concerns leads to a unique role definition	Numerous organizations and credentials exist with some overlapping content but development of NCFR Curriculum Guidelines and CFLE Criteria defines family life content areas.	Employers and the public are still unclear on what family life education is and how family life educators differ from social workers, therapists, counselors, etc.	3
6. The public served expresses some acceptance of the expertise of those practicing the occupation	The increased popularity of parent education and marriage education programs throughout the US reflects the public's increased acceptance of education related to family issues.	The public is often not aware specific credentials exist for family life educators.	3
7. Certification and licensure are the legal signs that a group is sanctioned for a particular service to society and that it is self-regulated	The CFLE designation was developed to regulate qualifications of family life education providers. CFLEs must meet continuing education requirements in order to maintain their designation.		5
8. A code of ethics is developed to eliminate unethical practice and to protect the public	The Family Science Section of NCFR established ethical principles and guidelines in 1995. In 1997 the Minnesota Council on Family Relations finalized their work on *Ethical Thinking and Practice for Parent and Family Educators*, which was adopted by NCFR for use with the CFLE program in 1997.		5

From Bredehoft & Walcheski (2003). Copyrighted 2003 by the National Council on Family Relations, 3989 Central Ave. NE, Suite 550, Minneapolis, MN 55421. Reprinted by permission.

CHALLENGES IN THE FIELD OF FAMILY LIFE EDUCATION

What needs to happen in order for family life education to be as widely understood and recognized as social work or counseling? Perhaps the biggest struggle faced by family life educators is the lack of awareness and understanding of who they are and what it is they do. What problems need to be overcome to make parent education commonplace, for all engaged couples to take marriage education courses, and for marriage and relationship enrichment weekends to be the norm? Imagine the personal and societal problems avoided if all high school graduates had completed a course in communication skills, money management, and conflict resolution? What if all expectant parents took parenting classes as part of childbirth preparation?

Lack of Identity as a Discipline

As demonstrated, substantial progress has been made in establishing consensus on the content of family life education and the standards needed for effective practice. However, there is less agreement on what to call an academic degree meeting these standards. Very few degree programs are specifically titled "family life education." Rather, family-related degree programs carry a myriad of titles including family science; family studies; individual and family studies; family and consumer sciences; family and child development; human ecology; family, youth and community sciences; family and child sciences; child, adolescent, and family studies; family relations; and more. The overall field of family studies has struggled with the issue of identity for many years with no clear consensus: *The Graduate and Undergraduate Study in Marriage and Family: A Guide to Bachelor's, Master's, and Doctoral Programs in the United States and Canada* (Hans, 2005), includes over 100 different titles for family-related majors. The establishment of a core body of knowledge and standards of practice will help in establishing a clearer identity for family life education, but a more consistent name for the field is needed as well.

Diversity of Settings in Which Family Life Education Takes Place

There are probably numerous instances of family life education occurring in your community on any given day. There are family life educators working in health care settings, community education, faith communities, junior and senior high schools, colleges and universities, social service agencies, corporate settings, government agencies, corrections, retirement communities, and the military. (See box 2.1 for examples of employment settings for those trained in the family field.)

The multidisciplinary nature of family life education and the variety of settings in which it takes place are both an asset and a liability. On the positive side numerous opportunities fit the "generalist" training that is family life education. Negatively, this variety of settings can make it difficult to target efforts when job seeking and may occasionally require family life educators to develop an entrepreneurial approach to their careers that does not match their personality or comfort level. Do you apply with hospitals or through community education

Box 2.1   Employment Settings for Family Life Education

4-H development	Early childhood	Neighborhood youth
Adoption and foster care	family education	organization
Adult education centers	Economic opportunity	Parenting centers
After school programs	Emergency/disaster	Peace Corps
Child protection services	preparedness	Pediatric units
Civic groups	Employee assistance programs	Planned Parenthood
Colleges and universities	Faith communities	Pre-school/
Community action programs	Family and individual therapy	day care centers
Community education	Family law	Project Head Start
Community health centers	Fathering programs	Recreation programs
Consumer credit and family	Funeral and mortuary services	Schools—public
resource management	Girl Scouts/Boy Scouts/	and private
Cooperative extension	Camp Fire Girls	Schools for the deaf
Correctional facilities	Halfway houses	and blind
Courts	Health care	Senior citizen programs
Criminal justice	Healthy promotion	Social welfare programs
Crisis centers	organizations	Student services
Crisis or hotline services	Hospices	Vocational guidance
Disability services	Hospitals	Work life programs
Divorce mediation	International agencies	Women's centers
Domestic violence prevention	Long-term care facilities	YMCA/YWCA
Drug/alcohol rehab centers	Mental institutions	Youth organizations
	Military family support	

programs? Which job titles do you look for in the classifieds or when searching the Internet? The Department of Labor's 2006–2007 Occupational Outlook Handbook (http://www.bls.gov/oco/) does not include family life education as an occupation. In fact, the only occupations listed with "family" in the title include family and general practitioners, family child care providers, family services social workers, and family therapists. The occupation of family services social worker only includes information on social work with no reference to any other family-related positions. As those involved in family life education know, the social work field has done an excellent job of branding itself and incorporating social work training (and in many cases social work licensure) into state and federal legislation. While this works well for jobs focusing on intervention and case management, it excludes a great many well-qualified family professionals who possess the skills and knowledge needed to help families through a preventative approach. A new licensure requirement for non-social work family professionals is not likely in the near future. Generally, most legislators are interested in creating new licensure requirements only in fields that involve significant health or welfare risks to the public.

The National Council on Family Relations is working with the U.S. Department of Labor (DOL) to list the occupation of *family life educator* in their official coding system. Unfortunately it will likely be a number of years before the title *family life educator* receives its own specific listing with the Standard Occupational Classification (SOC) system. A profession is added to the system when the title or position appears with a certain level of frequency. "Family life educator" does not yet appear often enough in the labor environment and will only do so when people identify themselves by this specific profession or when employers identify their employees as such. NCFR encourages family life educators to start this process by using the title *family life educator*. This includes identifying their profession on their tax forms; adding their title to their Web sites, business cards, and publications; and encouraging other family life educators to use the term in job postings when appropriate.

The first step for professional identification within the DOL is to get the term connected with an existing SOC code. Identification with an existing code will alert DOL employees who gather occupational information to the existence of the profession. The more they see it being used, the more likely the DOL will cite it within the SOC system and, eventually, within the Occupational Outlook Handbook.

The long-term goal is for employers, college students, and job-seekers to be able to go to the Occupational Outlook Handbook (OOH, http://stats.bls.gov/oco), enter the term "family life educator," and pull up a page with information on the profession of family life education similar to that for the terms "social worker" or "counselor." This would include information on the nature of the work, working conditions, training, other qualifications, advancement, employment, job outlook, earnings, related occupations, and sources of additional information.

Hopefully, with a collective and focused effort, the term "family life educator" will one day be recognized specifically by the Department of Labor, which in turn will enhance family life education as a profession.

Strategies for Growth

A number of strategies can be implemented to increase the visibility and value of educational and preventative efforts focused on the family. Once established family life educators can further create niches or specialty areas.

Promoting and supporting standards of practice. CFLE and CFCS certifications are perhaps the most relevant and appropriate credentials for those working in family life education. Family professionals can support the field of family life education by recognizing the need for established standards of practice. This might involve pursuing certification themselves or hiring or promoting those who carry the CFLE or CFCS designation. Increasing the number of people who identify themselves as family life educators and actively promoting this identification through the use of CFLE and CFCS initials after their name in their promotional materials, resumes, vitae, and job titles will help increase awareness of family life education as a profession. Likewise, increasing the number of qualified Certified Family Life Educators and professionals Certified in Family and Consumer Sciences is an important strategy in recognizing the value of family life education. The CFLE and CFCS initials after a designee's name bring attention to family life education as a practice with identified standards and requirements.

Educating employers and the public.   Family life educators find that they need to do a fair amount of educating others about family life education and its value. They often need to be creative and proactive in finding employment settings and willing to market themselves to potential employers. Often employers do not really understand what a family degree or certification represents. They need to be educated on the fact that these credentials denote a solid understanding of families, a life span perspective, and the skills and knowledge needed to develop and present educational programs. Most family life educators trained specifically in family will work from a systems perspective, i.e., individual system; couple system; family system; and social service, business, and government systems. Graduates of family degree programs need to see themselves working as family life educators at *any* system level in *any* organization (Campbell, personal communication, 2002). They need to see themselves very broadly in terms of training and skills and encourage employers to do the same. Employers that benefit from hiring an employee with such skills and knowledge will be more likely to hire similar candidates in the future.

Incorporating family life education into intervention settings.   Family life educators working in settings that focus primarily on intervention or counseling might be able to identify opportunities for offering family life education within that same setting. For example, an agency that works primarily with families struggling with financial issues might want to offer money-management workshops to the community. Those offering home visits to parents identified as at-risk might also sponsor "family fun nights" that provide opportunities for all families to gather together to share information and friendship. There will always be families that need the assistance of a social worker or counselor. In addition, all therapists and social workers are aware that preventing problems is best for families and society.

Including family life educators as providers in legislation.   The growing fields of marriage education and parent education may provide opportunities to get family life educators legally recognized as well. A number of states have passed or are considering legislation that mandates or provides incentives for people completing marriage education or parent education classes. Typically this legislation includes a listing of recommended providers of these services. Unfortunately, legislators tend to favor bills that include a finite list of qualified providers. These providers are usually people who possess credentials such as licensure that are already sanctioned and recognized by state or federal bodies. It simplifies the passage of the bill, but may not provide the best measure of who is qualified to provide these services. For example, mandated parent education programs, required in some states for divorcing couples with children, often identify licensed social workers, counselors, and therapists as the only approved providers. While many of these providers may very well be qualified to provide educational classes dealing with parenting, being licensed as a social worker, counselor, or therapist does not guarantee any specific knowledge in parenting or the ability to develop and implement educational work-shops or work one-on-one with parents. Someone trained specifically in family life education is at least as qualified, and most likely more qualified, to provide mar-riage education or parent education than a social worker, therapist, or pastor who is identified as a provider simply by virtue of licensure in that particular state.

Fortunately, some legislators are beginning to recognize other options. Judges are beginning to recognize the skills and knowledge of those with family degrees and their ability to work with these families, whereas in the past they automati-cally enlisted the aid of a therapist or social worker.

Those interested in promoting family life education can monitor relevant leg-islation and take the opportunity to educate those who initiate the bills to include family life educators among the list of approved or recommended providers. Inclusion of family life educators as "approved providers" in federal legislation would open the door for recognition by state and local entities in the public and private sectors.

Increasing funding for programs focused on prevention.   Effectiveness of pre-vention can be difficult to prove. Granting agencies usually require thorough doc-umentation of program outcomes to support funding efforts. "The potential benefits of family life education must be more clearly linked to predefined pro-gram goals (e.g., the reduction of teenage sexual activity or pregnancy, more effec-tive parenting behavior, or stronger, more fulfilling interpersonal relationships) in a way that shows such education to be good for society by fostering the develop-ment of individuals and families" (Czaplewski & Jorgensen, 1993).

A recent study carried out by the RAND Corporation (2005) found that early childhood intervention programs including home visiting and parent education could yield long-term benefits for participating children and families. Specifically, they found:

> Well-designed early childhood interventions have been found to generate short and long-term benefits to participating children and families in multiple domains of well-being. When these benefits are valued in dollar terms, the return to society ranges from $1.26 to $17.07 for each dollar spent. The benefits that translate into the largest dollar values – educational attainment, earnings, and crime reduction – often accrue later in life. The best outcomes seem to be associated with programs that offer children better-trained caregivers, small child-to-staff ratios, and greater intensity of services. (RAND Corporation, 2005)

The emotional "costs" of family dysfunction are difficult to assess. However, the financial costs are clear. The costs to the courts and the social support system are well-documented. Problems stemming from divorce, substance abuse, teen pregnancy, child abuse, violence, bankruptcy, and many other individual and societal problems are all areas in which education and prevention programs could avert or ameliorate social ills.

Carving a niche.   As noted, family life education takes place in myriad set-tings. Its multidisciplinary nature means that family life educators might find themselves competing for jobs with, or working alongside, those trained in social work, psychology, child development, sexuality, or therapy. One approach to increasing the visibility of family life education is to establish or identify a setting in which family life educators are uniquely qualified to provide services. Health care providers are increasingly offering workshops on parenting and stress management. Community education catalogs list numerous classes related to family life. Youth programs and church and faith communities are some of the most common settings for family life education.

The area of work life holds tremendous potential for family life educators. More corporations and businesses recognize the interconnectedness of work and family life. They understand that the personal life of an employee can have a detrimental effect on his or her work life, especially if that personal life is riddled with substance abuse, domestic violence, or serious financial difficulties. However, less-serious or problematic issues can affect work life as well and can include issues related to normative family stressors, such as couple relationships, parenting, elder care, and more. Investment in brown-bag lunch workshops on "communicating with your adolescent" or "time management" can pay back in increased productivity or decreased employee absence. Family life educators are uniquely qualified to provide these types of workshops.

Few can argue with the merits of providing individuals and families with the knowledge and skills needed to lead satisfying and productive lives. But general acceptance of, or the lack of argument against, such efforts is not enough to ensure the advancement of the field. The challenge before advocates of family life education lies in converting this rather soft support of preventative efforts into acceptance and promotion of something that can be seen, felt, and truly understood. We need societal recognition of parent education, marriage enrichment, and life skill training and an appreciation for the value of participating in these activities on a regular basis. We need professionals in related fields to acknowledge and value the knowledge and skills possessed by those who identify themselves as family life educators and to recognize the place that family life education can hold in a variety of settings and situations. Family life education does not compete with social work, therapy, counseling, or ministry. Rather, it should be seen as a complement and part of a collaborative collection of resources and services available to help families function as effectively as possible.

Like all worthy goals, the elevation of family life education to a recognized and valued profession cannot be accomplished quickly or through the efforts of just a few individuals. It requires a grassroots effort of multiple players: individuals, agencies, organizations, businesses, schools, and government.

Another important piece in elevating the field of family life education is to ensure the professionalism of those who practice. The heart of professionalism lies in the skills and qualities of those that practice or deliver services to the public.

PERSONAL SKILLS AND QUALITIES OF THE EDUCATOR

By its nature, family life education often deals with personal and sensitive issues. Unlike an educator providing instruction in a "hard science" such as math or chemistry, the family life educator deals in matters of personal values, decision making, growth and behavior change, and such sensitive issues as sexuality, communication skills, parenting, and money management. The feelings, motives, attitudes, and values of the learners are central to the learning process (Darling, 1987). A major component of family life education involves helping participants to "analyze, clarify, and determine their own values and value system" (Family Service Association of America, 1976, p. 10). Participants may tend to respond with more emotion or defensiveness due to the personal nature of the topics discussed.

Awareness of Attitudes and Biases

Because of the sensitivity of these issues, family life educators need to be aware of their own feelings and biases. They need to be comfortable with other people's feelings and accepting of various points of view. Many family degree programs require students to examine and study their own family of origin and family roles, rules, and values to increase their awareness of the influence of their own family experiences (Bahr, 1990). This also helps to identify conflicts that may influence their ability to effectively practice family life education.

Awareness of one's own biases toward such things as culture, race, physical ability, gender, and socioeconomic status is necessary in order to practice effectively. Family life educators must consider the following questions: How do I view differences among people? Are differences something to value and celebrate, or to ignore or fear? When working with a population different from my own, do I see my role as helper, leader, advocate, or partner? Family life educators need to take time to seriously consider their perceptions and attitudes about such things as individual and societal responsibility for poverty. Are poor people poor because of the choices they've made or because of circumstances beyond their control? The educator's perspective on these issues can influence the way in which he or she practices and interacts with an audience. Often our perceptions and attitudes are so engrained that we don't even know we have them. It takes conscious effort and thought to examine how we see the world. This can be uncomfortable and challenging. But if educators fail to face these issues, they run the risk of compromising their ability to practice as effectively as possible, and they cheat themselves out of a wealth of opportunities to grow and learn from those around them.

Personal Skills and Qualities

The National Council on Family Relations (1994), as part of the Certified Family Life Educator program criteria, identified certain characteristics as crucial to the success of a family life educator. They include general intellectual skills, self-awareness, emotional stability, maturity, awareness of one's own personal attitudes and cultural values, empathy, effective social skills, self-confidence, flexibility, understanding and appreciation of diversity, verbal and written communication skills, and the ability to relate well with all ages on a one-to-one basis as well as in groups.

Clearly, personal traits and characteristics play an important role in the success of a family life educator. A self-assessment (box 2.2) gives the reader an opportunity to evaluate personal attributes and identify areas that need improvement. Working with a mentor or supervisor, peer evaluations, and observing experienced educators are some of the ways to enhance professional development.

Box 2.2   Assessing Your Personal Qualities as a Family Life Educator

Listed below are qualities seen as critical for effectiveness as a family life educator. Rate yourself on the following scale:

1 Needs much improvement
2 Needs some improvement
3 Average, but not well developed
4 Above average, moving toward competency
5 Competent in this area

- *General intellectual skills*. Ability to gather, read, and process information and to apply it to a topic and to group needs; to articulate concepts and ideas; to organize materials and stay on track when presenting them; to hear and incorporate ideas of others.

- *Self-awareness*. Ability to recognize and articulate one's own personal opinions, attitudes, and cultural values and not to assume that they are everyone's opinions, attitudes, and values; to understand personal tendencies to assume certain roles in a group, such as caretaker, controller, placater, dominant authority; to acknowledge one's own strengths and limitations.

- *Emotional stability*. Ability to recognize one's own level of emotional comfort or discomfort in a given situation; to express emotions in appropriate ways and at appropriate times; to maintain calmness in the face of crisis or confrontation and to refrain from personal attack on another person, either verbally or physically.

- *Maturity*. Ability to handle success, disappointment, frustration, or confrontation with dignity and understanding; to acknowledge one's own mistakes and weaknesses and not blame others; to move past grievances and continue to see each person as someone with value and potential.

- *Empathy*. Ability to put oneself in another person's place; to reflect the feeling to the other person; to understand her or his dilemma.

- *Effective social skills*. Ability to feel comfortable and enjoy the company of others; to share in group activities; to engage in conversation and to actively listen to others.

- *Self-confidence*. Ability to speak and act decisively in personal conversation or in front of a group; to accept the challenge of one's ideas without defensiveness and to state one's position with enthusiasm and documentation, not personal criticism or attack; to acknowledge personal strengths and accept words of appreciation graciously.

- *Flexibility*. Ability to adapt plans to suit a changing situation; to recognize when change is needed and be willing to try a new approach.

- *Understanding and appreciation of diversity*. Ability to acknowledge differences in others' values, attitudes, and lifestyles; to respect and appreciate cultural and ethnic differences in dress, customs, and language; to understand socioeconomic differences in income, education, and status and how these differences affect lifestyles and decision making; to actively resist gender, racial, and socioeconomic biases or stereotypes.

- *Verbal and written communication skills*. Ability to speak articulately, convincingly, and concisely; to write clearly in language that is not "over the head" of one's audience; to use illustrations and examples that support one's points; to know when an audience has been "overloaded" with information.

- *Ability to relate well with all ages and groups and on a one-to-one basis*. Ability to talk with and not down to any group or person; to resist judgmentalism and boredom; to appreciate humor and sharing; to practice patience in listening and interacting.

Developing a Personal Philosophy

Although certain personal qualities can enhance a family life educator's effectiveness, it is also important to develop a philosophical basis for teaching about families. Educators must thoroughly consider where their beliefs lie to be effective. How do they define a family? What is the purpose of family life education? They must be clear about the benefits of family life education and how it can most effectively be accomplished. Dail (1984) determined that a philosophy of family life education is important because: It provides a sense of direction and purpose; it allows the educator to be in touch with himself or herself; it enables assessment of educational problems; it clarifies the relationship of family life education to the needs and activities of the larger society; and it provides a basis for understanding the reality of the family, its value in society, the nature of family membership for the individual, and the role of family life education. Having a personal philosophy provides a deeper meaning to the educator's life.

Dail (1984) identified four beliefs that need to be addressed when constructing a philosophy of family life education. They include:

- Beliefs about the family and the quality and nature of family life
- Beliefs about the purpose of family life education
- Beliefs about the content of family life education
- Beliefs about the process of learning for families

Take a few minutes to consider your own beliefs about the following.

Beliefs about the family and the quality and nature of family life.   Family life educators must look at their own beliefs about how to define family. A family life educator who does not consider a gay or lesbian couple to be a family, for example, needs to be aware of this bias, as it could influence his or her ability to effectively work with such a couple.

> Family is like an inkblot test: we see in it whatever we think is important. . . . Families are this or families are that. . . . From "family values" to "dysfunctional families" the term family is so loaded with meanings that even the idea of families is quite messy and adds to the confusion of discussions. (Wigger, 1998, p. 16)

See box 2.3 for exercises to consider what criteria are used in defining a family. Each exercise describes a different group formation. Students should independently determine if they would consider each grouping to be a family. Class discussion often reveals varying opinions about what constitutes a family and what does not, often with fairly soft criteria.

In addition to how they define a family, educators need to have an understanding of how they think a family should be. What role does the family play in an individual's life? Where does the family fit within society? What needs to be in place for a family to function optimally? Understanding his or her own beliefs about the role of a family and the characteristics needed for healthy functioning provides the educator with a goal to strive for and a foundation on which to base his or her programs and other services. Allen and Baber (1992) contend:

Family life educators can strengthen family life by adopting a perspective that values diversity, equality, and full participation in society for everyone. This agenda may be accomplished . . . by a renewed commitment to professional accountability as a family life educator, the on-going reevaluation of personal beliefs about families that affect one's teaching and authenticity, and the meaningful involvement of teachers and students in political activities that actually contribute to empowerment and social change. (p. 383)

In our increasingly diverse society it is also important for the family life education professional to work toward cultural competence. Cultural competence, according to Orlandi (1992), is a "set of academic and interpersonal skills that

---

Box 2.3   What Makes a Family?

1. A newly married couple moves into their first apartment together. They have both agreed that they do not want to have any children. Are they a family?

2. A man and a woman have shared an apartment for the past two years. They share equally in the maintenance and cost of the household. They have made a personal commitment to each other and plan to stay together for the rest of their lives although they have no plans to marry. Are they a family?

3. A man and a woman have shared an apartment for the past two years. They share equally in the maintenance and cost of the household. They are good friends but are dating other people. Are they a family?

4. A group of 10 people (five men, three women, and two children) live together on a farm. They share responsibility for the maintenance of the household, including growing their own food. All household members take part in the care of the two children. The group is committed to living together harmoniously. Are they a family?

5. Two gay men live together in a house. They have made a personal commitment to each other. Are they a family?

6. Two gay women live together in a house. They have made a personal commitment to each other and were legally married in the state of Hawaii. Are they a family?

7. A divorced woman lives with her son from her marriage and her daughter from a relationship with another man whom she no longer sees. Are they a family?

8. A man and a woman share an apartment. They have a personal relationship and are committed to staying together as long as the relationship is beneficial to them both. Are they a family?

9. Two divorced heterosexual men live together in a house with their children and share the expense and maintenance of the household. Each man sometimes cares for the other's children while the other is working. Are they a family?

10. A woman lives alone but speaks daily with her sister and brother who live in another state. Are they a family?

11. A brother and sister live with their grandparents while their divorced mother attends school in another city. The mother stays with the children and her parents on the weekends. Are they a family?

12. A widower moves in with his son and his wife. Are they a family?

allows individuals to increase their understanding and appreciation of cultural differences and similarities, within, among, and between groups" (pp. 3–4). Asay,
Younes, and Moore (2006) developed a cultural transformation model, which illustrates the changes in cultural perspectives that people might experience as they
progress toward becoming culturally competent. The model includes five phases
progressing from cultural smugness to cognitive overload and emerging insecurity,
realization and surrender, self and cultural examination, and ending with adaptations. Recognition and appreciation of the differences and similarities between cultures enhances both the practice and personal life of the family life educator.

Beliefs about the purpose of family life education.   The family life educator
must understand the purpose of family life education in order to develop appropriate goals and objectives. Is the goal of family life education to change behavior? Is it to provide insight, skills, and knowledge? Is it proactive or reactive? Is it
to provide support? Is it to promote a particular ideology or belief system? Family
life educators must be clear about what it is they want to accomplish and why.

Beliefs about the content of family life education.   The family life educator
must consider which topics are appropriate to include in family life education settings. Are there certain topics that are inappropriate? When should a referral to
another type of professional be made? Is program content free of bias and stereotype? How appropriate and up to date are sources of information?

A professional family life educator needs to recognize when inappropriate
topics are being discussed. For example, although issues of sexual or physical
abuse may arise in family life education settings, these issues should be referred
for counseling, therapy, or possibly law enforcement. Professional family life educators need to be familiar with appropriate sources of information. They need to
be able to make referrals and to research topics when necessary. A family life educator who attempts to deal with such issues directly or allows lengthy discussion
in a group setting would not be acting professionally. Later in this chapter we discuss William Doherty's levels of family involvement model, which provides guidance for some of these issues.

Effective family life educators will want to be sure that their program content
is free of bias and stereotypes. Course content should consider family members of
all ages; portray nonsexist roles for family members; include information about
families of different racial, ethnic, and cultural groups; recognize the uniqueness
of individuals and families regardless of age, sex, race, ethnicity, and cultural and
socioeconomic background; recognize that composition of families varies; and be
based on current research (Griggs, 1981). Though focused on early childhood education, Louise Derman-Sparks's (1989) *Anti-Bias Curriculum: Tools for Empowering
Young Children* is an excellent resource for addressing these issues in any setting.
International Family Studies: Developing Curricula and Teaching Tools (Hamon, 2006)
includes discussion of developing and teaching family content with cultural sensitivity and respect.

Membership and involvement in a professional association can increase
awareness of relevant resources, organizations, programs, and individuals. In
addition, it can provide access to current research and literature in the field. It is

important for family life educators to have the ability to critically evaluate materials to ensure that they are based on solid and current research.

Beliefs about the process of learning for families. The family life educator needs to be concerned about how families learn and function as a group, as well as how the group affects the learning and thinking of individual members within it (Dail, 1984). Do groups learn differently than individuals do? How can small groups be used most effectively? Are the developmental, social, and emotional needs of the group important? How important are learning goals and evaluation? How does the education of one family member affect others in the family?

An understanding of human development and the learning process enables the educator to use the most effective techniques for each audience and each individual. In addition, an educator who understands families as a system knows the value of including all family members in the learning process. When that is not possible, he or she considers the implications of introducing new information, such as parenting methods, into the family and is prepared to help the other family members to adjust to a new way of thinking or acting. Chapter 3 discusses various teaching methods and learning experiences in more detail. The important methodology concept to consider in this chapter is awareness of one's own personal beliefs about how individuals and families best learn.

Constructing a personal philosophy can be a difficult process. It involves questioning, evaluating, and accepting and rejecting ideas. It is just that—a process—and it continually evolves as the educator grows and learns. The time and effort spent in developing a personal philosophy of family life education will be well worth it. The family life educator who has a solid understanding of his or her own personal philosophy of family life education will be better equipped to assist individuals and families to lead more satisfying and productive lives.

THE LEVELS OF FAMILY INVOLVEMENT MODEL

An important trait of a professional is the recognition and acceptance of one's own abilities and limitations. This issue has been referred to as *levels of involvement* between the educator and the learner (Doherty, 1995). A fine line often divides the roles and responsibilities involved in family life education and those involved in counseling and therapy. Professionalism can be questioned when an educator is perceived as stepping over the line by participating in activities beyond his or her level of knowledge and expertise. But where does education end and therapy begin? William Doherty developed a model to help educators identify appropriate levels of involvement for family life education. An understanding of these levels and one's own capabilities is another important component of professionalism.

Family life educators must deal with some level of personal and sensitive issues in order to be effective, but working beyond an appropriate level can have harmful effects. Doherty's model involves a "continuum of intensity, describing interactions and defining necessary skills and understanding for working successfully at each level" (Early Childhood Family Education Demonstration Site Coordinators, 1997, p. 2). Doherty presented this model to family life educators involved in early childhood education in Minnesota in 1993. The model allows

Working with a mentor or supervisor, peer evaluations, and observing experienced educators are some of the ways to enhance professional development.

participants to clarify their role with families, define the intensity of involvement desired, and identify personal development issues needed for optimum performance. Though Doherty's model tends to focus on parent education and the relationship between the family life educator and the parent, it is certainly applicable to the many relationships carried out under family life education.

The five levels of the family involvement model (box 2.4) are arranged hierarchically, from minimal involvement with families (Level 1) to family therapy (Level 5). Levels 1 and 5 are outside the range of involvement for the family life educator, as they include either too little personal interaction or too much.

Level 1: Minimal Emphasis on Family

This level of interaction is focused on the institution or organization rather than on a family or family members. Professionals develop programs with little consideration for the needs or interests of parents and family members. They are not considered important to the situation and are included only for legal or practical reasons. An example might be a school that brings in a child's parents for a conference only because they legally have to rather than as part of a team approach. The parents are not seen as playing an important or active role in the situation. The teacher does all the talking and gets little input or feedback from the parent. Another example of level 1 involvement might be a case manager who interviews a client about financial assistance but has no interest in other matters of personal family coping. The effectiveness of level 1 interactions is limited by the superficial involvement of the professional with the family or family member.

Level 2: Information and Advice

This level involves sharing of knowledge and information about relevant issues such as child development, parenting, and family interaction. This might include sharing literature, distributing a newsletter, or making presentations in classes and workshops. The family life educator operating at this level must have good communication skills, be able to facilitate discussion, answer questions, be aware of appropriate resources, and be able to make appropriate recommendations. The strength of this level is that it is relatively low risk, involving sharing information rather than value judgments and personal input. However, interaction is limited for this same reason, as little personal discussion occurs at this level.

Level 3: Feelings and Support

This level includes the information-sharing component of level 2 but adds consideration of feelings and personal experiences as part of the educational process. Level 3 combines cognitive (thinking) and affective (feeling) domains. Family life educators involved at level 3 are able to "listen empathetically, probe gently for feelings and personal stories, create an open and supportive group climate, engage in collaborative problem solving, and tailor recommendations to the specific situation of the parent or family member" (Doherty, 1995, p. 354). Level 3 is generally considered to be the optimal level of involvement for most family life education activities, because it involves a combination of information sharing, feelings, and support appropriate to most family life education situations. Involvement at Level 3 might occur in workshops ranging in length from 2 hours to 2 days, as well as ongoing classes and support groups.

An important facet of level 3 is that it generally involves the normative stresses of family life rather than more traumatic or irregular occurrences. For example, the difficulty of balancing work and family, parenting issues, and financial management issues all are considered to be normative stresses and are appropriately handled at this level through discussion, sharing of personal stories, and recommendations for action. More intense and irregular occurrences, such as physical or sexual abuse, require more extensive discussion and responses and are not appropriate for this level. Therefore, family life educators operating at level 3 must be able to protect participants from sharing too much personal information. This is important not only for the person involved but also for other group members who might be uncomfortable with a level of disclosure beyond their expectations. The family life educator needs to be able to identify when a participant's needs go beyond the scope of the group and be ready to identify an alternate setting outside the group that is better suited to the participant's need.

In order to operate effectively at this level, the family life educator must be aware of and comfortable with his or her own emotional responses. Doherty (1995) cites four mistakes that often occur at level 3:

- Moving back to the cognitive level too quickly when too much emotion or personal information is shared because of the educator's own personal discomfort

- Moving attention away from the individual to the group without adequate opportunity for discussion

- Giving advice or recommendations before the participant has provided sufficient information or adequately shared his or her feelings
- Pushing too deeply into the experiences or feelings of the participant

Level 4: Brief Focused Intervention

Level 4 includes the skills and activities found in the first three levels but goes further to include assessment of the situation and development of a plan of action that goes beyond the activities of level 3. Level 4 actions usually involve more extensive and systemic change and are therefore more appropriate for individuals and families with more serious and compromising situations or for high-risk populations. For example, suppose spousal abuse is uncovered as part of a parenting support group conversation that normally operates at a level 3 involvement. A skilled educator would want to move the client toward help outside of the parenting group, that is, to a level 4 involvement that might include counseling or intervention.

Family life educators operating at level 4 need skills in assessment and intervention. These skills require training beyond that provided in most nontherapy degree programs such as family studies or family life education. Level 4 "represents the upper boundary of parent and family education practiced by a minority of professionals who choose to work with special populations of parents and seek special training in family assessment and basic family interventions" (Doherty, 1995, p. 355). At this level it is important that there be an explicit understanding between the educator and the individual regarding the level of involvement both are engaged in.

The most common mistakes at level 4 include:

- Unintentionally moving from level 3 to level 4 and then getting stuck or overwhelmed
- Engaging in deeper problem-solving discussions without the permission or agreement of the person involved
- Moving too quickly from level 3 discussion into assessment and intervention
- Remaining at level 4 when it is not proving to be effective

Doherty argues that although level 3 is most typically the appropriate level of involvement for most family life educators, they also need to be familiar with level 4 in order to decide when involvement is or is not appropriate. Family life educators often work with families with special needs and issues that may not be sufficiently addressed through level 3 involvement. Professional family life educators need to be able to identify when a more active problem-solving approach is needed. They need to work collaboratively with professionals in related fields who may be better able to help. Level 4 "is an approach that requires careful programmatic decision making, staff preparation, acceptance by the parents and family members who participate and close working relationships with therapists and other professionals in the community" (Doherty, 1995, p. 356).

Level 5: Family Therapy

Level 5, family therapy, is clearly beyond the scope appropriate to family life education but is included in Doherty's model as part of a continuum. Family therapy involves more lengthy and intensive discussion of more personal and serious issues. Family life educators are not typically trained in issues and skills needed to operate at this level. It is when family life educators work at this level without the proper training that issues of professionalism can be called into question.

Doherty's levels of family involvement model provides a much-needed framework from which to address the sometimes overlapping issues involved in family life education and therapy. Professionals working in both fields must work collaboratively to best serve individuals and family members. An effective family life educator recognizes issues that go beyond the scope of family life education and is prepared to provide referrals to more appropriate professionals and resources.

Box 2.4   Levels of Family Involvement for Parent and Family Educators Model

Level 1: Minimal Emphasis on Family

Interactions with parents are institution-centered, not family-centered. Families are not regarded as an important area of focus, but parents are dealt with for practical or legal reasons.

Level 2: Information and Advice

Knowledge Base: Content information about families, parenting, and child development.
Personal Development: Openness to engage parents in collaborative ways.
Skills:

1. Communicating information clearly and interestingly.

2. Eliciting questions.

3. Engaging a group of parents in the learning process.

4. Making pertinent and practical recommendations.

5. Providing information on community resources.

Level 3: Feelings and Support

Knowledge Base: Individual and family reactions to stress, and the emotional aspects of group process.
Personal Development: Awareness of one's own feelings in relation to parents and group process.
Skills:

1. Eliciting expressions of feelings and concerns.

2. Empathetic listening.

3. Normalizing feelings and reactions.

4. Creating an open and supportive climate.

5. Protecting a parent from too much self-disclosure in a group.

6. Engaging parents in collaborative problem-solving discussion.

7. Tailoring recommendations to the unique needs, concerns, and feelings of the parent and family.

8. Identifying individual and family dysfunction.

9. Tailoring a referral to the unique situation of the parent and family.

Level 4: Brief Focused Intervention
Knowledge Base: Family systems theory.
Personal Development: Awareness of one's own participation in systems, including one's own family, the parents' systems, and larger community systems.
Skills:

1. Asking a series of questions to elicit a detailed picture of the family dynamics of a parent's problem.

2. Developing a hypothesis about the family systems dynamics involved in the problem.

3. Working with the parent for a short period of time to change a family interaction pattern beyond the one-to-one parent/child relationship.

4. Knowing when to end the intervention effort and either refer the parent or return to level 3 support.

5. Orchestrating a referral by educating the family and the therapist about what to expect from each other.

6. Working with therapists and community systems to help the parent and family.

Level 5: Family Therapy
This level is outside the scope and mission of parent and family education. The following description is offered to show the boundary between level 4 parent and family education and level 5 family therapy.
Knowledge Base: Family systems and patterns whereby distressed families interact with professionals and other community systems.
Personal Development: Ability to handle intense emotions in families and self and to maintain one's balance in the face of strong pressure from family members or other professionals.
Example Skills:

1. Interviewing families or family members who are quite difficult to engage.

2. Efficiently generating and testing hypotheses about the family's difficulties and interaction patterns.

3. Escalating conflict in the family in order to break a family impasse.

4. Working intensively with families during crises.

5. Constructively dealing with a family's strong resistance to change.

6. Negotiating collaborative relationships with other professionals and other systems who are working with the family, even when these groups are at odds with one another.

From Doherty, 1995, pp. 353–358.

ETHICAL GUIDELINES

Let us revisit two of the family life educators introduced earlier in this chapter to look at the issue of professional ethics.

Carl has a baccalaureate degree in art history. He has worked for the past 9 years as a youth coordinator for the YMCA and organizes activities and classes for neighborhood kids identified as high risk. Carl learns that Chris, a child he has a close relationship with, has become involved in gang activity. The child's parents have told Carl that they want him to keep close tabs on their son. They don't know about their son's involvement with the gang. Should Carl talk to the parents?

Gretchen has a degree in child development. She organizes a parent group in her neigh-borhood for other stay-at-home moms and dads with kids under two years old. The group meets regularly and discusses a predetermined topic each time. Members rotate responsibility for researching the topic and presenting information. Much of the meet-ing is spent in casual conversation and support. Lately, one parent, Connie, has been monopolizing the discussion and has disclosed information about her relationship with her husband. Some of the other group members appear to be uncomfortable with the level of disclosure going on but Connie seems to be in need of the group's attention and input. What should Gretchen do?

Professionals in fields ranging from medicine to law to auto mechanics are faced with ethical issues at one time or another. Family life education is no excep-tion and may, in fact, be more susceptible to ethical dilemmas due to the sensitive and personal nature of some of the issues faced in practice. Because family life education often deals with values and belief systems, it is imperative that the pro-fessional family life educator have an understanding of the role of ethics in his or her professional life.

The development of a code of ethics is an important indicator of the develop-ment of a profession (East, 1980). As professionals, family life educators need access to ethical guidelines for practice, as well as the capability to consider and act upon these guidelines. "Ethical codes guide our professional interactions with each other as well as with our constituents. A code lets the public know what it can expect from those who call themselves professionals and helps us as practitio-ners face with confidence some of the difficult decisions that come with our work" (Freeman, 1997, p. 64).

Codes of ethics are designed to prevent harm to consumers and professionals and to the professions themselves (Brock, 1993). Ethics codes for the helping pro-fessions commonly address five principles of ethical practice that are based on the teachings of Hippocrates (Brock, 1993). These are:

- Practice with competence
- Do not exploit
- Treat people with respect
- Protect confidentiality
- Do no harm

The concept of ethics and ethical guidelines has only recently entered the pro-fessional discussion and literature of family life education. For many years, litera-ture regarding family life education supported the notion that a code of ethics for family life education was unnecessary, because the nature of family life education did not involve an intensity level that could result in the potential for harm. Mar-riage and family therapy was seen as more intense and therefore more in need of control and regulation (Brock, 1993).

Research began to support the effectiveness of preventive and psychoeduca-tional efforts with individuals and families with more severe clinical problems, such as family illness, mental illness, and so forth. The diversity and complexity of today's families required family life educators to increase and modify their roles. With this increased complexity, the potential for doing harm grows as well (Palm, 1998).

In 1992, the Parent/Family Education Section of the Minnesota Council on Family Relations (MCFR) began work on developing a code of ethics specifically for use by practitioners in parent and family education. They recognized that family life education was an emerging field and that many practitioners faced ethical dilemmas in relative isolation and with limited guidance (MCFR, 1997). They based their efforts on a model used by the National Association for the Education of Young Children (NAEYC) to develop a code of ethics for early childhood practitioners.

The Ethics Committee of MCFR developed and carried out a series of workshops with parent and family educators from 1995 to 1997. These workshops involved the use of case studies to identify agreed-upon principles for practice within family life education, as well as steps to follow in dealing with ethical dilemmas.

The committee's discussion with William Doherty of the University of Minnesota resulted in a multiperspective approach to ethics. Such an approach blends the concepts of relational ethics, ethical principles, and core human virtues. Relational ethics emphasizes the context of the relationship between the people involved. It asks, "Who are the stakeholders?" and considers the role of each person in relation to the other. The principles concept considers agreed-upon principles for practice and such standards as "We will do no harm to children and insist on the same from others" and "We will define our role as family educators and practice within our level of competence."

Doherty's inclusion of a virtue approach is an exciting step in the process of developing ethical guidelines, for it recognizes the importance of considering the "greater good" for families and society as opposed to only considering the aspirations of a single individual. The previous definition of professional behavior focused on technical competence. The introduction of virtues into the equation recognizes moral competence. "Good practice in family life education should be tied to internal standards of excellence" (MCFR, 1997, p. 2).

Doherty identified core virtues that should exist in most professions, including justice, truthfulness, and courage. But other virtues also are inherent in family life education. Professionals attending the ethics workshops provided a long list of virtues, from which three essential virtues emerged: *caring, prudence/practical*

Box 2.5   Process for Considering an Ethical Dilemma

Step 1   Identification of important relationships
Step 2   Application of principles
Step 3   Identification of contradictions
Step 4   Application of virtues
Step 5   Consideration of possible actions
Step 6   Selection of action

From National Council on Family Relations (1999). Copyrighted 1999 by the National Council on Family Relations, 3989 Central Ave. NE, Suite 550, Minneapolis, MN 55421. Reprinted by permission.

wisdom, and *hope/optimism.* It is believed by some that these virtues need to be present within the practitioner in order for him or her to implement effective family life education.

Tools for Ethical Thinking and Practice in Family Life Education is available through the National Council on Family Relations (NCFR, 1999). It provides a more detailed description of the concepts, as well as a step-by-step process for their use in dealing with ethical dilemmas. Box 2.5 provides a summary of the six steps.

It should be noted that in 1995 the Family Science Section of the National Council on Family Relations approved ethical guidelines for family scientists. Although many concepts are similar or identical to those in family life education, the focus is more on academic teaching and research issues.

Personal morals are not sufficient when dealing with ethical dilemmas in a work setting. Practitioners need to understand and internalize their profession's core values. Because of the nature of their work, family life educators are expected to balance the needs of a variety of clients. They have an ethical responsibility to children, parents, colleagues, employers, and society. Oftentimes ethical dilemmas arise out of the conflicting needs or interests of those involved (Freeman, 1997). Consideration of ethical principles and the implementation of an ethical-guideline process can provide family life educators with guidance to help make decisions that are right for them and for the situation.

IMPORTANCE OF ONGOING PROFESSIONAL DEVELOPMENT

As you walk up to the stage to accept your degree and prepare to throw your mortarboard in the air, it is tempting to think that your time as a student is over. You have completed the course work needed for your degree, taken your last test, and submitted your last paper. Now it is time to roll up your sleeves, get to work, and put all the knowledge to good use!

Newly graduated professionals often give little thought to the need to continue their education beyond graduation (Darling & Cassidy, 1998), but it is an integral part of professionalism. Qualified professionals must stay current on research and developments within their field.

Continuing education and professional development can be accomplished through a number of avenues. Some examples include attendance at workshops, seminars, and professional conferences; review of current research through professional publications such as newsletters and journals; presentation of research at professional meetings; and networking with others in the field through membership in professional organizations and associations.

Most certification and licensing programs require professionals to earn a minimum number of continuing education credits (CEUs), sometimes called PDUs (professional development units), in order to maintain the designation or license (Knapp & Reynolds, 1996). Professionals need to actively seek continuing education opportunities and to maintain records that document attendance at meetings and professional activities. Membership in one or more professional organizations can provide numerous opportunities for continued growth.

SUMMARY

We have looked closely at the field of family life education and issues of professionalism. We have determined that the field of family life education does indeed meet many of the criteria set forth by experts in defining a profession. We have considered some of the challenges in getting the profession recognized. We have looked at the importance of developing a personal philosophy, including personal insights, values, and beliefs about families and family life education. Personal qualities and traits needed for effective practices were considered. Doherty's levels of family involvement model provided helpful parameters for identifying boundaries for effective practice. Finally, we discussed the importance of ethical guidelines in assuring best practices. These considerations provide the foundation for further discussion about the practice of family life education.

Questions/Problems for Discussion and Review

Class Discussion

1. Which of the people described on the first page of this chapter would you consider to be a "professional" family life educator? Why?

2. How do you define "family"?

3. What is the goal of family life education?

4. Can a person have a different set of values in his or her personal life than in his or her professional life? Why or why not?

Research Problems

1. Trace the development of another social science profession (e.g., social work, marriage and family therapy) applying East's criteria.

2. Interview a representative sample of family studies majors in your department and a sample of family life educators in your area. Compare their responses to the ethical dilemmas presented in the case studies in this chapter. On what bases do they make their judgments?

3. Using Doherty's levels of family involvement model, determine the proper course of action for a family life educator when a parent in a parent education group reveals having been physically abused by his or her spouse.

Case Study Design

Read through the two ethical dilemmas described on pages 49–50. What should Carl do? What should Gretchen do?

PART II

THE PRACTICE OF FAMILY LIFE EDUCATION

three

Relating Theory to Practice

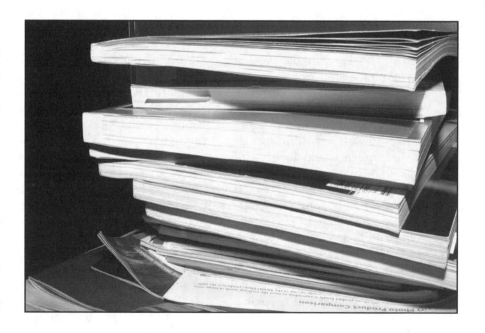

The trend is definitely disturbing: Teen pregnancies at younger and younger ages have been on a continual rise since the 1950s. Although the latest figures from the National Center for Health Statistics show an encouraging downturn in the number of teen pregnancies (Henshaw, 2004), the numbers still cast a long shadow. Young single parents tend to drop out of high school and have few marketable skills that would lift them out of poverty. Many of their children suffer from lack of resources and possible neglect. There is great national concern for the mothers, the children, the communities in which they live, and society as a whole.

What can be done to support these families and move them toward self-sufficiency and competent parenting? How can young men and women be influenced to postpone parenthood until they are adequately educated and able to make more mature decisions? Many things are being tried by various societal institutions: government, through changes in laws and policies; the education system, through more—and earlier—sex education in schools; the social system, through programs to get family members more involved with each other in positive ways.

Unfortunately, very few of the efforts to date have been based on established theories of social and behavioral change and proven effectiveness. "Too often, prevention efforts are based on common sense, good intentions, myths about adolescent development, and the heroic efforts of committed staff" (Bogenschneider, 1996, p. 127). For example, before the 1992 presidential election, an alliance of politicians pressed for adoption of governmental policies that they felt would reverse the breakup and decline of two-parent families. These included lowering the tax burden to reduce the financial stress that contributes to divorce; investing in education, job training, child care, and health care (social supports that would assist families toward self-sufficiency); and cutting welfare benefits to discourage welfare dependency and low-functioning families. Although some attention was given to reeducation and prevention services, they were not a major focus of the proposals (Zimmerman, 1995). This comes some 20 years after a rigorous assessment of a family support model conducted by the Yale Child Welfare Research Program determined that services to families can bring social benefits to children—and their mothers—but only if services are sustained and comprehensive (Ziglar & Gilman, 1990). The Yale project employed a multidisciplinary approach, including health care, monthly home visits for problem solving and parent education, and child care as required. The long-term effects on children and parents were very positive and measurable. After 10 years, children who had received intervention were better adjusted to school and had greater school attendance; mothers who had received intervention had a higher rate of self-support and employment. They also had pursued more education and had chosen to bear fewer children than the control-group mothers. "If we have learned anything over the decades of child study, it is the need to be broad-based and family-centered. There are no instant, one-shot solutions" (Ziglar & Gilman, 1990, p. 244).

As valid studies of healthy family functioning and family wellness accumulate, the family focus on education and preventive services is confirmed. Kilpatrick and Holland (1995), in developing a model for community human services, determined that education that reinforces family efforts is the most effective prevention tool. They outline three types of human-service agendas: (1) survival, (2) self-empowerment, and (3) self-realization and prevention of relationship problems. Agenda types (2) and (3) are especially related to the skills of family life educators who understand family dynamics and family systems theory. Coupled with knowledge of learning theory and effective teaching methods, education for positive behavior change should certainly be enhanced. Bogenschneider (1996), in presenting an ecological risk/protective theory for building prevention programs, stresses that our most effective prevention efforts are based on strong theoretical and empirical foundations that shape program conceptualization, design, implementation, evaluation, and institutionalization. Yet she laments that "promoting health or wellness is less effective in mobilizing parents, community leaders, and policymakers than is attacking problems or crises" (p. 129). Aulette (1994) points out that theory can serve not only as a guide to social change but also as a force for change, whether the societal concern is teen pregnancy, parent competency, or any other relationship issue.

THE ASSUMPTIONS OF FAMILY LIFE EDUCATION

The general goals of the family life education movement have been to encourage the growth potential of individuals and families and to reduce family-related societal problems through family-focused educational opportunities (Arcus & Thomas, 1993). Through the years, myriad family life education programs have been developed to address some part of this two-pronged focus, using a variety of objectives. The most common are (1) gaining insight into self and others, (2) learning about human development and behavior in the family setting over the life cycle, (3) learning about marriage and family patterns and processes, (4) acquiring skills essential for family living, (5) developing individuals' potentials in their current and future roles, and (6) building strengths in families. "One of the assumptions in family life education appears to be that, if these and other similar objectives are met through family life education programs, then families will be better able to deal with problems, to prevent problems, and/or to develop their potentials" (Arcus & Thomas, 1993, p. 5).

How this assumption influences program design depends upon the educator's perspective on the purpose of family life education (Miller & Seller, 1990). The *transmission* perspective equates accumulation of facts with mastery of subject matter and skills. Learners are expected to be attentive to their teacher and basically passive consumers. (They may ask or respond to a question, but no further involvement is expected.) The purpose of family life education from this perspective appears to be the transmission of facts, skills development information, and values information that prepare one to fit into society. The *transaction* perspective implies more involvement between the teacher and the learner. Learners are viewed as autonomous beings who are capable of rational thought and active involvement in their own learning experience. Therefore, the purpose of family life education from the transaction perspective would focus on developing cogni-

tive skills and critical-thinking abilities in order to use them in individual problem-solving situations. The *transformation* perspective recognizes the personal
element of knowledge and the strong influence of social interaction and cultural
context in determining personal behavior and values. Although learners are seen
as diverse and unique, they also share many basic human needs and concerns.
The purpose of family life education from this perspective is to facilitate social
interaction that results in personal and social change.

A review of the stated aims and objectives of family life education by Thomas
(1988) determined that most descriptions of family life programs reflect the transmission perspective, even though program designers often desire personal and
social transformation as an outcome. In a critical analysis of the assumptions of
family life education, Morgaine concludes that the practices of the field must be
"reconceptualized" if programs are to reach the ultimate goal of family life education, namely, to "strengthen and enrich family well-being" (Morgaine, as cited in
Arcus & Thomas, 1993, p. 5).

USING THEORY TO DESIGN PROGRAMS

In order to understand how growth and change in an individual or a family
occurs, it is important to be familiar with several major theoretical models related
to families. The process of change does not easily fit into any single model (Winton, 1995). Human beings and families are truly unique in their experiences and
makeup. Most family counselors conclude that no two children have the same
parents, because each child is born into a different time and context of relationships. Every person is unique and reacts somewhat differently to the same set of
circumstances because of other variables in her or his environment. So it is that
family scientists must always expect a certain degree of error in their conclusions
and discuss "probabilities" of cause and effect. With that qualification, we now
discuss the basic tenets of family systems theory, human ecology theory, exchange
theory, and family developmental theory.

Family Systems Theory

Earlier in this chapter, the Yale Child Welfare Research Program design
(Ziglar & Gilman, 1990) and the model for community human services (Kilpatrick
& Holland, 1995) were mentioned as programs that stress the important role that
the family plays in program success. Family systems theory helps us to understand why this is so. Basically, family systems theory views the family as a living
organism operating within certain boundaries, rules, expectations, and interaction patterns between its members. These patterns have been passed down and
adapted through many generations. They may be helpful or destructive to family
members, but regardless, they are very powerful in determining the behavior of
each individual. The family system exerts such a strong influence on the individual because the system depends on certain patterns of interaction to maintain its
familiar and comfortable "shape." Like the carefully balanced mobile that Virginia Satir (1972) used to describe the family, the system works to keep everything
in balance. When change occurs in any part of the system, the whole system is

affected and becomes unbalanced. The system then must either support and accommodate the change or resist it. Often it is easier to maintain the status quo (homeostasis) by resisting the change than to exert the energy it takes from every part of the system to accommodate a change. Furthermore, the family system is part of several larger systems, including the community, the culture, and peer networks. These also exert a strong influence on the shape of the family and may have to be confronted or altered if the family system changes.

Let us apply the family system concept to the topic of teen pregnancy prevention. Usually, programs of sex education and pregnancy prevention are designed by educators to involve the child or teen only. Little input from parents or program participants is sought in planning the program, and seldom is follow-up or long-term reinforcement included in the program design. The end result is scant family reinforcement of the ideas or skills presented in the program. The system remains uninvolved and unaffected. Furthermore, the teen functions within a peer system that emphasizes conformity and short-term gratification. Attempts to "buck the system" are quickly squelched through ridicule, intimidation, or isolation from the group. Is it any wonder that many of our programs show few positive changes, either short or long term?

On the other hand, if a family system functions in a healthy manner, it can reinforce and influence positive growth for the individual as well as the system. A classic and extensive study of psychological health in family systems by Lewis, Beavers, Gossett, and Phillips (1976) determined that families need to have access to preventive programs that are based on sound research about the types of interactions that build "healthy," well-functioning families. But "What is meant by 'health'? What is meant by 'normal'?" (p. 12). The authors proceed to discuss four perspectives of health that are used by behavioral and medical research: (1) health as absence of overt pathology, (2) health as "optimal functioning," (3) health as average or normal functioning, and (4) health as process, recognizing the ability of a system to change over time. Whether or not one chooses to define "health" from any of these four perspectives, the particular system's characteristics can serve as a basic reference point.

Lewis et al. (1976) also strongly stress that health cannot be studied independently of time, place, and cultural or ethnic context and values. Epstein, Bishop, and Baldwin (1984) give an example of this as it relates to understanding and evaluating certain family responses:

> [When] we describe how a healthy, or, in our view, a normal family should look on each of the dimensions, often such a description involves a value judgment. For instance, we would say that family members ought to be able to show sadness at the appropriate times and to the degree called for by the situation. The judgement of appropriateness with respect to sadness is not clear-cut and varies among cultures. We take the position that knowledge of the culture to which a family belongs is necessary for understanding a family and that judgements of health or normality are relative to the culture of the family. (p. 117)

Unfortunately for persons outside of the mainstream cultural group in America (i.e., the White middle class), many family life education programs or texts in the 1970s did not address differences in class, cultural values, or lifestyles (Rodman,

1970). The research of Scott-Jones and Peebles-Wilson (1986) uncovered a gender bias as well. They determined that many parent education programs were aimed at the middle-class, White female parent and that the scheduled times (plus fees charged and level of English-language competency needed to complete learning materials) automatically excluded those of a certain socioeconomic status and most males. Hopefully, increasing awareness of cultural and gender diversity—and its impact on program design and effectiveness—has addressed these earlier deficits.

The timing of educational intervention is another critical factor. Lewis et al. (1976) call this an "urgent need" for program design and stress the importance of focusing on the young family:

> In a useful analogy, young families may be likened to an infant. The family as an organism undergoes a series of developmental sequences. Over time a family's characteristic style of reacting may become increasingly "fixed." Young families, therefore, are reasonably unencumbered by family developmental events and may represent organisms unusually responsive to education. (pp. 4–5)

Because the new pair is forming a new family system, the probability of incorporating healthier patterns is much more likely than in a long-established system, provided new skills and options are presented effectively and reinforced through practice by the pair.

To summarize, the influence of the family system and external systems on an individual's behavior and choices is very powerful and should be considered and utilized in the design of family life education programs.

Human Ecology Theory

The external systems already mentioned (cultural context, time, place, gender, lifestyle) emphasize the interdependence of human communities and their various environments. This emphasis forms the basis of human ecology theory.

Families do not exist as isolated systems. They are constantly interacting with their environment and the resources (or lack thereof) it provides. These resources include useful goods and services that families must have for their own needs and also what they can give back, such as productive work and family and community support. Andrews, Bubolz, and Paolucci (1980) explain:

> The flow of energy to and through the family system activates the decision-making and decision-implementation processes. Internally, the energy is transformed to support the production, consumption, and socialization functions of the family. The outputs to the environment are used by other systems, activating reciprocal exchanges and bonds of interdependence. (p. 35)

For example, in planning a grief support group for widows, the family life educator must consider not only the group's emotional and social needs but also such factors as time, transportation, and health constraints. Cost of materials and supplies, reading levels, and child care are other typical ecological factors that must be considered when planning programs. On the "output" side of the ledger, it is important to remember that self-esteem is bolstered when persons feel that they have something to give back to the community and have power to make changes in their living environment. One small personal example supports this theory as an effective educational tool. I (Powell) was facilitating a welfare-to-work series of sessions on effective communication in the workplace. The meetings were taking place in a vacant apartment in the housing project where most of the women lived. Tables and chairs had been moved into the apartment, but unfortunately the apartment heater was not working. There were numerous voiced complaints, and the group's shivering and discomfort greatly affected their ability to engage in the sessions. Coincidentally, the lesson for the day was how to communicate and effect change in your home and work environments. The program leader had called the management office repeatedly with no results, and I suggested to the group that a letter might get more attention. Together, the group composed a letter; everyone signed it, and someone was dispatched to deliver it to the apartment manager. By that afternoon, we had a written promise from management that the heater would be fixed immediately. The group was elated. They received a "power boost" and a great lesson regarding how they could affect the environment in a positive way. Human ecology theory goes much deeper than that, considering natural, human-behavioral, and human-constructed environments and how each becomes an energy transformation system (Bubolz & Sontag, 1993). But the bottom line is that physical resources of families (air, water, land, food, temperature, space, and energy) are critically important factors that influence the ability to perceive problems and envision solutions (Rettig, 1988).

Exchange Theory

Whereas human ecology theory focuses on external factors of influence, exchange theory looks at internal influences on decision making and behavior, such as one's perception of self and internal motivations. Social exchange theory was articulated by behaviorist George Homans (1958, 1961) and sociologists J. W. Thibaut and H. H. Kelley (1959). They reasoned that all individuals are motivated to act on a cost-reward basis, seeking to minimize costs and maximize rewards. If a certain behavior is seen as rewarding, it will tend to be repeated; if it is seen as too costly (whether in terms of money, time, or emotional effort), it will be discouraged. Homans (1958) also surmised that people are drawn to those who possess desirable qualities or characteristics, such as people who have high income, status, or prestige or who are physically attractive. The qualities considered to be desirable may vary greatly from culture to culture, however. Reverence for the elderly and their opinions is a good example of this cultural variation. In some cultures, the elderly are considered wise and their input valuable; in other cultures, the elderly are generally tolerated or ignored. When applied to program design, the use of role models who have appeal for the particular group, either as group facilitators or guest speakers, can reinforce motivation for desirable change.

It is not always easy to ascertain who will inspire admiration and respect as a leader. In one situation I (Powell) personally experienced a group of learners of a different race and socioeconomic level, yet we seemed to get along quite well. I asked the program director if she had tried to recruit "successful" persons of the same race as the participants to serve as role models and teachers. "Yes, and we actually have had some come to lead the group, but the women didn't like them."

Rather surprised, I asked why. "Because they felt that the leaders were talking down to them," she responded. I am not sure what happened that resulted in the lack of connection, but it's important to remember that respect for what a teacher says is a quality that transcends cultural similarities or external trappings of success. Respect must be earned, not assumed.

Jane Vella (1994), a community development educator from North Carolina, has designed and led community education programs for adult learners in more than 40 countries around the world. The seminars often involve several hundred people and a language or culture different from her own. Vella recalls an invitation to come to El Salvador to teach what she knew about community development organization.

"I knew I could not do that with accountability if I did not first find out what they knew, what their life was like, how they thought about it, what they still needed to learn," she observed (p. 126). So Vella spent several days visiting clinics, schools, and farms in the area before she began her classes:

> We chatted with village leaders and priests and teachers and wives. We played with endless numbers of beautiful, brown-eyed babies, their mothers' eyes shining with pride as I praised each one. Again I saw how basic human courtesy, expressed in respect for each individual and for the cultural practices, is such a profound instrument for learning. I was learning because they respected me. They were learning through my respect. Perhaps, under the umbrella of respect, learning is always mutual. (Vella, 1994, p. 128)

Exchange theory is applicable in this example because it demonstrates how the role of respected leader and role model can be achieved through the exchange of information, sharing of opinions, and obvious respect for the culture and customs of the learners. As the two different cultures in Vella's experience came to admire each other, a sense of equality between teacher and learners developed, and everyone was then ready to learn.

The use of tangible or intangible rewards, also an emphasis in exchange theory, can enhance the effectiveness of educational programs as well. The age and identified needs of group members will determine what type of reward system will prove most effective. For example, adolescent drug treatment programs often use television privileges and weekend passes to encourage cooperation and group participation. Although the rewards may work to produce desired behaviors, they may also be viewed by the program participants as coercion rather than reward, and the desired behaviors will likely fall away after the participants leave the program. On the other hand, genuine acknowledgment by a respected leader of good work done or the discovery of personal gifts or talents that bring respect from others are often more lasting rewards. This may lead to sustainable behavior changes if coupled with a family and peer group system that support and encourage the new behaviors (another type of reward).

For adult groups, rewards will vary, but most will be intangible. The thrill of gaining new knowledge and personal awareness may be enough for some (and may be all the program was designed to do). For others, it may be the hope of a better self-image, a more peaceful household, better communication, more control over life deci-

Just as people in the same family have different personalities and preferences, so persons, old or young, have different learning styles.

sions, or a successful job search. If a new behavior is tried and gets positive results, it is likely to be repeated and reinforced. If it is tried and rebuffed, it is likely to be discarded. As a leader, I often remind program participants that new behaviors take work and practice in order to be successful. I did not learn to ride a bike on my first try (or my tenth!), but I wanted to learn badly enough that I was willing to suffer the wobbles and falls in order to keep on trying. The same is true of any new behavior.

Exchange theory is often used to explain why couple relationships last or end. If partners perceive that they are receiving benefits from the relationship that are equal to or exceed the costs of sustaining a long-term commitment, then they are likely to maintain the partnership. New behaviors can be taught and perceptions can change, but it usually takes commitment from both members of the couple to work at changing old interaction patterns. Some behavioral marital therapy programs design short-term rewards and contracts to encourage couples to keep trying to establish new relationship patterns. This use of exchange theory is one way to heighten the possibility of success for couple growth.

Family Developmental Theory

Family developmental theory proposes that the family unit grows and changes in stages and over time, just as individuals do. Winton (1995) points out that because families do not necessarily develop in a unilinear fashion (always proceeding in the same way and through the same stages), the division of family development into stages is "an arbitrary and artificial enterprise" (p. 13). For example, Duvall (1977) described an eight-stage developmental cycle that begins with the childless newlywed couple and ends with aging family members. For each stage, certain roles and developmental tasks are delineated (see table 3.1). One problem immediately seen is that not all couples begin new family development as childless newlyweds. There may be children present from previous marriages. One partner may have been married before and the other not. Many variables exist even for the first stage. Furthermore, all couples do not choose to

Table 3.1   Stage-Critical Family Developmental Tasks throughout the Family Life Cycle

Stage of the Family Life Cycle	Positions in the Family	Stage-Critical Family Developmental Tasks
1. Married couple	Wife Husband	Establishing a mutually satisfying marriage Adjusting to pregnancy and the promise of parenthood Fitting into the kin network
2. Childbearing	Wife-mother Husband-father Daughter-sister Son-brother	Having, adjusting to, and encouraging the development of infants Establishing a satisfying home for both parents and infant(s)
3. Preschool age	Wife-mother Husband-father Daughter-sister Son-brother	Adapting to the critical needs and interests of preschool children in stimulating, growth-promoting ways Coping with energy depletion and lack of privacy as parents
4. School age	Wife-mother Husband-father Daughter-sister Son-brother	Fitting into the community of school-age families in constructive ways Encouraging children's educational achievement
5. Teenage	Wife-mother Husband-father Daughter-sister Son-brother	Balancing freedom with responsibility as teenagers mature and emancipate themselves Establishing post-parental interests and careers as growing parents
6. Launching center	Wife-mother-grandmother Husband-father-grandfather Daughter-sister-aunt Son-brother-uncle	Releasing young adults into work, military service, college, marriage, etc., with appropriate rituals and assistance Maintaining a supportive home base
7. Middle-aged	Wife-mother-grandmother Husband-father-grandfather	Rebuilding the marriage relationship Maintaining kin ties with older and younger generations
8. Aging family members	Widow/widower Wife-mother-grandmother Husband-father-grandfather	Coping with bereavement and living alone Closing the family home or adapting it to aging Adjusting to retirement

From Duvall, Evelyn Millis & Miller, Brent C. *Marriages and Family Development* 6/E © 1985. Published by Allyn and Bacon, Boston, MA. Copyright © 1985 by Pearson Education. Reprinted by permission of the publisher.

have children in a "cluster," particularly if they are in a second or third marriage. And they may choose not to have children at all. There may be two separate sets of children, so that the family will be in two (or even three) developmental stages at the same time!

Hill and Rodgers (1964) determined a more general, five-stage model based on change in family size over time. Beginning with a stability stage for the childless married couple, the family expands with the birth of children, then stabilizes during a period of child rearing, contracts when the children start to leave home, and is stable again during the post-parental stage. This stage theory also has major exceptions, such as the tendency of many couples to divorce during the years of child rearing and the rising number of adult children who return home, many with children from a former marriage.

Later work by Mattessich and Hill (1987) stressed the importance of the theory for describing and explaining the processes of change in families. They noted that the sequence of stages is triggered by internal demands on the family—biological, psychological, and social—combined with external expectations and ecological restraints of the larger society. Rodgers and White (1993) suggested a revised theory that acknowledges that not all family change is developmental. At every level of analysis, the individual, the relationship, the family group, and the institution itself have an impact on the future direction of the family.

So what is the value of a family developmental model? Even with such numerous and widespread exceptions, developmental models can offer insight into the typical direction of development a family will take. Analyzing the new roles, adjustments, and developmental tasks that are needed in each stage can help families prepare to a degree for what is coming next. Noting typical development and the numerous exceptions can emphasize the complexity of developing and maintaining strong family systems. Discussing family development can also defuse unspoken simplistic myths about how a family ought to look or be.

Using developmental theory, family life educators can address programs to couples in a particular family developmental stage: newlyweds, new parents, parents with teens, empty nesters, or stepfamilies, to name a few. Such stage-specific programs have a greater probability of long-term effectiveness, because they address current issues that the person or family is facing and provide support and insight from other group members who are having similar experiences. Today, additional developmental stages have emerged for some families. There are grandparents raising a second family of grandchildren or the divorced older adult who struggles to redefine a family system. With few guidelines from the past, persons who are thrown into unexpected or unfamiliar roles may be eager for new insight and support from those in similar circumstances. A final word of caution: It is important that educators not assume that everyone in the group (even a group of newlyweds) has the same family developmental pattern. Educators should assure participants that differences in developmental paths do not mean deviance. Although some of the new developmental stages may be challenging, they can also be rewarding and growth-producing, provided individuals and families have good coping skills and a network of support.

MODELS AND PRINCIPLES FOR LEARNING

Educators who operate within a theoretical framework must still develop models and principles for program design. Vella (1994), after many years of experience in program design, implementation, and analysis, concludes that a program, even short-term or in less-than-ideal situations, can be effective if the following principles are incorporated:

- *Needs assessment*: uncovering the specific needs of the learners in the program through their participation in naming these needs
- *Safety in the environment and the process*: defusing fears of the group and establishing ground rules and ways of sharing that the group is comfortable with
- *A sound relationship between teacher and learner for learning and development*: persuading learners to trust and identify with the teacher in order to learn from her or him
- *Careful attention to sequence of content and reinforcement*: preparing and understanding how much (or how little) learners can absorb at any one time, with a variety of reinforcing activities
- *Focus on praxis*: acting and reflecting on the part of the learners
- *Respect for learners as subjects of their own learning*: "drawing in" and valuing the contributions of learners' life experience and insight
- *Cognitive, affective, and psychomotor aspects of learning*: incorporating ideas, feelings, and actions into the learning experience, if possible
- *Immediacy of learning*: making immediate application of the principles and information learned
- *Clear roles and role development*: accepting and honoring the "teacher" role but moving toward a "learners together" role, which encourages dialogue and freedom of application
- *Teamwork*: using small groups to complete tasks or projects
- *Engagement of the learners in what they are learning*: encouraging active, rather than passive, involvement, which results in new pathways of learning that the teacher can validate rather than ignore
- *Accountability:* validating their accomplishments through assessments, role-plays, praxis

To summarize, Vella (1994) emphasizes the basic educational concepts of Paulo Freire, who contrasts the "banking system" of teaching (in which the professor comes and tells you what she knows so that you know it too, with no reference to what you already know or what you need to know) with the "problem-posing approach" (in which the group works in and through dialogue; Freire, as cited in Vella, 1994, p. 126). She concludes that problem-posing dialogue structures a partnership for learning and is a much more effective model of education because it respects the learners and their needs.

Mace (1981) also points to several key concepts that have been demonstrated through theory and experience to create and enhance the climate for growth and change in educational settings:

- *Enough time together to build a sense of community and mutual trust*: a minimum of 15–18 hours of sustained time together, a time frame that can be met by a weekend seminar or a three-hour class five days a week

- *Trained leaders who can establish rapport with the group and who model the skills being taught*: ability to establish "connections" with the group and do more than present facts: to model, give examples from their own life history, and ask for examples from others

- *Dynamic presentation of a body of information based on a well-developed theoretical frame of reference*: information that is up to date, appropriate, and theoretically sound

- *Direct application of information to one's personal life and relationships*: each learner making the connection between the subject matter and the application, whether through writing assignments, role-plays, or sharing personal experiences

- *Follow-up and reinforcement of classwork with outside assignments or materials*: handouts, additional exercises, specific assignments to help the new information "stick" in the mind and encourage application of new principles

- *Opportunity for personal reflection and decision making*: a personal goal, a decision to start a new habit, and articulating steps on how to do this, to encourage personal reflection and application

The process of education with adults is sometimes referred to as *andragogy*—derived by combining the Greek noun *agoge* (the activity of leading) with the stem *andr* (adult). Gross (1993) delineates several methodologies that are highly effective with adult learners: buzz (task-oriented) groups, role-playing, and, most important, the discussion group. A discussion group can range in size from three to 15 participants. This small-group discussion allows optimum "two-way learning" to take place as both the teacher and the students share knowledge and participate in the learning experience. Vella (1994) adds that the small group provides an element of safety for the person who is reluctant to speak up in a large-group setting. The small group quickly becomes a learning team, building cooperation and support so that the team becomes a constructive competitor with other groups. Chapter 5 elaborates on the dynamics of group formation and interaction.

Moss and King (1970) point out that different approaches to family life education employ various methodologies. The *group-oriented approach* focuses on group processes in problem solving and decision making, the *sensitivity approach* on the development of individual awareness, and the *thinking-oriented approach* on intellectual development. The methodology and focus of andragogy obviously differ somewhat from effective methodologies used with children and young adolescents. The needs and limitations of other ages are reviewed in chapter 4.

DEVELOPING EFFECTIVE EDUCATION STRATEGIES

Does real education involve more than simple accumulation of facts? If you answered yes, then you agree with education specialists who emphasize that education involves the ability to actually use knowledge to make choices and to act on the basis of reason (Arcus & Thomas, 1993; Mace, 1981; Peters, 1967; Vella, 1994). "Making choices" and "acting on the basis of reason" imply a much deeper level of involvement by the student and certainly are required if many of the stated goals and assumptions of family life education are to be accomplished. Yet few teachers in our education system in general or family life education in particular consistently go beyond factual presentation and immediate audience response.

Mace (1981) stressed the original meaning of the word *education*, which is derived from the Latin verb *duco* (to lead, conduct, draw, or bring) combined with the prefix *ex* (out of, from). Thus education originally referred to drawing out of the student what was already there but unknown or unarticulated. Mace observed:

> This is not, however, the sense in which we customarily use the word "education" in academic circles. We place the emphasis less on drawing out what is already there, and more on pumping in what is definitely *not* already there. What we pump in is *information*, so that the student may process it as *knowledge*, which is simply information systematically filed in the brain's computer system in such a way that it is later available for instant recall. (p. 599)

Although such ability to recall facts is certainly necessary for cognitive/intellectual growth, Mace stressed the importance, particularly for family life educators, of distinguishing between "learning for knowing and learning for living."

"As family life educators, therefore, we have to ask ourselves how our students make the transition from the classroom, where they learn to *know*, to the more private environment in which they learn to *live*" (Mace, 1981, p. 600). Mace offered a model for the journey from factual input to behavioral change, although it is a difficult road for any individual:

> I asked myself whether I really believed that the people who heard me speak, or who read my books, were somehow released from their paralysis, and set free to change their relationships for the better . . . but I could not persuade myself that I . . . made any significant difference in the way they behaved at home—the tight bonds of long-established habits are just too powerful. (p. 600)

So what are the established levels and necessary environments for learning that motivate personal behavior change? Mace proposed that one must go through several steps: from the *acquisition of knowledge* (the gathering of facts that "stick" in the brain and are available for recall) to *insight* (the understanding of how a certain piece of knowledge could apply to one's personal life and situation) to *experimental action* (the actual application of a new piece of knowledge to personal behavior to see what will happen) to *commitment to change* (the determination to make a behavior change and the ordering of one's life to accommodate this change) to *relational reorganization and acceptance* (the acceptance and support of the change by significant others in one's life).

Let us apply these steps to the straightforward behavioral change needed for "Ann" to lose weight. Ann has read books and seen programs on the health hazards caused by obesity (acquisition of knowledge). She is also aware of feeling unhappy with her body image and believes that she would feel better and get better responses from friends and coworkers if she were slimmer (insight). She decides to try a new diet that she read about in a magazine (experimental action).

Box 3.1   Family Life Education Is Most Effective When It . . .

- promotes the functions of healthy family systems
- supports and encompasses the family in its unique social and cultural context
- reinforces family efforts
- is sustained and comprehensive (over time, over life experiences)
- focuses on prevention rather than remediation
- builds in levels of learning that encourage personal transformation and behavioral/attitudinal change
- includes at least 15–18 hours of learning experience, followed by options for long-term reinforcement
- incorporates learning activities for all learning styles
- engages the learner in praxis (action with reflection)
- applies information to personal life experience and demonstrates immediate usefulness
- respects learners' experiences, culture, and values orientations
- models learning skills and invites discussion/commentary
- uses a small-group discussion format
- is well prepared and up-to-date
- involves short "lectures" followed by prepared learning activities and discussion
- is based on the assessed needs of the group

The first couple of days go well, but then she begins to long for her favorite comfort foods and finds it to be a lot of trouble to always be counting calories and fat grams. Her resolve weakens, and she starts to give in and give up. But she goes back and reads the article again. It suggests she make a list of the good things that will come from losing weight. It also suggests new menus that sound interesting and not too difficult. Some of Ann's friends are not very helpful. They applaud her efforts but say she shouldn't let the diet control her life; it won't hurt to cheat now and then. They urge her to eat a little more when they go to lunch together. Some say her personality will change if she gets too thin. For now, Ann decides not to listen to them. She is determined to follow through (commitment to change and growth). She calls a friend who has decided to go on the diet with her. They talk about the temptations, and they encourage each other. They decide to share cooking duties during the week and to make larger quantities that they can freeze to eat later. They set a date to go shopping for new clothes after a month has passed. As Ann's weight drops, she begins to get compliments from some of her coworkers and friends. Others seem to be jealous and make comments about how long it is taking and so forth. But Ann is getting enough reinforcement to keep going (relational reorganization and acceptance).

For illustration's sake, this story has a happy ending, but Ann's successful journey has not been an easy or a guaranteed one, as any of us who have tried to lose weight can testify. When the learning model is applied to topics such as parenting or enhancing interpersonal skills, the challenge is even greater. It takes sustained attention and consistent reinforcement to incorporate new behaviors. Yet many times the family life educator is asked to present programs of one hour or less on family life education topics ranging from developing intimacy to parenting the difficult child. Is anything accomplished by such short-term contact? What about the weekend seminar or retreat? Or the 50-minute sex education class once a week for six weeks? Do people retain any of the facts presented long enough to apply them and incorporate them into their lives? Malcolm Knowles's research (1989) concluded that average people retain 20% of what they hear, 40% of what they hear and see, and 80% of what they do or discover for themselves. He also determined that learning is most effective when the learner feels respected by the teacher, can relate the information to his or her own life experience, and can see immediate use for the information.

Learning Styles

Just as people in the same family have different personalities and preferences, so persons, old or young, have different learning styles. Emphasis on learning styles has been a recent focus of education research, and several explanatory models have emerged (Gregorc, 1982; Kolb, 1984; Sternberg, 1988). The Gregorc model encompasses learners of all ages and is based on a two-pronged assumption:

1. We take in information (perception) in two ways: concretely and abstractly.

2. We use information (ordering) in two ways: sequentially and randomly.

This results in four primary learning style combinations: concrete sequential (CS); abstract sequential (AS); abstract random (AR); and concrete random (CR).

Concrete sequential (CS). CS learners are generally perceived as orderly, disciplined, and organized persons. They prefer a plan that leads from point A to point B, and they become uncomfortable veering from that plan. CS learners are usually dependable, hardworking, and stable. They are often tempted to "pick up the slack" or "do it for" less organized or slower paced learners:

> Mary is always on time to the seminar and has her homework assignment ready to hand in. She keeps all of her notes and assignments in a special notebook that she brings with her every time. She usually brings extra paper and pens for her group members who may have forgotten, although they pay the price of enduring Mary's smug expressions. Mary prefers lectures, handouts, and personal work assignments to small-group discussions, which she describes as "a waste of time."

Abstract sequential (AS). AS learners tend to be analytic thinkers who prefer to acquire knowledge through a vast number of sources. They are usually thorough, logical, and deliberate in their consideration of a topic. They do not like to be rushed and generally take more time to make decisions than other learners:

> Joseph wants extra reading assignments on the seminar's topic for the week. He sometimes brings in news articles related to the topic and he enjoys discussing the pros and cons of any idea. He is hard to pin down, however, espe-

cially when the group has to reach consensus on a question within a short time period.

Abstract random (AR).   AR learners are defined as sensitive, compassionate, and perceptive. They are quick to pick up on the needs of others, and they are natural nurturers. If people are upset, AR learners readily assume guilt and work to avoid open conflict. They are spontaneous, flexible, and idealistic:

> Earl is quickly bored with lectures and paper-and-pencil tasks. He prefers small-group discussion and brainstorming about problem solutions. It fascinates him to hear other group members' personal stories, and he enjoys sharing his own personal experiences. He has little patience with someone who hogs all the time (either as presenter or discussant), but he doesn't know how to voice his frustration without making someone angry. When decisions have to be made Earl may voice his opinion, but he will "go with the flow" and quickly adapt to what the majority wants to do rather than risk an argument or disapproval from someone in the group.

Concrete random (CR).   CR learners are the most challenging for a teacher or presenter. They are strong-willed, curious, and realistic. Their quick and creative minds are easily bored. CR learners crave adventure and innovation. The CR learner, whose independent and innovative thought processes challenge traditional teaching situations and methodologies, may often wind up in trouble with the teacher.

> Susan is often late to the seminar and usually arrives in a state of agitation. Her life seems to go from crisis to crisis, and she much prefers to recount this real-life experience to the group than to focus on the topic being discussed. When she settles down and is given a specific task that allows for creative expression and personal application, she works intensely and quickly. She is often ready to move on to another task before most of the members have finished. Susan is also quick to laugh and to make jokes or puns, often interrupting the flow of the session with her spontaneous creativity.

Although no one style is the "right" one, the concrete sequential learner tends to be seen as the "model student." Learners who do not fall naturally into the CS category are often judged to be undisciplined, disorganized, or unmotivated. Their learning strengths go unrecognized and unrewarded. Furthermore, teachers tend to approach a topic using their own learning style and ignore all others, with frustrating results for both teacher and many learners. As greater understanding of personality types and preferences has developed in the last 20 years, the awareness that people also learn in different ways has grown. Other styles of learning have been identified and are better understood. The learning styles are further defined in figure 3.1. Before reading on, consider which combination best describes your own learning style. Each style has strengths and challenges. What would you say are the challenges of your style?

Sensory Modalities

Learners also perceive and take in information using a variety of senses. These modalities have been categorized as auditory, visual, and kinetic (Barbe, 1985).

Figure 3.1   Gregorc Learning Style Combinations

Concrete Sequential (CS)	Abstract Sequential (AS)
hardworking	analytic
conventional	objective
accurate	knowledgeable
stable	thorough
dependable	structured
consistent	logical
factual	deliberate
organized	systematic
Abstract Random (AR)	**Concrete Random (CR)**
sensitive	quick
compassionate	intuitive
perceptive	curious
imaginative	realistic
idealistic	creative
sentimental	innovative
spontaneous	instinctive
flexible	adventurous

Based on the work of A. F. Gregorc. Reproduced with permission of Anthony F. Gregorc.

Although each person may have a dominant modality, she or he can use all three in the process of learning. Retention and application of information is enhanced when all sensory modalities are incorporated into the learning experience. How various learning techniques can be applied to the modalities is illustrated in figure 3.2. Some of the learning exercises obviously involve more than one modality, serving to enhance effectiveness. Ideally, family life education presentations and programs incorporate all three learning modalities in creative combinations.

What about the Short-Term Program?

We return now to the question of the value of the one-hour program for effective education. Although the brief, one-time program is severely limited in its effectiveness, it can be the starting point for developing individual awareness and intellectual development. It may be a safer way for people who are skittish about attending long-term parenting or marriage enrichment programs to "test the waters," have negative stereotypes challenged, and lay a positive foundation for future involvement. Unfortunately, many institutions assume that they have done all they need to do to educate when they have a speaker come to talk about parent education or sex education. Our own educational challenge as family life educators is to raise awareness among community leaders regarding the limitations of short-term programs and encourage alternatives that we know from theory, educational models, and experience that will be more lasting and life changing.

Figure 3.2   Learning Modalities and Classroom Experiences

Auditory Learning	Visual Learning	Kinesthetic
Presentation/lecture	Computer graphics	Puzzles, games
Songs, poems, stories	Demonstration/modeling	Note taking
Discussion	Personal	Question cards
Humor	inventories/assessments	Role-plays
Audiotapes	Brainstorming on charts,	Pencil-and-paper tests
Debate	blackboard	Journaling
	Cartoons	Drawing
	Books, reading assignments	Manipulative materials
	Slides, transparencies, posters	(clay, pipe-cleaners,
	Films, videotapes	dominoes, etc.)
		Movement into groups
		(dyads, triads, etc.) or lines
		(opinion continuums)
		Reporting assignments
		(give a task to do in class
		or out of class)

Source: *Growing Up Learning* by W. B. Barbe, 1985, Washington, DC: Acropolis Books.

SUMMARY

The value of theory-based program design and development was discussed in this chapter from the viewpoint of the educator and the learner. This discussion included a review of family systems theory, human ecology theory, exchange theory, and family developmental theory. Basic teaching assumptions and how assumptions relate to teaching effectiveness were addressed. The experience and conclusions of Vella (1994) and Mace (1981) stressed the importance of models and principles of learning that focus on interactive learning and build retention. A review of the learning styles typology developed by Gregorc (1982) and a discussion of sensory modalities for learning concluded the discussion.

Questions/Problems for Discussion and Review

Class Discussion

1. Recall and describe the best teacher you ever had. How did her or his methods correspond with the list of effective teaching strategies listed in box 3.1?

2. Determine which of Gregorc's learning styles (figure 3.1) best describes your personality. Then, as a group, discuss the different learning styles among the group members. How can a group with so many different styles learn to work effectively together? How would you as an educator or group leader design a program that affirms all of the learning styles?

3. Using your own family constellation, how do you see it fitting with the developmental stage theory articulated by Evelyn Duvall and Brent Miller

(table 3.1)? If there are exceptions in many families, does that make the theory invalid or useless? Why or why not?

Research Problems

1. The area of emphasis on family wellness and family strengths has been prominent in family research during the last few years. Review several of these studies. Are there commonalities between them? What overarching principles seem to be incorporated in all? Compare with the characteristics of healthy family systems.

2. A book by Judith Rich Harris, *The Nurture Assumption* (1998), has stirred much discussion over the value of parental influence on children in the course of their development. Read the book and consider the research on which Harris bases her conclusions, looking particularly at its thoroughness and possible bias. Are there influences or issues she may have ignored? What counterarguments have been presented in journal articles and Internet discussions? Are these arguments or defenses supported with valid research? What conclusion do you personally reach about the issue?

Case Study Design

If you are developing a program based on the case studies in chapters 1 or 11, review the program now by applying the criteria for effective programs listed in box 3.1. What might you want to add or change about the shape of your program design?

four

Addressing the
Needs of Your Audience

An important first step in establishing programs for children, youth, adults, and families is to determine the needs of the specific group you are working with (National Commission on Family Life Education, 1968). This allows the educator to determine program priorities and to know more about the major concerns of the learners, thereby developing more effective programs.

The first two "operational principles" of family life education, as defined by Arcus, Schvaneveldt, and Moss (1993), support the value of the needs assessment process (p. 14). Principle 1 states: *Family life education is relevant to individuals and families throughout the life span.* At all ages and stages, people experience normative changes (births, deaths, moves) and nonnormative changes (divorce, parenting a special-needs child, serious accident or injury). Each of these situations brings the need for certain resources and education in order to most effectively cope and adjust. Principle 2 follows logically after: *Family life education should be based on the needs of individuals and families.* But needs are not as easy to pin down as it may first appear.

Let us look again at designing a sexuality education program for adolescents. One teen, when asked what she needs to know about sexuality, might say: "I need more information about birth control and what to do if I get pregnant." Another teen could answer, "I need to know how to say 'no' without hurting someone's feelings." Yet another teen responds, "What I really want to know is how to satisfy my girlfriend: Where are the 'spots' that turn her on?"

A parent, if asked about the program design, could say: "My children need to know more about what causes pregnancy, how to protect yourself, and why you shouldn't have sex before you're married." Another may say, "He needs to learn respect for other people and their choices." A third parent speaks up: "They don't need a lot of information. They just need to know that sex before marriage is wrong." The educator will probably have her or his own agenda of needs, based on developmental stages and tasks and the knowledge of adolescent stressors. He or she believes that adolescents need information on pubertal changes in their bodies and emotions; they need practice in good decision-making skills; they need to know the difference between love and infatuation; and they need to know what it really means to be a parent to an infant. A special-interest group or a government grant may put limitations on the program content. Guidelines could specify that the adolescents be taught only certain information, such as how to prevent sexually transmitted diseases. They may also prohibit discussion of other related topics, particularly those that are seen (by at least some of the community) to go against the community's prevailing value standards. So how does the educator sort out all of the various voices and expectations? How does the educator decide what the needs are and which ones to address in the program? You can see why it is easier not to ask in the first place! Yet educators must not overlook this important first step in developing a program that really fulfills its primary objective: to promote "learning for living."

RECOGNIZING TYPES OF NEEDS

Three basic types of needs are addressed in family life education programs: felt needs, ascribed needs, and future needs (Arcus et al., 1993). All are important in determining program design, and all are assessed in different ways. Additionally, the educator must identify the developmental needs and the abilities of the audience to take in and process information. Otherwise, a program with good, relevant content will still miss the mark of providing relevant, useful information and experiences.

Felt Needs

These are the needs that potential learners specifically tell you about. Felt needs are very personal and based on the learners' experience with the topic. They may be not only individualistic but also culture-centered. Felt needs tend to address immediate problems with a hope for quick answers—which may or may not be possible. Regardless, the needs and concerns of the learners should be acknowledged by the educator and addressed in some fashion during the program. Otherwise, the learners will feel frustrated and doubtful about the value of the program to their personal situation, and they will "vote with their feet," says program developer Jane Vella (1994). Expression of felt needs helps the leader to get to know the learners better and to establish rapport and empathy with them. It also provides points of reference for moving from the specific issue or concern to a more general topic of discussion or a deeper level of need. "Modeling a true attitude of inquiry and learning is perhaps the most useful thing a teacher of adults can do" (Vella, 1994, p. 50).

Ascribed Needs

"To ascribe" is defined in the WordNet Vocabulary Helper as "to assign" or "to attribute." Ascribed needs are those identified by someone other than the learner and assigned to the person or group as a need. For example, a pediatrician may determine that an infant is undernourished and conclude that the young mother needs information on nutrition, even though the parent has no awareness of that need. A parent educator who has studied the latest research on brain development may determine that the new parents' group he is leading needs to learn more about the importance of infant stimulation and giving affection—even though the group may not have mentioned this as a felt need. A teacher in the university knows that her students need information on family systems theory because their future career plans will draw upon such knowledge, whether they know they need it or not!

The area of ascribed need also has its risks, particularly when cross-cultural programs are being planned. Past history can be a valuable teacher about what *not* to do. Up until the 1970s a cultural deficit model was most often used to design programs. The main objective of such programs was to remedy a problem, or what was seen by the researchers and educators as a problem: low achievement on mainstream cultural norms. "Such an approach not only undermined the strength that characterizes various cultural groups but also robbed them of their dignity as a people" (Hildreth & Sugawara, 1993, p. 177).

One of the harshest examples of this approach involved the American Indian children who were placed in boarding schools run by the Bureau of Indian Affairs. For more than a century, the philosophy of the schools was to "kill the Indian and save the man" (Youcha, 1995, p. 222). Children were often taken forcibly from their families and totally cut off from their cultural traditions. In some schools they were forbidden to speak their native language and were given new Anglo names. The school directors decided the children "needed" this in order to become assimilated into the dominant culture: to become "real," that is, "White," Americans.

More recently, the recognition and appreciation of cultural differences and family strengths has been emphasized:

> This approach makes no value judgement about the relative "goodness" of each cultural group, and there is no intervention into the life of such a cultural group for the purpose of remediation and modeling. Instead, all cultural groups are valued for their uniqueness, so that programs change to meet the needs of individuals and families rather than vice versa. As a result, the dignity, integrity, and diversity of all cultural groups are preserved. Family life education programs that are sensitive to the diverse needs, expectations, and strengths of various cultural groups and are flexible enough to adjust their programs to meet this diversity are more likely to achieve success in aiding individuals to live meaningfully and effectively in a diverse society. (Hildreth & Sugawara, 1993, p. 178)

Adjusting to a multicultural society may yield a different set of needs and program goals than just focusing on the cultural group alone. Often, groups need to work together on common goals for school, community, and society at large. Family life educators can play a critical role in designing and implementing successful programs for culturally diverse societies if they are sensitive and knowledgeable about cultural diversity (Hildreth & Sugawara, 1993).

Because one third of the population in the United States are members of an ethnic or cultural minority group (U.S. Census Bureau, 2004b), it is important to spend time observing and listening to their opinions and their needs. To simply ascribe a set of needs to them based on one's limited experience with the cultural group would be counterproductive and disrespectful. Because differences within a main culture group can be vast, no one or two persons can validly "represent" the group's opinions and needs. Surveying a large representative sample from the target population produces a more valid needs assessment and is vital for working effectively.

Future Needs

Addressing future needs is one way of preparing children and adults for the tasks and normative developmental changes that come later in the life span. Even highly stressful events can be better handled if one understands fully what to expect in the future and what resources are available.

"Ms. Jones," a former preschool teacher at a college laboratory school, had joined a parent support group in her community. Now, as the mother of two toddlers who were born within ten months of each other, she had her hands and lap full of squirming, crying, pushing, poking babies. The group was sharing personal experiences on the topic of "What I wish someone had told me before I had children." When it was Ms. Jones's turn, the harried mother observed, "I have a master's degree in child development and taught 20 three-year-olds every day for four years, but nobody ever told me it was going to be this bad!" She explained that she wouldn't change her decision about motherhood, but she would have been better equipped to handle the stresses of a difficult role if someone had told her what to expect.

Older adults need to consider the possibility of ill health and reduced income; children who are about to become the "big sister or brother" need to think about the changes that will take place in their family when the baby arrives; parents whose last child is leaving home need to consider empty-nest challenges. The Framework for Life Span Family Life Education (appendix A, this volume) outlines in detail the developmental tasks of four distinct times of life: childhood, adolescence, adulthood, and older adulthood. Education programs developed around the various themes and developmental tasks can be very effective, but timing is everything! Scheduling programs too soon or too late can sabotage their effectiveness (Arcus et al., 1993). For example, teaching middle-school adolescents about parenting skills is largely ineffective unless they are pregnant. Even then, their ability to realistically conceptualize what parenting will be like is limited by their level of cognitive development. A better approach is the one-on-one home visitor who starts her visits in the hospital after the young mother has given birth and is available when crises and questions arise. A support group for new mothers would also catch the teachable moment.

Developmental Needs and Abilities

A different kind of need category involves the educator's awareness of the developmental abilities of the participants. If a group of adults who are basic readers are asked to read complicated material or assessments, their needs and abilities are not being considered. If children or teens are expected to sit still and listen to a long lesson that involves little kinetic activity or interaction with the speaker, the teacher does not understand the cognitive and developmental abilities of this age group. An understanding of cognitive development, abilities, limitations, and interests (as long as this understanding is not based on stereotypes) will help the educator to assess the needs of the group and address them more effectively.

Ages and stages of need.   Gross (1993) observes that we have different educational needs at different ages and stages of family development but that the stages also overlap as families are more often now dealing with four-generation issues. Schaie (1977/1978) succinctly summed up the basic questions and issues of four main stages of life (childhood/adolescence, younger adulthood, middle adulthood, and older adulthood) in two broad categories (see table 4.1). For children and adolescents, the broad category is "What should I know?" For adults, it is "How should I use what I know?" This is not to imply that adults are closed to new knowledge, but that their basic concern is with the application of knowledge to their lives. Irwin and Simons (1994) point out that Schaie's basic schema is compat-

Table 4.1   Schaie's Stages of Adult Cognitive Development

I. "What Should I Know?"	II. "How Should I Use What I Know?"		
Childhood and Adolescence	**Young Adulthood**	**Middle Adulthood**	**Later Adulthood**
Acquisition (Get Knowledge)	Achieving (Use Knowledge)	Responsible (Concern for Others) Executive (Concern for Social Systems)	Reintegrative (Wisdom)

Source: Toward a Stage Theory of Adult Development by K. Warner Schaie, 1977/78, *International Journal of Aging and Human Development* 8:2, pp. 129–138. Baywood Publishing Company. Reprinted with permission.

ible with the cognitive stages of Piaget and the psychosocial stages of Erikson. In this chapter, we focus on how to apply learning concepts to life experiences, the basic focus of family life education. But it is important to understand how people of various ages and abilities learn best. Cognition, according to Santrock (1992), is the process of receiving and interpreting information from our environment, through either our senses or our perception. How it is stored in memory and acted on is also a part of cognition. Piaget stressed the "acting on" part and theorized that humans act on information through assimilation, the incorporation of new information into one's existing knowledge, and accommodation, adjustment in one's attitudes and behavior because of the new knowledge. The more recently developed information-processing approach breaks cognition into smaller segments.

The information-processing approach.   This approach has been influenced and refined through considering how computers store and process information and then comparing it with the human brain (Santrock, 1992). The physical brain is seen as similar to a computer's hardware and cognition to its software. A person takes information from the environment through sensory and perceptual processes (touch, taste, smell, sight, sound, emotional environment, relational interactions). This information is stored in the memory (short- and long-term) and used to expand thought (knowledge) and determine future behavior, which includes, first and foremost, language. This interaction and interpretation of the environment through language in turn creates more sensory and perceptual stimulation, more memory, more thought, and, hopefully, application to one's attitudes and behavior. It is at this last point—the application to one's attitudes and behaviors—that humans exceed computers, and it is at this point that family life educators hope to have a role and an influence.

Information processing in children.   Children are constantly bombarded with sensory stimulation that they interact with and interpret in ways that are often quite different from the ways adults interpret the event (having had many more years of accumulated input, memory, thought, and interaction). It is important, however, for the adult to learn to understand what the child is saying and respond in a way that the child can incorporate into memory (Santrock, 1992). Three important learning processes enhance a child's long-term memory:

rehearsal, organization, and imagery (McGilly & Siegler, 1989). Rehearsal, the repetition of information after it has been presented, improves memory. Because children enjoy repeated stories and activities, incorporating rehearsal is easy if the educator is attuned to the children's natural rhythm. Organization fits knowledge into categories: from naming five kinds of dogs to identifying the capitals of all the states to recognizing nonverbal signs of anger, distress, or approval. As with the rehearsal process, children in middle and late childhood are usually more capable of spontaneous organization, which improves memory retention. Imagery—the ability to picture in one's mind a scene, a story, an anticipated activity—enhances both memory and thought processes. Imagery encourages children to engage in the rehearsal of societal roles and behaviors and to play out their fears and dreams, both in the present and in the future.

The extent to which these processes function efficiently is determined by many influences. Age is the obvious one, but attitude, motivation, accessibility, past experiences, external and internal feelings of oppression, and health are others. Santrock (1992) summarizes: "The best way to nurture this motivation for knowledge is to allow the child to spontaneously interact with the environment. Education needs to ensure that it does not dull the child's eagerness to know by providing an overly rigid curriculum that disrupts the child's own rhythm and pace of learning" (p. 310).

Information processing in adolescents. As cognitive development continues, adolescents can use new skills for processing and using information. They can think more abstractly, logically, and idealistically. They are keenly aware of their own thoughts and what others are thinking about them, and they are very absorbed in their own social context. This may explain why research studies show that the knowledge that adolescents and young adults have about a subject does not necessarily coincide with their behavior. They may know all the facts about how pregnancy occurs, for example, and they may know that unprotected sex is very risky, but some still engage in this risky behavior. Why? For one thing, not all adolescents have reached the level of formal operational thought that fosters abstract thinking about logical consequences. Further research and testing of Piaget's original theory of the development of formal operational thinking in adolescence shows that there is much more variation in the level of formal operational thought than was first believed (Lapsley, 1989; Overton & Byrnes, 1991). Only one in three adolescents was determined to be a formal operational thinker. Many adults in American and other cultures never develop this level of thinking (Santrock, 1992). It is therefore wrong to assume that all adolescents and adults process information in a way that automatically leads to a change in behavior. Even highly educated adults are "guilty" of knowing the facts about exercise and good nutrition and yet never practicing those important habits. Why then would we assume that teens change their behavior because they learn new facts?

A second reason why adolescents may fail to act on new information is that they have had little experience with the newly developed ability to think critically. Although definitions of critical thinking vary, they all address the ability to think more deeply about problems and issues. This includes looking at varying points of view and discussing the merits and disadvantages of each. Critical thinking stresses the connection between cause and effect and the importance of making one's own decision about an issue, thought, or belief. Unless this critical thinking process is encouraged and nurtured, it does not develop. Adolescents must have the freedom to speak their opinions without ridicule or judgment, but they should be challenged to state why they hold these opinions and to follow the course of an argument to its logical end. Adolescents must be regarded as persons moving toward total independence and therefore be allowed to make more of their own decisions and experience the consequences of those decisions. Programs that use people who share their stories of struggle, decision making, and the ultimate consequences make much more of a lasting impression on teens than any carefully structured lecture. Role-play, a chance to practice a social script and to discuss it afterward, also brings more lasting impressions to adolescents and adults who are striving to develop critical thinking skills.

Information processing in young adults.   The young adult of today is more likely to be single and mobile than in any previous period. In the past 30 years, the number of single adults living independently has doubled and includes three-fourths of all men and women between the ages of 20 and 25. More than 20 million adults in the United States are never-married singles (Irwin & Simons, 1994). Do these changing lifestyles affect the way one processes information? Schaie (1977/1978) proposed that young adults are in the achieving stage of cognitive development. They use the knowledge they have acquired earlier to further their education, careers, leisure activities, and relationships. So family life education programs aimed at young adults should certainly utilize the small-group interaction format. Minilectures, which provide new schematics of information, followed by group discussion appeal to the young adult's desire to acquire and use knowledge.

Information processing in middle adulthood.   Is there a difference between young adult and middle-aged adult thinking? Labouvie-Vief (1986) contends that the middle-aged adult is more pragmatic and at ease in a variety of situations than is the young adult. Three distinct characteristics of mature thinkers are:

1. complex thinking that knows and can allow inconsistencies in thought and action to exist

2. practical thinking that deemphasizes the idealistic "ifs" and "whens" of fantasizing

3. subjective thinking that feels free to disregard formal, logical rules in favor of intuition (Labouvie-Vief, 1986)

In general, when compared with young adults, middle-aged adults are superior in answering questions based on real-life situations that require subjectivity and self-reliance. Whereas young adults are generally better at decision making through logical thought, some theorists and researchers term the middle-adulthood stage of life as the most creative (Cole, 1979; Simonton, 1977). Schaie (1977/1978) characterized middle-adulthood thinking as responsible and executive (see table 4.1). The responsible aspect addresses the middle-aged adult's concern for others in the family and in society. This is the age of heavy involvement with children, aging parents, and church and/or civic organizations. Career advancement is also a primary concern. The executive aspect, defined by Schaie as concern for social systems, includes the leadership roles that middle-aged adults assume in business and community. Both aspects challenge the capabilities of middle-aged adults, who are very busy people. The effect on family life education programs is obvious: They need to be concise, well-planned, and accessible. Programs must demonstrate their usefulness and be time-efficient.

The ability to use creative problem solving to solve practical problems or improve a situation has been termed *postformal thinking* (Arlin, 1984). Postformal thinking recognizes the overlapping nature of the demands of everyday adult living in the contexts of work, home, friends, and society. It draws upon past experiences to define problems in better ways and to offer creative solutions. Yet it is believed that less than half of middle-aged adults engage in postformal thinking. Much of midlife thinking is more practical in nature: paying bills, raising teens, planning weddings, attending to needs of grandchildren and aging parents. It is easy to get into ruts of habituation. Kastenbaum (1984) described habituation as the growing tendency of middle-aged adults to depend on daily routines and limited expectations. They have become comfortable and complacent. This makes them less open to adaptation to new situations or challenges. Although dependence on routine can free one to focus on other tasks that require more energy, it can also become extreme—a condition termed *hyperhabituation*. At this point, any change in routine or habitual experiences is strongly resisted and feared. Fortunately, this condition is also extremely rare (Datan, Rodeheaver, & Hughes, 1987).

Information processing in older adults. Current activities of many older adults are blasting the stereotype of the "failing granny." More than 340,000 Americans aged 65 and older are enrolled in college (Peterson, 1985). Schaie (1978) describes this cognitive stage as *reintegrative*, or the age of wisdom. Many learning experiments with older adults show that comprehension is still keen, although reflexes are slower than in younger adults (Clark, Lanphear, & Riddick, 1987). Older adults tend to emphasize personal experience over straight logic. They are cautious about trying new things if the "old ways" are satisfactory to them. They tend to prefer practical solutions over "ideal" ones (Botwinick, 1967). In general, older adults are slower at problem solving and tend to ask more inefficient questions when trying to solve a problem. This is not true of more educated adults, particularly those who have continued to read, study, and remain actively involved with others (Irwin & Simons, 1994). Short-term memory is somewhat impaired. In one study, older adults had more problems reporting details of a story just heard or a passage read. However, they did well in summarizing the essential meaning of the material. They may become distracted if material that is being read or recited contains a number of pronouns or auxiliary phrases. Short sentences using basic sentence structure communicate best. Long-term memory remains strong, although recall may take longer than in the past. "Priming," or "prompting," greatly improves recall. Bahrick (1984) reported on a research study that compared recall of Spanish by younger adults who had completed a Spanish class in the past three years with that by older adults who had studied Spanish 50

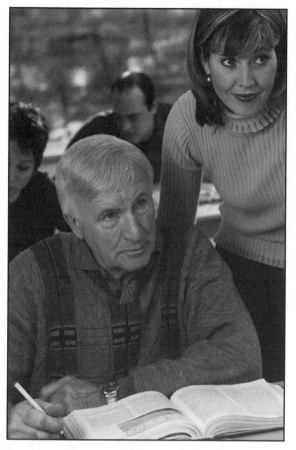

Learning experiments with older adults show that comprehension is still keen.

years previously. Not surprisingly, the younger adults did better; but what was surprising was that the older adults recalled 80% of what the young adults remembered, even though more than 47 years had elapsed! The slope of decline in intelligence that psychologists of the 1960s assumed to start right after college has been greatly overrated. The most consistent finding is that a person's response rate to questions or problems slows as one ages, but, given no time limits, performance on many mental tests is equal to that of young adults.

Self-actualizing creativity is a term coined by Abraham Maslow (1959) to describe the personal intelligence that comes from experiencing a long life. Such creative wisdom can be passed from older to younger individuals, forming a valuable network of interconnectedness.

The conclusion about information-processing ability is that it varies widely among all ages. Many factors, including educational level, test-taking style, health, personality characteristics, and exposure to information through many sources, have an influence on a person's level of cognitive reasoning. But overall, problem-solving abilities are very much tied to life experience—gained through repetition, rehearsal, memory, envisioning, and creativity.

CONDUCTING AN ASSESSMENT

The Process

Vella (1994) considers the process of needs assessment to have three distinct components: asking, studying, and observing. There are two basic kinds of asking to be done. First, to start the "investigation" process, one must first seek permission from appropriate authorities—and the participants themselves—to conduct an assessment. The appropriate authority might be a school board or a principal, a church youth minister, and/or parents (if the participants are under 18). Determining which type of permission is necessary—formal or informal—is governed by the sensitivity of the topic and the age of the participants. The prevailing cultural and political climate also have a bearing on the type of permission one should seek to conduct a needs assessment.

In a formal permission process, a written permission form explains who you are and what the purpose of your assessment is. The form should assure the consenting party and the participant that all participation is voluntary—no one will be forced to participate—and that all information gathered will be used anonymously. There should be a place for the consenting party to sign (see appendix C, this volume, for an example).

Many types of consent to conduct a needs assessment are more informal and do not require a written form. For example, you may verbally request that a group of adults at a PTA meeting fill out a brief questionnaire about the upcoming program topic or explain to a school class that the teacher has given you a few minutes to ask some questions about smoking or teen dating. It may be as informal as asking an already assembled group how many are grandparents or who has teenagers, school-aged children, and so forth.

The second type of "asking" is used to uncover the felt needs of the target group for whom you are designing a program. The purpose of such asking goes far beyond getting answers to the basic question, "What do you want to know about . . . ?" Asking opens up room for relationship and the building of trust between teacher and learner. It sends the message that you really care about what they think and feel. Asking allows you to discern attitudes and cultural values of the group and to see what topics might be of interest to them that you, or they, may not have thought about before. Freire (1970) termed this "thematic analysis." It is a way of listening and understanding the themes of importance in a person's life. "When . . . learners are bored or indifferent, it means their themes have been neglected in planning the course. Motivation is magically enhanced, however, when we teach them about their own themes. People are naturally excited to learn anything that helps them understand their own themes, their own lives" (Vella, 1994, p. 5). Vella recounts an example of a phone-interview needs assessment that a colleague conducted:

> A colleague of mine, Dr. Paula Berardinelli, doing training in time management skills with a group of secretaries at a major industry, sent a number of them the draft program for the training a month before the event. She indicated that she would be calling them for a ten-minute conversation on a specified day. When she spoke with them, one by one, she heard a similar set of themes about their work. She also heard, over and over, how delighted they were by her call. They cited many incidents she could use in the training—as stories for analysis, praxis material for reflection—and helped her understand some of the unspoken variables they were working with. The result was a course that was accountable to the industry and to the adult learners, who knew themselves to be subjects in a healthy relationship with the teacher. Although she spoke with only one-tenth of the group, the entire unit had heard of her needs assessment and were prepared at the outset of the day to offer their ideas spontaneously and creatively. Virtually all of the secretaries said this had never happened to them before. (pp. 5–6)

The needs assessment can be conducted in a variety of settings: as a small focus group, a phone interview, or a written questionnaire, to name a few. Types of assessments are discussed further in the next section of this chapter.

The second step in the needs assessment process is to study. The educator should take time to research and read about the age group and the culture. Read some of their popular literature. Get to know their heroes and their interests. Put assumptions and prejudices aside and study for insight and understanding. This takes time and patience, but it is invaluable for designing truly effective programs.

The third step in the process is to observe. While observing implies a passive spectator stance, it actually demands involvement and immersion by the potential teacher in the culture and values of the reference group. It also requires a willingness to become the one being taught: to "get inside their skins" in order to understand the pressures, dilemmas, and challenges that they face in their life themes.

Suppose you are asked to design a parenting program for teen parents in the local high school. Spending a day or two as an unobtrusive observer in the school's classrooms and halls can give you some idea of the teens' situations and cultural values. Going with the teacher on home visits can further clarify what the teen has to cope with as both a student and a new mother. It is important to be introduced to the situation by someone who is trusted and accepted by the prospective learners. Also, you must be able to convey interest and warmth when persons approach you with questions or comments. Genuine smiles and a relaxed attitude are a must!

One question remains: In cases in which program material is sensitive and the issues politically charged, how do you determine what needs will be addressed? If you are designing a program that is being funded through a grant or research project, you must function within the parameters of the specified content that can or cannot be discussed. To do otherwise would be unethical and would destroy your credibility. It is possible to preface your program with some words about the scope of the program to be presented. Acknowledge that all topics gleaned from the needs assessment will not be covered but that you will address certain issues. All of the information you collected from the assessment, shared anonymously, of course, could be useful to parents and policy makers as they consider what type of programs to plan in the future.

Assessment Techniques

There are many ways and many times to do needs assessment. Adapting the type of assessment to the group is the first step in a creative process of engaging each individual in a mutual learning experience. The amount of time you have, the context, and the available resources are some of the factors that will determine your choice of a needs assessment technique for a particular group. Vella (1994) also stresses that needs assessment is an ongoing process that continues as the leader comes to know the learners and their current levels of knowledge of and experience with the topic being discussed. Some ways of gathering information about learners' concerns have been mentioned already. This section discusses the main techniques for beginning the needs assessment process.

The focus group.   A focus group is composed of a small group of representative persons (six to eight) drawn from the pool of potential participants in the program. The purpose of a needs assessment focus group is to gather information from participants about their concerns and attitudes on issues related to the program topic. The value of the group format versus an interview is that it provides opportunity for feedback from members about the opinions of other members. It allows for clarification and a better understanding about whether one person's opinion is representative of the group. Group interchange also generates questions or issues that might not have been thought about by one person or by the facilitator alone.

The group facilitator is usually the educator who is planning the program and leading the group. However, when a focus group is used at the end of a program for program evaluation, it is important for participants to feel that they can speak freely about program effectiveness. In that case, a neutral third party who is skilled in leading group discussion should be chosen as focus group facilitator, and the program facilitator should not be present.

Ask someone who works with the target group and knows them well to choose a cross section of participants to visit with you for a specified time (30 minutes to one hour). Include at least 10 minutes extra in the schedule for gathering time. Arrange also to have someone present to take notes during the discussion, preferably a colleague rather than the person who selected the group or a participant. In order to encourage a relaxed atmosphere, the setting for the focus group should be carefully planned. Spend some time arranging the room beforehand. Put the chairs in a circle, prepare light refreshments, and provide name tags. Greet the participants as they arrive, introduce yourself, and thank them for coming. Start the meeting at the appointed time (don't wait around for latecomers). Explain who you are and who the recorder is. Thank the participants for coming, and let them know that you need their help: You want to get to know them better in order to plan a program that really meets their needs. Start with the "easy" questions that are basically demographic: Ask for each person's name and ask a simple question or two, such as, "How many people are in your family?" "Are you the youngest, oldest, middle?" "What grade are you in in school?" "What's your favorite thing to do with your brother/sister/mother/father?" This gentle process can ease anxiety and helps to develop rapport between you and the future participants of your group.

The second-stage questions are more directly related to your planned program topic and are generally open-ended questions (not answered by a "yes" or "no"). For example, "What do you think will be the hardest thing about being the parent of a newborn?" "If someone made a video about child management, what do you think they should include?" "How do you handle a disagreement between you and your spouse—or you and the grandparents—over how to discipline your child?" "What areas seem to cause the most disagreement?" Questions such as these should not be posed to any particular person but should be voluntarily answered. Encourage all to participate, but be sure to keep participation voluntary and to acknowledge appreciatively any contribution from a group member. For example, "Let's hear from some of the rest of you. What do you think is the biggest stress in parenting?" Never ignore or slide over someone's comment. All contributions are important and worthy of being acknowledged, even if they're a little "off-base." Generally, this should include a verbal restatement of what was said. This lets the person know he or she has been heard and gives time for the recorder to write the comment and time for other group members to consider their own responses. Avoid expressions (either verbal or nonverbal) of judgment or belittling. Listen to what is not being said as well as to what is being verbalized.

For groups of children or teens, the best type of question poses a hypothetical situation: "Suppose you are about to bring your new baby home from the hospital. What are the main things you will need to know how to do? What would you like to ask someone about being a parent?" or "What would you like your younger brother or sister to know about sexuality?" or (for a class on ethical decisions) "If you found a $50 bill on the sidewalk, how would you decide whether to keep it or not?" A question like this will help you understand the level of clarity or confusion about decision making. Children and teens are also good at listing things that "bug" them (about living with brothers and sisters, about dating, about being part of a stepfamily). To keep things on a positive note, you might follow a "bug" question with, "What do you like about (dating, etc.)?" With adult groups, a straightforward question will usually be effective, such as "What would you like to know more about in the area of (handling stress, managing your time, parenting adolescents, etc.)?"

The interview technique.   Interviews to determine participant needs and interests can be conducted either in person or over the phone. Randomly select a sample of persons from the target participant population to be interviewed regarding the design of a planned program. About 10% of the participant group provides a good sample. Advantages of this technique include the sense of safety in speaking to one person instead of the whole group and a stronger sense of dialogue between two persons. Effectiveness is also enhanced by sending a letter ahead of the interview outlining the scope of the planned seminar, as in the example of the phone-interview technique in the previous section on the needs assessment process. By giving persons time to think ahead about the topic, the interviewer is likely to get more thoughtful and thorough feedback. The major disadvantage is the amount of time it takes.

Another way to use the interview technique, but only as a supplement to other needs assessment, is to interview persons who work with the target group, such as social workers, schoolteachers, or ministers. Their experience can often detect patterns of questions or behaviors that need to be addressed in a program.

The questionnaire.   A written needs assessment can "poll" the group on their most pressing needs and allows every potential participant to respond. It can also bring issues to the surface that a person or group may not think about during an interview or group session. The questionnaire should be easy to understand and relatively short. Preferably, it should be filled out on the spot—at the beginning of a class or in the office cafeteria, with the interviewer waiting nearby. Any time people have to do it at home, survey participation drops. It can be as simple as: *Below is a list of issues that parents of newborns usually have to deal with.*

Please check the ones that you would like to have discussed in the upcoming seminar on "Baby Bliss and Baby Blues." You may check as many as you wish. At the end of the questionnaire, always invite other suggestions or comments by leaving several blank spaces for write-ins. These comments will address some of the most pressing needs of your group. You may already be thinking that a questionnaire like this could generate too many topics to cover in one seminar (unless it's very long). What can you do about that?

In order to be responsive to all the expressed needs, you can do several things. First, collate the returned questionnaires and determine which items have been checked most often. These should determine the major topics for seminar discussion. Next, see if any of the other needs expressed, particularly those write-in comments, can be subsumed under major categories. Finally, build in a Q-and-A time to deal with the expressed needs that do not fit into other categories. One parent educator has developed a technique for dealing efficiently with a number of parents' questions that also involves the whole group rather than just himself as responder. The parent (or the group leader) poses the question, and then the group is asked to provide individual responses, preferably from their own experiences. The responses are not evaluated or discussed but are simply recorded on a sheet of newsprint. The leader can of course add her own comments as well, but the ground rules state that there not be a discussion of the suggestions. The questioner is encouraged to take the suggestions, consider them, and see if any can be adapted to his or her situation. This structured-response Q-and-A time allows the group to have an opportunity for input while dealing with several issues rather than getting bogged down in just one or two.

Finally, when dealing with a long list of needs and interests, the leader can provide books, articles, and brochures that address some of the issues, particularly those that fall outside the parameters of the time and topic coverage of the seminar. It is always good to include in your introductory remarks a statement of appreciation for all of the input. Explain that many issues were checked as being of interest to members of the group and that there was only time enough to cover a few of these. Outline your basic seminar plan and topic coverage and invite the participants to review the books and pamphlets you have available. Another idea is to plan a second seminar to deal with a major topic of expressed concern, such as "Protecting my child from sexual abuse."

Other creative techniques. Your constant challenge as an educator is to design creative ways to do the three needs assessment tasks: asking, studying, and observing. You may be visiting in a home, office, or classroom. You may be calling on the phone or handing out questionnaires or polling participants. Or you may be doing something even more innovative, such as posing a "three wishes" question to children about their family life or asking a group of pregnant teens to draw their greatest fears about becoming a mother. It may be asking a group of new parents to take a pretest about infant development during the first hour of a seminar. This is a wonderful method, incidentally, because it gives the leader a chance to note knowledge gaps and also to provide accurate information while involving the group in a "kinetic" activity. The point of all of this is to form warm, caring connections with the participants so that you become an informed friend instead of the "sage on the stage."

LISTENING EFFECTIVELY

In his book *The Miracle of Dialogue*, Reuel Howe (1963) tells the story of an architect who was hired to build a house. The owner met with the architect to discuss the particular features she wanted in this new home, but when the architect returned with the plans, none of the special features had been included. "Why have you not included the things I told you about?" queried the homeowner. "Well, I didn't think they were that important, and you probably would regret spending the extra money. After all, I'm the one with experience in building houses," the architect replied. The architect was fired, and a new one hired. This new architect listened carefully to the owner and took her wishes seriously while offering feedback and suggestions that would make the features less costly. Together, they built a house that was of outstanding design, better than either could have done alone.

Keys and Barriers to Effective Listening

Howe emphasizes that one of the biggest obstacles to communication is the tendency for one participant to carry on both sides of a dialogue. We draw conclusions in advance or make assumptions about the other person's response. Such communication then becomes a calculated monologue, which robs the other person of his or her freedom to be heard. Learning to really listen to another person involves a conscious decision to put aside one's personal agenda and assumptions. Virginia Satir (1988) explains that to listen fully means to:

- Give full attention to the speaker and be fully present
- Put aside any preconceived ideas of what the speaker is going to say
- Interpret what is said descriptively, not judgmentally
- Be alert for any confusion in the message received and be ready to reflect or ask questions to get clarity
- Let the speaker know that she or he has been heard and also the content of what was communicated

To effectively combine all of the elements of active listening takes concentration and practice, because a number of barriers can block the pathways. Howe (1963) lists four major barriers: language, image, anxiety and defensiveness, and contrary purposes. Language barriers are not limited to two people speaking in different tongues. Even people speaking the same language can be confused because of the various connotations and hidden meanings each person attaches to particular words and phrases.

Satir (1988, p. 71) illustrates with this simple exchange:

"I think it's hot in here."

"Do you mean that you're uncomfortable?"

"Yes."

"Do you mean that you want me to bring you a glass of water?"

"No."

"Do you mean that you want me to know that you are uncomfortable?"

"Yes."

"Do you want me to do something about it?"

"Yes."

There was certainly more being communicated in that one sentence than was readily apparent.

The barrier of image involves one's prejudices and preconceived ideas about the other person. Whether the images are negative or positive, they block out the possibility of true dialogue and understanding. The speaker and listener respond to ghosts and shadows, always holding something back, failing to hear and understand the other's needs and concerns.

The barrier of anxiety and defensiveness follows naturally on the heels of image. I (Powell) decided many years ago to take each person's comments at their best interpretation rather than their worst. I have been amazed at how often I was more on target with my better interpretation and have found that the hurtful remark was seldom really caused by dissatisfaction with me but rather arose out of the other person's history of past hurts or current stress.

Finally, the barrier of contrary purposes arises to block communication effectiveness. The speaker and listener must both be honest with themselves about their agenda. If the educator is doing a needs assessment in order to fulfill a requirement rather than to truly find out what the learner thinks, wants, and needs, then there will be no dialogue—only two people talking. Have you ever had to make a complaint to a store manager or supervisor? Typically, the manager starts explaining or making excuses before the customer finishes speaking. There is very little real attention to the customer's concerns. Rather than seeing this as an opportunity to improve customer service now and in the future, the manager tends to see his or her purpose as a defensive one. So the "conversation" of contrary purposes usually ends in frustration for both parties, one of whom will probably not patronize that business again.

Counselor and author Robert Doyle (1992) states that the primary role in establishing a trusting relationship is being able to communicate the message *I am interested in what you have to say and I am available to you.* Once that attitude is genuinely felt by the listener, there are some verbal and nonverbal listening techniques that will help to get the message across.

Types of Listening Skills

Verbal cues. The simple minimal verbal statement is a primary way to convey the message that the listener is tuned in to what is being said. "I see," "umhumm," "go on", and so forth are the verbal equivalents of a head nod and encourage the speaker to continue without interrupting his or her train of thought.

Reflective statements.   In this kind of "feedback," the listener acts as a mirror for the speaker's words without any interpretation. The listener simply repeats a phrase or sentence or summarizes what the speaker has been saying. Here are some examples:

> SPEAKER: I really get uptight when my children start fighting. It makes me want to just run away and never come back.
>
> LISTENER: So their fighting makes you want to run away.
>
> SPEAKER: What I really need to know is how to get my children to go to bed and stay there after I put them there.
>
> LISTENER: Getting the kids to stay put!
>
> SPEAKER: I don't really care about all that information on nutrition and exercise that our teacher keeps talking about. I want to know how to earn a living for myself and my baby!
>
> LISTENER: Nutrition and exercise are not that important to you. You just want to know how to earn a good living.

Note the lack of judgment or advice giving. The reflective statement requires a neutral listener stance. Amazingly, a speaker often rethinks or qualifies an opinion when it is repeated in this way.

Accent.   This listening technique is especially helpful when getting feedback from a focus group or directing a class discussion. The listener accents—picks up on—some part of what the speaker has said and encourages the listener, or the group, to elaborate on that point. Not only does this demonstrate attentive listening, but it also validates the contribution of the speaker. For instance, the listener/facilitator may say, "Mary, I'm really interested in your comment on the difficulty you have in knowing how to discipline Mandy without spanking. Could you say some more about that?" Or, "Do others of you have the same problem?" Or, "Sara, I'm glad you mentioned the issue of decision making between you and your husband. You know, this is one of the major reported stressors among new parents. What do you think causes it to be so stressful?"

Paraphrasing.   Here the listener restates the elements of the conversation using different words that go beyond the speaker's words and include underlying meanings. Unless you are in a counseling setting, psychological interpretations of the speaker's statements should be avoided.

To further examine your listening skills level, score yourself on the "How well are you listening?" assessment (box 4.1). After determining your strengths and weaknesses, choose one or two areas at a time to focus on improving. Empathic, active listening is an art and a skill that can be learned.

Box 4.1   How Well Are You Listening?

Listening is an art and a skill you can learn. Score yourself on the following statements by using: 1–Never   2–Hardly ever   3–Usually   4–Always

___ 1. I am interested in what other people have to say.

___ 2. I don't interrupt while someone is speaking.

___ 3. I listen the same way to men and women, young people and old.

___ 4. I listen without prejudice, even though I may not like the person or her or his opinions.

___ 5. I can stay focused on the conversation so that my mind doesn't wander.

6. I ask for clarification of words when they are used.

___ 7. I ask questions to get the other person to fully explain what she or he is saying.

8. I listen attentively, even though I think I know what is going to be said.

9. I listen with neutrality and reflect the person's statements without judgment or put-down.

___ 10. I look at the person who is talking.

11. I can ignore distracting influences.

___ 12. I listen attentively, even though the person's manner of speaking and choice of words is not the best.

___ 13. I encourage the speaker with smiles, head nods, and other verbal cues.

___ 14. I consider and evaluate carefully what the person is saying, reserving judgment until the end.

___ 15. I acknowledge every speaker and every comment when conducting a group discussion.

___ Total Score

If your score is between 50 and 60, you are an accomplished listener. Keep up the good work!

If your score is between 40 and 50, you are well on your way. Focus on areas to improve.

If your score is between 30 and 40, you are an average listener. Hone your skills!

If your score is below 30, get to work immediately to consciously improve.

SUMMARY

This chapter addressed the issue of assessing needs of program participants through a process and an understanding of developmental needs and abilities. Techniques for conducting needs assessments were reviewed and the role and skills of empathic, active listening emphasized.

The importance of timing was also stressed. To address a future need too soon or a felt need too late will sabotage a program's effectiveness. Thorough knowledge of developmental tasks at each age level, as well as acquaintance with the cultural and social contexts of the learners, keeps the program on target and the learners' life themes in focus.

Questions/Problems for Discussion and Review

Class Discussion

1. Look again at the introductory example of expressed needs in regard to a sexuality education program. Which would be categorized as felt, ascribed, and future needs? Is one type more important to address than another in a program for adolescents? Explain your answer.

2. Persons have many different ways of processing information, and they are at many different stages. In light of this, how do you go about designing an effective program that takes this variability into account?

3. Think of a time when you worked together with someone of another culture or age group. What things did you or they do that helped you to work well together?

Research Problems/Activities

1. Choose an ethnic group from your community to research in the library and on the Internet, looking particularly at marriage and family experiences and customs. Then set up interviews with three or four persons from that ethnic group. Using the Life Span Family Life Education Framework (appendix A, this volume), choose one of the categories (e.g., interpersonal relationships or families in society). Formulate a set of interview questions about the category across the life span that will help you examine how the developmental tasks articulated under that category are experienced by the chosen ethnic group.

2. If possible, audiotape your interviews from the previous activity so that you may critique your listening skills. How often did you make reflective statements or ask open-ended questions? What verbal cues and other attending behavior (smiles, nods, eye contact) did you use? What areas do you want to improve?

Case Study Design

1. If you are developing a program for a specific group, now is the time to conduct a needs assessment. Determine the type of assessment technique you want to use. Preferably, the class should divide into several groups, and each group should conduct a different type of assessment (focus group, questionnaire, interview, creative idea) to share with the class.

2. When the needs assessment is being conducted, assign two people as observers to evaluate the interviewers' listening skills. Have them note strengths and areas for improvement to share later with the group.

3. Review your experience with the class. What generally did you learn about the participants (about their developmental needs and abilities, their learning styles and unique characteristics) through the process of "ask, study, observe"? How would you evaluate your rapport with the group? Observers should share, without identifying specific people, what strengths and weaknesses in listening skills they observed.

4. Discuss the felt needs that were identified through the assessment process. What other needs (ascribed, future, developmental) should also be addressed in the program?

CHAPTER FIVE

Understanding
Group Process

Author Anna Quindlen, in her book *Thinking Out Loud* (1993), cites a fortune cookie message as having had a major impact on her life. The cookie read: "To remember is to understand." "I have never forgotten it," said Quindlen. "A good judge remembers what it is like to be a lawyer. A good editor remembers being a writer. A good parent remembers what it was like to be a child" (p. 222). And a good group leader remembers what it was like to be a part of a group or a class directed by someone who knew the secrets of effective leadership. Stop reading now, and think for a moment about the best teachers or group leaders you ever had. What made them so effective? List the qualities in the margin of your book or on a separate sheet of paper. How did being a part of that class or group make you feel? Record that, too. Then remember and refer to these experiences as you consider your own potential for group leadership.

The capability to lead groups is listed by Gross (1993) as one of the main tasks of an effective family life educator. In this capacity, the educator is expected to:

- Provide learning experiences and activities that will help participants develop their own skills to more effective levels

- Maintain a balance between the presentation of information and the personalizing of the information through group discussion

- Cope with interpersonal problems that inevitably arise in groups

- Have an understanding of life-cycle development

- Have a good grasp of group development theory

Gross doesn't list *leap tall buildings in a single bound*, but it may seem like an unspoken expectation. Does a group leader have to be superhuman? No. Effective leadership skills can be learned. But most of all, a group leader must continually *remember* what it was like to be in a group that worked well. And by putting yourself in the place of the participants, you will develop empathy with them and understand more clearly what to do.

DEFINING A GROUP

As a family life educator, you will be called on to address all types of groups, from the civic group who gather for lunch and a 20-minute speaker to the stepparent support group that meets together monthly for the next year. Some of these experiences will be purely presentational, whereas others will involve long-term, interactive small-group facilitation. We discuss the latter in this chapter.

Although definitions of small groups differ, Shaw (1981) offers what might be termed the most generic definition of a small group: "Two or more people who are interacting with one another in such a manner that each person influences, or is influenced by, each other person" (p. 8). Shaw lists several essential elements of a small group:

1. 5 to 7 participants ideally, certainly not more than 20;
2. interaction between group members and with the facilitator;

3. a common purpose;

4. mutual influence by talking and listening to each other and sharing values, expectations and resources, thereby becoming interdependent.

It is important to note that small groups are formed for a variety of reasons. Bertcher and Maple (1996) enumerate several basic types. *Treatment groups* have as their primary purpose changing significant psychosocial problems that affect the group members' personal functioning and well-being. Leadership is by highly trained human service professionals, and the intensity of interaction is high. *Support groups* consist of individuals who strive to cope with similar issues and who support and encourage one another. Examples include alcohol or divorce recovery or parent support groups. Intensity of interaction is considered moderate. Leadership can be provided by a group member who may have been informally trained or by human service professionals, or by representatives of both categories. *Educational groups* are designed to increase knowledge, teach skills, consider value issues, or all three. No assumptions are made of personal involvement or that the material will be difficult to grasp. It is assumed that the learning will affect behavior. There is little selectivity about who participates, and intensity is low to moderate, depending on the topic and the amount of time allotted for the group to interact. *Task groups* assume no personal involvement with an issue and no change in the participant's daily life. A task group is formed to address a specific task. Leadership is usually elected or appointed from within the group, or it may be supplied by an administrator who needs input and group problem solving. An educational or support group can sometimes take on a task-group role, to carry out a specific project, for example. A *residential group* can be considered a subgroup of one of the other groups. The main difference is that participation in a residential group (e.g., at a prison or hospital) often may not be voluntary and could pose a particular challenge for the group leader. *Groups on the Internet* are a relatively new phenomenon by which groups form to discuss a variety of topics, including family relations and services. For example, potential adoptive parents may join an online group to discuss adoption issues. Anonymity can prompt some persons to share deeply with other anonymous persons. Bertcher and Maple (1996) see such groups as having "amazing potential" for dealing with personal issues, particularly for persons who are hesitant to join a face-to-face group.

Shaw (1981) and Bowman (1990–1995) emphasize that having a common purpose does not imply that all group members think alike or that they come together with the same expectations or levels of need. Other personal and societal factors also influence receptivity or response. The recognition of this point is seen as one of the many signs of growing sophistication in the family resource movement. More attention is now being given to the impact of differences in life circumstance, learning style, and history of the participants. In the not-too-distant past, participating in a group was the only choice that many agencies had to offer to parents, regardless of their distinctive differences. According to Bowman (1990–1995), "Frequently, the primary distinctions in program choices were in ages of children, not parental circumstance, need, or tradition. . . . There was little recog-

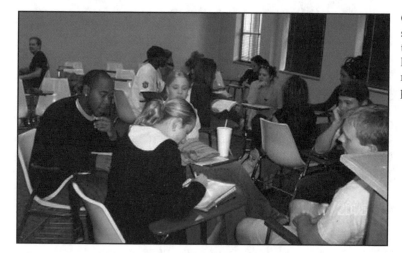

Group interaction stimulates application of personal knowledge and experience to common problems or tasks.

nition that stress, grief, gender, race, age, life circumstance or education could make a significant difference in the ways people might be able to learn" (p. 1).

Myers-Walls (2000) stresses the diversity of backgrounds and cultures that often makes up groups of learners today. She notes that a major factor in a group's success is the facilitator's comfort with self and with differing lifestyles and social values. Does the leader view diversity as a problem or an opportunity? The "frame" through which one views life often determines the outcome of interactions.

Today, many more options for education and intervention are available to family case managers, such as peer helping, home-based services, video check-outs, and telephone "warm lines," call-in lines for parents in crisis or who need parenting information. "Virtual" family life education through Internet connections is bringing diverse audiences together in new ways (Morris, Dollahite, & Hawkins, 1999). Family life educators are now much more aware of certain life realities of the community members they seek to serve.

THE VALUE OF GROUP PARTICIPATION

Eric Berne (1963) proposed that *survival needs* are the basic reason that people join groups. He explained that as social beings, the motivation to join together with others actually fulfills four basic human needs: (1) a biological need for stimulation of the physical senses, especially touch, sight, and hearing; (2) a psychological need for time structuring—talking, working, playing together; (3) a social need for intimacy—being close, sharing thoughts and feelings; and (4) a physiological need for safety—the protection and support of others. Schultz (1989) described the appeal of the group to human needs in different terms: (1) the need for inclusion—to be wanted, to belong, to be recognized as a person of worth; (2) the need for control—over one's personal choices and over the environment in which one lives; and (3) the need for affection—to both give and receive personal warmth and esteem, to get close to others.

All of these needs are powerful forces in human life. To provide a context in which such basic needs can hopefully be met is indeed a worthy endeavor. But groups are valuable for other reasons as well. Schultz (1989) points out the power of the group to effect change and to accomplish tasks that the individual might find impossible or at least much more difficult to achieve. The term *synergy* describes the concept of the whole being greater than the sum of its parts. The group, as well as its members, is stronger when individuals bring a variety of backgrounds and perspectives to bear on a problem:

> The hallmark of effective group process is mutuality, reciprocity, give and take. When it occurs in a group, power is unleashed.... Some give something they have. Others receive. And like popcorn popping, mutual help moves from person to person. At its best, reciprocity is energizing, empowering, and enduring. (Bowman, 1990–1995, p. 58)

THE FACILITATOR ROLE

Although the titles *leader* and *facilitator* denote basically the same role, the term *facilitator* is preferable because one who facilitates is less likely to be seen by the group as the expert with all the answers. Falling into the answer trap can short-circuit the group interaction process, and personal involvement with the issue ceases.

This is not meant to imply that groups work better without leadership. According to Schultz (1989), group leadership is necessary because groups need direction. They do not progress naturally in an organized fashion but tend to alternate between task needs and social needs. Issues also need clarification, and the impact of social-emotional relationships must be understood. An effective leader-facilitator helps to keep the group on track and functioning efficiently.

Napier and Gershenfeld (1983) point out a fundamental difference between the role of group facilitator and the role of teacher. The facilitator is not in charge, as is the teacher in a typical classroom. The group is in control of their learning and use of materials. Although the facilitator definitely must plan beforehand and have a goal in mind, it is the interaction of the group, which is not always predictable, that makes the group experience work.

Attributes of Effective Group Leaders

A classic study by Leiberman, Yalom, and Miles (1973) identified several important attributes of effective group leaders. *Caring* conveys friendship, protection, affection, and the invitation for members to receive feedback, support, and encouragement. This caring must be more than warm regard. It involves action that demonstrates the leaders' commitment to support families. This type of support aids them in building on their strengths in their neighborhoods and communities. But caring alone is not sufficient to sustain a lasting positive outcome. *Meaning attribution* helps the members to understand the plan, the purpose, and the importance of the group. Tasks include clarifying, interpreting, and providing frameworks for change. The leader understands that people learn by instruction as well as by doing. *Emotional stimulation* encourages but does not force emotional involvement of group members. Moderate-level sharing of the facilitator's personal feelings and life story is also received positively by group members. The *executive* function includes the ability to set goals, direct the flow of the meeting, and set necessary limits and structure. This function involves inviting, questioning, suggesting procedures, and decision-making functions.

But a group leader is not a perfect person, and mistakes in tactics or judgment do happen. In order to continually check one's congruency of motive and behavior, Bowman (1990–1995) suggests that facilitators regularly ask themselves the following questions:

- *Do I see the group members as clients, registrants, students, or partners?* A vision of collaborative learning and problem solving that does away with hierarchical roles will create the environment and results we desire. Collaboration doesn't mean that the facilitator discards skills, training, or the facilitator role. It does mean an attitude change and the ability to see persons as people with resources, ideas, new thoughts, and experiences that can be combined with yours to bring about learning and growth.

- *Do I see problems, weaknesses, and blame, or strengths and resiliency?* It is hard to move past prejudices and stereotypes, whether of homeless people or abused women, to a point of encouragement for small strengths and possibilities of new directions. Because we all bring our own beliefs and values to the group, it is difficult to lay judgment aside, but effectiveness for meaningful group participation will be curtailed otherwise.

- *Am I exploring options, or giving answers and solutions?* When the leader assumes the role of fixer, the individual takes no ownership or lasting interest in the solution provided. It is important to resist the temptation to provide answers and instead to encourage the group members to explore possibilities.

Leadership Can Be Learned

Wood (1977) and Napier and Gershenfeld (1983) stress the fact that leadership behaviors can be learned. The primary requirement of anyone who wishes to learn to lead groups is adaptability. Effective leaders know how to adapt their contributions to the needs and expectations of the group. In other words, they have learned to diagnose and respond to what is going on in that particular group. They remain open to change and growth (Wood, 1977). Bertcher and Maple (1996) point out that some people work better with certain populations—for example, senior citizens, children, the terminally ill. Generally, a person who matches the demographics of the group (gender, race, age) is most likely to be accepted quickly, but this is not always the case. Deliberately mixed groups probably fare better with cofacilitators who represent the major diversity factors.

Although the task of group leadership may seem daunting, fledgling leaders can cope with anxiety and build confidence by being thoroughly prepared and practicing activities beforehand. Starting small and building up, working with a co-leader, and getting experience as a group participant under an experienced group leader are also advisable (Napier & Gershenfeld, 1983). Finally, it is absolutely vital to be genuine and available and willing to ask for feedback from the group. Bowman (1990–1995) stresses the importance of leader self-care throughout the course of one's career as a group facilitator. Failure to care for one's own needs will result in burnout and fractured personal relationships. Establishing a mentor relationship with a colleague and interspersing group times with periods of relaxation can provide important self-care. Other stress reducers might include a standing lunch date with a good friend following a stressful group time or blocking out preparation time before a group time.

DEVELOPING A CLIMATE FOR PARTICIPATION

Getting Started

Recruiting group members. Not everyone is totally comfortable being part of a group, particularly at first. If the group membership is required, rather than voluntary, anxiety and reluctance to participate will definitely be heightened.

Bertcher and Maple (1996) note that recruiting members may be the most difficult part, because people often have preconceived notions about what the group will be like. They may have had a previous bad experience with a group that has left them uneasy and afraid. They may simply be overwhelmed with other obligations and see this as just one more thing to add to a very busy schedule rather than as something that could help them manage other stresses. It is very important to provide information to potential participants about the nature of the group, a statement of purpose that clearly states how this group will meet the needs of the individual, what time and how often the group will meet, and who to call if there are other questions.

Recruitment can be done directly through personal contact by the group facilitator (the person creating the group) or indirectly through referral resources. Either way, do not assume that one contact or announcement about the planned group will yield enough participants. Follow-up with referral resources and repeated announcements about the planned group are often necessary. Direct contact is preferable because it allows the group facilitator to determine personal roadblocks by asking if the person has ever participated in a group before and, if so, what the experience was like. If it was bad, the leader can then point out how this group will differ from his or her past experience. Getting personally acquainted with participants so that they have a chance to voice any reluctance can greatly enhance willingness to participate. Groups that are time-limited (four sessions or one weekend, for example) may get greater participation, because the person is not obligated for an extended period of time. A group can always be extended for those who want to continue.

Choosing a meeting site. In choosing a meeting location, it is essential to have privacy, audibility, comfort, and an absence of distractions. A meeting site that is close to the participants' neighborhoods or workplaces and therefore convenient is another important factor.

It is also important to choose a room size that matches the size of the group (Bertcher & Maple, 1996). Six people meeting in a banquet hall does not invite intimacy! Room arrangement also is a major consideration for enhancing group participation. Chairs in a circle or around a table (if this is a task-oriented group), rather than in rows, is always preferable. Bowman (1990–1995) points out that even the placement of the facilitator's chair—whether it is set apart or included as part of the circle—sends a message about the group climate.

Size of the group. The size of the group also affects the amount and quality of communication within the group. With only six members and one facilitator, for example, each person has to manage 21 different relationships (Bertcher & Maple, 1996). The relational complexity increases exponentially with each addition to the group. Size also affects group members' motivation to get involved in group work. There appear to be higher satisfaction and cohesiveness in smaller groups and an increase in disagreement and antagonism as size increases. Although a large group has more resources (knowledge, skills, and abilities) to call on, people often feel intimidated and unable to participate in a large group. The dominant members become more talkative, and their ideas tend to dominate decision making and the overall group climate. Research has shown that the more each member actively participates in the group, the more he or she will be affected by the group experience. If the group must be larger than six to eight people, the facilitator should divide the group into smaller units to discuss topics and have the large group reconvene at the end to reconnect with each other.

The First Meeting

Introductions. The first session sets the tone and direction the group experience will take. It is important to get acquainted and to address needs, expectations, and fears that group members might have. Napier and Gershenfeld (1983) note the importance of the first hour of the first session as a "grace period" during which the group reserves judgment and is cooperative and friendly. This is the time to establish yourself as an effective facilitator. There should be some review of your experience and an indication of your openness and humor. Let them know you have a plan and are well prepared. Convey a sense of confidence that you can handle any situation that arises because you believe in the competency of the group members to assist in working out the kinks in the plan. Be responsive to questions and comments, and learn their names.

Ground rules. Addressing ground rules and expectations for participation is another important topic to cover in the first session. This helps group members to feel safe as participants. Bowman (1990–1995) also emphasizes the value of group rituals, such as expected ways of beginning and ending the group and of ending relationships when members leave the group. Rituals are important because they establish needed boundaries and remove distractions to full participation. They aid in handling expressions of conflict or grief and give comfort. Gross (1993) summarizes some basic ground rules, which should be reviewed and posted at the first session: (1) everyone is encouraged to participate, but participation is voluntary; (2) we share our experiences, not our opinions; (3) every contribution is valuable and should not be judged or criticized; (4) you are free to ask questions and express concerns as we go along; (5) confidentiality and respect for each other is expected.

The importance of variety.   Bowman (1990–1995) emphasizes the value of variety in fostering group vitality: variety of methods, of tasks and groupings, and of follow-up questions. Sharing the discussion center, managing and encouraging input from everyone, and checking back after someone has received input are other ways to show appreciation for a wide range of feedback and participation.

Levels of Self-Disclosure

Sharing in a group setting is a new experience for many people. It is important for them to see the group as a safe place for taking the risk of self-disclosure. If the experience is rushed, some people may be scared off. The first session should structure opportunities for each person to share personal information without feeling exposed. In most cases, your modeling of appropriate levels of openness will encourage others to be open. Writing the answer to a question and then sharing it with a partner or a small group is one way of encouraging participation by everyone. One caution about pairing people, learned from personal experience, is that you may have people in your group who dislike each other. Forced pairing can cause friction to erupt. If a person seems especially reluctant to pair off, you might ask him or her to be your partner. Another way to handle this is to ask the group members to pick someone they don't know very well to be their partner.

John Powell (1969) enumerates five levels of self-disclosure, with level 5 being the least disclosing and level 1 the most. Level 5 is called "cliché communication." It acknowledges the other's presence: "Nice day, isn't it?" "Hi, how are you?" "Fine, how are you?" Level 4 consists of facts and biographical information about self: name, occupation, marital status, number of children. Level 3 moves to personal attitudes and ideas. This involves more risk of rejection or disapproval. Level 2 shares personal feelings, particularly those considered "negative" (anger, guilt, sadness, hurt). Level 1 is considered by Powell to be peak communication. The person shares private truths about him- or herself: Fears, behaviors, and thoughts that could bring rejection or disapproval are revealed. This level of sharing involves the most risk but also the most possibility for intimacy and close relationships. It is usually reached only when there is a high level of trust between people.

The European American cultural assumption that sharing personal stories and feelings is beneficial is not an assumption shared by every culture, or even every European American (Bowman, 1990–1995). The concept of saving or losing face is very important to personal esteem in many cultures. "Saving face" can range from not admitting weakness under any circumstance to a sense of personal privacy that does not allow discussion of personal issues in public. As we relate to more diverse groups, techniques that allow for discussion of personal matters without personal exposure need to be developed. Indirect methods, such as case studies, stories, or hypothetical situations, can allow group members to examine personal issues without the risk of "losing face." If you are working with a culture different from your own, it is very important to find out ahead of time about its particular cultural norms. The best resource is talking with representative members of the culture group, who can share their perspective with you.

The Time Factor

One of the major tasks of a group facilitator is to structure and set parameters for the group's time together. To start and end the group promptly at the time arranged, right from the first day, lets the members know they can trust you to control the boundaries of the group. This trust will carry over to other issues as the group develops. Some structure and a predictable routine create a safe space for risk, change, creativity, and handling of stress. Responsibility for the process lies with the group leader (Bowman, 1990–1995).

Napier and Gershenfeld (1983) emphasize the importance of taking breaks and not overloading a session or a program:

> Often what the group needs is less, not more: less information, fewer experiences and fewer lectures. The one ingredient participants need more of is time: time to regenerate their own energy and interest, time to think and integrate, time for psychological and physical rest, time for a change of pace, time to be reflective about the questions, and time to let go and have fun. (pp. 101–102)

THE GROUP PROCESS

Effective group process can be compared to a dance in which persons are acting and reacting in response to other persons: synchronized and in touch (Bowman, 1990–1995). As studies of learning have shown us, the higher the level of engagement and involvement by the learner, the greater the impact and retention. Group members also learn more when they feel respected and when the new learning is related to their life experience and has some immediate usefulness to them.

Theories of Group Dynamics

Whereas some theorists (Bion, 1961; Lewin, Lippitt, & White, 1939; Moreno, 1953) have focused on the individual's role and responses within the group, Bales (1950) turned his attention to the interaction within the group itself. Bales's work was accomplished through the use of an observational scheme that came to be known as IPA (Interactional Process Analysis) and a later version, called Systematic Multiple Level Observation of Groups (SYMLOG). Using this schematic, Bales and Cohen (1979) were able to chart the tasks and socioemotional activities of a group, phases in group development, and the types of roles group members assume. A major finding was the important role that communication plays in producing effective or ineffective groups. The research also confirmed that the most effective groups were those in which all members were essentially positive in their interactions with each other and in which power was shared rather than being in the hands of the leader or a few dominant members. The effective group was also fairly task-oriented: There was direction and active work on individual or group goals. An effective facilitator recognizes that he or she must operate two domains of leadership: administrative (group management and task orientation) and affective (person-centered, feelings focus, and "climate control"; Bowman,

1990–1995). Leaders who are aware of these needs and value them will realize their role in several areas: tension and release of feelings and differences of opinion, "gatekeeping" during complex communication interactions, and encouraging and mediating so that all people can make their views known and no one dominates or is nonparticipative (Beebe & Masterson, 1990).

Systems theory has also been used to analyze group interactions and understand outcomes of group experience (Fisher, 1975). Just as a family operates as a system, with each member functioning in relation to all others and forming a whole unit, so it is with groups that become interdependent and cohesive. Input, process, and output variables can be identified; roles can be established; and the group can operate as an open or closed system.

In studying the developmental process in groups, Tuckman (1965) developed a set of descriptors that define a four-stage process: forming, storming, norming, and performing. Each of the four stages is discussed as it applies particularly to educational and support groups.

Forming

A number of aspects of group formation were discussed earlier in the chapter. This section focuses on the leader's role in facilitating the formation process. There is always a tension between being well prepared and organized and being flexible and open to the group's ideas.

Recently, I (Powell) was asked to lead a four-session program on interpersonal relationships for women who were victims of domestic violence. The staff counselor had arranged the experience and given me some idea about the things she saw as topics that needed to be discussed. However, I had had no prior contact with the group before the evening of the first session. I definitely wanted to get their ideas and involve them in setting the agenda, but I could not go in empty-handed. By sketching out a four-session program beforehand, with a major topic assigned for each night, I had some feeling of preparedness. I also planned several get-acquainted exercises that involved low-level sharing of personal feelings and thoughts. But the main item on the first night's agenda was to ask them what they wanted to talk about in regard to personal relationships during the next four weeks. They were brimming with ideas. Their focus was not always the same as mine. It was easy, however, to incorporate their concerns into my basic outline (which I gave to them the following week, with their topic suggestions included). The result was an enjoyable experience of interchange and new awareness, most of which I drew from their own comments as we focused on various topics.

One aspect often overlooked by group facilitators in the process of group formation is the ethical dimension of leadership. Miles (1981) developed some rules of thumb that can guide thinking about ethical decisions in groups. As facilitators, we have various styles, but these guidelines should undergird all our efforts (see box 5.1)

Box 5.1   Ethical Guidelines for Group Facilitators

Awareness of Ethical Choice

If your beliefs and values run counter to those of the group that has invited you to present, you must make a choice: to refuse the offer or to hold your own views in abeyance, which is actually impossible to do. Just as judges disqualify themselves from certain cases, facilitators should be aware that working with certain systems that are contrary to their beliefs can cause ethical problems.

Awareness of One's Own Power

The facilitator is often viewed as the expert on everything. You must resist the temptation to dominate or manipulate. Playing favorites is also unwise and tends to cause jealousy and antagonism among other group members. Ask for anonymous, written feedback from the group regarding how they see your role in order to provide a safeguard against falling into the "power-trip trap."

Truth in Packaging

Avoid false advertising about what the group experience will accomplish or what the possible risks are. Accept and acknowledge your limitations and those of the group.

Voluntary Participation

When a group member is forced to do anything, it can build resistance to future involvement. Ground rules that stress this point can emphasize the importance of this concept for you and them.

Privacy and Confidentiality

This is expected of leaders and group members. You should not obligate yourself to any sort of written report that reveals personal confidences. If group participation is required by court, you may have to write a general statement about a person's involvement in the group. This should be noted at the outset.

Competence

The leader is expected to have the training and certification he or she claims to have. It is one thing to feel new and apprehensive, to know the material but be fearful about having the ability to work with the population. It is quite another thing to be so overwhelmed with an assignment that prayer and the fact that you are a good person are all that sustain you. Going beyond your level of competence is dangerous. It is not taking a risk; it is inviting disaster.

Value and Behavior Congruence

The leader who advocates a certain value but whose behavior contradicts that value is acting incongruently. Examples include incongruent values/behavior in managing conflict, self-disclosure, or confidentiality.

Avoidance of Harm

The member's right to not participate in any exercise should be stressed. Goading, sarcasm, or scapegoating can cause psychological harm to a person and to program effectiveness.

Source: *Learning to Work with Groups*, by M. B. Miles, 1981, New York, Columbia University. Permission granted by Teachers College Press.

Storming

As group members become comfortable with each other and with the leader, the "honeymoon" period of social niceness wanes, and people begin to express a genuine range of personal responses, including disagreement, slight, and frustration. Everyone has a personal investment in what she or he believes. If an idea seems to challenge those beliefs, we tend to reject it as a way of upholding our self-worth (Schultz, 1989). This need to defend oneself is just one of the reasons group members may get into conflict. Opposition to new ideas and insufficient time to process an idea or task may also cause friction and discomfort. An ineffective group tends to focus on the flaws of any proposal being made. Also, many group members may not actively participate and may even sabotage the group's work if their own needs are not met (Schultz, 1989). When a group member expresses strong emotions, either verbally or nonverbally, it is good to ask, "How can the group be helpful to you right now?" (Bowman, 1990–1995). Then offer some types of support: listening, giving suggestions, sharing similar experiences, telling the member that we understand. This produces a thoughtful pause and emphasizes personal needs and awareness.

Gibb (1961) determined that small groups were more effective in managing conflict when conditions were supportive rather than defensive. Such a climate of support is possible when people (1) listen and respond in nonjudgmental terms; (2) participate actively and show an understanding of each other's views; (3) are willing to experiment with new ideas; and (4) recognize their interdependence, as well as their dependence. Defensive climates occur when (1) attempts are made to control the behavior of others; (2) people fail to understand others' feelings; (3) communication is self-serving and competitive; (4) criticism is directed at persons, not at ideas; and (5) statements are delivered with such certainty and dominance that a negative climate results. Conflict is not necessarily a bad thing to happen in group interaction. Schultz (1989) points out that healthy conflict can foster consideration of diverse ideas and perspectives. It encourages participation by more people and fosters more intense involvement with the task or subject. Conflict can also clarify problems.

When conflict occurs, the leader's task is not to squash it, but instead to manage it. Gross (1993) suggests that leaders discourage labeling an approach as right or wrong, good or bad. General statements, such as "Some of us feel strongly about. . . . Let's hear/explore other viewpoints," will keep the discussion from getting out of hand or being dominated by one or two persons with very strong opinions. The leader may have to keep emphasizing that within the group individual differences, values, and attitudes are respected.

Beebe and Masterson (1990) identified three types of common interpersonal conflict: pseudoconflict, simple conflict, and ego conflict. Pseudoconflict, as its name implies, is not really conflict but more likely a misunderstanding in communication or a misperception of the problem. Simple conflict arises when individuals disagree over which course of action to pursue. Ego conflict involves a person's sense of "losing face" or being personally attacked by another. Each type of conflict is best managed when it is identified and dealt with in a specific way. Table 5.1 summarizes the suggested approaches to each type of conflict.

Table 5.1   Managing Different Types of Conflict

	Pseudoconflict	Simple Conflict	Ego Conflict
Source of conflict	Misunderstanding individuals' perceptions of the problem.	Individual disagreement over which course of action to pursue.	Defense of ego: Individual believes he or she is being attacked personally.
Suggestions for managing conflict	1. Ask to clarifiy perceptions. 2. Establish a supportive rather than a defensive climate. 3. Employ active listening: *Stop* *Look* *Listen* *Question* *Paraphrase content* *Paraphrase feelings*	1. Listen and clarify perceptions. 2. Make sure issues are clear to all group members. 3. Use a problem-solving approach to manage differences of opinion. 4. Keep discussion focused on the issues. 5. Use facts rather than opinions for evidence. 6. Look for alternatives or compromise positions. 7. Make the conflict a group concern rather than an individual concern. 8. Determine which conflicts are the most important to resolve. 9. If possible, postpone the decision so additional research can be conducted. This delay also helps relieve tensions.	1. Let members express their concerns but do not permit personal attacks. 2. Employ active listening. 3. Call for a cooling-off period. 4. Try to keep discussion focused on issues (simple conflict). 5. Encourage parties to be descriptive rather than evaluative and judgmental. 6. Use a problem-solving approach to manage differences of opinion. 7. Speak slowly and calmly. 8. Develop rules or procedures that create a relationship that allows for the personality difference.

Norming

When conflict situations are managed forthrightly and calmly, the group moves to a new level of working together. Ground rules established at the beginning then have more meaning, and the group may even decide to adopt others. But norming does not ensure that the unpredictable will never happen. The unexpected crisis will inevitably come. It may be a crisis in the community or a disclosure of personal hurt or discomfort. Sherwood and Scherer (1975) label this a *pinch*, which can be managed more effectively if it is expected and if certain norms are followed. First, address the disruption directly and kindly. If it is a personal issue, deal with it empathetically (put yourself in that person's place and space). Second, invite shared group responsibility and affirm the ability of the group to deal with the issue and move on. The tendency is to gloss over or avoid pinches instead of dealing with them. Then they become crunches that can seriously disrupt group effectiveness (Bowman, 1990–1995).

Other group norms should include periodic feedback or evaluation from the group and the setting of limits by the group facilitator. Setting limits is often viewed negatively, but it is really a positive. It helps the group to focus attention and move toward a goal.

Performing

Because this aspect of group process constitutes the majority of time spent in a group, it is discussed in its own section below.

EFFECTIVE GROUP WORK

Basic Design

Gross (1993) suggests a basic design for facilitating a group session. At the beginning of the session, the facilitator should announce the topic and plan for the day. Be prepared to ask open-ended questions to invite group participation and discussion. Do not be surprised if you are met with silence (as often happens). Be ready to rephrase the question or ask another one after waiting an appropriate time for a response. Facilitators are often uncomfortable with silence and may fill up the silence too quickly after a question is asked. But silence can be a rich time for personal reflection, tension release, and collecting one's thoughts. Give the participants time to think and perhaps to get a little uncomfortable with the silence themselves. Otherwise, you undermine the possibility of group response. They will get in the habit of letting you "fill up the space." Asking members to first write their response encourages group participation and gives everyone a chance and a reason to really think about the question. I would not use this method exclusively, but it can be a good way to begin group discussion.

When a person does share a response, acknowledge it appreciatively by reflecting back what has been said or by writing the answer on a chart or board. Then ask for other responses, without pressuring anyone. Dividing into dyads or small groups of three to five also encourages more personal responses and involvement.

The Minilecture

Family life education implies group interaction rather than a classroom lecture format. Research confirms that lecture has the poorest rate of effective retention. Knowles's (1989) research, discussed earlier, stated that we retain 20% of what we hear versus 80% of what we see and do. Nevertheless, there are times when information and input are needed. The minilecture allows for input and group interaction. Strive to keep the lecture time at 10 minutes or under, interspersed with response or a kinetic activity related to the topic.

Praxis

Praxis is defined by Vella (1994) as "action with reflection" or "learning by doing" (p. 4). The best type of action is not contrived but drawn from the life experience of group members. The next best is involving the group in a project or group task that illustrates your learning points and then reflecting together on the process and the outcome.

Good Communication Skills

Gross (1993) stresses the importance of teaching good communication skills and personal sharing by modeling these skills when appropriate. It is important not to monopolize or redirect a group member's concerns. Stay with a topic as long as it seems important to the person or the group to continue the discussion. Again, just because the group is silent for a little while does not necessarily indicate that they are ready to move to a different topic. Often, asking a second question related to the first will help gauge whether there is more to be said on the topic.

The use of active listening skills by the facilitator provides an important model for group members who may have poor listening skills, a common deficiency in our society. Active and effective listening skills can be learned by everyone in the group. The main requirements are good modeling and lots of practice.

The largest part of human communication is nonverbal. Many gestures, such as smiles, frowns, yawns, clenched fists, movement of legs or body, raised eyebrows, and eye contact (or the lack of it), are subtle and ambiguous pieces of communication. We cannot immediately conclude that the restless person is bored or that a raised eyebrow means disapproval of what is being said. It is up to the leader to take notice and move to a kinetic application of the topic or to ask the group if they are ready for a break. Again, do not put an individual on the spot. Instead of, "John, I see you're yawning. What's up?" you might comment, "Well, I'm noticing some restlessness and signs of boredom. Is it time for a break?" The raised eyebrow could prompt you to ask, "Joe, do you have something to add?" Then allow time for response.

A leader's own nonverbal communication is also very important. Smiles beget smiles. Eye contact conveys that you are confident and can decrease the psychological distance between you and the group members. Directness and warmth, a sense of humor, and a relaxed stance can reduce tension and encourage relaxation among members.

Follow-Up

Follow-up of unfinished business or a recapitulation of what went on in the last group meeting allows for continual correction of misconceptions and reinforces concepts taught. Another type of follow-up may occur after the program is completed and can be built into the original plan or contract. For example, the group may be asked to assemble again in a month or so to see how they are doing with their newfound insights or skills. Box 5.2 lists questions for reflection that can assist the facilitator in determining if the group is functioning effectively.

> **Box 5.2   Checklist for an Effective Group**
>
> ❑ Does everyone have a chance to talk?
>
> ❑ Are comments understood? Is everyone given feedback?
>
> ❑ Are group members open-minded about ideas and opinions? Do they allow arguments to surface?
>
> ❑ Does each person get recognition even if his or her idea was not accepted?
>
> ❑ Does the group avoid "win-lose" situations?
>
> ❑ Do members help the group examine the process of exploring problems and making decisions?
>
> ❑ Do members urge others to confront their differences rather than simply agreeing to disagree?
>
> ❑ Do members assist the group in working toward the group's goal?
>
> From Schultz, Beatrice G. *Communicating in the Small Group: Theory and Practice.* Published by Allyn and Bacon, Boston, MA. Copyright © 1989 by Pearson Education. Reprinted by permission of the publisher.

FREQUENTLY ENCOUNTERED PROBLEMS

Experienced group leaders are often asked to comment on a number of topics that seem to be common challenges to group facilitation. The following problems and responses are a few that may help the reader in the future.

- *What do you do when the group depends on you to be "the expert"?* It is flattering to have persons asking your opinion, but it is very costly, because they come to depend on you for every decision or administrative detail. They become like children instead of collaborators or colleagues. There is definitely a balance that must be struck between "taking over" and being "out of it." When should you give answers and when should you not? When a question is asked by a group member, always return it to the group if possible. Or give several options and ask the group to evaluate. Continually remember your role as that of facilitator and resource, but not the "answer person."

- *How do you deal with discussion dominators?* Some people are by nature more verbal than others. You don't want to squelch, just manage. Ideas for doing this include dividing into small groups for discussion or task assignment, having everyone write a response before asking for verbal response, or specifically asking for others to comment. The "fishbowl" discussion method is another good technique. Have the group divide themselves into two categories: the Mostly Talkers and the Mostly Listeners. Then have the Mostly Talkers sit in an outside ring to observe the Mostly Listeners discuss a topic. Then switch observers and discussants. Finally, have each group share what they noticed about what happened in the group they observed and the group they participated in. This is a good example of praxis.

- *How do you deal with frequent interruptions?* Again, the goal is not to squelch, but to manage. It is important to acknowledge the person's statement or question and to eventually deal with the topic at a more appropriate time. A quick way to acknowledge is to ask the person to hold the question until you finish the current discussion. You might also comment, "That's a good question, but one we can't answer quickly. Let's get back to it." Then don't forget to do that. If the interruption has to do with a question about a task assignment, you probably need to halt everyone, go over the instructions to clarify them for everyone, and ask for further questions.

- *How do you handle a disruptive member?* This is not an easy or a pleasant task, but if the problem is not attended to, the group's effectiveness will be gravely diminished. It is also a caring thing to do, because it is a matter of courtesy, it is respectful of all group members, it is excellent modeling, and it is crucial to group morale. Disruptions can include crying, put-downs of other people, personal disclosure in a way that others have not done, getting angry with someone in the group, interrupting with inappropriate laughter, or other behaviors that control or disrupt conversation between the facilitator and the other members. There are several ways to address this problem. First, make an effort to hear what the person is saying by reflecting back his or her comments or general concern. Then have the person respond. You might offer to meet after group to discuss it further. There might be a need to refer the person for counseling. The facilitator can also set limits with firmness and remind the group about the ground rules if someone begins to overstep them. Or, for the constant talker, "I'm going to have to call time here so we can move on to hear from others in the group."

Disclosing a painful experience can be especially disruptive if the news is shocking to the group or if it's the first time a person has become extremely emotional. It is not unkind to interrupt the speaker and acknowledge the difficulty of his or her situation and the group's concern with listening carefully and being supportive. In rare instances, a person may start to divulge a serious secret about himself or herself, one that could be inappropriate for a support or education group. Often people in distress may be unaware of the level of disclosure they are making. If this is not a therapy situation, it is a kindness to offer them a time to pause to reconsider their words.

- *How do you deal with a person in crisis?* Assess the immediacy of the crisis. Often group time spent in supporting a hurting member is time well spent. For vast, chronic needs, referral to other resources would be best. In private, provide names and phone numbers and affirm the person's worthiness to get the resources he or she needs.

- *What about the person dealing with deep emotions of grief and loss?* Grief is better handled when it is recognized and shared, but group facilitators are still sometimes uncomfortable with its expression. Most life transitions incorporate some type of loss. It is a predictable and legitimate component of group work (Bowman, 1990–1995). The primary task of the facilitator is to encourage the grieving person to "put words to their tears" so as to bring understanding and a sense of being heard and comforted. There is no one right order or manner of handling grief. Don't push or judge the person. Sometimes denial or distraction is a healthy response. You are not here to confront or evaluate but to provide empathy and acceptance. Don't expect him or her to "get over it" in a hurry. Stay clear about the purpose of the group and gently return to the topic.

Another major problem can arise when deep grief is shared in the group. Some members will rush in to express similar experiences and draw the focus away from the one who has brought up the issue. Also, a member may compare her or his coping mechanism to that of the grieving person and imply that it is superior. As a result, the other person may come away from the group feeling inferior rather than supported. It is up to the leader to bring the focus of attention back to the original speaker and affirm his or her unique perspective.

ENDINGS

Whether closing one session or ending the group experience, the time of closing is often neglected or rushed. Yet what happens during this period either completes or fragments the effectiveness of the session (Bowman, 1990–1995). If you start your planning by thinking about closure, it directs the flow of the meeting. Think first of where you want the group to be when the session or program is over. Be very aware of the time your closing will take and be willing to stop discussion and move to closing when it is time. A good closing includes recapping what has been said and concluded, checking about hurt feelings or disgruntled members, and pointing ahead to the next meeting. Take time after closing to reflect on and note lessons learned, new insights, and other needs to attend to. Then give yourself credit for what you were able to accomplish and move on.

If this is the final session of a group experience, it is better not to introduce new topics but to use this as a time of closure and tying up loose ends. Always include time for group members to comment about the group and to ask any lingering questions, time to say good-byes and affirmations to one another, and time to fill out an evaluation questionnaire. Where to go from here is also an important topic for the last session. Suggestions of available community resources and other ways of sustaining growth should be offered. Family resource centers are a good example of community support. Bowman (1990–1995) notes that family therapy gurus Carl Rogers and Virginia Satir were asked in 1970 (independent of each other) what they projected as a base of support for families in the twenty-first century. Both described the family resource center concept, to which people in all stages of life could come for assistance in dealing with a variety of family issues, from child care and parent education to literacy and job skills training to anger management classes to having coffee and conversation with friends. Just knowing such resources are available is all many people need to cope with life's challenges.

SUMMARY

This chapter looked at the various elements and dynamics that make up effective group processes. The definition of a group and the individual perspectives that members bring to a group were discussed. The value of group participation and the hesitancy of some persons to join a group were examined in light of human needs and human fears.

The setting, the room arrangement, the introductions, the time factor: All of these contribute to whether the group climate is chilly or warm and inviting. In order to provide a climate of safety so that persons are willing to risk sharing with others, the facilitator must be able to balance the maintenance of boundaries with openness to the interests and ideas of the group.

Theories of group dynamics point to the value of positive regard and individual involvement as keys to learning within a group. But effective group process does not proceed along a constantly smooth track. Generally, a working group can be expected to travel through stages of forming, storming, norming, and performing. The facilitator's ability to handle the various stages with calmness and respect for all the members will certainly influence the rate at which a group arrives at the performing stage, or if they arrive at all.

Aspects of effective group strategies, from the basic design to the value of good communication skills and the use of praxis, were discussed. Suggestions about how to address specific problems the facilitator may encounter should provide assistance to new and veteran group facilitators.

It is obvious that the facilitator has the major role in establishing a climate for full participation and in guiding and inspiring the group members to discover new resources within themselves. Leadership is a skill that can be learned if the person is honest and flexible and genuinely cares for the group members. That caring must go beyond sympathy to a willingness to set aside preconceived ideas about certain groups of people and to the ability to empathize with each individual as he or she strives to grow at his or her own pace.

"There is considerable agreement in the literature to support the claim that the educator's personal qualities are potentially as important as any specific technique he or she employs in facilitating the group process" (Gross, 1993, p. 25). Each educator-facilitator's preparation must start with his or her own personal awareness and comfort with the leadership function and with expressions of feelings, conflict, and criticism. Remembering your own experience as a group member in a well-led group—and getting feedback from mentors and colleagues—will work to help you develop the skills you need to do successful and effective group work.

Questions/Problems for Discussion and Review

Class Discussion

1. Review the questions asked in the first paragraph of this chapter. Share your answer with others in a small group. Choose what you consider to be the top three attributes of an effective teacher or group facilitator.

2. How are the roles and the tasks of a classroom teacher different from those of a group facilitator?

3. Consider again the definition of praxis. Give an example of praxis in your own life. Why is this such a powerful learning tool?

Research Problem

A great deal of research on group dynamics and group process was done during the 1960s and 1970s, a time when encounter and sensitivity groups were popular. Choose a text on small-group process from that time period and one from the 1990s or 2000s to compare in terms of emphasis and methodology. What is different? What is the same?

Case Study Design

Consider carefully the known characteristics of a group you will be facilitating. Determine a plan for recruitment and assess the quality of the location and the anticipated size of the group. What can you alter to improve the anticipated group climate?

Consider also your personal readiness for leadership, based on the ethical guidelines in box 5.1. Discuss with your group how comfortable you are in a conflict situation or a boundary-setting situation. How might you develop more comfort?

In a Nutshell
Designing Your Program

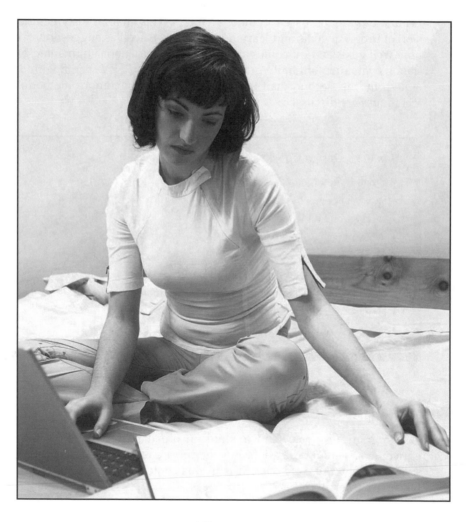

The time has come. You've been on the job for two months as program director for a teen parent support organization. The executive director has now asked you to design a new parent education program. What basic information do you need to get started? Before you read further, jot down some ideas.

KEEP THE BASICS IN MIND

It's easy to overlook the obvious, so let's not do that here. This chapter provides a framework for program design that you can hopefully use and adapt for any program you are called upon to design and present. Many of the elements of design and presentation (needs assessment; group interaction; theories of change; evaluation) are discussed in other chapters. This chapter also includes a discussion of program goals and learning outcomes as well as suggestions for assessing how well goals and outcomes are met. The discussion is augmented by the material on evaluation of family programs (see chapter 7). We begin with design principles; in the second half of this chapter presentation methodologies and techniques are discussed.

Box 6.1   Design Checklist

- What is the subject/topic?
- How much time has been allotted?
- Who is your audience?
- What content do you want to include?
- What do you want the outcome for learners to be?
- What teaching materials/equipment do you need?
- How do you present the materials for best comprehension?
- How do you get feedback/assessment/evaluation?
- What type of follow-up/follow-through do you do?

WHAT IS THE SUBJECT/TOPIC?

Program designers tend to think in broad terms: Sex education; marriage enrichment; parent education. But the most effective designers must *relate more specifically to real-life problems.* It is in this context that learning is most likely to take place (Merrill, 2002).

Box 6.2

> Consider our opening scenario; how can you be more specific—and appealing—to the new teen mothers? What real-life problems are they facing? How can you find out? How can you work that into a topic that will appeal to young mothers?

HOW MUCH TIME HAS BEEN ALLOTTED?

While this seems to be a simple question, let us not forget how much time behavior change takes. To expect too much from too little (too little time, training, advance preparation, and investigation) is a recipe for ineffectiveness. On the other hand, a program that seems to go on endlessly does not appeal to the contemporary American lifestyle where "instant" is the byword and "commitment" for more than a few weeks is rarely seen. More people will come to a one-shot program than will commit to a long-term group experience, where learning and change can actually occur.

I (Powell) and my spouse have been a facilitator couple in an established marriage enrichment organization for more than 30 years. We know that the best climate for learning and practicing new relationship skills is an ongoing group in which both members of the couple participate in regular meetings to "work on their marriages." We also know that many couples are skittish about committing to a monthly meeting. Furthermore, they are uncertain about what will happen if they spend that much quality time together! Often we are told, "We would certainly participate, if we could find the time." (An aside, they will never "find" the time, since so many other things compete for their time—children, jobs, education. Time must be prioritized. It can't be "found.")

The real-life problem here is how to present even the basic philosophy and objectives of marriage enrichment in a way that will catch a couple's attention and make them want to get more of this good stuff. Recently, we designed a two-hour program that included a light supper and a program of fun and togetherness. We advertised through a hospital continuing education program, and the pastoral care department underwrote part of the meal cost so that the couples paid only $10 total for "an evening of marriage enrichment." We billed it as "tired of getting the leftovers of time and energy for your relationship? Here's a chance to have the main course: a date night for you and your spouse."

Some 24 couples attended and 12 of them signed an information card expressing an interest in an ongoing group. We followed up with the 12 to set up such an ongoing group. Sadly, only four couples signed up. We know that several have conflicts on the night we chose, which is always a problem. But the good news is that the concept and the seed of interest in relationship enhancement/marriage enrichment have been planted.

Box 6.3

Consider how much time you can realistically allot to the teen parent program. Is a two-step (intro plus ongoing) sequencing possible? What accommodations, such as child care, will be needed in order for participants to easily attend?

WHO IS YOUR AUDIENCE?

A program design that doesn't address the needs of its audience is about as useful as wearing an outfit that is too big or too small. It just doesn't fit, and you probably won't ever wear it again! Knowing your audience and their needs is crucial to designing effective programs. Chapter 4 addresses needs assessment in great detail. Considering the limited amount of time and resources you sometimes have, how can you get "a feel" for the audience before you begin your program design?

A great starting point is to talk to someone who works with the target group and get their impressions. In addition, talk to potential participants themselves, if at all possible. As larger numbers of diverse ethnic and culture groups relocate from their original homelands into new towns and cities across America, the need for specific education and understanding of their unique backgrounds is critical. Many of the families have endured extreme conditions and traumatic events. We cannot assume that we know or understand the needs of so many divergent family forms and experiences. It is crucial to avoid stereotyping. Some culture groups may be reluctant to speak about what they want or need from an education program. An alternative or second stage assessment might incorporate a printed checklist to determine one's interest in specific topics (e.g. "check all of the topics that you would be VERY interested in talking about"). Always include a blank space asking for other suggestions.

Another way to know the audience is to research and read about similar groups. Popular literature often provides insight into first-generation experiences and cultural values. Research literature may report on successful programs that have been designed and implemented for similar groups. Always ask yourself: What's missing here? How is the audience the same? How is it different? Avoid assumptions.

Box 6.4

Consider what books and research articles can be found about the teenage parent. Does the teen father need to be considered? What differences are likely between culture groups? What universal mothering needs, roles, and challenges are there?

WHAT CONTENT DO YOU WANT TO INCLUDE?

This is probably one of the hardest questions to answer, particularly if you are new to the job with few resources in your files. The Internet can provide a wealth of information on practically any family topic, but how do you determine which information and ideas are sound and how do you turn content into session topics, goals, and objectives?

Let's say you are browsing the "family" section of the local bookstore or the World Wide Web for ideas for your program. A variety of catchy titles and Web sites grab your attention. Some programmatic materials provide videotape support and participant workbooks. But how do you know for sure if the material is sound?

First, is the information supported by current research? Look for books or articles on the general topic written by persons with academic credentials and experience in the field. While non-academic persons can certainly design credible programs, check their affiliations and other books published. Who does the author refer to and how are ideas supported? Check the references for recent dates of publication (preferably within the last ten years). An excellent source of credible information, professional development, and program assistance is Family Information Services, edited for the past 20 years by Dr. Joan Comeau. Subscribers to the service receive regular volumes of current information, research updates, and program aids on a variety of family topics. Libraries as well as individuals may subscribe to FIS, either online or on computer disks (see www.faminfoserv.com for more information). A cumulative index allows educators to go immediately to information they need about specific or general topics.

The CFLE (Certified Family Life Educator) e-mail list is a service of the National Council on Family Relations for persons who have achieved this professional credential. It offers CFLEs the opportunity to pose questions about potential program needs and receive feedback from other CFLEs who have designed similar programs. The list also sends announcements about training events and special conferences that might be of interest to family life educators. Training programs in parent education are available from NPEN (National Parent Education Network). The Association for Couples in Marriage Enrichment (ACME) offers a highly credible leader training program for couples who want to be leaders of marriage enrichment events (see www.bettermarriages.org).

Affiliation with a professional organization that studies and supports families, such as the National Council on Family Relations, the American Association of Family and Consumer Sciences, or Cooperative Extension Services, offers members national conferences, teleconferences, and other opportunities for training in specific programs. Most conduct state as well as national meetings where you can network with colleagues, review new books and materials that have been published, and attend workshops on diverse family issues.

Once you have relevant, sound content, how do you turn it into a learning experience? As has already been pointed out, receiving information is not the same as learning something. How many millions of hours have been spent with information floating across rooms and bouncing off the ears and eyes of bored listeners in classrooms and business conferences and across kitchen tables? Turning passive information dissemination into active learning requires thought and skill on the facilitator's part as well as interest and motivation for the participant. Of course the facilitator's presentation during the opening session has a significant influence on the learner's continued interest and motivation.

Here are some basic guidelines to enhance the first session:

1. Involve the learner early and often. Introductions provide a natural starting point. Ask for more than name, rank, etc. Always be the first to introduce yourself. Ask questions such as: Who has been the biggest influence on your life? What is the hardest thing about being a teen parent? If possible, match the opening question to the topic of the seminar. It may be as simple as: How many children/grandchildren do you have? Have you ever been part of a group like this? If so, what benefit was it to you?

Do something to get them talking! Remember to keep self-disclosure low so that no one feels threatened. Use a handout with thought questions or examples to discuss. Let them take a self-assessment test. Be sure to listen carefully to their experiences and what they want to know.

2. Keep the amount of new information low and digestible. Take plenty of time to chew on each new idea and get feedback, examples, and self-assessments. Don't rush to another point before you have thoroughly examined the first one. Relaxation, humor, and interaction with one another all send the message that "this person is comfortable with me and I can trust him/her."

Duncan and Goddard (2005) suggest using a general principle or truth to hold together your individual sessions and link them into a program. Merrill (1994) calls this the *expository generality*. In a teen parent program, such a generality might be "infants need loving and patient response to all of their needs." The *how* of internalizing that truth in ways that influence behavior in the future is the hard part. This brings up the next basic element of good program design: Developing goals, objectives and learner outcomes.

What Do You Want the Outcomes for Learners to Be?

Have you ever asked yourself in the middle of a higher math class, "Why am I here? What good is this going to do me?" At that time you deeply desired knowledge about the goals and objectives of the class. You were also worried about whether you would be able to perform well enough on the tests to pass the course! These are learning outcomes. All learners want to know what they are going to get out of their experience. Is it worth their time and effort? The facilitator/teacher wants to know whether he or she is having any long-lasting effect on the attitudes and behaviors of the learners. Instructors in formal education settings can require students to do certain assignments and take tests to evaluate application of knowledge. Educators in informal, non-compulsory settings—but often with grant and program accountability—must articulate goals and objectives and assess learning outcomes in a somewhat different way.

Let us define some important terms, starting with the word *vision*. Duncan and Goddard (2005) define this as "the larger picture" (p. 64). Also called the "mission statement," a well articulated vision should be at the center of any organization's planning and programming. *Goals* of a program are still very broad and general, but they should relate to the vision and to the desired program and program participants. *Objectives* articulate specific steps and principles to achieve the goals of the desired program. *Learning outcomes* are similar to objectives, but they address the response of the learners to the program: observable behaviors that indicate their understanding and application of the objectives.

I (Powell) recently conducted a two-hour leadership seminar for officers in the student professional organization where I am an advisor. In planning for the seminar, first I gathered materials that seemed appropriate for student leadership competencies and expectations. Then I wrote down the vision of the sponsoring organization (the College of Human Sciences) as well as the vision of the organization with which I was working, and my goals, objectives, and learning outcomes for the seminar:

- **Vision for the College of Human Sciences:** to improve and enhance the human condition.

- **Vision for the organization**: to engage students in an understanding of the profession of family social science and to enhance their abilities to lead and to serve families in the community.

- **Program goal:** to assist students in developing leadership skills for use in the student professional organization and in daily life.

- **Program objectives:** Participants will:
  1. Consider qualities of leadership and how to develop
  2. Consider practical habits of effective people
  3. Consider the value of student professional organizations
  4. Consider officer responsibilities and planning for the year

- **Learning outcomes:** Participants will:
  1. Name and discuss qualities of leadership and assess themselves on each dimension.
  2. Review practical habits of effective people and apply them to themselves, identifying one new habit to practice during the next month. They will reflect on their progress in developing this habit in a report to the leader at the end of four weeks and again at the end of the year.
  3. Brainstorm about the value of involvement in student professional organizations. They will apply this discussion to our organization by filling out the affiliate reaction form (from AOC/NCFR). They will learn about the resources of NCFR and be able to name three of these on an assessment/review form at the end of the year.
  4. Each participant will review her officer responsibility and develop a 3-step plan to successful execution of that responsibility. She will share this plan with the group, and it will be kept in a notebook for review at the end of the year.

Before you read on, how do the visions, goals, objectives, and learning outcomes relate to each other? How do they differ from each other? What may be lacking here?

Suskie (2004) provides some helpful guidance by identifying three major characteristics of learning outcomes.

1. They specify an action by the learners that is *observable*.

2. They specify an action by the learners that is *measurable*.

3. They specify an *action by the learners* and not subject matter delivered by the professor.

Go back and evaluate the learning goals articulated for the leadership seminar. How could they be improved?

Below are some statements that reflect either vision, program goals, objectives, or learning statements. Identify which is which by marking as V, PG, O, or LS. For answers, see the end of the chapter.

1. _____ Learners will role play three discipline techniques other than physical punishment that they could use in a particular parenting situation.

2. _____ We provide nurture and support to at-risk children and their families.

3. _____ Present options for positive child guidance in the home; explain nutrition and physical fitness basics for healthy families.

4. _____ Learners will develop a weekly menu for healthy snacks using food stamp staples.

5. _____ This program will address ways to cope with the stress of being a new parent.

6. _____ Foster parents will be able to list three sources they can call in an emergency.

7. _____ Participants will list ten food items that are food stamp eligible.

8. _____ Participants will evaluate their own learning styles and list one advantage and one disadvantage of that style of learning.

9. _____ Participants will identify with 90-percent accuracy acceptable and unacceptable ways of expressing anger.

10. _____ Help teens to develop assertive behaviors for dealing with peer pressure.

Box 6.5

What would be an appropriate vision statement for the teen parent support organization from the opening paragraph of this chapter? What would your specific educational program have as its goals, objectives, and learning outcomes? Remember that the initial thought process should be broad and not too restricted. Brainstorm freely. You can always come back to fill in, define specifically, and "operationalize."

WHAT TEACHING MATERIALS AND EQUIPMENT DO YOU NEED?

Teaching materials should always include pencil, paper, and a folder or notebook to write on and to keep materials and notes in. A flip chart, white board, and working markers are also very useful. Beyond those basics are the specific handouts, objects, and props to involve the group in active learning. The choice of teaching methods and the size of the group will determine other needed materials. Be sure to spend adequate preparation time reviewing the process in your mind. How will you need to divide the group? What handouts, props, writing materials, and surfaces will be needed? If you need technical equipment, be sure to request it ahead of time and arrive early enough to check it out and understand how it operates. Always have a backup plan!

Recently, I (Powell) was the presenter of a luncheon program that depended primarily on a video presentation. I had planned to give a brief introduction, share some statistical information, and then let the video tell the rest of the story. I had checked two weeks beforehand about the availability of a TV/VCR. When I was told that none were available, I sought someone who had access to a laptop and projector who could convert the videotape to a DVD format. She came early to set up the equipment, but she could not get the DVD to play through her laptop. We were down to five minutes before presentation time, so I went to Plan Three! I gave my introduction, explained the program concept using the brochure I had handed out, and asked for questions. There was an excited time of sharing and offers to help getting the new community program started. It actually may have worked better than my original plan.

Remember that as the presenter/facilitator, you are the main ingredient in a successful learning experience. If you are enthusiastic and believe in the concepts you are presenting—and you realize you don't have to do all the talking—you will be successful.

HOW DO YOU PRESENT FOR BEST COMPREHENSION?

It is important to first consider the size of the group you are working with. The ability to engage in large amounts of discussion and group interaction is limited with groups larger than 10 or 12 persons. If the group is larger than 20, you should plan more in a presentation mode than an interactive mode. This does not rule out small-group sharing or audience involvement, but the presentation must be handled differently. I (Powell) once participated in a seminar led by Dr. Jane Vella before an audience of 300 people. She used large-screen projection to present her major points and information, but then gave us a series of small-group tasks to do with our tablemates (we were seated at round tables in an auditorium). Each table was asked to appoint a recorder/reporter, and results were tallied on the large screen. I was amazed at the amount of personal sharing and engagement that occurred. A small group, on the other hand, may feel intimidated by "large-screen" methods (PowerPoints overheads, etc.). Content is more effectively presented in handouts and posters and audience input recorded on a white board. In other words, formal presentations tend to downplay or discourage audience input and interactions. Conversely, informal, relaxed methods encourage more group interaction. Large groups can still address and apply the content to their own life situations, particularly through self-assessment quizzes and other techniques that do not require much group interaction.

Consider the Time Allotted

One of the most common offenses of new program presenters is trying to stuff too much information into too short a time. When you are planning, decide on one or two learning outcomes that you think are most important and then present and reinforce them in several different ways during the time you have. If the program design includes several sessions, then more learning outcomes can be addressed. Be very respectful of the time given you and do not run over! Doing so will severely damage your effectiveness with the program planners and the participants. Keep an eye on the clock. If you can't finish what you have planned, acknowledge that there is much more that could be said, move to your concluding statements and sit down!

Scope and Content of the Program

Simple lecturing employs what is known as the "still" method of learning: You sit still while I instill. It is the least effective teaching method. Very little of the information given is retained or even absorbed. So plan a variety of presentation methods, including personal experiences and illustrations. If possible include some activity that will engage the listener with the content, even if it is a short T/ F quiz. Remember to appeal to a variety of learning styles (see figure 3.2). The visual learner wants to see what's being presented. The auditory learner wants to hear information, questions, and discussion. The kinesthetic (active) learner wants active participation through tests, discussion, games, and object lessons. The less "sophisticated" your audience, the more kinesthetic they will tend to be. However, *all* learners retain more when more of the senses are involved. You can develop matching or identification games to pair personal needs with community resources or design a bingo game with anger management statements or positive parenting behaviors. "Test your knowledge" quizzes can effectively introduce knowledge you plan to present, and role-playing problem behavior can motivate for

The Internet can provide a wealth of information, but the planner must know how to discern solid, research-based concepts from personal perspectives or biases.

needed changes without putting anyone on the spot. Follow the game/assessment/role-play with a written response statement: "What did you learn from this exercise?" A second written response could reflect on "What do you still have questions about?"

Before reading further, consider the two questions above. Why would it be helpful for the program leader to review the written answers to these two questions? What does this illustrate about the learning process?

When you reflected on the two evaluation questions, did your response include the following ideas?

- Learning is an active process that includes personal reflection and application of information.

- We learn from the experience and thoughts of others who share things in common with us.

- We learn best when we are relaxed, unhurried, and having fun.

- We learn best when we engage more than one sense or learning style.

- We learn best from a leader who values and respects our own experience and expertise. We learn best from someone who does not feel threatened by our questions or the new direction of our thinking and who sees questions and comments of the learners as valuable contributions to the learning process.

Appropriate Teaching Methods.

Although the list of possible teaching/learning methodologies is extensive, a selection of some of the most commonly used interactive methods is discussed in this section.

Audiovisual with discussion/feedback. AV methods are generally defined as any presentation method that the group both hears and sees together. AV methods can range from a low-tech chart or poster to slides, videos, or sophisticated PowerPoint presentations. The important distinction in using AV methods for active learning is that discussion or feedback must follow the presentation. The presenter is responsible for "priming the pump" with her presentation. Then she should ask the audience specific open-ended questions about what they have seen and heard. For example: "Can you think of other ground rules we might want to include here?" "What do all these statistics have in common?" "Why do you think there is such an increase in cohabitation among young adults?" When persons respond to such questions, it is important to have a board or flip chart and marker ready to record their answers. And you *must* acknowledge and record every answer—even if it seems far afield from your question—or responders will get the unspoken message that "my response doesn't count."

Box 6.6

Should you read aloud what you are presenting visually to a group? Why or why not?

Group discussion. This common method is quite effective if used correctly. It takes more than "Does anyone have a comment or question?" to get a good discussion started. Discussion questions tend to be open-ended with enough of a "tickler" to trigger active thought. They can ask to recall personal experiences. For instance:

"What have you found that works when your child balks at going to bed?"
"How do you handle temper tantrums?"
"What are some ways that we say 'I love you,' besides actually saying it?"
"What things get in the way of *really* listening to your spouse?"

If you find your group reluctant to respond to your questions, try a "write, then share" technique. I (Powell) often use this in my classroom discussions where people are hesitant to respond to a group invitation for discussion.

Dyadic discussion. Another variation is for learners to write and then share with their neighbor. You might bring the group back together by inviting each dyad to share one thing they came up with—of course, write these down. Be sure to use the discussion responses to full advantage. Not only acknowledge the group's responses, but work them into your teaching points.

Paper-and-pencil assessments. These "little tests" can recall and evaluate personal experience, competency, attitudes, values, or knowledge. One of this author's most frequently used techniques is a "test your knowledge" quiz, usually with true-false answers. This can be an excellent pretest/posttest, tied to a knowledge-based learner outcome. It also introduces the learner to specific points of knowledge that you want to emphasize. The time when you share correct answers can be used to elaborate on these points of knowledge. A true-false quiz regarding teen sexuality has proved to be a very effective way to get across some major points about high risk behaviors to teens without being "preachy." (See box 6.7.)

Role-play. This technique can be used in several ways. The facilitator can ask for a volunteer to role play a frustrated new mother, a difficult mother-in-law, a spouse who won't listen, or a stubborn teenager while the facilitator demonstrates active listening skills. To be effective, the role-play must be followed by questions and comments from the group on the interpersonal skills and family dynamics exhibited (not on the acting skills!). A lead-in question can be as simple as, "What's going on here?" You may be surprised at how perceptive observers can be! Questions and comments are critical to using role-play as a teaching methodology, so be sure not to rush them. A variation on this method is the *dyadic role-play.* This technique is especially effective when teaching active listening and reflecting skills. One person of the dyad is the designated listener, who must use reflection and appropriate nonverbal responses to respond to the speaker. A third person added to the group (dyad plus one) can serve as observer to give feedback after the short conversation. Then the roles rotate, so that each person gets a chance to speak, listen, and observe. Finally, the whole group processes their experience. Once again, the facilitator should solicit comments from the group. How did you feel when the listener was focusing her full attention on you? As the listener, what was the hardest part of this exercise? When you were the observer,

---

Box 6.7   Sex Knowledge Quiz

True or False?

1. It is possible to get pregnant the first time a couple has sex.
2. There are only three known sexually transmitted diseases (STDs).
3. A girl can get pregnant even if the couple is not actually "having sex."
4. Birth control provides 100 percent protection from pregnancy or STDs.
5. Most pregnant teens who deliver decide to place their babies up for adoption.
6. Most of the time, the teen father is supportive and faithful to his pregnant girlfriend.
7. It is not possible to get a sexually transmitted infection from oral sex.
8. Most teens who have sex don't use birth control for at least six months after they start having sex.
9. Teens who date and/or go steady before age 16 are more likely to have sex before they finish high school.
10. Most teen sex takes place in the back seat of a parked car.

Answers: 1. T; 2. F; 3. T; 4. F; 5. F; 6. F; 7. F; 8. T; 9. T; 10. F.

---

what listening behaviors did you notice that encouraged conversation? What did you notice about body language?

Modeling.   Closely akin to role-play, the facilitator usually uses modeling to demonstrate skills to be learned by others. The facilitator may model affirmation, openness, or listening—and she may never actually comment on what she is doing. On the other hand, she may want to follow up with questions to pinpoint the specific skills being demonstrated.

Box 6.8

Modeling is one of the strongest teaching methodologies. Why is this? Are there any qualifications for being a good model?

Handouts.   Handouts are used frequently by teachers and facilitators, but they are often used poorly. Why is this? Effective handouts are actually utilized by the presenter in some way. For example, a handout on "Blocks and Bridges to Good Communication" can be reviewed by the learners as they mark three things they think they do very well and three things they think they need to work on. This makes the learners read and process the handout information in order to complete the task. Other handouts might include diagrams or case studies that are then used by the learners to write notes on or discuss in small groups.

Interactive kinesthetic experiences. Activities that get the group moving around can be fun and effective as icebreakers or a change of pace. One of my favorites is a differences continuum that asks people to position themselves in a line according to how much they agree with a certain statement, for example, "I'm a night owl or I'm an early bird to bed." (It's amazing how many couples have one person on each end of this line!) It could be statements about managing children, handling money, assertiveness, or free time. I have used clay and markers very effectively in presentations about creative arts. Pieces of newsprint scattered around the walls of a room can be very effective for brainstorming. One word of caution: Be sure your exercise does not overshadow your main point or presentation. Always process afterward and reiterate your main points.

How Do You Get Feedback, Assessment, and Evaluation?

It is easy for a program presenter to overlook this element of the design, yet feedback, assessment, and evaluation are at the heart of quality, effective presentation. Reviewing the feedback or self-reports of participants gives you ideas for future presentations and helps to clarify fuzzy parts of the program. While everyone may fear the possibility of negative feedback, it is rarely the overwhelming response. A large number of negative comments signals a need for serious restructuring of your approach. Take that as a positive possibility! Feedback can be as simple as two questions: "How was this program helpful to you?" and "What suggestions would you make for next time?" Some audiences may not respond to open-ended questions very creatively. They might prefer a rating scale approach: "Please rate the following sessions of the program as either (1) excellent; (2) good; or (3) needs work," with a comments line beneath each statement for explanation. Another rating scale option is "What was your favorite part of the program?" and "What was your least favorite part of the program?" with a checklist of the program elements such as speaker, handouts, movie clips, small group time. The feedback approach is most useful in judging the group's personal reaction to the program itself. To assess the effectiveness of the program, refer to the learning outcomes that you established at the beginning. Did your group show evidence of achieving these outcomes? At what level?

Program evaluation is discussed at length in chapter 7 of this text. Such evaluation involves careful planning and observable results. If funding sources and program permanence are high priorities, then an evaluation plan is a must.

Follow-Up and Follow-Through

Many family life education programs fail to follow up with program participants after the program is completed. Although educators have always known that new skills and attitudes must be reinforced, this second stage of educational effectiveness is often lacking in program design. Granted it is not easy; many participants assume that once they take a course or go to a program, they have "finished." But who learns to play ball or cook well by taking a few lessons and never practicing? Support groups are a natural follow-up offered by many FLE programs. The Association for Couples in Marriage Enrichment offers retreats and mini-retreats for couple education and enrichment, but the leaders know that no real change occurs in one weekend. Leaders encourage couples to become part of a marriage enrichment group that meets regularly over an extended period of time. Not everyone is willing to commit to an ongoing program, but those that do testify to its effectiveness. An innovative mother-daughter program for sixth-grade girls, designed by the College of Education at the University of Texas at El Paso and co-sponsored by the public schools, brings the girls to the college campus on weekends for an entire year. These young girls show promise for college but have never had a family member attend. The mother-daughter pairs must *commit* to participate for the entire year. In subsequent years, the young girls are mentored by older girls and come together at intervals for special programs throughout their junior and senior high school experience. A very high percentage of the program participants complete high school and go on to attend college. The *extended program* and *follow-up* are the keys to success.

So begin your program design with the ending: How will you encourage participants to follow through on their newly acquired knowledge? It's well worth your time to think about. If you can involve members of the community in planning and reacting to your program design, you will be even farther down the road toward successful and effective education.

SUMMARY

Designing a program demands careful planning and an understanding of the needs and interests of the audience. The best practice and valid information rely on research and theory in the hands of well-trained practitioners who know how to present and how to evaluate the effectiveness of their presentations. Help and resources are available, if you know how and where to look. Continuing your professional development will provide stimulation and networking that will multiply the influence of your programs.

Questions/Problems for Discussion and Review

Class Discussion

1. What do you think the author means when she says "We expect too much from too little"?

2. Why is the "still" method of education still used in many classrooms if it really is so ineffective? Does that mean that the facilitator should never present a body of material to the group?

3. Illustrate three ways (visual, auditory, and kinesthetic) to teach basics of infant nutrition.

Research Problem

Search the Web to find an example of family life programs that are popular but not evidently grounded in research or that do not use an interactive or praxis approach. Now find a program that is grounded in research and provides interactive learning. Which of the two was easier to find and to use? Conduct a random survey of parents or couples and ask them which program is most appealing and why. What conclusions would you draw from this?

Case Study Design

Using the teen parent population suggested in the chapter text, divide the class into small groups to develop a program step by step for this population.

Answers to questions on p 126.
1. LS; 2. V; 3. O; 4. LS; 5. PG; 6. LS; 7. LS; 8. LS; 9. LS; 10. O.

Evaluation of
Family Programs

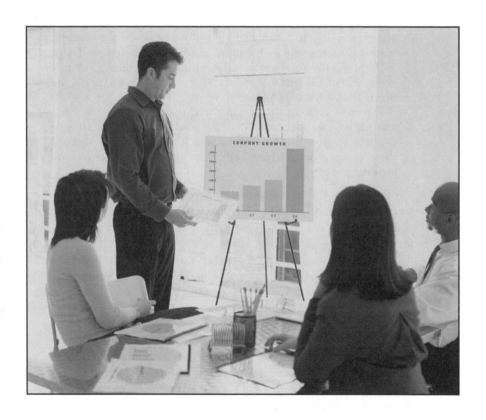

INTRODUCTION

Imagine that you are the director of the Southwest Family Center, a neighborhood resource center located in a large metropolitan city. Funded by the United Way, the Southwest Family Center serves residents with children from before birth to age 6 living in the nine neighborhoods that make up the southwest section of the city.

The overall goal of the Southwest Family Center is to increase school readiness for children entering kindergarten. It was developed through the efforts of professionals at a lead agency and the input of community residents and business and service providers. The developers of the program have determined that one way to increase school readiness is to provide families with formal and informal support systems.

The Southwest Family Center provides formal and informal support through a number of activities, events, resources, and services. Activities and events include an Indoor Playground, a Family Fun Night, numerous baby and toddler classes, and parent education and support groups. They also offer a resource and toy library, make home visits, and produce a monthly newsletter and calendar of events for families with small children. The Southwest Family Center has been operating for five years.

Overall, things seem to be going well. But how do you know for sure? How do you and your staff know if you are meeting your goals? How do you know if you are making the best use of your limited staff and resources? How do those funding your program know if the program is effective and if it is making a difference?

A family agency or organization can spend a great deal of time and money promoting and carrying out programs designed to meet the various needs of families. But without conscious, systematic evaluation efforts, it might be time and money misspent. This chapter provides an introduction to the evaluation of family programs. The intent is not to make you an evaluator but rather to familiarize you with the concepts and steps that make up this sometimes complicated, but always important, aspect of family life education. Throughout this chapter we use the Southwest Family Center as an example to help you to understand and apply the concepts discussed.

The number and scope of family education programs has increased substantially in the past decade. However, efforts at evaluating these programs are relatively new, and debate over terminology, techniques, and approaches is ongoing. Greater evidence of the effectiveness of family programs is needed, as is increased understanding and knowledge of how to evaluate programs.

Few issues present a greater challenge to parenting education and family support than those surrounding evaluation and accountability. There may be thousands of programs nationwide and in many of them important things seem to be happening. But, except for a few pilot programs and focused research on individual dimensions of parenting, we haven't provided the conclusive evidence. Nowhere is the "adolescence" of this field more apparent than here: the maturity, clarity and confidence that comes with measured accomplishment and proven effectiveness is still ahead of us. (Carter, 1996, p. 58)

A number of national parent education models have been studied over the past 25 years. These important studies have served as benchmarks in helping us examine the effectiveness of parent education and family support programs. Studies examining the effectiveness of such programs as Parents as Teachers; Parent Effectiveness Training; Home Instruction Program for Preschool Youngsters (HIPPY); Minnesota Early Learning Design (MELD), which merged with Parents as Teachers in 2005; and Minnesota's Early Childhood Family Education (ECFE) have provided important groundwork for replicating and understanding program effectiveness in the broader context of family education. The combination of small- and large-scale studies has shown us that "there is solid evidence on the critical role parents play in raising healthy children and that well-designed, controlled programs can have positive impacts on parenting outcomes" (Carter, 1996, p. 59). Family life educators must continue to carry out thoughtful and careful evaluation to ensure that family programs reach their goals in the most efficient manner possible.

In recent years, the political climate in the United States has become more accepting and supportive of preventative efforts as opposed to the service and intervention approaches of the past. In light of this, we need to design evaluations to record individual program effectiveness, as well as to collectively address questions on the minds of policy makers about which family support and education programs work, for whom, how, when, where, and why (Weiss & Jacobs, 1988). Especially where public tax revenues support parent and family education programs, taxpayers and legislators expect accountability and evidence of measurable benefit to the community. The development and recognition of effective prevention programs could serve to restructure the delivery of human services in this country. Although great strides have been made in recent years to increase the thoroughness and effectiveness of family program evaluation, there is still much to learn.

DEFINITIONS

We begin the discussion by looking at the definition of evaluation as articulated by several contributors to the literature on program evaluation. Patton (1997) defines evaluation as "the systematic collection of information about the activities, characteristics and outcomes of programs to make judgments about programs, improve the program effectiveness, and/or inform decisions about future programming" (p. 23).

Littell (1986) considers program evaluation to be "the systematic collection, analysis, and interpretation of information designed for use in program planning and decision-making. It is concerned with the types of interventions used, by whom, toward what ends, under what conditions, for whom, at what costs and with what benefits" (p. 17).

Finally, evaluation is defined by Weiss and Jacobs (1988) as: "the systematic collection and analysis of program-related data that can be used to understand how a program delivers services and/or what the consequences of its services are for participants. . . . It is both descriptive and 'judgmental' of program merit, with the emphasis on designing an evaluation that fits the program" (p. 49).

Though the definitions vary, they contain similar concepts, namely, that evaluation is a systematic collection of various types of information and that the results of the collection and analysis of information are used to modify programs, increase effectiveness, and aid in decision making.

It is important to note that evaluation is different from research. Evaluation is used to determine the value, quality, or effectiveness of a program. It is judgmental, and the results are usually program specific. It is usually motivated by the program's needs. Information gathered can be subjective. The major reasons for conducting evaluation are for planning, improving, or justification. The goal of evaluation is to come to some sort of recommendation.

Research, on the other hand, looks more at the relationships among variables and cause and effect. It is nonjudgmental and conclusion oriented. The intent is to have information that can be generalized rather than specific to any one particular program. Evaluation answers the question of *what*, whereas research answers the question of *why*. (See box 7.1.)

Box 7.1   Evaluation or Research?

The staff of the Southwest Family Center wants to know if babies who attend a program like the Indoor Playground (which includes opportunities for climbing and exercise on playground equipment) on a regular basis show more advanced motor skills than babies who do not attend such a program. This type of study would be considered *research*.

The staff of the Southwest Family Center wants to know how the parents who attend the Indoor Playground feel about the program and if they find it to be a good opportunity to connect with other parents in their community. This type of study would be considered *evaluation*.

CHALLENGES OF EVALUATION

For many family life educators, evaluation provides quite a challenge. Thorough evaluation takes planning, time, and money, often beyond the capabilities and resources of the average family education program and the technical expertise of the staff. And there can be resistance to evaluation. Program directors and staff may be concerned that evaluation will divert resources away from the program's activities, that it will increase the burden for program staff, or that it is too complicated. Some fear that it may produce negative results, which jeopardizes the funding of the program.

So why should evaluations be conducted? The reality is that evaluation is imperative to the success of a program. "Program providers are becoming increasingly aware of the need for program evaluation and for practical program evaluation strategies that will: (1) yield information of use to them for program improvement and (2) answer questions about program effectiveness" (Cooke, 1991, p. 13). Through evaluation you can find out what is and isn't working with your program. You can improve the efficiency and effectiveness of your staff's efforts by identifying strengths and weaknesses. You can increase the likelihood that resources are used effectively and goals are reached. Evaluation can show those who fund your program, as well as community members, how your program is benefiting its intended audience. And when results are shared with others running similar programs, it can contribute to knowledge in the field. If consciously incorporated into the design and ongoing operation of a program, evaluation does not need to be overly complicated or time-consuming.

TYPES OF EVALUATION

Assessing Needs and Assets

Perhaps one of the most important concepts about evaluation is the need to incorporate an evaluation plan into the development and initial planning stages of a program. A well-developed program begins with a ministudy (sometimes referred to as a needs assessment, a feasibility study, or an assets inventory). These ministudies (part of the research and evaluation continuum) often include examining the current situation, that is, why or to what degree is this program justified? Who is the target audience for this program? What resources are available? What are the strengths or assets of this community? Do similar programs exist in this community? Will the community support our efforts? What benefits are likely to be produced through our program? It is important to be clear about the need for and goals of your program. If you don't have a clear picture of what your program is trying to accomplish, you won't know how to tell if you've been successful! Think seriously about what it is you want to learn from the evaluation, and integrate the evaluation into the ongoing activities of your program. Always remember that evaluation is a process, not an event. Consider its place in the ongoing implementation of your program.

Formative Evaluation

Evaluation efforts can have different goals and can be conducted at different points throughout the development and implementation of a program. Evaluations may be considered to be formative or summative in nature. Formative evaluations generate information for the purposes of planning, monitoring, and improving programs. Formative evaluations describe a program and provide feedback on how it is doing while the program is still in progress, often prompting changes in timing, approaches, and so forth. Formative evaluation might include surveying participants midway through a scheduled program to see if the program is meeting their expectations.

For example, imagine that your agency holds a monthly meeting to provide education on infant development to mothers of newborns. You notice that although the participants seem very enthusiastic about the meetings, attendance has been sporadic. By surveying the participants, you find that the availability of transportation is a defining factor in whether or not they are able to attend. You arrange a car pool that provides rides for everyone who wants to attend the meeting. Attendance increases dramatically. Had you waited until the end of the program to survey participants, it would have been too late to implement the car pool, and a number of possible program participants would have missed out on the program. The use of formative evaluation throughout the program allows you to make changes that increase the likelihood that you will effectively implement your program and reach your goal.

Box 7.2 gives an example of a formative evaluation of the Indoor Playground program. With this information the staff can determine if the Indoor Playground is meeting the needs of the participants. They can make changes in scheduling and format. They can also determine which marketing efforts are working best. This formative evaluation has provided them with information that they can use to modify the program while it is still in progress.

Box 7.2   Formative Evaluation

The Indoor Playground is held each Friday at the Southwest Family Center. Once each month the staff distributes a survey to the attendees. The survey includes questions such as:

- How many times have you attended the Indoor Playground?
- What is your main reason for attending?
- Is this a convenient day for you to attend?
- Is this a convenient time for you to attend?
- If not, when would be better?
- What changes would you like to see in the Indoor Playground?
- How did you hear about the Indoor Playground?
- Do you attend any other Southwest Family Center events?

Summative Evaluation

Summative evaluations are concerned with the end results of a program. How did it affect the people it served? Were the program goals met? Summative evaluations can be used to determine if a program should be replicated, expanded, or perhaps discontinued. In the example given in box 7.3, a summative evaluation carried out at the end of the program cycle could determine if participants in the New Parents program had increased their knowledge of infant development.

Box 7.3   Summative Evaluation

The Southwest Family Center sponsors a New Parents support group for parents of newborns. The meetings are facilitated by parents in the community who have completed a 16-hour small-group-facilitation training program. Parents enter the program before their babies are born or just after. The program meets twice a month for two hours for a two-year period. A *summative evaluation* of the New Parents program would be carried out at the end of the two-year period. Participants might be interviewed or asked to complete a questionnaire to determine how the parents benefited from the program. Did they learn new skills regarding parenting? How about new knowledge about child development? Did their participation help them to feel more confident about their abilities as parents? Did they feel less alone and isolated? Do they feel more connected to their community, having met other families in a similar situation? Results of this summative evaluation will help the staff of the Southwest Family Center know if their goals have been met. The results may determine if the program will be replicated.

COMMONLY USED TERMS IN EVALUATION

Although the specific terminology varies, some common terms and concepts are used in the literature on evaluation. The United Way publication *Measuring Program Outcomes: A Practical Approach* (United Way of America, 1996) provides a helpful conceptual framework for understanding evaluation. It defines the following measurement terms.

Logic Models

Programs can be developed and outcomes identified with a *logic model* (United Way of America, 1996), or an "if-then" method of looking at a situation. Logic models can help you think through the progression of steps taken by program participants and can give you a more realistic view of what to expect of your program. Logic models also help you identify key components that must be kept track of in order to determine if the program is effective. Logic models include inputs, activities, outputs, and outcomes. An example of a logic model might be: *if* classes (activities) can teach about child development and parenting skills (output), *then* parents can acquire knowledge, gain skills, and change their attitudes about how to care for their children (initial outcomes). *If* they learn new approaches in dealing with their children, *then* they will change their behavior to reflect these new methods (intermediate outcomes). *If* they change their behavior, *then* they will increase the likelihood of positive results. Applying this method can help you to identify the steps needed to reach your goals and link your activities to program outcomes.

Inputs.   *Inputs* include resources dedicated to or consumed by the program. Examples are money, staff and staff time, volunteers and volunteer time, facilities, and equipment and supplies (see box 7.4).

Box 7.4   Inputs

Inputs at the Southwest Family Center include financial support provided by the sponsoring agency, staff members and staff time, and members of the community who volunteer their time to various programs and services offered through the Southwest Family Center. The site at which the Southwest Family Center is located, including meeting space, materials, supplies, playground equipment, and toys available through the Indoor Playground would also be considered input.

Activities.   The program uses its inputs to fulfill its mission through *activities.* Activities include the strategies, techniques, and types of treatment that make up the program's service methodology. In our example of the Southwest Family Center, activities center on providing education and support to families with small children. These activities include the Family Fun Night, the Indoor Playground, the community calendar, and other events and services intended to provide education and support to parents of small children.

Outputs.   *Outputs* are the direct products of program activities and usually are measured in terms of the volume of work accomplished—for example, the number of classes held, brochures distributed, and participants served (see box 7.5).

Box 7.5   Outputs

How many people attended the Indoor Playground? How many sessions of Family Fun Night were held? How many people used the toy library? How many brochures or flyers about the Southwest Family Center were distributed at neighborhood festivals and community events? These questions attempt to gather information about *outputs*—the direct product of programs and activities carried out by the Southwest Family Center. In addition to attendance, further qualitative information might reveal interesting results. Program observers could tally specific parent-child behaviors.

Outcomes.   *Outcomes* are the benefits or changes to individuals or groups that emerge during or after participation in program activities. Outcomes are influenced by outputs. Outcomes are reflected through modified behavior, increased skills, new knowledge, changed attitudes or values, improved conditions, and other attributes. They represent changes in the participants from the time they started the program to the time they completed it. For example, outcomes of the program described in box 7.6 are a better understanding of infant development and a resulting change in parenting behavior, such as the use of more appropriate discipline strategies. Program evaluation should include consideration of initial outcomes, intermediate outcomes, and long-term outcomes.

Box 7.6   Outcomes

Parents attending a monthly class, "Discipline and Your Child," learn new techniques for directing the behavior of their toddlers. The staff hopes that providing comprehensive information about child development and discipline alternatives will expand parents' understanding of these topics. By increasing parents' knowledge, the staff hopes that parents will make better choices about strategies when disciplining their child. Because making better choices about discipline strategies includes approaches to preventing misbehavior, the staff believes that parents will use less punitive means and employ more appropriate choices with their children. By preventing misbehavior, the staff hopes that parents will have a more positive attitude about discipline, feel more confident about being able to prevent misbehavior, feel more successful as parents, and enjoy their child more. These are all examples of *outcomes*—the benefits and changes experienced by the participants of the parenting class.

Indicators

An *indicator* identifies the factors that are being measured as a way of tracking the program's success on an outcome. An indicator is observable and measurable (see box 7.7).

Box 7.7   Indicators

One of the goals of the Indoor Playground is to provide opportunities for parents in the community to connect with each other. Staff at Indoor Playground events might observe parents to see if they interact with each other and if they form relationships. This interaction between the parents, especially if the same parents sit together and talk to each other at subsequent events, could be considered an *indicator* that the parents are connecting with each other. Staff might observe other Southwest Family Center events to see if some of the same parents attend and if they interact with other families.

An overall goal of the Southwest Family Center is to increase learning readiness of children entering kindergarten. One indicator of learning readiness is having received all recommended shots before entering kindergarten. Another indicator might be that children have been screened for hearing, vision, or speech problems and have received appropriate interventions. These problems should be identified early enough for actions to be taken so that the children are ready to learn by the time they enter kindergarten.

Qualitative Data

Qualitative data describe and interpret happenings or emotions. They are verbal or narrative and can be collected by observing participant behavior or by interviewing participants, for example. Methods for collecting qualitative data include focus groups, interviews, case studies, and direct observation. Although they are hard to measure, they address the kinds of effects that influence positive human behavior and that family programs hope to affect. Qualitative data might include descriptions of how parents teach children to play with a new toy; stories about how a support group changed a parent's perception of a crisis situation; or a series of excerpts from a parent's journal that describe what was learned during a year of being involved in a home visiting program (see box 7.8).

Box 7.8   Qualitative Data/Evaluation

If the staff of the Southwest Family Center wanted to gather *qualitative data* or carry out a qualitative evaluation, they could interview or survey the participants of the programs to collect information on how they feel about the programs and how they think they have benefited. Another option would be to observe parents at various activities and record information about their interaction with their children or other parents. Or they might hold a focus group of parents of 4-year-olds to determine what issues are of most concern for them at this stage in their children's lives. This information could be used to help them design future classes or determine what resources might be most helpful.

Quantitative Data

Information gathered through quantitative methods is typically reported numerically and is easier to measure than qualitative data. *Quantitative data* are typically, although not always, objective. Age, education level, and attendance counts for various events are all considered to be quantitative data. Quantitative data can be gathered through questionnaires, forms, tests, and surveys and sometimes simply by counting the number of participants in the program (see box 7.9). They can also be gathered by observation. For example, one measurement of a quantifiable change in the parent-child relationship may be inferred by an increase in the number of minutes that mothers spend interacting with their children as opposed to socializing with the other mothers.

Box 7.9   Quantitative Data/Evaluation

At each event held by the Southwest Family Center, a sign-in sheet for the participant's name and address is provided. The staff uses this information, in addition to attendance, to monitor how many people are attending each event. They may collect information on how many kindergartners had received all their shots when entering first grade in 2000 and compare that number with the number of kindergartners inoculated in 2005. This would be considered *quantitative data*.

Although evaluators with different educational backgrounds are likely to continue to debate the best approach to evaluation design and data collection methods (i.e., qualitative vs. quantitative), many evaluators believe that the questions that focus the evaluation study should lead to a discussion about which types of approaches are used. It is also important to note that many studies employ a mixed-methods approach, that is, a design using both qualitative and quantitative methods. The needs and interests of the stakeholders in your program may influence the evaluation design and methodology as well. Stakeholders include anyone who is affected by the results of the evaluation and can include decision makers, policy makers, staff, people in the community, and the clients themselves (Rader & Cooke, 2006).

LEVELS OF OUTCOMES

In some instances there is just one desired outcome for a program. But often there is a series of outcomes, each of which can contribute to the accomplishment of another and, ultimately, to the final outcome goals of the program. Different programs use different terms to describe these same levels. The important concept to consider is that there are varying levels of outcomes.

Initial Outcomes

Initial outcomes are the first changes or benefits that a participant experiences as a result of the program. It may be a change in attitude, knowledge, skills, or all of these. In most programs these initial outcomes would not be ends in themselves but important steps toward reaching the desired ends.

Intermediate Outcomes

Intermediate outcomes connect a program's initial outcomes to the longer-term outcomes intended for its participants. Intermediate outcomes are often exemplified by changes in behavior as a result of the new knowledge, skill, or attitude.

Longer-Term Outcomes

Longer-term outcomes are the lasting outcomes that a program wants to achieve. These are usually significant changes that are often longitudinally apparent and related to condition or status. An example of a longer-term outcome might be that since the program began, parent attendance at parent-teacher conferences in the community has increased significantly. (See box 7.10.)

Unfortunately, many programs have the resources to measure only initial outcomes. The cost of carrying out evaluations to include intermediate and longer-term outcomes is sometimes prohibitive for organizations operating on limited budgets.

STEPS IN CONDUCTING AN EVALUATION

The Five-Tiered Approach to Program Evaluation (see appendix F), developed by Francine Jacobs (2000), is perhaps the most widely used evaluation approach. It provides a useful rubric for family life educators to ensure that a pro-

---

Box 7.10   Levels of Outcomes

Initial Outcomes

After attending "Terrific Threes" and "Fabulous Fours" parent education classes, there is a measurable increase in the number of minutes that most parents spend reading to their child in one-on-one parent-child time during future classes.

Intermediate Outcomes

Several months into the program, the staff member who oversees the program's lending library notes that the library is busier. When she checks her records, the librarian notes that library usage has more than doubled for most parents.

Longer-Term Outcomes

Two years into the future, as kindergarten teachers collect information about their students' preschool experience, they discover that children who participated in "Terrific Threes" and "Fabulous Fours" with their parents scored significantly higher on all school readiness assessments.

---

gram is evaluated comprehensively. It prompts evaluators to think about the purpose of evaluation, its audience, and the procedures for collecting and analyzing data. The step-by-step tiers serve as a guide for developing a systematic strategy for evaluation. Tiers one through three guide users through assessing needs and ensuring accountability, quality, and clarity. Tiers four and five explain the process of translating data into new outcomes, applying findings to further research, enhancing the program, and determining areas for public policy action. The National Parenting Education Network (NPEN, www.npen.org) and the Children, Youth, and Families Education and Research Network (CYFERNET, www.cyfernet.org), among others, provide helpful resources for the evaluation of family programs.

Cultural Considerations in Evaluation

Regardless of the method of evaluation chosen, it is important to keep cultural contexts in mind. Most standardized instruments were designed for White, middle-class populations. These are often not appropriate when English is not the primary language of the individuals who complete them or if Western cultural concepts would not be well understood or do not carry the same value. The issue of language is complex. For example, not everyone from a particular ethnic group can read and write even in their native language. Dialects and regional language differences exist. Communication skill-levels differ among generations, across socioeconomic groups, and among people with different educational histories.

Some Western concepts are difficult to translate and require data collectors to clarify survey items for study participants. For example, self-esteem is not only a concept that is challenging for U.S. researchers to define and measure but it may also be a concept unfamiliar to new or recently arrived immigrants. In addition, evaluators should be mindful of any participants' reluctance to "fill out a form."

Participant Questionnaire

The following evaluation is a simple example of a participant survey. This evaluation builds-in marketing information (question 1), assurance of anonymity, and an incentive to respond in the form of a babysitter memo pad. Open-ended questions (versus Yes/No responses) encourage subjective comments and more detailed information. Note that in this questionnaire, there are no numerical choices, such as rating the items on a scale of 1–5. While the numerical survey would reveal quantitative ratings—which might be of use with other evaluation goals—this survey elicits more qualitative information. Either type of survey is valid, depending on the evaluator's objective for the instrument. Any survey questions or design should be developed keeping in mind the community's educational and literacy level, ethnicity, lifespan stage, and other characteristics that would speak to the sensitivities and needs of the audience.

Thank you for participating in the Southwest Family Center Family Life Education Program. In order to assure that our program is meeting the needs of our clients, we encourage you to provide feedback to our staff. If you would take just a few minutes to complete this short survey, we would appreciate hearing your views. To assure anonymity, please do not sign this form and return it to the survey box at the front desk. To thank you for participating, please pick up a free pad of Babysitter Information Forms. These convenient memos help you organize information for your babysitter and they are magnet mounted for convenient posting on your refrigerator.

1. How did you hear about the Southwest Family Center and its programs?

2. What did you expect to experience or gain from activities at our Center?

3. Did the program meet your expectations?

4. What was the most valuable part of participating?

5. What was less helpful?

6. How would you describe the effectiveness of the group leader/facilitator?

7. Is there anything that we could do to make your participation more enjoyable, more informative, more convenient or more positive in any way?

8. Would you recommend the programs at Southwest Family Center to a friend?

9. Are there any additional services or programs that you would like the Southwest Family Center to offer?

Please add any additional comments you have that would help us enhance our services and classes at the Southwest Family Center. Thank you! And don't forget to pick up your free Babysitter Information pads!

Created by Nancy Wicklund Gonzalez, M.Ed., CFLE, MN Licensed Parent and Family Educator

This qualitative survey collects information on how participants *feel* about the program and how they think they have benefited.

Among undocumented aliens, parents may be fearful of revealing any identifying information that might be available to immigration enforcement. Carrying out pretesting interviews and surveys or setting up advisory group review committees can determine the best approach for examining questionable words or concepts. This procedure is sometimes referred to as pilot testing.

It is also important to be aware of the possibility of cultural response sets. In some cultures, professionals may be seen as authority figures deserving of respect. Participants in this situation may feel uncomfortable or unwilling to provide any negative feedback even if encouraged. In some cultures, asking for help or appearing needy is inappropriate. Participants from such cultures may not feel comfortable revealing what they consider to be weaknesses. There may also be cultural taboos against revealing too much personal information.

Other things to be considered within varying cultures might be gender, age, and socioeconomic status. Are family programs experienced differently by men than by women or by people at different economic levels? Awareness and sensitivity to such factors will increase the effectiveness of your information-gathering strategies.

SUMMARY

As you have no doubt surmised after reading this chapter, evaluation can be a complicated issue. But its value and importance cannot be underestimated. If you find yourself involved in family programming in any way, you will be directly or indirectly involved in evaluation. Take the time to assess the needs and strengths of your audience. Identify existing resources. Consider stakeholders and their expectations. Develop a logical model that thoughtfully considers the relationship between actions and results. Build formative evaluation into the design of your program. Identify your activities, inputs, outcomes, and indicators. Carry out a summative evaluation at the end of your program or class to help you determine what worked and what could be improved.

By following these important steps and considering the multiple aspects of evaluation, you will increase the likelihood that your program will improve and enhance the lives of its participants.

Questions/Problems for Discussion and Review

Class Discussion

1. Describe how you would do a needs assessment, a formative evaluation, and a summative evaluation for a one-night, three-hour workshop on "Balancing Work and Family."

2. Identify possible inputs, activities, outputs, outcomes, and indicators for the same program.

3. How would you gather qualitative data in the above situation? Quantitative data?

4. Describe possible initial, intermediate, and long-term outcomes that may occur as a result of attending the "Balancing Work and Family" workshop.

Could all be carried out at the end of the workshop, that is, at the end of that same day?

Research Problems

1. Locate one or more of the evaluation studies cited on page 137. What were the results regarding program effectiveness? Is there a common characteristic of successful programs?

2. Identify a large federal grant opportunity that focuses on prevention rather than intervention. How would evaluation be different for a program that focuses on prevention?

3. Read Francine Jacobs's description of the Five-Tiered Approach in Jacobs and Kapuscik (2000). Provide examples of evaluations performed at each tier.

Case Study Design

1. Your six-week workshop, "Sexuality and Your Teen," has not been going as well as you had hoped. Attendance has dropped. Attendees seem distracted, and it has been difficult to engage them in group discussion. How would you best go about finding out what the problem is?

2. What are some of the possible reasons for their discontent?

PART III

CONTEXTS FOR FAMILY LIFE EDUCATION

eight

Foundations of Sexuality Education

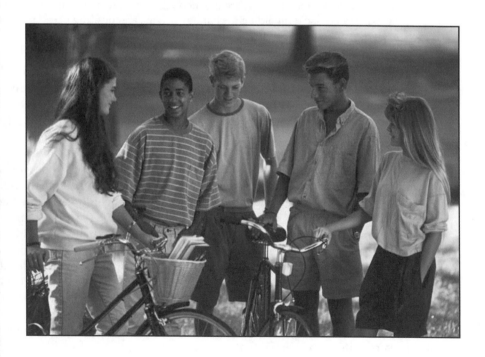

HISTORY

Compared to parent education, sexuality education is a relatively new field for family life educators. In 1984, as part of the twentieth anniversary of the founding of the Sex Information and Education Council of the United States (SIECUS), cofounder Lester Kirkendall (1984) recalled his own personal history of "sex education":

> In my boyhood, [if] there had been an organization such as SIECUS, it might have helped me with some of my sexual problems. Mainly I was distressed over my inability to cease masturbating. This was around 1914 or 1915 and I had discovered hidden away in an attic an old book published in 1897, *What a Young Boy Ought to Know* by Sylvanus Stall. It was intended to help males "avoid vice and deliver them from solitary and social sins." After I had read the pages on the "abuse of the reproductive organs," I realized that I was on my way to having a "sallow face, glassy eye, drooping form, [lacking in] energy, force or purpose, [being] a laggard in school, shy, avoiding the society of others, disliking good books, avoiding the Sunday-School, and desiring to escape from every elevating Christian influence." I was unsuccessful in stopping my "solitary sinning," but I did watch fearfully for these terrifying symptoms. (p. 1)

Kirkendall's subsequent tenure as a public school teacher, from 1927 to 1933, and as a resource for male students who had sexual concerns, further convinced him that "much of what had been taught [to them] was erroneous and that there was a need for organizations that could promote and direct sex education" (Kirkendall, 1984, p. 2). Kirkendall wrote several books, including *Sex Education as Human Relations* (1950), which proposed the unique idea that sex education should be considered an integral aspect of complete and satisfying living. "I became totally aware that the methods we use in relating to others, sexually and otherwise, are of highest importance. I knew then that the rest of my life would be devoted to helping people learn how to build relationships" (Kirkendall, 1984, p. 3). In 1960, he initiated one of the first university courses in human sexuality for undergraduates, at Oregon State University. In 1961, he met physician Mary Calderone, and the two shared their visions of an organization to promote sexuality education in the schools. As a result of their leadership, SIECUS was established in 1964. During the first 18 months of active promotion of materials and information, from January 1965 to August 1966, SIECUS received 3,930 requests from schools, the medical profession, religious groups, parent-teacher associations and individuals from every state in the United States.

The decade of the 1960s was a time of revolutionary change in attitudes and public interest in education about healthy sexuality. It contrasted greatly with the reception of William Masters's initial research on the basic physiology and psychology of sexual functioning. In 1954, after more than a year of deliberation, the Washington University Board of Trustees reluctantly approved Masters's research proposal "on the basis of academic freedom" (Allgeier, 1984, p. 16). When Masters, then an associate professor in the medical school, went to the library to begin his research, he found that only full professors could check out the sexual anatomy texts. Eventually he began a collaboration with Virginia Johnson to interview populations of women, including prostitutes, who were willing to be research participants in the physiology lab and who would talk openly about physiological sexual response. In 1960, Masters and Johnson submitted the first article on their research to the obstetrics and gynecology (OB-GYN) and psychiatric journals. "Psychiatry rejected the material outright as pornographic, and OB-GYN banned me for life in both [its] journals. That ban has since been rescinded voluntarily" (Masters, cited in Allgeier, 1984, p. 18). His medical school course on reproductive biology, which included information on female sexual physiology, also was not well received in 1960. More than 20% of the medical students asked the dean to discontinue the lectures, as did three of the executive faculty. Masters's and Johnson's laboratory equipment was repeatedly sabotaged and their families verbally attacked and socially ostracized.

Adults who were adolescents in the 1950s recall a sexual climate filled with "major doses of silence, embarrassment, ignorance, and fear. For many, parent-child talks were nonexistent, and sex was seen as an activity to which women submitted in order to satisfy their husbands" (Selverstone, 1989, p. 7). Girls who got pregnant before marriage were seen as shameful, "bad girls." They usually dropped out of sight (visiting a "relative") during the pregnancy and placed the baby for adoption, often keeping the dark secret to themselves for the rest of their lives.

Although these children of the 1950s speak gratefully of the current openness about sexuality and access to good information, they express concern about the increased sexual involvement of their children and grandchildren and the subsequent rise in teen pregnancies and sexually transmitted diseases. Overwhelmingly they also support sex education in the public schools. A 2000 study by the Kaiser Family Foundation found that four out of five parents surveyed wanted school sex education program content to include discussion of how to use condoms; how and where to get other birth control; how to talk to a partner about birth control and STDs; abortion; and sexual orientation and homosexuality (Henry J. Kaiser Family Foundation, 2000). While one-third of the parents said they wanted their children to learn abstinence as the only option until marriage, many of the same parents also wanted their children to learn preventative skills, such as how to use condoms and other birth control methods.

Yet it was not until 1965 that it became legal everywhere in the United States to purchase, sell, or use contraceptives. And as late as 1972, it took both houses of the Connecticut legislature to rescind a state law that made it illegal to have intercourse on Sunday (Selverstone, 1989). Box 8.1 recounts a time line of significant events in the "sexual revolution."

THE CURRENT SITUATION

"More than any other variable, concern over teenage pregnancy, HIV/AIDS, and other sexually transmitted diseases (STDs) is transforming the debate over sexuality education in the U.S. to a consensus around public health. Seventy-two

Box 8.1   Timeline of Significant Events in the "Sexual Revolution," 1948–2006

1948   *Sexual Behavior in the Human Male* (Kinsey, Pomeroy, & Martin) published by W. B. Saunders

1950   *Sex Education as Human Relations* (Kirkendall) published by Inor Press

1953   *Sexual Behavior in the Human Female* (Kinsey and colleagues) published by the Institute for Sex Research

1960   "The pill" first marketed in the United States

1964   Sex Information and Education Council of the United States is founded

1965   *Griswold v. Connecticut.* The Supreme Court establishes the right to privacy and married women's right to contraception

1966   *Human Sexual Response* (Masters and Johnson) published by Little, Brown National Organization for Women is founded

1968   Feminists protest at Miss America pageant

1969   *The Sensuous Woman* (by "J") published by Dell
         Stonewall riots in Greenwich Village help launch gay rights movement
         Woodstock festival celebrates era of free love, drug culture, and antiwar protests

1970   Title X Family Planning Program established

1972   *The Joy of Sex* (Comfort) published by Crown. Selling more than 5 million copies, it is on the *New York Times* best-seller list for 8 years, longer than any other book in the history of the list
         Title IX establishes sex equity in education
         U.S. Commission on Population and the American Future established
         Open Marriage (G. O'Neill and N. O'Neill) published by M. Evans

1973   *Roe v. Wade.* The Supreme Court establishes women's right to choose abortion
         Our Bodies, Our Selves (Boston Women's Health Book Collective) published by Simon & Schuster

1974   American Psychiatric Association removes homosexuality from list of mental illnesses

1978   Louise Brown, first test-tube baby, born

1979   Moral Majority founded

1980   Ronald Reagan elected president

1981   First cases of AIDS diagnosed

1982   Reagan administration proposes "squeal rule" to require clinics to notify parents of teens who have received contraception

1985   U.S. Attorney General appoints Commission on Pornography

1986   *Bowers v. Hardwick.* The Supreme Court sustains constitutionality of sodomy laws
         Surgeon General C. Everett Koop publicly advocates that sex education, including AIDS education, be directed toward preadolescents and adolescents

1990   *The Kinsey Institute New Report on Sex* (Reinisch & Beasley) published by St. Martin's Press, based on national statistically representative sample research conducted in 1989
         Title X of the Health Service Act and the Adolescent Family Life Act mandates that sex education content that promotes abstinence as the primary sexual value for adolescents be required for the agencies receiving federal funds for sex education

1995   The National Coalition to Support Sexuality Education established (see appendix D)

1996   Section 510b of Title V of the Social Security Act, the state entitlement for abstinence-only-until-marriage programs, established under "Welfare Reform." Between 1998 and 2006, more than $1.1 billion of federal grants would be awarded to abstinence-only programs in public schools

1998	AIDS public education mandated in 42 states; 23 states and the District of Columbia mandate sexuality education programs in public schools
1999	Nationwide randomized study reports that 70% of Americans surveyed support the teaching of age-appropriate, comprehensive sexuality education in schools
	Statistics reveal a 20-year low in the teen birth rate and a significant drop in the abortion rate. Researchers say fewer teens are having sex and that those who are are more likely to use contraceptives
	United States still leads all industrialized nations in the highest rate of teen pregnancies, more than 1 million per year
2001	Surgeon General David Satcher issues *Call to Action to Promote Sexual Health and Responsible Sexual Behavior*, which underscores the evidence that comprehensive sexuality education programs that provide information about both abstinence and contraception can help delay the onset of sexual activity in teens, reduce their number of sexual partners, and increase contraceptive use when they do become sexually active
2004	Analysis of Youth Risk Behavior Surveys concludes that significant declines in adolescent sexual risk-taking behavior occurred between 1991–1997 but have not continued to decline significantly since that time
2006	Rhode Island Department of Education bans an abstinence-only-until-marriage program, concluding that it violates students' rights, embraces sexual stereotypes, and isolates GLBT youth, and that accompanying materials promulgate religious views
	House of Representatives' Committee on Government Reform—Minority Staff declares that the majority of abstinence-only programs provide false and misleading information

percent of all Americans agree that 'preventing HIV/AIDS and sexually transmitted diseases are public health issues and should be left to scientists and experts, not to politicians'" (Advocates for Youth, 2000, p. 1). Yet the political debate over the content—and effectiveness—of public school sex education programs rages on. In the past ten years, over $1.1 billion in federal grants has been directed toward abstinence-only or abstinence-only-until-marriage sex education. Such education specifically prohibits teaching the use of condoms and contraception for the prevention of unintended pregnancy, HIV/AIDS, and STDs. When Congress passed the Personal Responsibility and Work Opportunity Reconciliation Act (PRWORA) in 1996, over half a billion dollars in grant money was earmarked to fund state sponsored abstinence-only programs in public schools. Funding for abstinence-only-until-marriage education has increased nearly 3,000% since the entitlement program was begun in 1996 (Dallard, 2000).

A national survey conducted by Hickman-Brown Research (1999), indicated that there is great support (90% of respondents) for including a strong abstinence discussion in public school sex education programs. At the same time, 70% of the sample opposed using federal money for programs that did not also provide information on contraception for the prevention of unintended pregnancy and disease. Respondents also saw a strong distinction between abstinence-based and abstinence-only-until marriage programs.

In order to determine how effective both program approaches were, the National Campaign to Prevent Teen Pregnancy thoroughly reviewed the situation. The organization contracted with Dr. Douglas Kirby to evaluate programs designed to "delay the initiation of sex, increase condom or contraceptive use, and reduce teen pregnancy" (National Campaign to Prevent Teen Pregnancy, 2001, as quoted in Kirby, 2002, p. 1). The report, *Emerging Answers: Research Findings on Programs to Reduce Teen Pregnancy* (Kirby, 2001), gives high praise to "abstinence-plus" programs (where abstinence is stressed as the first and best choice for teens, but also encourages condom and contraceptive use if teens do have sex). Kirby found that many programs with strong research designs do persuade teens to delay sexual intercourse, reduce its frequency, and increase condom and/or contraceptive use. This is linked to reducing teen pregnancy and sexually transmitted diseases. A study of abstinence-only programs revealed that there was too little evidence and too much diversity in abstinence-only programs to know whether these programs are effective in delaying the initiation of sex. "It seems likely . . . that sooner or later studies will produce strong evidence that some abstinence-only programs are effective at delaying sex and that others are not" said Kirby (2002, p. 6). "However, until needed research is completed, we won't know which programs delay the initiation of sex nor will we know whether they affect contraceptive use and teen pregnancy."

Findings about the effects of comprehensive sex education programs should allay fears of those who see stressing abstinence while explaining contraceptive choices as incompatible messages. In 1997, the UNAIDS Review examined 68 reports on sexuality education from eight developed nations including the United States, the United Kingdom, Thailand, France, Mexico, Switzerland, and several Scandinavian nations. They concluded that sexuality and HIV education curricula that discuss abstinence and contraception do not encourage or hasten the onset of sexual behavior and do not increase the frequency of intercourse or the number of a person's sexual partners (UNAIDS, 1997). Kirby's review of nationwide sex education programs (2001) reached a similar conclusion: Skills-based programs (those that stress contraceptive use and communication skills among other things) do not increase the frequency of intercourse and do not encourage increased sexual activity. They do tend to increase the use of condoms and other contraception when youth choose to have sex.

On the other hand, abstinence-only programs and virginity pledges are showing a disturbing "sleeper" effect. Not only do these programs demonstrate little success in delaying teen sexual activity, they may actually discourage sexually active teens from using condoms or other contraception by giving the impression that the contraceptives are unreliable (Bearman & Bruckner, 2001; Hauser, 2004; Kirby, 2001). The result is obvious: higher risk of unintended pregnancy and STDs. With 61.6% of all U.S. teens reporting at least one sexual experience by the twelfth grade, that risk is significant (Center for Disease Control and Prevention, 2004). Furthermore, the encouraging decline in teen sexual activity and teen pregnancy that began in 1991 has stalled, and in the years since abstinence-only programs have been instituted across the country, the percentages have started to rise again (1–2%) among students in grades 10–12. Interestingly, the decline in sexual activity by ninth-grade students continues to fall, from 39% in 1991 to 32.8% in 2003, which could indicate that sex education programs are indeed encouraging postponement of initial sexual experiences. In the same year, the percentage of sexually active tenth-graders rose to 44.1%, an increase of 3.3% since 2001.

Despite wide support for comprehensive sex education, the vocal minority (less than one in five) of adults and parents who object to comprehensive programs, combined with the federal government grant incentives, have had a significant impact on what U.S. children are taught about sexuality and decision making. According to Darroch, Landry, and Singh (2000), the proportion of sex education teachers who taught abstinence as the only way to prevent pregnancy and STDs increased from one in fifty in 1988 to one in four in 1999. At the same time, 90% of teachers personally believed that sexuality education should include topics of sexual decision making, abstinence, and birth control methods, as well as pregnancy and AIDS prevention. Leading public health organizations—the Society for Adolescent Medicine, the American Medical Association, the American Academy of Pediatrics, and the Institute of Medicine—support this thinking (Advocates for Youth, 2006). A 2001 national survey of state sex education requirements revealed that the number of states requiring STD/HIV education, the most universally accepted sexual health topic, has dropped from 42 states in 1998 to 36 states and the District of Columbia (Kaiser Family Foundation, 1998). And teens continue to take risks for getting pregnant and/or contract an STD. Of the approximately 950,000 teenage pregnancies that occur each year, three out of four are unintended. Over one-fourth of these pregnancies are terminated by abortion (Alan Guttmacher Institute, 1999).

Although the rate of pregnancies has declined in the last 15 years, the United States still has one of the highest teen pregnancy rates in the developed world: over twice as high as those in England, Wales, and Canada and nine times as high as in the Netherlands and Japan. New STD infections in the U.S. each year top 4 million, indicating an "extremely high" rate of gonorrhea and chlamydia (Alan Guttmacher Institute, 2001).

This continues to confirm what Engel, Saracino, and Bergen observed in a 1993 study:

> Pre- and posttest research on the effectiveness of school-based curricula usually report evidence of increased knowledge but little or less evidence of changed attitudes or behaviors. Thus it appears that, while school-based curricula may be effective in accomplishing the traditional educational goals of schools (i.e., to increase knowledge), other interventions may be necessary to accomplish social and health-related goals (i.e., behavior change and problem prevention). (p. 67)

Fortunately, sexuality education programs are not limited to public school education. A number of youth-serving organizations, such as the Boys and Girls Clubs of America and the American Red Cross, have developed their own sexuality education programs, as have many religious groups and organizations. Although the goals and length of programs vary widely (from five to 30 hours), their content usually is more comprehensive than in public schools. Topics typically include family relationships, drugs and alcohol, consequences of adolescent pregnancy, dating relationships, and myths and stereotypes. Skills such as values clarification, communication, and assertiveness are also frequently covered. Frequently excluded from objective discussion are more "controversial" topics such as homosexuality, abortion, masturbation, and contraception, as well as a knowledge of health care systems (Engel et al., 1993). Yet these are the very areas in which youth make choices every day.

Even in the "free speech" arena of media coverage (television, radio, music CDs, movies), many aspects of sexuality—particularly those aspects that call for responsibility and that look at the consequences of risk-taking behavior—are rarely covered. The late 1970s saw a vast increase in the number of media references to seductive behavior and implied acts of sexual intercourse. Verbal references to intercourse increased from two to 53 per week during this time (Haffner & Kelly, 1987). A national analysis of sexual content on prime-time television conducted in 1978–1979 (Sprafkin & Silverman, 1981) determined that more than 20,000 scenes of suggested sexual intercourse and behavior, sexual comments, and innuendos appeared in one year of evening television broadcasting. Yet it was not until the mid-1980s that birth control or particular types of contraception were mentioned on network television, even in advertisements (Haffner & Kelly, 1987).

Are teens "educated" by the media? More than 40% of youth believe that TV gives a realistic picture of sexually transmitted diseases, pregnancy, and the consequences of sexual activity (Harris, 1986). Compared with the time spent on computers and watching television every week, the sex education teens receive in school or community or church programs, over a year or over a lifetime, hardly weighs in at all.

In light of the rapid sexualization of society over the past 40 years, a National Coalition to Support Sexuality Education was formed in the mid-1990s. Composed of more than 100 national nonprofit organizations concerned with health education and social concerns of families and individuals, the coalition sees its mission as assuring that comprehensive sexuality education is provided for all children and youth in the United States (SIECUS, 1997b). See appendix D for the list of participating organizations.

This chapter explores definitions of sexuality education, including comprehensive sexuality education; the need and contexts for sexuality education; and theories and methodologies that have proven to be helpful in understanding and designing effective programs. Chapter 9 continues the discussion of sexuality education with a look at types of programs, a discussion of cultural-specific concerns, and suggestions for evaluating program effectiveness.

SEXUAL CAUTIONS OR SEXUAL HEALTH?

The terms used by a community or school program are often defined by the specific concerns of the program planners. This is particularly true in the area of sexuality education. Because of the critical health risks of premature sexual involvement, sexuality education is often "defined" by program planners as that type of education that will reduce and prevent unanticipated teen pregnancy and sexually transmitted diseases, HIV and AIDS most particularly.

There is wide consensus among politicians, health educators, parents, and professionals about what is sexually unhealthy: premature and unprotected sex-

A successful program must address the underlying values and decision-making thought patterns of the learners.

ual intercourse, exposure to sexually transmitted diseases, sexual abuse, and date rape. Yet there is wide disparity about what is sexually "healthy" for children and youth. The public debate about adolescent sexuality has often focused on which sexual behaviors are appropriate or inappropriate for adolescents and ignored the complex dimensions of healthy sexuality (Haffner, 1995).

In 1994, the National Commission on Adolescent Sexual Health was convened to focus attention on the development of healthy values, attitudes, and skills, as well as the avoidance of unhealthy decisions and behaviors (Haffner, 1995). The commission adopted a consensus statement that defined sexual health and reproductive health as encompassing "sexual development and reproductive health as characterized by . . . the ability to develop and maintain meaningful interpersonal relationships; appreciate one's own body; interact with both genders in respectful and appropriate ways; and express affection, love, and intimacy in ways consistent with one's own values" (National Commission on Adolescent Sexual Health, cited in Haffner, 1995, p. 3).

Are these concepts of sexual health appropriate for adolescents only? Gradually, the realization is dawning that education about sexual health is appropriate and necessary for people of all ages. Sexuality education has thus been described as "a lifelong process of acquiring information and forming attitudes, beliefs, and values about identity, relationships, and intimacy . . . encompassing sexual development, reproductive health, interpersonal relationships, affection, intimacy, body image, and gender roles" (National Coalition to Support Sexuality Education,

1999). Such a definition confirms the role of parents as the primary sexuality educators of their children and reinforces the idea that responsibility and obligation for sexuality education are shared community-wide. Sexuality education does not, and should not, occur just within the classroom or home. It is most effective when each arena (home, school, religious setting, community group, media) accepts its unique role in teaching and reinforcing concepts of sexual health and responsibility.

THE NEED FOR AND CONTEXTS OF SEXUALITY EDUCATION

In spite of continuing protests, national surveys consistently indicate that the vast majority (more than 80%) of parents and adolescents in the United States desire sexuality education that is more comprehensive in scope and age range and that they support it being offered in a variety of settings.

The National Guidelines Task Force (SIECUS, 1997c) outlined four main goals of comprehensive sex education:

- to provide accurate information about human sexuality
- to provide an opportunity for young people to develop and understand their values, attitudes, and beliefs about sexuality
- to help young people develop relationships and interpersonal skills
- to help young people exercise responsibility regarding sexual relationships, including addressing abstinence, pressures to become prematurely involved in sexual intercourse, and the use of contraception and other sexual health measures

Parents also express the desire to know how to communicate better with their children and teens about all aspects of sexual health and values. And, despite myths to the contrary, teens also want to be able to talk to their parents. A 1999 study by the Kaiser Family Foundation reported that 59% of children ages 10–12 and 45% of adolescents ages 13–15 said they personally learned the "most" about sexuality from their parents. This then is the first "need" for comprehensive sexuality education: the need to be better informed and comfortable with one's sexuality.

A second aspect of need revolves around concern over the unhealthy consequences of premature, unprotected, or inappropriate or unwanted sexual activity. Poverty exacerbates teen pregnancy and affects both mother and child. Among teens 15 to 17 years old, 46% of those with family incomes below the poverty line are at risk for unintended pregnancy, compared with one-third of teens with family incomes 2.5 times or more above the poverty level. Only 70% of teen mothers complete high school, and 25% are on public assistance by their early 20s (Henry J. Kaiser Family Foundation, 1998). Thirty-five percent of all pregnancies among women 19 years of age or younger are terminated by abortion. Young age and low income are the reasons most often cited for the abortion decision (Alan Guttmacher Institute, 1994).

Sexually transmitted diseases are also a major concern to be addressed by sexuality education. The public and private costs of STD infection are tremendous: over $17 billion annually in the United States alone. Complications of STDs include various cancers, infertility, ectopic pregnancy, spontaneous abortion, and possible infection of the newborn baby. STD infections also increase susceptibility to HIV, a fact that less than half of Americans under age 65 are aware of. Although chlamydia is the most common bacterial STD, only 23% of American adults under 65 who were surveyed even cited chlamydia when asked to name kinds of sexually transmitted disease (SIECUS, 1997a). There is great need for more information.

Sexuality education also is needed to protect persons of all ages, particularly children, from sexual abuse. Although many sexual abuse prevention programs were introduced in the 1980s, there is still great uncertainty regarding both the positive and the potentially negative outcomes of such programs (Engel et al., 1993). If this is the only sexuality education that children receive (as it is in some school districts), it may engender unwarranted attitudes of fearfulness or interfere with appropriate expressions of affection with significant adults (Krivacska, 1991). "To avoid this, abuse intervention programs should be offered in the context of (or as a component of) comprehensive health-focused sexuality education" (Engel et al., 1993, p. 75). On the other hand, even a one-time classroom presentation about sexual abuse has helped many children to recognize that their situations are harmful, resulting in them finally telling someone about it. The value of the intervention aspect of sexual abuse programs should not be overlooked. Nor should the program occur only once in a child's 12 years of public education.

TEACHER EDUCATION

Providing clear and positive sexuality education across the life span requires well-trained, competent professional educators. This obvious need was stated as far back as 1912, when sexuality education consisted mainly of information about "venereal" diseases. Margaret Mead echoed the concern for special training of teachers in 1968:

> We're faced with a serious problem in the whole sex education field. This problem is the tremendous shortage of people who by their background and training and experience are able to stand up in front of a mixed group of people—a diverse set of parents, a bunch of adolescents—and talk simply and clearly, without embarrassment *and with emotion* [italics in original], about sex relationships, those relationships which we split off so badly from the rest of life. (Mead, 1985)

In 1991 the National Education Association passed a resolution favoring special training for sexuality education teachers (Krueger, 1991). So how has this need been addressed in the ensuing years? A recent survey study determined that very few college and university teacher education programs (14% of the 169 surveyed) require a health education course for all new teachers, and no universities require a sexuality education course (Rodriguez, Young, Renfro, Asencio, & Haffner, 1996). This is true in spite of the fact that a high percentage of states now mandate at least an HIV/AIDS-prevention education for all students in public school. As a result, most of the sexuality education offered in public schools is given by persons with little or no training in the subject. Physical education teachers most often have the responsibility, followed by health educators, biology teachers, family and consumer sciences teachers, and school nurses (Forrest & Silverman, 1989).

The good news is that 94% of the higher education institutions surveyed do offer at least one sexuality course, and 87% at least one health education course. With courses already available, many new teachers could have at least minimal training in sexual health education if state certification requirements mandated such training.

Although the emphasis of this discussion has focused on public school teachers, the need for adequate and comprehensive training for community family life educators is just as acute. If programs are offered by an organization, such as the Boys or Girls Clubs, or by a religious denomination, there is usually a teacher-training component included, although the training may vary widely in length and coverage. Many programs for parents are one-shot or short-term programs in which no curriculum guide is used, and the presenter may or may not be trained or well versed in the components of effective sexuality education.

USING THEORY TO DEVELOP PROGRAMS

In listing the attributes of effective sexuality education programs, longtime researcher Douglas Kirby (1994) emphasized the importance of theory-based program designs and needs assessments. Three levels of theory are particularly appropriate.

General Sexual Development Theory

General sexual development theory can provide a foundational philosophy for all program designs. Such theory proposes that experiencing one's sexuality is appropriate at every age and stage of life and that sexual learning can enhance healthy, sexually positive attitudes (Engel et al., 1993). Sexually positive attitudes are described as attitudes that promote experiences that are noncoercive, nonexploitative, risk-free, and mutually pleasurable (Haffner, 1990).

This is contrasted with sexually negative attitudes, which promote fear, guilt, manipulation, avoidance of discussion, and denial of sexual feelings and which often result in participation in risky behaviors. These attitudes have also resulted, over the years and centuries, in lack of enjoyment of sexual lovemaking, particularly for females, who were expected to be passive and disgusted by the whole business. David Mace (1970) recounted an experience that happened to a physician colleague in 1943 at the first Marriage Guidance Center that opened in London. The physician was conducting an intake interview with a middle-aged woman. When he asked the woman if she enjoyed sex with her husband, she hung her head shamefully and replied, "I'm afraid I do."

Another example of sexually negative attitudes comes from my (Powell) own experience: As a preteen in the 1950s I received a harsh scolding from my mother for using a dirty word: *passion.* Later, when passion became an experience instead of just a word, I had no basis for analyzing my rush of conflicting feelings or for talking with my boyfriend about how we should handle a potentially risky situation. So, as a college student in the early 1960s, I decided I needed more information. I was afraid to be seen looking up such a subject in the library (I was at a church-sponsored college), so I ordered a sex "encyclopedia" by mail in a plain brown wrapper. The publishers sent the book to me, but for some reason they sent the bill to my mother! When she mailed the bill to me (with no word of encouragement for wanting to know more), I was so embarrassed at getting "caught" that I sent the book back! My sexually negative education put me at high risk at a time when the normal feelings of sexual excitement yearned to be expressed. I didn't know what to do except either to try to resist and risk losing the person I cared about so much or to give in and keep my fingers crossed that nothing "bad" would happen. He too was torn between the pleasurable sensations of natural desire and the guilt of even having these new feelings. Neither of us could talk to the other about it. We had little sexual vocabulary and no experience at discussing sexual issues. So there we were, trying to cross a minefield with no map.

Haffner (1990) lists eight concepts of a sexually positive developmental paradigm:

1. Begin sexuality education at birth.
2. Promote the development of a healthy self-concept.
3. Acknowledge a wide range of values and experiences.
4. Talk honestly and openly about sexual questions and issues.
5. Prepare for realistic long-term relationships.
6. Value the future: career achievement, personal fulfillment, and personal health.
7. Focus on shared responsibility: home, school, community, religious organizations.
8. Address the political implications of change.

Engel et al. (1993) stress the importance of providing more sexuality education for neglected audiences and clienteles. This includes adults of all ages—young adults, parents, and older adults, to name a few—and of all circumstances. Gay and lesbian couples and persons with physical disabilities are examples. For cases of sexual dysfunction because of ignorance or prior traumatic experiences, counseling or therapy should also be available.

Many times it is assumed that adults do not need or are not interested in sexual education and enrichment. My personal involvement as a leader with my husband in marriage enrichment conferences says otherwise. As one of very few couples who are willing to talk openly in front of a group about our own sexual experiences, we have found our conferences to be always well attended and appreciated.

Social Learning Theory

Social learning theory examines how people learn and incorporate behaviors and attitudes through societal interaction and influences. Learning takes place through a series of steps. *Knowledge* is the first step, whether it be accurate or inaccurate, comprehensive or sketchy. I often remind parents that their children are getting sexuality education from the time they turn the radio on in the morning until they turn the television off at night. The questions are whether that is all the sex education they need and if it is the kind of sex education the parents want them to have. *Motivation*, the desire to act on the knowledge received, is the second step in social learning. Both internal and external motivations can be present: from curiosity to fantasy to the desire to please a favored one to wanting to fit in with the group or to prove something to oneself or to stay true to one's values. *Outcome expectancy* is a powerful determinant of behavior that also relates to cognitive development theory. When one can think rationally about the consequences of certain behaviors and whether these consequences are deemed to be good and pleasurable or harmful and risky, better decisions can be made. Social influence theory focuses on the social pressures that may override rational thinking about outcomes and how persons act. Brown (1995) and Bearinger (1990) have looked particularly at media influences on adolescent sexual attitudes and behaviors.

The final step in social learning is *self-efficacy*: the belief that one has the power to learn new attitudes and behaviors and to control one's choices. Self-efficacy does not come quickly, nor just by hearing "you can do it" or other positive messages, encouraging as they are. Self-efficacy takes practice and support, from a peer group, a mentor, a therapist. Self-efficacy also has a cognitive component. One must be able to "self-talk" in ways that are encouraging and rational and to be self-forgiving when mistakes are made in order to claim personal power and achieve goals.

Kirby (1994) has determined through his review of sexuality education programs that effective programs are designed on a solid theoretical base of social learning and behavioral theories. In other words, just giving children and teens "the facts" and expecting them to make their own decisions about behaviors and attitudes is not taking into account the higher steps in social learning theory. Programs must send a very clear message about the role of sexuality and sexual behavior in the lives of adolescents, and this message must be reinforced by the other experiential, interactive elements of the program. Kirby articulates the message very simply: Kids should be abstinent, but if they do have sex, they should always use condoms; or kids should always use condoms but should keep in mind that abstinence is the only means of preventing pregnancy and sexually transmitted diseases that is 100% effective (Kirby, 1994, as cited in Settles, 1998). Because too much information can be confusing for teens when they are struggling with difficult choices, discussion of comprehensive issues, such as gender roles, dating, and parenthood, were not included in the programs that Kirby studied.

Kirby (1994) identified other elements of adolescent sexuality programs that were shown to be effective in delaying the onset of sexual activity among participants and/or that increased the use of contraceptives among participants who initiated sex after being in the program. In addition to a strong learning theory basis and a clear message, the other common elements were (1) teaching resistance skills through role-playing and group discussion; (2) instruction on social influences and pressures; (3) setting peer norms and challenging normative myths (such as "everybody is doing it"); and (4) using activities that increase relevant skills or confidence in those skills.

Settles (1998) observed:

> It is important to note that these expectations do deviate from the typical sex education program which teaches only biological facts or decision-making skills in a value-neutral environment. Sex educators are now concluding what

advertisers have known for years: too much information obfuscates. It's possible to sell ideas to people, but you can sell only one primary idea at a time. (p. 5)

Kirby (1994) and Settles (1998) also stressed the importance of tailoring the message to the target audience. If the audience is teenage girls who are at high risk for pregnancy and sexually transmitted diseases, the emphasis on how to protect oneself and how to say "no" is critical. On the other hand, a strong focus on abstinence, with information about avoiding pregnancy and STD risks, is effective for young audiences or for high school groups in which most of the youth are not already engaged in sexually risky behavior. If the school has a high rate of sexual activity, then the primary focus should be on protection from pregnancy and disease, with the option of abstinence also encouraged.

Moral Development Theory

If programs designed to influence behaviors have any hope of succeeding, they must also address the underlying values and moral decision-making thought patterns of the learners. An understanding of the stages of moral development as proposed by Kohlberg (1984) and enhanced by Gilligan (Brown & Gilligan, 1992; Gilligan, Taylor, & Ward, 1988) is helpful. Based to some degree on the cognitive development theory of Piaget, Kohlberg proposed three levels of moral development. The first level, preconventional, is consistently practiced by young children. Obedience and other "right" actions are governed by fear of punishment and self-preservation. The second level, conventional morality, is seen more often in older children and adolescents. Moral decisions are based on good interpersonal relationships and good motives, which help to maintain the social order. There is more concern for society as a whole and for the importance of laws, social responsibility, and values such as love, empathy, and trust. Kohlberg saw a higher, third, level of morality, one which very few people attain and which he called postconventional morality. People who live and operate at this level may value but also challenge the views of conventional society. They are less willing to accept a "law" at face value if they think a higher good is being jeopardized. They also consider the living conditions and rights of other people to be equally as valid as their own. Gilligan (Gilligan et al., 1988) added new moral considerations to Kohlberg's stages based on her studies with girls and women as they responded to moral dilemmas. She contended that men and women may have alternative moral frameworks from which to base their decisions. A deep concern for making and maintaining relationships determines the actions of many female adolescents and adults. In close relationships, this concern may override other interests, such as self-preservation or societal norms, particularly if these have not been clearly discussed or supported.

Although one's cognitive development stage does influence one's moral development stage to some extent, persons do not necessarily advance in their moral thinking as they grow older. Clarity in moral thinking and decision making requires the opportunity to discuss, with some guidance, dilemmas and options and the moral high ground. Such guidance is not meant to be an exercise in authoritarian judgment by an outside "expert," however. Learners must be respected and their differing views acknowledged and accepted even as they are considered in the light of high moral standards. Settles (1998) points to Robert Coles's interviews with children and adolescents about moral issues. Coles (1997) observed that the young people raised various ethical questions that showed their concern about not only how they should behave but also why, in accordance with a larger scheme of things. Coles marveled at their "tenacious moral seriousness," even though most had no idea where to go from there.

Kohlberg maintained that moral development was not a product of socialization but of one's own serious consideration of ethical questions and behaviors (Crain, 2000). However, social experiences do promote development by encouraging each person to articulate his or her position and then to consider other viewpoints in a nonjudgmental context. Kohlberg also saw role-taking opportunities as a very effective way to consider others' viewpoints. But whatever the context, the interactions should be open and democratic. Gilligan et al. (1988) emphasize the importance of mentors who have clear values and a moral philosophy that is not hypocritical or condemning but that demonstrates caring and genuine interest. She points out that adolescents are keen discerners of contradiction and sham. Settles (1998) summarized a discussion of sexuality and moral development theory: "The clearest lessons learned are that we, as educators, must be clear about our students' needs and knowledge, we must be clear about our own values and goals and we must take a stand that incorporates both concerns in order to most clearly benefit the healthy growth of the adolescents in our charge" (p. 17).

THE PRAXIS PRINCIPLE

In all of this, it is important to see the learner as an active, not a passive, participant. When learners begin to interact with a subject and with each other and to practice *praxis*—action with reflection—amazing changes in attitudes and behaviors can occur. "If we follow what we know about learning, we would 'teach' in a way that activates the learner because we know that people 'learn best by doing,'" observed an experienced sexuality educator (Rudrauff, 1999):

> The droning lecture needs to end forever for any group of people including adults. Replace it with activity and skills-based exercises such as simulation games, role plays, performing arts experiences, game shows, demonstrations, student-led discussions, small group projects, service learning in the community, experiments, interviews of interesting people, and a myriad of other teaching and learning events. . . . When we mobilize the "student as leader" in their own learning process, we hook their emotional selves for internalization of the messages so behavior change might occur. (p. 4)

Evaluation of programs in which praxis occurs shows positive change in learners' attitudes, increased family communication, behavior changes in relation to relationships, and lower risk-taking behavior, as well as an increase in knowledge.

SUMMARY

Clear, comprehensive, positive sexuality education continues to be an urgent need for people of all ages and cultures in our society. The life-changing—and life-threatening—consequences of premature and unprotected sexual involvement have motivated much of the focus on sexuality education thus far. Yet it is obvious that developing children and older youth long for opportunities to learn about their bodies and their feelings in a context that is not threatening or embarrassing. Discussion of moral and ethical issues and decision making with mentors who can offer guidance and acceptance should also be included. Surveys continually confirm that parents want this type of education for their children and that children value what their parents have to say. Yet most parents and teachers express anxiety at the thought of actually doing the education. Teacher training and parent education are both elements of sexuality education that must be addressed by teacher-training institutions, teacher-certification bodies, and community and religious organizations. Many resources are now available for information and education; the challenge is getting them all connected. Chapter 9 elaborates on how that is being done in a variety of settings and with emphasis on valid evaluation of effectiveness.

Questions/Problems for Discussion and Review

Class Discussion

1. Looking at the 60 years of history of sexuality education and the "sexual revolution," what have been the benefits and the detriments of this societal movement? Could education have had a greater positive impact? In what ways?

2. If teacher education certification should require a course in health education, what teachers should be required to take it? Is a general course in health education sufficient to teach sexuality education? Why or why not?

3. If the majority of parents desire sexuality education in the public schools, do you think that a vocal minority who oppose it should be allowed to control the decisions of school administrators? Why is sexuality education such a hot topic?

Research Problems

1. Review the theories presented in this chapter as bases for sexuality education. Then search the current scholarly journals for program design reviews. Identify at least one program that exemplifies each theory, and give examples to support your answer.

2. Take a random sample survey of students at your university regarding their level of sexuality education and its perceived effectiveness. Develop a phone survey or questionnaire that will allow you to define which type of education experience they had and how they would evaluate it.

Case Study Design

Using the contexts of sexuality education discussed in the chapter, divide the class into small groups to design educational programs that would be appropriate for different ages and societal contexts. Be sure to include programs for adults and for persons with disabilities. How would you address the issues of sexual orientation and sexual abuse?

Approaches to
Sexuality Education

Although it is usually assumed that sexuality education takes place in the public school classroom with adolescents, this is not the only setting in which it occurs or is needed. This chapter discusses the focus of various program types and the audiences they address. A review of the elements of effective programs and concepts of evaluation concludes the chapter.

TYPES OF PROGRAMS

For Education

Programs designed primarily to educate have at least five major objectives: to promote sexual health in persons of all ages and sexual orientations; to reduce teen pregnancy and sexually transmitted disease; to prevent child sexual abuse; to assist parents in talking with their children and youth; and to assist teachers in preparing to teach sexuality education courses.

Promoting sexual health.   The desire to promote sexual health in persons of all ages and sexual orientations acknowledges that all persons are sexual beings but that all sexual experiences are not alike. The Life Span Family Life Education Poster (see appendix A), developed by the National Council on Family Relations (1997a), addresses the content of human sexuality education programs for children, adolescents, adults, and older adults. Obviously, developmental capabilities and needs determine what content is presented; however, a sexual health perspective begins with the assumption that one's sexuality involves far more than sexual arousal and sexual intercourse. A model by Dennis Dailey (figure 9.1) presents a holistic view of the elements that compose understanding of one's sexuality. Set within the context of sociocultural and family relationship settings, the areas of sexuality, sensuality, reproduction, intimacy, and identity overlap and influence one another. Certain aspects of one's sexuality come more into focus at various times of life, and depending on the sociocultural and family relationship settings, these aspects develop in either positive or negative ways. For example, research has determined that uncertainty about sexual orientation declines with age as students move through adolescence: About one fourth of 12-year-old students report uncertainty about sexual orientation, but only about 5% of 17-year-old students (Remafedi, 1992). At the same time, the sociocultural setting for many gay and lesbian students is certainly less than positive. One in five school health teachers said that students in their classes often used abusive language when describing homosexuals. In a 14-city survey of lesbian and gay youth, 46% said they lost a friend after disclosing their sexual identity to them, and less than 20% of the adolescents said they could identify someone who was very supportive of them (Telljohann & Price, 1993).

Persons with disabilities or chronic illnesses should also be affirmed as sexual beings who have the same feelings and desires as all other persons. "All too often adolescents [and adults] with developmental disabilities or chronic illnesses are viewed as nonsexual beings by professionals, peers, and parents" (Heighway,

Figure 9.1   A Model for Understanding Human Sexuality

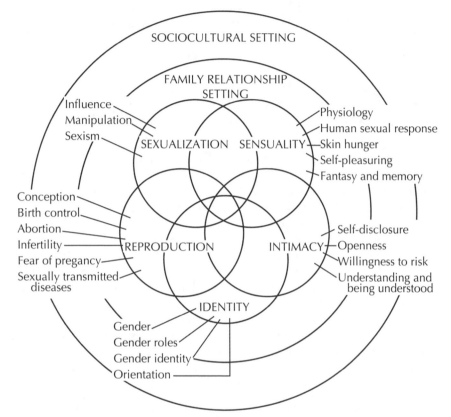

Developed by Dennis Dailey, University of Kansas School of Social Welfare. Based on "The Components of Sexuality," by H. L. Gochros, J. S. Gochros, and J. Fischer, in *Helping the Sexually Oppressed*, edited by H. L. Gochros, J. S. Gochros, and J. Fischer, 1986. Englewood Cliffs, NJ: Prentice-Hall. Reprinted with permission of Dennis Dailey.

1989, p. 4). Education about healthy sexual development for students with disabilities should include all of the elements of a typical comprehensive sexuality education program, as well as opportunities to learn and develop social skills and the teaching of appropriate touch.

Family context certainly has a great influence on one's sexual health. From the way a child's simple questions about body parts are answered to attitudes toward nudity to the roles of men and women in the family and society: All provide a foundation for positive or negative attitudes about one's sexuality. When incest and other inappropriate sexual behaviors are present in the family, a child's self-image and sense of control over her or his life can be so seriously affected that it may take a lifetime of therapy to overcome the negative messages.

Sexual health addresses the aspects and context of one's sexual development in ways that are affirming and teach respect for one's own body and the rights of others. Sexual health acknowledges the pleasurable aspects of sensuality but resists the sexualization of society that treats persons as objects for drawing attention and making money. Sexual health looks at health risks, as well as at ways to avoid those risks. The *Guidelines for Comprehensive Sexuality Education* (SIECUS, 1997c), developed by a task force of SIECUS in 1990, articulated four primary areas for sexuality education that focus on the promotion of adult sexual health: (1) information; (2) attitudes, values, and insights; (3) relationships and interpersonal skills; and (4) responsibility. These goals are based on a set of specific values that relate to human sexuality and that reflect the beliefs of most communities in a pluralistic society (SIECUS, 1997c). Box 9.1 lists the values articulated by the task force.

Preventing health risks.   Adolescents are at high behavioral risk of acquiring most sexually transmitted diseases. They are more likely to have multiple sex partners and less likely to use condom protection. Each year, approximately 4 million new sexually transmitted disease infections occur among teenagers in the United States. Biologically, younger women are more susceptible to contracting chlamydia, gonorrhea, and HIV (Centers for Disease Control and Prevention, 2001). Young women are also the most affected, healthwise and in future decision-making, by an unintended pregnancy. Of the approximately 950,000 teen pregnancies that occur each year, more than three in four are unintended (Henshaw, 2004). Young people's attitudes toward oral sex also contribute to high-risk behaviors. In a sample of 510 adolescents aged 12–17, 31% of females and 44% of males agreed or somewhat agreed with the statement "oral sex is not as big a deal as sexual intercourse" (Hoff, Greene, & Davis, 2003). Oral sex may eliminate the fear of pregnancy but it does not take away the possibility of STD infection. Although the media have spread alarm about this new trend, data to support the claims are yet to be collected (Grunbahm et al., 2002).

Preventing sexual abuse.   A survey of students who had already completed sex education classes asked students what they wanted to learn more about. *Knowing what to do in case of rape or sexual assault* headed the list of topics checked by the respondents (55%). Yet this subject was not even on the list of parent-preferred choices for sex education topics (Henry J. Kaiser Family Foundation, 2001). This writer (Powell) was asked several years ago to present a program on sexual abuse and incest at a national church gathering of adolescent girls. Naively, I assumed that I was speaking to the wrong audience about this topic, and I was astonished at the number of girls who talked with me afterwards about their problems with male family members who were sexually harassing or abusing them. Obviously more education for adolescents is needed in this area.

Child sexual abuse prevention programs vary widely in content, length and number of sessions, age of students, methodology, and context. According to Engel et al. (1993), most programs focus on delivering the following messages: (1) children have a right to control their own bodies; (2) there are different kinds of touch, good and bad, and not all kinds need to be tolerated; (3) children can trust their feelings and recognize inappropriate touching; (4) children can learn to say "no" to touching that makes them feel uncomfortable or afraid and can run away; (5) children should tell an adult they trust about confusing or inappropriate

Box 9.1   Common Values Concerning Sexuality Education in a Pluralistic Society

- Sexuality is a natural and healthy part of living.
- All persons are sexual.
- Sexuality includes physical, ethical, social, spiritual, psychological, and emotional dimensions.
- Every person has dignity and self-worth.
- Young people should view themselves as unique and worthwhile individuals within the context of their cultural heritage.
- Individuals express their sexuality in varied ways.
- Parents should be the primary sexuality educators.
- Families provide a child's first education about sexuality.
- Families share their values about sexuality.
- In a pluralistic society, people should respect and accept the diversity of values and beliefs about sexuality that exist in a community.
- Sexual relationships should never be coercive or exploitative.
- All children should be loved and cared for.
- All sexual decisions have effects or consequences.
- All persons have the right and the obligation to make responsible sexual choices.
- Individuals, families, and society benefit when children are able to discuss sexuality with their parents and/or other trusted adults.
- Young people develop their values about sexuality as part of becoming adults.
- Young people explore their sexuality as a natural process of achieving sexual maturity.
- Premature involvement in sexual behaviors poses risks.
- Abstaining from sexual intercourse is the most effective method of preventing pregnancy and STD/HIV.
- Young people who are involved in sexual relationships need access to information about health care services.

Developed in 1990 by the National Guidelines Task Force, which consisted of 20 professionals in the fields of medicine, education, sexuality, and youth services. The guidelines were updated in 1996 to reflect societal and technological changes that had occurred during the subsequent five years. From "Fact Sheet: Guidelines for Comprehensive Sexuality Education: Kindergarten–12th Grade," 1997, *SIECUS Report 25*(6). Copyright 1997 by the Sexuality Information and Education Council of the United States. Reprinted with permission of the Sexuality Information and Education Council of the U.S.

touching; (6) the abuser may be someone the child knows, not a stranger; (7) "secrets" about touching need not be kept; and (8) any abuse that occurs is not the child's fault.

Teaching methods usually go beyond traditional classroom instruction and include booklets that children and parents can read together, comic books, video and theater performances, puppets, role-playing, and coaching sessions (Engel et al., 1993). Another reason that education must go beyond the classroom is that child victimization occurs at a very young age, usually before age 7 (Finkelhor, 1984). It happens to young males, as well as females, at about a 1:3 ratio. Although there are no conclusive studies on the effectiveness of such child abuse prevention programs, preliminary research indicates that the learners do gain knowledge, but the knowledge may be short-lived and needs to be reinforced (Graham & Harris-Hart, 1988). In order to enhance retention and desired protective behavior, children need to have opportunities to practice and interact with the teacher and the materials. This type of learning tends to increase desired behaviors in the face of potential danger, such as responding to strangers' playground requests (Graham & Harris-Hart, 1989). Also, as previously mentioned, sexual abuse programs tend to have an intervention function also, with children being offered the opportunity to confide their "secret" and their fears to someone. Although current programs tend to focus on education for the child only, it is thought that education for parents and other caregiving adults might enhance effectiveness. Other potential program areas could focus on the offender, who is rarely considered in educational programming (Gilgun & Gordon, 1985).

The need for education in sexual abuse prevention certainly does not end with puberty. Programs for adolescents and for developmentally disabled youth and adults should also be considered. Ryerson (1984, p. 6) defines sexual abuse as "rape, attempted rape, incest and indecent exposure," although legal definitions vary from state to state:

> We cannot wait . . . to respond to the educational needs of developmentally disabled individuals in regard to self-protection. Nor can we shy away from the issue because it is a sensitive one, difficult to approach with children. . . . Regardless of their disability, these people can learn reporting and self-protective practices, both of which should be a critical part of every disabled student's basic education. (Ryerson, 1984, p. 7)

Assisting parent/child/adolescent conversation.   The largest study of adolescent behavior conducted to date (Annie E. Casey Foundation, 1998) confirms the findings of other major studies over the past two decades: Parents are the earliest and most important influence in their children's decision making about risk-taking behaviors. Over 90,000 adolescents participated in a study sponsored by the Institute for Youth Development and the National Teen Pregnancy Prevention Research Center. The study found that teens who know their parents strongly disapprove of risky adolescent sexual behavior are much more likely to abstain from that behavior. Miller (1998), in reviewing two decades of research on parent-child relationships and influence, added that teens who are relationally close to their parents are also more likely to remain abstinent or to postpone sexual intercourse. They also are more likely to use contraception if they do have intercourse. Evidence also indicates that strong parental attitudes and values that disapprove of adolescent sexual intercourse and pregnancy and that caution about the dangers of unprotected intercourse are related to lower adolescent pregnancy risk.

Teens have stated consistently that they prefer to talk to parents about sex and health and rank that source of information as the most reliable. Only one in 10 said a friend was most reliable. And when teen mothers were asked about why they had participated in risky sexual behavior, 75% cited lack of communication with their parents as a primary reason (Annie E. Casey Foundation, 1998).

At the same time, numerous studies confirm that parents are uncomfortable discussing sexual issues with their children and welcome help from more formal programs and from other sources. Educational seminars that target parents as the primary sexuality educators of their children are usually well attended and appreciated. The Zero Adolescent Pregnancy (ZAP) program in Cortland, New York, is a good example. The series of workplace lunchtime seminars focuses on improving communication between parents and children of all ages on all kinds of subjects, including sexuality and relationships. A needs assessment, administered before the program starts, helps the facilitator to tailor the program to the particular parent audience. Parents who attend the seminars report that they are "mobbed" after each session by coworkers who were unable to attend asking for advice and information. So the program has a definite spillover effect (National Campaign to Prevent Teen Pregnancy, 1998).

Other sources of material for parents abound. These include books, booklets, videos, and age-appropriate books for parents and children to read together. Yet many parents admit being at a loss when it comes to finding information. Appendix E lists selected clearinghouses of resources that are continually updated.

It is important to note and to emphasize in parent education seminars that the most important factor in influencing children and adolescents is not being a "sex information expert." Rather, it is the cultivation of an ongoing, positive relationship with the child (which includes focused attention and listening skills) and an ability to state one's opinions and values on many subjects, including sexual behavior, clearly and succinctly.

Educating teachers of sexuality education. Hickman-Brown Research conducted a national poll in 1999, which revealed that a distinct majority of parents, 70% or better, support age-appropriate sexuality education in the public schools (Figueroa & Hanock-Jasie, 1999). Ninety percent believe that abstinence should be taught as the best sexual decision, but 70% oppose an abstinence-only education and want both abstinence and contraception to be taught, as well as other age-appropriate topics. The Kaiser parent survey (Henry J. Kaiser Family Foundation, 2001) found that parents overwhelmingly approved of including the following topics and skills in high school sex education classes:

- HIV/AIDS and other STDs (98%)
- Basics of pregnancy and birth (90%)
- How to deal with the pressure to have sex and the emotional issues and consequences of being sexually active (94%)
- How to talk with a partner about birth control and STDs (88%)
- How to use condoms (85%);
- How to use and where to get other birth control (84%)
- Abortion (79%)
- Sexual orientation and homosexuality (76%)

Engel et al. (1993) listed three essential qualifications for sexuality educators at all levels of public education: (1) comfort with sexual communication; (2) the ability to listen, understand questions, and assess needs; and (3) appropriate education and knowledge about human sexuality.

Rodriguez et al. (1996) identified six key concepts of a comprehensive sexuality education program: human development, relationships, personal skills, sexual behavior, sexual health, and society and culture. When teacher education courses available at colleges and universities were evaluated for inclusion of these concepts, the researchers concluded that 93% of teacher education majors would not receive training in all six areas, even if they took every related course available.

In their recommendations, Rodriguez et al. urged colleges and universities to ensure that human sexuality courses are comprehensive in scope, covering all six of the key concepts. For current teachers, in-service and continuing education programs are vital. "Whether the explanation is lack of funds, lack of time, or lack of thorough understanding, the states which have mandated sexuality education are, with few exceptions, neglecting their teachers' cries for guidance, training, and professional preparation" (Krueger, 1991, p. 3). In addition to joining the Sex Information and Education Council of the United States, teachers may seek certification through the AASECT and through the CFLE program of the NCFR. New Internet technologies also offer opportunities for sharing resources, training opportunities, and program guides.

Service and Youth Development Programs

Service programs typically combine education with access to health services. School and neighborhood clinics often provide basic health care and, in some high-risk areas, contraceptive information and access. Some programs are designed to assist pregnant teens with basic child development education, infant care, and parenting skills. These programs may also have school-hour child-care services, usually on a time-limited basis, for young mothers who might otherwise drop out of school for lack of child care. Sara McDonald Rohar directs the Young Mother's Program in Birmingham, Alabama, and has been involved in services to pregnant teens for more than 13 years. She believes that such services are highly effective as education and prevention tools:

> This critical time in an adolescent's life is also a period of intense interest in sexuality education and family life education. We have a window of opportunity to reach and teach young mothers about contraception and risk prevention, positive parenting and self-sufficiency. The self-sufficiency component is vital to avoiding poor decision making in the future. It involves learning to manage their personal lives and finances and developing employment skills. It is this combination of services and education, presented in ways that relate to the teen's current environment, that has made our program work. A strong comprehensive program has the potential to help young parents become high school graduates who are responsible nurturing parents, able to support themselves and their families. The payoff is certainly worth the effort. (personal communication, April 5, 1999)

Parent and Child/Adolescent Programs

Recognizing the importance of parent-teen communication, many pregnancy prevention programs have developed components that involve both parent and child. The National Campaign to Prevent Teen Pregnancy (1998) gives several successful examples:

> In rural Missouri, the Family Planning Department of the Family Guidance Center for Behavioral Health Care created "Parents and Kids Learn Together," a comprehensive family life education program for parents and their teens and preteens. Working with parent groups, youth organizations, local religious institutions, and area educators, the Family Guidance Center designed a six-class curriculum for both mothers and fathers with youth aged 9–12 and 13–17. The first class in each series is for parents only, in which they place anonymous questions in a "question box" for group discussion. The remaining classes bring parents and kids back together for learning that is active and fun. (p. 2)

> Girls Incorporated, a national youth development program, developed "Growing Together," a four- to five-session curriculum that seeks to delay the onset of teen sexual activity by fostering mother-daughter communication. Mothers and daughters who attended the program in Cobb County, Georgia, say the safe, supportive environment helped them build stronger relationships. Planned Parenthood of Los Angeles has trained their lay health workers to conduct "growing together" workshops in Spanish. (p. 2)

> In Fayetteville, North Carolina, the "Steel Magnolias" program, part of the Support Our Students (SOS) initiative, has served sixth-, seventh-, and eighth-grade girls and their mothers over the past four years. This collaboration of middle schools, the community, and Fayetteville State College provides six weeks of structured workshops in which mothers and daughters interact. After "graduating," they move to an "alumni group" with ongoing opportunities to learn and practice new skills. Many of the "Steel Magnolias" women are single mothers or guardians who welcome the support. The program was so successful and popular that boys at the middle schools wanted a similar opportunity. "Brother's Keeper," stressing self-confidence, spirituality, and knowledge, now offers activities for boys three nights a week. On the fourth night, the boys and their parents discuss healthy human growth and development and sexuality issues. (p. 3)

Culturally Specific Program Designs

As with other types of family life education programs, no generic program of sexuality education will "fit" all or appeal to all cultural groups. Because of cultural distinctions in norms and behaviors, an intervention that is effective with one culture group may fall flat with another.

> In McAllen, Texas, the Planned Parenthood Association of Hidalgo County, which serves a low-income Latino community near the Mexican border, has trained a cadre of Spanish-speaking lay health workers (*promotoras*) who go door to door to reach underserved women with a "friend and neighbor" approach. *Entre Nosotros* ("Just Between Us") is a ten-year-old peer education program run by 12 women, four men, four teens, and one mother-daugh-

ter pair who offer reproductive health education, family planning techniques, and information on how to avoid sexually transmitted diseases and AIDS to their friends, family, and neighbors. The peer leaders attend monthly training sessions. Promotoras are also available at clinic sites to welcome people referred by the projects, help with paper work, answer questions, and provide emotional support. Promotoras serve 25,000 people a year. (National Campaign to Prevent Teen Pregnancy, 1998, p. 9)

It is important for educators who design and present programs to become well acquainted with the cultural distinctions of the various groups with which they are working. The following discussion is not meant to be exhaustive or to provide all the information that the program designer needs, but it is meant to heighten awareness of the multicultural nature of our work.

Another important variable that must be considered is the economic status of differing cultural groups. More than 70% of children in "communities of color" live in extreme poverty (Columbia School of Public Health, 1996). Research studies show a direct correlation between poverty and parental education levels and pregnancy rates. The birthrate for Latina and African American teens is 108 per 1,000 females aged 15–19, compared with 40 births per 1,000 for Caucasian females of the same age, who have a youth poverty rate of only 14% (Child Trends, 1996).

> Growing numbers of adolescent voices [in impoverished communities] are now saying, "There is no hope. There is no one who values me. There is no one who cares." Under such conditions, it is no wonder that some young people, instead of becoming industrious and hopeful, become sexually intimate for a short-term sense of comfort, and ultimately become profoundly fatalistic. In such cases, intercourse is used as a coping mechanism. Youth workers, teachers, and counselors must replace the use of that coping mechanism with concrete and hopeful (not rhetorical) alternatives such as decent employment, a bank account, improvement in school, a place in college, or a meaningful career or vocational track. These are the elements that produce desirable outcomes in young people and reduce teen pregnancy, teen violence, and teen substance abuse. (Carrera, 1995, p. 16)

A researcher and sexuality education specialist, Carrera assisted in designing a long-term, holistic, multidimensional pilot program with young people, parents, and adults in the Harlem community. The program, sponsored by the Children's Aid Society of New York, addressed sexuality education within a context of cultural and poverty awareness. It was highly effective and is now being replicated in several states. According to Carrera, the most well-attended module in the program was the one on employment, with an attendance rate of 89%. This even exceeded the attendance rate for the program's sporting events!

Added to the poverty factor are the cultural norms, customs, and mores that various culture groups value and adhere to. Latinos, Native Americans, Asian and Pacific Islanders, and African Americans all operate as distinct culture groups within American society, and yet it is risky to generalize any particular characteristics to all persons within that larger group. One major point made by all the writers on cultural distinctions is that within each group are smaller subgroups with which individuals identify. For example, the Latino population, the fastest growing minority in the United States at an estimate of more than 20 million people, includes individuals who speak many different languages and come from very different regions, races, classes, and cultures of the Americas and Europe (de la Vega, 1990). The same is true for the other major culture groups. Yet there are some points of distinctiveness that apply generally to each major group. The reader is urged to refer to primary sources for more in-depth discussion of the cultures presented here.

Latino culture groups.   "We must become sensitive to the differences that exist among Latino groups, respond appropriately to nuances of Latino behavior, and most importantly, become aware of perceptions Latinos have about human sexuality and their own sexuality" (Medina, 1987, p. 1). Medina lists several areas of special importance in working with Latino groups:

1. The educator must be bilingual. Even Latinos who are quite proficient in English will choose to address sensitive subjects in their native tongue and usually in private, if at all. Sexual topics are especially sensitive, and the establishment of *confianza* (trust and breaking down of barriers) will rarely be achieved if the language barrier is not crossed.

2. Religion and family are primary values. Some 85% of all Latinos profess the Catholic faith, and religious experiences are deeply embedded in their culture. Family loyalty that extends to several generations and relationships is also a major value. Child-rearing responsibilities are often shared, lifting some of the parental burden from single parents especially. *Compadres*, or godparents, are also considered to be family and have an interest in the children's welfare. Living in an Americanized culture raises fears for parents about the corruption of their children by drugs or violence or by learning different sexual mores, values, and customs. They often shy away from public school sexuality education programs because of this.

   School-based comprehensive health care programs, which include sexual health, must invest time to sensitize Latino parents and their children to the meaning of preventive health care and health maintenance. Anything that may threaten traditional family stability and challenge parental authority will be rejected by Latino parents (Medina, 1987). Programs that address child safety, rather than child abuse prevention, for example, will be more positively received and attended.

3. Gender roles, usually traditional and male-dominant, are an important factor to be considered in educational interventions with Latino adolescents or adults. The best intervention involves both the males and females, engaged educationally at the same time, even if they are in different rooms (de la Vega, 1990).

Culturally sensitive programs conducted by persons who have gained the trust and respect of the community have a good chance of success.

Native American culture groups.   Because of stereotyping, Native American people have not been considered to be sexual in the same way as the rest of humanity (i.e., including persons who are homosexual or bisexual), so AIDS/HIV prevention programs were slow in coming (Rowell, 1990). Another misconception that has hampered sex education interventions is the idea that the federal Indian Health Service takes care of the health needs of Indian people and that they receive generous health benefits from the government. Actually, the Indian Health Service is a small, poorly funded agency that is unable to provide health services for even half of the Indian population. The result is that Native Americans have a poorer health status than the general U.S. population on almost every health indicator. Persons under age 65 are more likely to be uninsured when compared with all other racial and ethnic groups except Hispanic (National Center for Health Statistics, 2005).

Prompted by the rising number of HIV/AIDS cases among their people, Native Americans took the initiative to develop educational strategies that would work in their communities. The skills of traditional Native American healers, many of which are preventive in nature, have been used, as well as Western medicine. Indian artists and musicians have also been invited to bring their talents to bear on the problem. As a result, a number of Native American-targeted materials have been produced, capitalizing on the culture's common values: respect for elders, teaching children survival skills, focusing on the extended family, strong spiritual traditions, storytelling, and humor (Rowell, 1990). An award-winning health education publication and video, *We Owe It to Ourselves and to Our Children* (National Native American AIDS Prevention Center, 1990), brought together traditional poetry, Native American stories, and artistic images to present the message about STD prevention and treatment in a subtle and beautiful way. Focus groups have shown that Native Americans feel embarrassed to discuss most materials on STDs. Culture-sensitive resources are available from the National Native American AIDS Prevention Center (www.nnaapc.org).

Asian and Pacific Islander American culture groups.   Making up more than 15% of the nation's total population growth since 1990, Asian and Pacific Islander Americans represent a vast diversity of languages and traditions from more than 40 countries and territories, speaking over 100 different languages (Lee & Fong, 1990). Recognizing and understanding the distinctions among the different groups is especially important when attempting to address their needs and to reach them with appropriate information and education programs. Differences between American-born and foreign-born, young and old, new immigrant or refugee status, and English proficiency among these groups are also nuances that must be considered.

At the same time, some basic similarities characterize most Asian and Pacific Islander subgroups: a strong sense of priority of family and community over individual rights; a taboo on sexual discussions; unacceptability of homosexuality by either the family or the community; and avoidance of discussion of illness and death. The reason for the latter is that discussion of such topics is considered a self-fulfilling prophecy.

So how might sexuality education be presented in an acceptable way? Lee and Fong (1990) urge more involvement by Asian and Pacific Islander health professionals, researchers, and community activists in one-on-one encounters, realizing that acceptance of new ideas comes slowly and depends on trust relationships. Television educational campaigns also have high potential for effective communication, because this is the most popular source of information for many new citizens who may not be able to read or even have a written language, such as the Mien and the Hmong. But programming must be culturally sensitive and linguistically specific. Media educators must engage the concerns of Asian and Pacific Islander communities and not just use a "token" Asian representative. They must also go beyond the "model Asian" myth of the family who is highly self-sufficient and skilled and understand that many families are struggling with limited resources, a

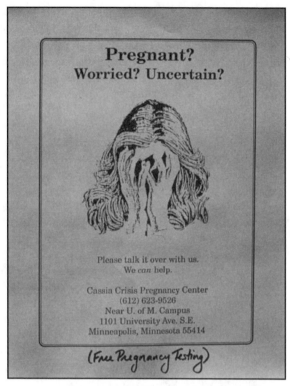

Competent health educators respond to clients' needs with empathy and active listening, as well as accurate information.

very different language and way of life, and possibly a traumatic past that would make them afraid to trust "outsiders."

African American culture groups. In a 1997 national survey of high school students, approximately 61% of all high school seniors reported having engaged in sexual intercourse at least once. This is a drop of 9% from 1990 survey figures. Yet among African American youth, the percentages actually increased by 1%, to 73% (Annie E. Casey Foundation, 1998). The risk factor for this culture's youth is further increased by the number who live in poverty situations: some 41.9% of all African American families, as compared with a rate of 35.2% for Latino families and 14% for Whites (Columbia School of Public Health, 1996). The National Adolescent Sexuality Training Center and the Children's Aid Society of New York surveyed 200 Harlem youth who were involved in their comprehensive sexuality education program. Three-fourths did not live with both their mother and father, and one-fifth did not live with either parent. Twenty-two percent have been homeless. Thirty percent were born to teen mothers (Carrera, 1995).

Programs designed for African American youth must take into account the high-risk contexts and the hopelessness that results, as well as cultural norms and values. Consider the example of AIDS prevention programs. Currently, the incidence of AIDS and the death rate because of it is 10 times higher among African Americans than among Whites. Smith (1999) notes that part of the problem has been misinformation: The disease was originally seen as a White gay disease, so Black communities took few precautions. This was especially true in heterosexual relationships. Furthermore, many young African American males still view condoms as a challenge to their manhood (Smith, 1999).

Several recent program designs have addressed these issues and have statistically monitored immediate and long-term effects. The Harlem project model is a unique, intensive, and comprehensive preventive model approach. Program participants are involved in the program's activities for years on a regular, daily basis. Components include the Job Club and Career Awareness; Family Life and Sex Education; Medical and Health Services; Mental Health Services; Academic Services and Homework Help; Self-Esteem Through the Performing Arts; and Lifetime Individual Sports. Most participants record 20 or more contacts with the program per month. Outcomes on measures of educational achievement and aspiration, substance abuse, parental involvement, and rates of sexual activity and contraceptive use indicate significantly higher achievements and much lower rates of high-risk behavior for program participants.

"Although abstinence is emphasized throughout all program activities as the most desirable behavior for young people, some make the personal choice to have intercourse, especially as they get older. Therefore, this program cannot accurately be called abstinence-based; rather it is based on the realities of the young people we serve" (Carrera, 1995).

The effectiveness of abstinence-based sexuality education versus a "safer-sex" condom education program for African American youth was compared recently, using a randomized controlled trial study with middle school students in Philadelphia, Pennsylvania (Jemmott, Jemmott, & Fong, 1998). This study used a vastly different approach: a short-term, one-day program, focusing on cognitive-behavioral intervention. The researchers compared the short- and long-term results of an abstinence approach that stressed delaying sexual intercourse or reducing its frequency and that was not fear based (a definite turnoff for this culture group) with those of a safer-sex intervention that emphasized sexual responsibility and condom use. A control group intervention concerned health issues unrelated to sexual behavior. Both adults and peers were used as cofacilitators to test leadership model effectiveness. Learning activities were designed to be educational but also entertaining and culturally sensitive. Many had been previously tested for successful response with other inner-city African American adolescents. Each intervention incorporated the "Be proud! Be responsible!" theme that emphasized personal and community esteem and considerations of future goals and consequences. After surveying the program participants at 3-, 6-, and 12-month intervals, the researchers concluded that the safer-sex strategy may hold the most promise, particularly with those adolescents who are already sexually experienced (Jemmott et al., 1998).

Samuels (1995) also noted that educational models that place emphasis on social norms and commitment to social responsibilities are more appealing to African American students and encourage responsible sexual behaviors. This contrasts with models that emphasize individualistic rational reasoning and/or a health belief model. For many African Americans who grow up in contexts of severely limited resources, sexual expression becomes a source of power that leads to a more positive sense of self and a bond to the community at large (Samuels, 1995). Therefore, the typical educational models that emphasize individualistic, direct, rational behavioral decisions do not work well with African American youth. The evaluation results of the innovative models presented here seem to bear that out. McAdoo (1993) reiterated the impact that economic inequality has had on African American families. This poverty factor has contributed to an unfavorable depiction of the culture that fails to recognize the strong resilience and cooperative nature of African American communities. When middle-class Black and White families are compared, many of the stereotypical differences fall away.

EVALUATING EFFECTIVENESS

Whereas the effectiveness of most educational programs is proven by learners' scores on written tests, family life education programs are typically designed to alter behaviors and attitudes as well as increase knowledge of facts and consequences. The vast majority of well-designed programs do indeed show significant knowledge increase by the learners. They have also been found to clarify values, increase parent-child communication, and help young people delay the initiation of sexual intercourse. Additionally, they may increase the use of contraception and condoms by sexually active participants while not encouraging young people to begin intercourse or to increase the frequency of sexual activity (Frost & Forrest, 1995; Grunseit & Kippax, 1993; Kirby et al., 1994; Moore, 1995; Powell & Jorgensen, 1985).

Behavior and attitude changes are more difficult and elusive goals. They are also much harder to assess. Self-reporting by participants is often unreliable, because many persons will report socially desirable answers to questions about their attitudes and behaviors. This is particularly true in the area of sexuality education evaluation, in which topics are often very personal and embarrassing for some participants. Many schools and communities do not want personal behavior questions included on assessments. And yet the great majority of sexuality education programs have been designed with the hope that they will change attitudes and prevent high-risk behaviors that lead to early pregnancy or sexually transmitted diseases.

Another major problem with evaluating effectiveness of sexuality education programs is how to statistically control for outside influences such as peer values and the media, which are especially pervasive in the area of sexual behavior and decision making. And because the act of conception involves two people, the ultimate outcome of a pregnancy prevention program will be affected by the attitudes and behavior of the program participant's partner, who often does not participate in the program.

Additionally, the level of rigor that constitutes valid scientific research is very expensive, time-consuming, and difficult to implement. Kirby (1997) lists the key components of rigorous evaluation:

- A sufficient number of participants
- Random assignment to experimental and control groups
- Long-term follow-up
- Appropriate statistical analyses
- Use of independent evaluators
- Replication of successful programs
- Reporting of both positive and negative results

Because very few programs have had the resources to conduct such rigorous evaluation, definite conclusions about program effectiveness cannot be made. Nevertheless, enough programs have now been conducted with some level of valid evaluation and published information that sexuality education researchers can draw conclusions based on reasonably strong evidence of effectiveness or ineffectiveness. In the case of some program designs, insufficient evidence exists to make a judgment of effectiveness or ineffectiveness, and further study needs to be done.

Recognizing these constraints, a 1996 symposium of prominent researchers in sexuality education and pregnancy prevention programs identified the following common characteristics of effective programs:

1. Using a theoretical model for behavior change
2. Targeting specific behaviors
3. Providing information about the risks of unprotected sexual intercourse and how to reduce risk
4. Providing opportunities for student input and interaction; practicing communication and negotiation skills and discussing situations that are realistic and meaningful
5. Addressing the influence of media, peers, and culture on teens' sexual behaviors and decisions
6. Developing and reinforcing beliefs and values among students that support their decisions to be abstinent and/or to protect themselves (Haffner & Goldfarb, 1997)

A review of research by Miller (1998) stressed the value of parent involvement in program design, reinforcement by community and religious programs, and addressing socioeconomic and cultural factors that may intervene in what would otherwise be a successful program. The "bottom line" is that reducing adolescent pregnancy is possible, but challenging (Kirby, 1997). Programs that focus on only a small number of sexual beliefs or skills or even on access to contraception are not likely to have a dramatic effect on pregnancy rates.

Based on a study of program evaluation designs and constraints, the symposium participants made the following recommendations regarding evaluation (Haffner & Goldfarb, 1997):

- Doing no evaluation is better than doing a bad evaluation
- Rigorous outcome evaluations are appropriate only after a program has been successfully implemented for a period of years

- Evaluations must be consistent with the expressed goals of the program and the course content
- Evaluations of comprehensive sexuality education should go beyond measuring changes in whether young people are having intercourse or whether they are using contraceptives
- Evaluations of school-based sexuality education should focus on changes in knowledge, attitudes, and skills. Be cautious about measuring outcomes outside the classroom
- Simple programs should be evaluated by simple measures; complex outcome measures on behavior change should be reserved for multiyear, intensive strategies
- There is a need for new instruments to measure the sexual health objective
- Qualitative methods are an important supplement to quantitative methods

SUMMARY

There is no doubt that more sexuality education is desired by youth, parents, and other adults for a variety of reasons, both personally enhancing and preventative. Yet, although the majority of parents want age-appropriate, comprehensive public school programs for their children, attempts to incorporate new programs face several barriers. Strong opposition from a vocal minority in the community often intimidates school administrators, who would rather ignore the need than risk the public spotlight. Most school programs currently have a very narrow focus: most prominently on AIDS/HIV prevention education or abstinence-only education. The lack of trained teachers also hampers program effectiveness, even though sexuality education is now mandated in four out of five states. Fortunately, other community and religious groups can and do address a wider range of topics and offer programming for parents and for parents and teens. Because parents' attitudes and involvement with their children have proven to be a major factor in curbing high-risk adolescent behavior, these programs hold great promise for community education, a major domain of family life educators.

Increased understanding of the distinctive learning styles and values of various culture groups increases program effectiveness. The results stress the importance of incorporating culturally relevant ideas and educational styles into program designs and identifying more indigenous leaders to seek training in family life education.

After some five decades of research refinement, effective evaluation of programs is now better understood. The ability to draw conclusions about characteristics that effective programs have in common will provide valuable assistance to program designers in the future.

Questions/Problems for Discussion and Review

Class Discussion

1. In public school programs, how should administrators determine what subjects and value approaches to cover?

2. How can family life educators promote nonschool programs and culturally diverse programs of sexuality education in the community? What can boost your confidence to conduct such programs?

3. Look at figure 9.1. Are there areas of sexual experience that Dailey has failed to include? Why and how do contexts of the family and society impact each of the overlapping circles of sexual expression?

Research Problems

1. What research has been done on the effectiveness of parent-teen programs? What areas seem to show the most improvement?

2. Using the values articulated in box 9.1, develop and administer a questionnaire to several diverse audiences to assess their level of agreement with the statements. Write a report of your findings.

Case Study Design

Divide the class into several groups, each representing a board of education. Assign a person in each group to represent one of the following: a member of one of two different ethnic minority groups, a religiously conservative person, a bank vice president, a parent whose child was molested at a school playground, a member of Planned Parenthood, a young teacher in the school system, and a veteran school nurse. Each board has the task of determining the level of comprehensiveness of sex education courses and programs in their school. How do they come to consensus?

ten

Education for Relationships and Marriage

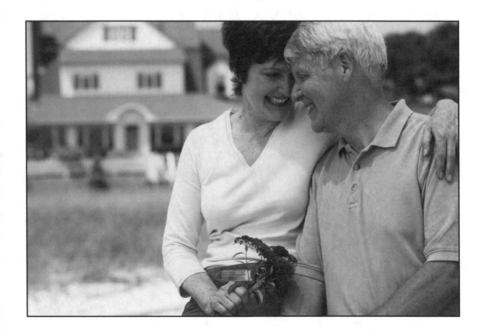

"For better or worse, marriage hits a low." This headline appeared in the July 2, 1999, *Washington Post* (Fletcher, 1999). The article cited a publication from Rutgers University's 1999 National Marriage Project (NMP) that reported the nation's marriage rate had dropped by 43% since 1960. The 1996 rate of 49.7 marriages per 1,000 unmarried women was the lowest in recorded history. Ten years later, the unprecedented decline continues. In 2004, the marriage rate plunged to 39.9 (Whitehead & Popenoe, 2005).

Although Americans still hope for long-term marriages, researchers report that increasing numbers of young people, particularly women, are skeptical about finding a lasting marriage partner. Many young people are far more accepting of alternatives to marriage, including cohabitation and single parenthood (NCHS/CDC, 2002; see tables 10.1 and 10.2).

"Young people today want successful marriages, but they are increasingly pessimistic about their chances of achieving that goal," commented Barbara Dafoe Whitehead, codirector of the NMP (Fletcher, 1999). Young people have good reason to be pessimistic about marriage. Although the divorce rate in the United States has declined slightly but steadily since the late 1980s, it has risen more than 30% since 1970 (National Center for Health Statistics, 1996; see table 10.3). A young person entering marriage today is projected to have only a 50% chance of avoiding divorce. More disconcerting, Norval Glenn, a sociologist at the University of Texas, estimates that only about 25% of couples in first marriages are still together and happy after the first 10 years (Glenn, 1991).

Table 10.1   Percentage of High School Seniors Who Agreed or Mostly Agreed with the Statement: "It Is Usually a Good Idea for a Couple to Live Together Before Getting Married in Order to Find Out Whether They Really Get Along"

Year	Boys	Girls
1976–1980	44.9	32.3
1981–1985	47.4	36.5
1986–1990	57.8	45.2
1991–1995	60.5	51.3
1996–2000	65.7	59.1
2001–2004	64.1	57.0

Number of respondents for each sex for each period is about 6,000 except for 2001–2004, for which it is about 4,500. The overall trend is significantly upward for both girls and boys ($p < .01$ on a two-tailed test).

Source: Monitoring the Future surveys conducted by the Survey Research Center at the University of Michigan.

Reprinted from http://marriage.rutgers.edu/Publications (2006 *State of the Unions* Report). Used with permission.

Table 10.2
Number of Cohabiting, Unmarried, Adult Couples of the Opposite Sex, by Year, United States, per 1,000

Year	Number
1960	0.439
1970	0.523
1980	1.589
1990	2.856
2000	4.736
2004	5.080

Source: U. S. Bureau of the Census, Current Population Reports, Series P20-537; America's Families and Living Arrangements: March 2000; and U. S. Bureau of the Census, Population Division, Current Population Survey, 2004 Annual Social and Economic Supplement (http://www.census.gov/population/socdemo/hh-fam/cps2004).

Table 10.3   Number of Divorces per 1,000 Married Women Age 15 and Older, by Year, United States

Year	Divorces
1960	9.2
1965	10.6
1970	14.9
1975	20.3
1980	22.6
1985	21.7
1990	20.9
1995	19.8
2000	18.8
2004	17.7

We have used the number of divorces per 1,000 married women age 15 and older, rather than the Crude Divorce Rate of divorces per 1,000 population to help avoid the problem of compositional changes in the population. Even this more refined measure is somewhat susceptible to compositional changes.

Source: Statistical Abstract of the United States, 2001, Page 87, Table 117; National Vital Statistics Reports, August 22, 2001; California Current Population Survey Report: 2000, Table 3, March 2001; Births, Marriages, Divorces, and Deaths: Provisional Data for 2004, National Vital Statistics Report 53:21, June 26, 2005, Table 3, (http://www.cdc.gov/nchs/data/nvsr53/nvsr53_21.pdf) and calculations by the National Marriage Project for the US less California, Georgia, Hawaii, Indiana, Louisiana and Oklahoma using the Current Population Surveys, 2004.

THE NEED FOR RELATIONSHIP AND MARRIAGE EDUCATION

If we as a society value marriage, and the NMP report suggests that we do, then we must find ways to better prepare people of all ages to build successful relationships that sustain long-term happy marriages. According to the NMP report, "Marriage is weakening but it is too soon to write the obituary" (National Marriage Project, 1999, p. 15). One of the reasons for hope offered by the researchers is that a marriage education movement seems to be emerging among marriage therapists, family life educators, schoolteachers, and clergy. An example of this movement is the Smart Marriages: Happy Families conferences sponsored annually by the Coalition for Marriage, Family, and Couples Education. Recent conferences have drawn hundreds of mental health professionals and more than 300 clergy, educators, and government policy makers, as well as a host of reporters from such media outlets as CNN, *USA Today*, *Time*, and the *Washington Post*. Diane Sollee, founder of the coalition, says the work she and her colleagues are doing represents a marriage and family education movement:

It's an optimistic, cost-effective approach to reversing the epidemic of divorce and family breakdown. The idea in founding the coalition was to put marriage education on the map. I thought there was a whole body of knowledge that wasn't getting out there. The threatening thing [to some therapists] is that we've known for 20 years that you don't have to be a behavioral health provider to teach marriage education. ("Special Report," 1999)

This report points out that Smart Marriages: Happy Families is not antitherapy, but it does explore educational alternatives to therapy. Behind most of these approaches is the basic premise that if couples can master basic skills that are present in good marriages—communicating effectively, resolving conflicts, and being good friends—they can work on building healthy marriages. Howard Markman, a leading marriage researcher and cofounder of the marriage course Prevention and Relationship Enhancement Program (PREP), has found that clergy and laypeople may actually be more successful than therapists in helping troubled couples. Couples struggling with their marriages do not frequently see therapists, but they do see other professionals in the community. Markman found that couples trained by clergy and lay leaders had more positive communication skills after training than did those trained by marriage counselors at the University of Denver (Markman, as cited in "Special Report," 1999).

The federal government also entered the arena of marriage promotion in an unprecedented way in 1996 when the Healthy Marriage Initiative was established by a congressional decision to fund marriage promotion projects in all states (Administration for Children and Families, 2006). According to its mission statement, the initiative is meant "to help couples, who have chosen marriage for themselves, gain greater access to marriage education services, on a voluntary basis, where they can acquire the skills and knowledge necessary to form and sustain a healthy marriage" (p. 2). The report defines a "healthy marriage" as having two common characteristics: It is mutually beneficial to both spouses and children (if present) and it is committed to ongoing growth through use of effective communication skills and conflict management skills. A full discussion of the goals and activities can be found on the Administration for Children and Families Web site (www.acf.hhs.gov). A comprehensive menu of options for writing and presenting on marriage education is also offered on the Web site of the National Healthy Marriage Resource Center (NHMRC) (www.healthymarriageinfo.com). Links direct visitors to general topics of marriage education, community action, research and trends, policies and laws, multimedia, conferences and events, and free downloads.

Today's youth remain optimistic about the future of their own marriage relationships. *Monitoring the Future,* a national representative survey, has collected data from high school seniors since 1976 (Whitehead & Popenoe, 2005). A high percentage of teens, both female (84%) and male (78%), continue to agree with the statement that "a good marriage and family life was *extremely important*" to them (see table 10.4). A recent study stresses the economic advantage to being—and staying—married. Married people accumulate financial resources 93% faster than single or divorced persons, and when persons divorce, they lose on average three-fourths of their personal net worth (Ohlemacher, 2006).

Table 10.4   Percentage of High School Seniors Who Said Having a Good Marriage and Family Life Is "Extremely Important"

Year	Boys	Girls
1976–1980	69.4	80.2
1981–1985	69.0	81.3
1986–1990	69.7	81.9
1991–1995	72.0	83.2
1996–2000	72.9	82.1
2001–2004	70.2	82.1

Number of respondents for each sex for each period is about 6,000 except for the 2001–2004 period for which it is about 4,500. The trend for both boys and girls is statistically significant (p <.05 on a two-tailed test).

Source: Monitoring the Future surveys conducted by the Survey Research Center at the University of Michigan.

Reprinted from http://marriage.rutgers.edu/Publications (2006 *State of the Unions* Report). Used with permission.

HISTORY OF RELATIONSHIP AND MARRIAGE EDUCATION

Stahmann and Salts (1993) report that historically four approaches have been developed to educate people for marriage: generalized educational programs, premarital counseling, enrichment programs, and marital and premarital therapy. Marriage enrichment and premarital counseling programs in which education is the primary objective are the central focus of this chapter. General marriage preparation programs differ widely due to the varying developmental age levels of the participants and are more academic in nature than are marriage enrichment and premarital counseling. Therapy is not generally considered to be a function of family life education; consequently, marital and premarital therapy are not addressed.

Education for marriage is not a new idea. Stahmann and Salts (1993) report that the first formal marital education program was instituted in the early 1930s, when the Merrill-Palmer Institute established a premarital educational program. Mudd, Freeman, and Rose (1941) report that a premarital counseling program was in existence at the Philadelphia Marriage Council at least as early as 1941. The program was designed to provide education and information about marriage to couples planning to be married and to help them work through interpersonal problems. For more than 50 years general marriage preparation content has been available in high school family life education courses and in colleges through departments of family studies, sociology, and psychology and more recently through adult education courses and extension programs (Stahmann & Salts, 1993). Although some courses are becoming more experiential and skill based, in the past they were primarily didactic. For the most part, they were taken by women and often stressed traditional male and female roles. Most were designed to teach about marriage rather than provide education for marriage.

David and Vera Mace were strong advocates of education for marriage. Pioneers in the development of marriage counseling, the Maces established marriage counseling programs on several continents. After coming to the United States from England in the 1950s, the couple served as joint executive directors of the American Association of Marriage Counselors, now the American Association of Marriage and Family Therapists (AAMFT). After a long career of trying to rehabilitate relationships through therapy, the Maces in frustration concluded that an army of marriage therapists could not turn back the tide of divorces occurring in the United States in the 1960s and 1970s. David Mace raised the question, "Could not all young people be trained to perform these operations [interpersonal skills] competently before they marry?" (Mace, 1982, p. 189).

Mace pointed out that young people in our society already spend a major portion of their lives in compulsory education acquiring knowledge intended to make their later lives productive and rewarding. "If it is important that young people be qualified for their future vocations, is it not equally important that they be qualified for their future roles as founders of families?" (Mace, 1982, p. 186).

Mace (1982) recalls an observation by an anthropologist friend who spent many years studying a West African tribe. The anthropologist noted how different the educational system of tribal people is from that of "civilized" societies. Tribal people tend to carefully teach their children about the art of living and cultural traditions and leave them to pick up information about the outside world on their own. By contrast, so-called civilized people spend most of their education on providing information about the external world and leave children to pick up living skills on their own.

Although Mace had spent many years as a classroom lecturer, he reluctantly concluded that the classroom offered limited opportunity for effective marriage and family life education (Mace, 1982). He argued that the key to better marriage was acquiring "interpersonal competencies," or basic relationship skills such as communication, anger management, and conflict resolution. Essential relationship skills such as these cannot be developed simply by hearing about them or in two or three easy lessons. Mace's alternative to the classroom was to teach these interpersonal skills to couples in small groups using experiential learning methods. He called the approach *marriage enrichment*. We look at this particular approach later in this chapter.

PREVENTIVE VERSUS REMEDIAL APPROACHES

Over the past 30 years there has been a proliferation of programs to prevent the breakdown of marriage relationships (Berger & Hannah, 1999; Dyer & Dyer, 2003; Guerney, Brock, & Coufal, 1986; L'Abate, 1981; Mace, 1983; Olson, 1976; Stanley, Blumberg, & Markman, 1999). Many family researchers have struggled to define the differences between approaches designed to prevent relationship distress and those designed to repair seriously damaged relationships. Berger and Hannah (1999) point out that preventive programs for couples, married and unmarried, have appeared under different titles throughout the years. Prominent titles have included "family life education" (Groves & Groves, 1947), "marriage enrichment" (Mace & Mace, 1975), "relationship enhancement" (Guerney, 1977), "couples communication" (Miller, Nunnally, & Wackman, 1975), "skills/competence training" (L'Abate, 1986; Markman, Stanley, & Blumberg, 1994), and "psychoeducational programs" (Leveat, 1986). More recently, Olson (2006) has developed "marriage mentor training." Trained mentors provide one-on-one support to engaged and newlywed couples using the Prepare/Enrich inventory. A common thread in all of these programs is that they are preventive in nature. They are designed for couples whose relationships are not in crisis and who want to maximize the potential for relationship wellness in their marriages. *Remedial programs* are therapy programs aimed at dysfunctional couples whose relationship satisfaction has been compromised and the stability of the marriage undermined.

Berger and Hannah (1999) describe *preventive programs* as being based on the strengths of couples rather than on pathology. They employ psychoeducational or skill competency models and are: cognitive, experiential, structured, programmatic, time limited, affirmative, relatively economical, and primarily small group oriented. In contrast, remedial or therapy models are less structured, nonprogrammatic, minimally didactic, more confrontational, open ended, and much more costly.

During the past decade or two, programs with an educational orientation have been integrated into remedial approaches to couples therapy so that it is now difficult to establish a clear demarcation between prevention, enrichment, and therapy. Berger and Hannah (1999) conclude that the best way to view the commonalities between preventive and remedial programs is to see them as falling at different points along a continuum of interventions.

Levels of Prevention

L'Abate (1983) has been one of the strongest advocates of preventive approaches to helping couples avoid marital breakdown. He argues that prevention is cheaper, more innovative, easier, happier, and cleaner, and he has called for prevention and those who practice it to be raised to the same status as practitioners of remedial approaches. Berger and Hannah (1999) document an even stronger rationale for preventive programs. They cite longitudinal studies that demonstrate that early premarital and marital conflict is a major risk factor for future marital dysfunction and that once negative patterns become entrenched it is difficult to eradicate them.

L'Abate (1983) applied three historical levels of prevention—primary, secondary, and tertiary—to couples programs. Primary prevention programs intervene with couples before they experience difficulties. An example of this level is a program for the parents of entering college freshmen that two CFLEs have facilitated at Baylor University for the past 20 years. The purpose of the program is to help parents deal with the transition to the empty nest and the resulting changes in parenting and marital interaction. Most premarital counseling programs, such as Prepare/Enrich (Olson & Olson, 1999) and the Saving Your Marriage Before It Starts (SYMBIS) model (Parrott & Parrott, 1999), also fit into this category in that they are designed to identify potential relationship problems and to provide early intervention in the transition to marriage.

Secondary prevention involves interventions with couples "at risk": couples who are already experiencing some degree of relationship distress. Programs at this level are designed to prevent further loss of satisfaction and to increase friendship and intimacy. Gottman and Gottman's (1999) Marriage Survival Kit workshop and the PREP program developed by Stanley, Blumberg, and Markman (1999) are examples of this level of program, although neither program screens couples. Most marriage enrichment programs are aimed at "healthy couples," but many participants actually need secondary prevention.

Tertiary level programs are designed to keep serious relationship problems from getting worse and leading to separation. Such programs are more likely to be carried out by trained therapists and not by family life educators. Most family life education programs address levels 1 and 2, but identifying which couples are best served by levels 1, 2, or 3 is beyond the scope of L'Abate's typology.

Berger and Hannah (1999) include 13 preventive approaches in their recent work, none of which claims to be directed toward couples at level 3. In only 1 of the 13 is it claimed that couples are carefully screened (L'Abate, 1999). The others are open to all couples without screening. Mace (1983) concluded that preventive approaches overlap and cannot be precisely distinguished from one another, and Berger and Hannah (1999) concluded that distinctions are somewhat artificial.

Obstacles to Prevention

If educational approaches to relationship competence have so many advantages, why then are they not more popular? What is it that blocks couples from taking advantage of programs designed to improve their relationship before they begin to experience relationship-threatening problems? Clark Vincent's concept of the *myth of naturalism* (Vincent, 1973) sheds some light on these questions. The myth of naturalism asserts that people are born with all the knowledge and skill necessary to have successful relationships. Successful marital relationships should come naturally and effortlessly to normal adults. Anyone who has difficulty in relationships, then, must be inadequate. Consequently, participating in a communication course or attending a marriage enrichment event is admitting that one is in some way defective. Even if the myth had been true in the past, when marriages were more institutional in nature, it would not be true today, when the marital bond is so clearly dependent on a couple having the interpersonal competencies essential to maintaining a passionate friendship.

Mace & Mace (1976) coined the term *intermarital taboo* as a further explanation of why couples do not take advantage of preventive programs. The intermarital taboo says, "as a married couple, you shall not reveal to other married couples what is going on inside your marriage" (p. 329). The intermarital taboo is based on the concept of privatism, which refers to cultural attitudes that declare that anything that occurs within the family is too private to be shared outside the family. This belief might have been functional when large extended families were the norm and there were many family members around to discuss issues. Most families today, however, are nuclear and tend to be more isolated. For these couples, practicing privatism is like shutting themselves in a box. It prevents them from seeking marriage preparation or help in figuring out how to relate to each other in mutually satisfying ways. Privatism also fosters the idea that "other couples must be perfect [after all, they look and act perfect in public], so we must be the only ones having a problem with this issue." In designing educational programs for marriage, both the myth of naturalism and the intermarital taboo must be overcome. This is especially true for programs that focus on couples' groups.

Berger and Hannah (1999) have identified an additional barrier to the use of preventive programs: the "if it ain't broke, don't fix it" motto:

> The most obvious and perhaps formidable barrier involves the couple's motivation to change. Attempting to prevent future distress in nondistressed couples creates an inherent paradox: Because preventive programs are geared toward at-risk couples who have not yet developed significant relationship problems, what would motivate such couples to pursue and invest in preventive programs? (p. 9)

Marriage enrichment leaders, in promoting marriage enrichment programs, have frequently heard potential participants comment, "If my marriage was any better, I couldn't stand it." This comment illustrates the motivation problem in recruiting participants to preventive relationship and marriage education programs. One response to such a comment is, "That's great! We need you to come and share your secrets of success with the other couples." Such a comment attacks both the motivation issue and the intermarital taboo.

Another strategy is to link relationship education programs to life cycle transitions or to "teachable moments." The program for parents of entering college freshmen mentioned earlier would be an example of this strategy. The program is offered on move-in day during student orientation. The focus is on parenting the adult child and on the transition to the empty-nest stage. One certified leader couple in the Association for Couples in Marriage Enrichment (ACME) convinced the leaders of a hospital childbirth class to allow them to add three marriage sessions at the end of the usual series of classes. A parent educator suggests that several marriage enrichment sessions be added to parent education classes and that the participants then be moved into ongoing marriage support groups. In this case, the more threatening marriage education program is being linked to a less threatening and more acceptable family life education program.

PHILOSOPHIES, THEORIES, AND PROCESS

Relationship and marriage education programs vary widely, and to describe the philosophies and theoretical underpinnings of all would be impossible. The purpose of this section is to present the underlying philosophies and theories common to the majority of programs that have been described in the professional literature.

Philosophies

The common philosophical thread among these programs is their educational and preventive nature. Guerney (1977) and Hof and Miller (1981) describe programs based on an educational model as those that teach attitudes and specific skills in a structured and systematic fashion and that have clear behavioral objectives and appropriate evaluative measures included. Certainly not all relationship programs meet these standards, but all have an educational orientation, with the primary objective to prevent the emergence, development, or recurrence of interpersonal dysfunction (Hof & Miller, 1981).

Because of their educational nature and preventive focus, most marriage and relationship education programs use a core philosophy that is oriented toward growth and potential. This perspective sees people and relationships as possessing numerous untapped strengths and resources that can be developed. Hof and Miller (1981), describing marriage enrichment programs, elaborate:

> People are viewed as having a natural drive towards growth, health, and personal development. Given the appropriate environment people can learn how to choose and change behaviors and attitudes which will improve their interpersonal relationships, and allow them to experience increased satisfaction in life and in relationships with other people. (p. 8)

Emphasis on strengths or potential does not mean that conflictual issues are ignored. To the contrary, an emphasis on growth affirms that couples can learn to resolve the negatives in their relationship in positive and creative ways.

Mace and Mace (1976) did not use the term *enrichment* to mean the provision of additives from the outside, as in "vitamin-enriched" bread. Enrichment is something that comes from within the couple's relationship. They believe the emphasis on growth and potential best communicates the idea that in each marital dyad there exists an inherent capacity for mutual fulfillment and development, which in most instances remains largely untapped. The Maces believe that in many cases marriages end in divorce because couples are unable to access these resources. It follows, then, that marriage education programs designed to help actualize relationship potential not only prevent some marriages from failing but also improve the quality of many mediocre but stable unions in which interpersonal relationships have never gone beyond a superficial level (Mace & Mace, 1976).

The concept of the "companionship family" has influenced the thinking behind many marriage education programs. In the late 1940s Burgess identified a new form of the family emerging in the United States that he called the *companionship model* of the family (Burgess, Locke, & Thomas, 1971). He contrasted this new model with the traditional model, which he called the "institutional model." The institutional model is seen as rigid and patriarchal, with a hierarchical role structure. The companionship model is relationship driven and characterized by intimacy, equality, democratic decision making, and flexible role structure. The institutional model's unity and strength come from traditional rules and regulations, specified duties and obligations, and community support. Unity in the companionship model depends on the internal cohesiveness of its interpersonal relationships rather than the external coercion of custom and community opinion.

Unfortunately, many of the factors in the companionship marriage that make it appealing also make it less stable and more vulnerable to divorce. Many people in marriages with companionship expectations lack the interpersonal skills necessary to sustain a marriage based primarily on relational characteristics such as mutual affection, sympathetic understanding, comradeship, and mutual respect. As much as a couple may want a marriage based on a loving companionate relationship with a passionate best friend, few actually have the skills to make it work (Dyer & Dyer, 1999). The minimum skills needed are:

- A commitment to individual, relationship, and partner growth
- A means of communication that leads to understanding
- The ability to use conflict to stimulate creative change
- The ability to create and maintain intimacy

Mace (1982) identified the first three of these skills as a couple's primary coping system. The fourth was added by contemporary practitioners in recognition of the importance of intimacy in relationships (Dyer & Dyer, 1989). Most marriage education programs today address one or a combination of these essentials. Hof and Miller (1981) maintain that the ultimate goal and underlying value of most marriage enrichment programs is the attainment and maintenance of an intentional companionship marriage.

The majority of marriage and relationship education programs use a group format. Some, however, are offered to a single couple, and some use both an individual and group format. For example, the Couple Communication Program (Miller & Sherrard, 1999) can be used with a single couple or a group of couples. Prepare/Enrich: Version 2000 (Olson & Olson, 1999), a premarital counseling program for individual couples, is also offered in a group format called Growing Together (Olson, Dyer, & Dyer, 1998).

Interaction among couples is central to the philosophy of many programs. One way to overcome the intermarital taboo is to provide a safe environment in which couples can share relationship experiences. Interaction occurs at three levels: from the leader to the total group, among couples in the group, and between the partners in the couple. The degree to which this interaction occurs varies among programs. In ACME-style marriage enrichment, couple leaders openly discuss their marriage with the couples in the group and encourage the other couples to do the same (Dyer & Dyer, 1999). By contrast, marriage encounter, another approach to marriage enrichment, limits interaction among couples in the group but encourages a high level of interaction among partners (Elin, 1999). In all cases the hope is that couples will become comfortable communicating positively with each other and will continue the practice at home.

Theories

Stahmann and Salts (1993) stress the importance of basing family life education on a strong scholarly foundation, an approach that requires current theoretical and empirical knowledge and application. Unfortunately, few creators of marriage and relationship education programs explicitly document their research or theoretical base. Significant exceptions to this general statement include two early programs, Guerney's (1977) Relationship Enhancement (Rogerian, social learning, and interpersonal) and Miller, Nunnally, and Wackman's (1975) Couple Communication Program (communication systems). These programs were exemplary in clearly identifying their theoretical bases. Three more recent programs with strong scholarly foundations are John Gottman's Marriage Survival Kit (Gottman & Gottman, 1999), based on his 25 years of research at the University of Washington; the PREP program (Markman, Stanley, & Blumberg, 1994; Stanley et al., 1999), based on research at the University of Denver; and the Prepare/Enrich inventory (Olson & Olson, 1999), which also has a strong research base and has been subjected to numerous reliability and validity studies.

Berger and Hannah (1999) compared preventive approaches on seven dimensions, including theoretical bases. Six of the programs identified their theoretical base as eclectic, including in some form humanistic, systems, and empiricistic theories. Cognitive-behavioral theory was the most frequently cited single theory (seven times), followed closely by learning theory (five times). Others included religious mentoring, religious reflective sacramental, self-psychology, Adlerian, communication systems, Rogerian, Bowenian systems, and object relations theories.

Humanistic psychology and Rogerian psychotherapy have had a strong influence on the development of marriage education and particularly on the marriage enrichment movement (Hof & Miller, 1981). Important concepts in marriage, such as the emphasis on the emotional life and the expression of feelings, the importance of interpersonal relations on personal well-being and the need to create effective relationships, and fulfilling personal and couple potential, are contributions from these theoretical traditions (Guerney, 1977). Marriage education programs generally attempt to create a safe and empathic environment in which participants can freely express feelings, experience acceptance from spouse and others, and acquire new knowledge and skills with a low personal-risk factor. Doing this often employs Rogerian techniques, such as leader congruence, modeling respect, and complete acceptance of participants.

Because relationships are the focus of marriage education programs, all programs owe some debt to systems theory. Bertalanffy (1950) defined a system as any whole with interacting parts. The system concept, that relationships are not static but dynamic living entities that strive to balance stability and change, is central to relationship education programs. "System properties and principles provide a framework for understanding relationship development and dysfunction" (Miller & Sherrard, 1999, p. 127).

The majority of the programs reviewed by Berger and Hannah emphasize communication. Most programs, then, incorporate some form of communication systems theory. Many have relied on the work of Miller, Nunnally, and Wackman (1975), the originators of the Minnesota Couple Communication Program, now known as Couple Communication. Miller and his colleagues, drawing on the earlier works of Virginia Satir, Don Jackson, Paul Watzlawick, and Sidney Jourard, created an integrated, systematic approach to interpersonal communication that is highly teachable.

Attitudinal change and skill development are key objectives in relationship education. To accomplish this, family life educators have drawn on social learning theory, behavior modification theory, and cognitive-behavioral theory. Marriage educators believe couples can learn new patterns of interaction and correct deficiencies in social learning. New communication and conflict resolution skills can be taught and learned.

"Deficiencies in social learning are thus viewed as important components in relationship discord, and the learning and continued practice of appropriate skills is viewed as an important component in marital and relationship health" (Hof & Miller, 1981, p. 17). Modeling, behavior rehearsal, prompting, and reinforcement

Couple dialog is a key to intentional growth and marital enrichment.

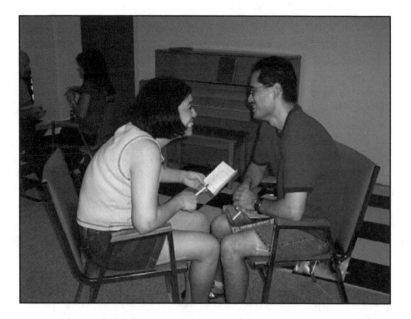

are frequently used techniques in marriage education. They reflect behavior modification approaches that incorporate social learning theory. Marriage educators have also recognized the importance of reeducation in the area of attitudes and other cognitive functions. Many programs are based on the cognitive-behavioral tradition of change:

> Therefore, the focus is on ways of thinking (attitudes and expectations) and behaving (communication and conflict management) that are associated with marital success and failure. The skills-oriented approach rests on the assumption that couples can learn new behaviors that can help them prevent the deterioration in relationship quality commonly seen in marriage. (Stanley et al., 1999, p. 280)

Experiential learning models are used extensively in relationship and marriage education programs. Experiential learning is based on the assumption that people learn best by doing. The underlying premise is that experience precedes learning and that involved learning is more potent than vicarious learning. Much of what has been done in the past in family life education has depended on didactic methods and vicarious learning. This kind of information exchange may be effective for some types of knowledge and may change behavior in some areas of life, but it has very limited value in behavioral change in the area of interpersonal relationships. Most therapists long ago gave up on advice giving as an effective means of producing behavior change. Behavior change in interpersonal relations is more likely to occur when learning is a dynamic process in which learners are active participants. This method requires leaders to use techniques that actively involve couples in experiencing new situations, experimenting with new methods, and practicing new skills (Dyer & Dyer, 1989).

Process

The dynamics of group process provide an environment in which experiential learning can take place. Didactic learning is passive; experiential learning is active. Listening to a lecture or watching a film allows learners to remain anonymous and not risk vulnerability. Experiential learning, on the other hand, always requires some risk. Used effectively, group process encourages and supports the learner's ventures into new territory. It is a vehicle of affirmation of new discoveries that provides immediate reinforcement for behavior change. The focus of such programs is on the relationship.

Group process takes on an additional dimension when working with relationship and marriage education programs designed for groups of couples. Leaders must keep in mind that they are dealing with a group of relationships, as well as with individuals. These relationships have a past and a future. The partners are connected to each other in a systemic arrangement that makes it inevitable that change in one partner requires corresponding change in techniques that primarily focus attention on the relationship itself. Maintaining this balance is essential. The relationship cannot grow without corresponding individual growth by both partners, but failing to keep the focus on the relationship risks disrupting the marital system the couple came to improve (Dyer & Dyer, 1989).

APPROACHES TO EDUCATION FOR RELATIONSHIPS AND MARRIAGE

The purpose of this section is to discuss in some depth two of the four types of approaches to education for relationships and marriage: marriage preparation and marriage enrichment. Marriage preparation, or premarital counseling, is designed to help couples before they marry to face marriage realistically and to identify and begin to address specific issues in their own relationships. "Marriage enrichment" is a generic term that refers to preventive programs designed to help couples in functioning marriages increase their relationship satisfaction and avoid marital breakdown.

Marriage Preparation

Marriage preparation, or premarital counseling, has existed in some form for a long time. Mudd and her associates (Mudd, Freeman, & Rose, 1941) at the Philadelphia Marriage Council are generally credited with creating the first program developed by family professionals. Unfortunately, their pioneering efforts did not catch on, and for the most part premarital counseling has been left to pastors and other ministers. Estimates are that in the United States ministers provide approximately 50% of all premarital counseling (Stahmann & Hiebert, 1987). In the past, many ministers were not well prepared for this part of the ministry and had little time to devote to working with couples considering marriage (Olson, 1983). Often preparation for marriage consisted of one or two meetings with the pastor just before the marriage. The content of the meetings focused mostly on planning the wedding and discussing the spiritual and religious aspects of marriage and included little or no education for marriage.

Premarital counseling started to change in the early 1980s, when researchers began to develop scientifically reliable and valid relationship assessment tools for premarital couples (for example, see Olson & Olson, 1999; Markey & Micheletto, 1997). These instruments allowed practitioners to give specific feedback to couples on the strengths and weak areas of their relationships and to focus their efforts on the troubling issues that are likely to create problems later in the marriage. Most of these inventories require some degree of training to be used, and some practitioners have incorporated the assessment tool into structured programs such as Prepare/Enrich: Version 2000 (Olson & Olson, 1999). Increasingly, ministers, family life educators, counselors, and therapists are taking advantage of this training and offering more premarital programs to couples. These programs can be a major intervention to help couples begin their marriages with adequate knowledge and skills to prevent future marital breakdown.

Premarital approaches with couples take many forms. Some are individualized and similar to traditional therapy, some are like classroom courses that depend primarily on lectures about marriage, and others are structured to some degree but focus on strengths and are skill-based and experiential in orientation. This section discusses the latter.

Premarital education programs are designed to encourage individuals planning to marry to take a serious look at marriage and at their relationship. The objectives of premarital education differ with various programs; however, all programs are preventive in nature. A primary goal is to enhance the premarital relationship so that the couple might develop a satisfying and stable marriage relationship and avoid marital dysfunction.

Couples seeking premarital education are taught interpersonal skills, such as communication and conflict resolution, to help them in the development of their marriage relationship. Premarital programs should offer an opportunity for couples to assess their strengths and growth areas and to identify potentially disruptive issues. Working together on their relationship may help some couples decide they should delay their marriage or not marry at all.

It is essential for couples to learn effective ways to deal with current issues so that these same skills can be used to attack those issues that occur after marriage. They need to learn that they can resolve issues more easily while they are small rather than allowing them to become major battlefields in their relationship. Premarital programs should attempt to help couples become aware of the potential issues in their relationships and to give them specific skills to resolve these issues.

An important component of premarital education is to alert couples to the idea that good relationships take time and energy (Olson, 1983). Many couples believe that you are just lucky if you have a good relationship. Others think that relationships will be satisfying if they are "in love." Premarital education begins the process of giving attention to the relationship and encourages couples to continue to do so into their marriages.

Content.   The topics covered in premarital education vary from program to program, but most give attention to the essentials of a healthy marriage identified earlier in this chapter: a commitment to growth as individuals and as a couple, a communication system that leads to understanding, the ability to resolve conflict creatively, and the ability to create and maintain intimacy (Dyer & Dyer, 1999). Research suggests that couples with satisfying, well-adjusted marriages have positive communication patterns that exhibit low levels of anger and resentment. They also have relatively low rates of arguing and communicate positive feelings more often than negative feelings, both before and after marriage (Kelly, Huston, & Cate, 1985; Markman, 1979, 1981). Emotional and sexual intimacy is an important component of contemporary companionship marriage and is expected by most couples. Most individuals want a "sexy best friend" as their marriage partner. Knowing how to create emotional and physical closeness in a long-term relationship is an important skill for couples anticipating marriage to learn.

Stahmann and Salts (1993) suggest that premarital education should focus on topics that research has connected to marital satisfaction (see box 10.1). In general, content should focus on education *for* marriage, not education *about* marriage. Skills should be demonstrated, and participants need to have ample opportunity to practice and become proficient in their use. Just talking about skills provides little help.

Formats.   Couples generally seek marriage preparation during their engagement, many times only a few weeks before their wedding. Couples marrying for the first time, as well as those who have been married previously, participate in

---

Box 10.1   Premarital Education Program Topics

The following list includes topics presented in marriage preparation programs that research has connected to marital satisfaction:

• Marriage as a commitment
• Family of origin and individual backgrounds
• Temperaments and personalities of partners
• Communication skills
• Role expectations
• Couple interaction patterns
• Conflict resolution
• Decision-making skills
• Financial resources and financial management skills
• Leisure and recreational interests
• Goals and expectations
• Sexuality and affection
• Children and parenting
• Religious or spiritual values and expectations
• Identifying relationship strengths
• Plans for wedding

premarital programs. In a survey of college students, Silliman and Schumm (1995) found a high interest in brief, high-quality, low-cost voluntary premarital programs led by well-trained professionals.

Some churches require a couple to have premarital preparation in order to be married in the church and by the minister. The Roman Catholic Church has such a requirement for all persons marrying in a Catholic church. The couple may choose individual sessions or participate in Engaged Encounter, a program sponsored by the church. In 1998, the state of Florida led the way in a new trend by establishing governmental support for premarital education. Currently, several states are considering similar policies that support premarital education by offering incentives such as reduced marriage license fees to couples who participate in a premarital program.

Programs are offered by a variety of individuals and groups. As noted previously, pastors have historically been the primary providers of marriage preparation, but more recently family life educators, counselors, and therapists have begun to engage in marriage education. Community agencies and organizations such as family service agencies, mental health clinics, community counseling centers, extension service groups, women's clubs, churches, and schools have provided the opportunity for couples to receive premarital education programs. Lay couples with good marriage relationships who are interested in helping other couples are a potential resource for premarital preparation leadership. With training, lay couples can teach relationship skills, as well as share from their marital experience. They may also serve as a useful resource and support for the couples as they enter their first year of marriage (Olson, 1983).

Premarital programs are offered in several formats. A number of programs are designed for individual couples. An individual couple may contract with a family life educator, marriage counselor, therapist, or pastor to receive premarital education. The sessions are conducted according to the provider's specifications, which may include a defined number of sessions for a specific amount of time, usually from one hour to 1 1/2 hours.

Other programs are designed for groups of couples. The group most often consists of six to eight seriously dating or engaged couples but may also include some newly married couples. Some couples groups meet once a week for six to eight weeks. Other groups may meet in extended sessions for one weekend.

There are advantages to working with individual couples rather than with a group of couples. The facilitator is able to give more attention to the individual couple than would be possible in a group setting. Issues that are foremost in the couple's relationship may be addressed in more depth in an individual-couple session. The couple may be more focused on their own issues and not get involved in other couples' problems. A disadvantage is that the couple does not have the opportunity to see how other relationships function or to learn from the group (Gleason & Prescott, 1977).

Couples groups also have advantages. Couples groups help to overcome the barriers to relationship enrichment: the myth of naturalism and the intermarital taboo (Mace, 1982). Small groups also encourage people to become active in the learning process. Couples may share their views on marital issues, listen to how the views of others might be similar to or different from their own, and explore as a group a variety of options for working through problems. Perhaps most important, couples find that they are not alone in their struggles. They can appreciate the chance to observe how others handle the same issues they are experiencing. The group helps reduce isolation for couples and often results in the development of new couple friends (Dyer & Dyer, 1999).

Limitations of the group format include the lack of time to address all of the issues that are raised by the couples in the group. Also, if one couple has a problem in a particular area, they may tend to dominate the group in their attempt to resolve the issue. Some people are not comfortable in a group and therefore may be unwilling to disclose in the group situation (Gleason & Prescott, 1977).

What Makes Marriage Preparation Programs Effective?

Based on studies investigating the effectiveness of premarital programs, David Olson (1983) suggests a three-step model for marriage education that takes about six to eight weeks. First, a couple takes some type of premarital inventory and receives feedback on the results of the inventory. Second, the couple participates in a small support group in which they express their feelings and concerns. Third, they are provided with communication and conflict resolution skills to use in dealing with issues in their relationship. A problem with this three-step model is that many times couples do not come for premarital education until a few weeks before the wedding, thereby not allowing time for the entire program. Olson suggests that these couples begin the program prior to marriage and continue six months to a year after the wedding. Some research has suggested that couples may be more motivated and better able to use the skills if they are trained a few months after their marriage (Bader, Microys, Sinclair, Wilett, & Conway, 1980).

Marriage Enrichment

Marriage enrichment represents a new paradigm in our approach to helping families. It is a positive, dynamic, and preventive philosophy that focuses on the active pursuit of growth and is directed toward "healthy" marriages. Programs in general have emphasized the development of interpersonal skills with which partners can identify, appreciate, and develop the latent strengths they possess within themselves and their relationship to build a satisfying and fulfilling marriage (Dyer & Dyer, 1989).

Marriage enrichment exists today in many secular and faith-based forms. Two of the best known programs are Marriage Encounter and ACME-style marriage enrichment. Marriage Encounter is a faith-based program started by the Roman Catholic Church and now supported by three national organizations: National Marriage Encounter, Worldwide Marriage Encounter, and United Marriage Encounter. ACME-style marriage enrichment is a community-based program sponsored by the Association for Couples in Marriage Enrichment, a nonprofit organization.

Father Gabriel Calvo, a Catholic priest, is credited with beginning Marriage Encounter in Barcelona, Spain, in January 1962. Frustrated in his attempts to work with youth in an urban parish, Calvo decided to focus his attention on married couples:

> I began to realize that . . . I would have to go to the heart of the family—the couple. They are the key to the love revolution the world needs. . . . In many families I could see a characteristic, something special they had that was lacking in other families. I tried to discern what these special qualities were, and I concluded in time that the unique quality was the confidence and trust these couples had in each other. (Calvo, cited in Mace, 1982, p. 121)

A few months after Calvo's first Marriage Encounter groups began and without any knowledge of them, David and Vera Mace stumbled onto an approach to marriage education to which they would dedicate the remainder of their professional lives. In October of 1962, they were invited to meet with a group of eight Quaker couples for a weekend marriage retreat. Mace relates that this was entirely an experiment. He was fully aware of the difficulties of counseling couples with serious marital problems, but his extensive attempts to identify literature on the subject or any individuals who had led programs for couples with working marriages was fruitless. He was fascinated with the potential of finding ways to prevent marital breakdown by working with couples before they became alienated from each other. This retreat led to others, and from these experiences the Maces developed what they called the Quaker Model for marriage enrichment. On their fortieth wedding anniversary in 1973, they founded the Association for Couples in Marriage Enrichment, or ACME, as it became known. This nonprofit, nonsectarian organization is the primary promoter of and training source for the Maces' approach to marriage enrichment. It is not clear whether the Maces originated the now generic term "marriage enrichment," but they certainly did much to place it into popular usage.

Although working in two different parts of the world in two different styles, Calvo and the Maces shared two central beliefs: (1) that the husband-wife relationship is the key to a successful family life, and (2) that preventive, educational interventions are more efficient and more effective than treatment delivered after problems arise.

Marriage Encounter.   More than 2 million couples worldwide have now participated in a Marriage Encounter weekend experience, making it the largest marriage education program in the world (Elin, 1999). A Marriage Encounter weekend generally begins on a Friday evening and lasts through Sunday afternoon and includes 10 to 25 couples led by a clergyperson or a couple and two or three volunteer couples. All members of this team have had a previous weekend encounter experience. They have had training in the encounter process and instructions on how to prepare and present their written talks. During the weekend the team gives presentations on 13 specific topics, including discovering oneself, talking to the other, mutual trust, growth in knowledge of each other, growth in understanding of each other, learning to accept each other, learning to help each other, growth in love and union, opening up to each other, and transcendent love (Elin, 1999).

The team couples describe their personal relationship experiences and struggles with the topic at hand. After each presentation, the participating couples are given one or more questions, generally called dialogue questions, on the topic presented. They are asked to spend time as individuals reflecting on and writing about their personal feelings in response to the questions. After a time of personal reflection, spouses come together in private to share their reflections and what they have written. Several low-key religious services are held during the weekend, and the retreat ends with the renewal of marriage vows (Elin, 1999).

No group sharing is done among couples during the entire weekend. The emphasis is on personal reflection and communication between the marital pair. Couples are encouraged to focus on feelings and not on judgments and thoughts. The concentration of approximately 40 hours of time together without interruption is a unique experience for many of the couples.

Although Marriage Encounter began as a program of the Roman Catholic Church, it has now been adopted by many religious organizations. In addition to the three national organizations mentioned previously that support Marriage Encounter, many independent churches and denominations use the program.

ACME-style marriage enrichment.   The Maces' long experience in marriage counseling and their experimental work with nondistressed couples in small groups led them to the conclusion that marital partners need help long before their marriages develop severe problems that seriously damage the relationship. Acting on this belief, they formed ACME to give married couples a way to join together in expressing their support for successful marriage. ACME took the slogan, "To work for better marriages beginning with our own" (Mace & Mace, 1974). Although religious themselves, the Maces purposefully created ACME as a nonsectarian organization based in communities.

ACME supports a wide variety of marriage enrichment activities that include weekend retreats; two- to three-hour monthly group meetings; state, local, and international conferences; and four- and five-day training events for leader couples. These events differ in structure, setting, and format but must conform to the following parameters (Association for Couples in Marriage Enrichment, 1995):

- Marriage enrichment events are for couples who have a "healthy" marriage; in practice this translates to couples who are not in immediate marital crisis and not seeking couples therapy for marital problems

- The event is led by one or more ACME-trained and certified couples, whose leadership reflects an interacting, participatory style

- The method is basically experiential and dynamic, rather than didactic and intellectual

- Participants have an opportunity for couple interaction in private couple dialogue and within the context of the group

- Use may be made of structured experiential exercises

- Participant couples usually have some voice in determining the agenda for the event

ACME-certified leaders generally follow a five-stage process model in designing marriage enrichment events. The stages are: security and community building, development of individual and couple awareness, development of knowledge and skill, planning for intentional growth, and celebration and closure (Dyer & Dyer, 1989).

Marriage potential is a core concept in marriage enrichment theory. The Maces coined the term *marriage potential* to describe the relationship quality of couples (Mace & Mace, 1978). Lederer and Jackson (1968) noted that "Marriage is a continuous process involving constant growth" (pp. 128–129). Marriage potential changes as expectations and experiences in the marriage either enhance or erode the relationship. Cole (2002) points out that couples capture higher levels of marital functioning when they use marital resources, which in turn leads couples to increase their expectations for greater marital functioning and exert more effort to achieve their marital goals. Conversely, when couples fail to access marital resources, they tend to try less and expect less from their relationship, which in turn decreases their marriage potential. Research by Cole, Cole, Fort, and Robertson (in press) showed that couples' marriage potential increases as a result of active involvement in marriage enrichment. Figure 10.1 illustrates the process of marital growth. This model depicts the intended impacts of marriage enrichment on perception of marriage potential. Marriage enrichment provides couples with an environment to acquire skills, build affection, and intentionally increase their interpersonal relationship quality with other supportive couples who are mutually committed to nurture and maintain marital growth.

Figure 10.1   Marriage Potential Growth Process in Marriage Enrichment

From Cole, Cole, Fort, & Robertson (2004), as reproduced in Powell et al. (in press).

ACME-style marriage enrichment differs from Marriage Encounter in several significant ways. Trained leader couples always lead ACME programs. Many ACME-trained leader couples are clergy, but there is no requirement that clergy be involved. Leader couples are considered participating facilitators whose role is to lead a process rather than to provide scripted presentations. As in Marriage Encounter, the couple leaders openly share their marital experiences. However, in ACME style, this is done through a dialogue between the two leaders, with group members listening. Generally, ACME events are much smaller—5 to 12 couples—

and a high degree of interaction among couples, as well as interaction between partners, is encouraged.

The Marriage Enrichment Group (MEG) model, as it has been developed through the Association for Couples in Marriage Enrichment, contains all of the elements which social learning theory and couple enrichment researchers have identified as necessary for attitudinal and behavioral change to occur. Couples *learn skills* through seeing them *modeled* by a leader couple. They *practice* the skills and focus on positive relationship interaction in individual and group couple dialogue in a safe environment of support. They *reinforce* the learning by intentionality of participation in an ongoing MEG, which meets regularly over an extended period of time. *Intentionality* is also stressed as couples choose issues for group discussion and share individual and couple dreams, which they are encouraged to turn into *achievable steps toward a goal*. Small accomplishments are shared and celebrated, which leads to *increased positive regard* and motivation to try harder.

EVALUATION OF PROGRAMS

Many of the programs designed to prevent breakdowns in relationships were not designed by family scientists or others with a strong interest in systematic program evaluation. Markman, Floyd, Stanley, and Lewis (1986) found that clergy and faith-based organizations were the most extensive providers of marriage preparation programs. Consequently, solid research on the effectiveness of a wide range of marriage and relationship programs is not available.

Several programs developed by practitioner-researchers have been exemplary in providing quality evaluations of the outcomes of their programs. These include Relationship Enhancement (Guerney et al., 1986), PREP (Markman, Floyd, Stanley, & Storaasli, 1988), and Couple Communication (Miller & Sherrard, 1999). These three programs have consistently shown effectiveness with premarital and married couples.

One of the most cited studies of marriage and relationship education was a meta-analysis undertaken by Giblin, Sprenkle, and Sheehan (1985). Eighty-five prevention and enrichment programs representing 3,886 couples and families were included in the study. Across all studies, the average participant improvement from pretest to posttest was more than 67% compared with those in the corresponding control group. The Relationship Enhancement program demonstrated the largest effect, followed by Couple Communication and Marriage Encounter. Giblin et al. (1985) concluded that programs of the type they studied were effective. Guerney and Maxson (1990) drew similar conclusions in their review of a decade of marriage education literature. Essentially, these studies strongly suggest that skill training is effective in increasing marital satisfaction and reducing the probability of divorce even after the program is over (Cole & Cole, 1999).

Other findings showed that the longer the training lasts, the more emphasis the program puts on the development of skills, and the more practice under competent supervision it allows, the greater chance the program has of producing a positive effect on couples that could be sustained over time (Guerney & Maxson, 1990). A pilot study by Powell and Powell (2003) found that verbal and nonverbal skills were higher—nonverbal significantly higher—for couples who had been regular participants in MEG groups that had met regularly for at least a year.

Gottman, Coan, Carrere, and Swanson (1998) have challenged the efficacy of skill-based models of marital education and therapy. They have specifically suggested that the popular communication technique of "active listening" should be abandoned because healthy couples do not use it. They further suggest that it is probably unrealistic to expect couples to use active listening in conflictual situations when faced with negative affect from a partner. These suggestions have created considerable controversy in the field, and Gottman and his associates have been confronted by researchers and practitioners from the fields of therapy and of relationship and marital education. It should be noted that Gottman and his colleagues have not said the technique is not effective, just that it is not used by the typical couple. Cole and Cole (1999) are among those who have come to the defense of skill-based programs in therapy and education. They argue that skills such as active listening, using "I-statements," and nondefensive listening and speaking are skills that must be learned and thus may not be used by typical couples who have not been taught to use them. Gottman's challenge is one that can be answered only by replication of his research and by more thorough research on the efficacy of relationship and marital education programs. Research is particularly needed into the long-term effects of educational programs (Berger & DeMaria, 1999; Kelly & Fincham, 1999).

Practitioners of relationship and marital education models should not dismiss the challenge of Gottman and his colleagues too quickly. Basic assumptions about models and theories should be reexamined. Theory must be linked more closely to interventions. Research such as Gottman's into what makes marriages succeed or fail must be taken seriously and incorporated into program development. In a plenary session at the 2003 conference of the National Council on Family Relations, Gottman presented a theoretical model based on his years of observing couples in satisfactory and unsatisfactory couple interchanges. Gottman's Sound Relationship House theory addresses seven components of a quality couple relationship (Gottman, 2000, pp. 31–50). He posits that the first three components of the Sound Relationship House—Love Maps (internal complementary maps of partners' relational world), a strong Fondness and Admiration System, and Turning Toward emotional connections—are the foundational components upon which romantic affection and intimacy are built. In other words, even if a couple learns good communication and conflict management skills, they will not be effective in changing the level of positive interaction in the relationship if the other foundational components are not present. A discussion of "best practice" in couple relationship education by Halford et al. (2003) also concluded that a stable, satisfying couple relationship involves much more than just being able to manage conflict. A best-practice relationship education program should include a discussion of the natural tendency of couples to take their relationship for granted and should help couples develop strategies for making and keeping their relationship the top priority in their lives. New programs should build on what has been shown to be effective in existing programs such as Relationship Enhancement, Couple Communication, and PREP. Finally, researchers and practitioners need to work more closely together to create and evaluate relationship and marriage education programs.

SUMMARY

Marriage preparation and marriage education offer hope to a society disenchanted with its ability to establish and maintain close relationships. Although the marriage education/enrichment movement is now more than 40 years old, it is still a relatively new phenomenon in the United States and worldwide. But momentum is gathering as counselors, educators, and ministers begin to bring pressure on schools and legislatures to emphasize marriage preparation courses and counseling. Effectiveness of preventive programs is also being evaluated by serious researchers, and positive results are emerging. Certification for marriage educators is also under consideration by several professional organizations.

Although traditional education can introduce principles, all marriage education experts emphasize the necessity of personal motivation, commitment to intentional work on the relationship, praxis, and reinforcement of skills learned. The short-term program has little hope of success. Fortunately, increasing numbers of couples are being trained as group leaders and mentors for newlyweds. The future is promising.

Questions/Problems for Discussion and Review

Class Discussion

1. What could be done by universities, communities, and churches to encourage or motivate more engaged couples to participate in premarital education programs?

2. Why is it important to have trained leadership? Isn't having a satisfactory marriage enough to qualify as a leader couple?

3. Review the myths about marriage that discourage premarital and marriage education. Which do you think is the strongest and why?

Research Problems and Activities

1. Interview 20 engaged couples (males and females separately) about their interest in a premarital education program. If possible, find an ethnically diverse sample. Using the content areas in box 10.1, assess their level of interest in each area. What do they see as the value of such a program? How do the responses of males and females compare? What about ethnic groups? A second, related, survey might interview engaged couples who have been married before. What differences do you notice in their responses?

2. Review the research on one of the programs mentioned that has undertaken some rigorous evaluation of program results (by Olson, L'Abate, or Gottman, for example). Consider the assumptions and objectives of the program and how they were carried out. If more than one person works on this activity, choose different programs to assess and then compare differences in assumptions, objectives, and program design.

Case Study Design

1. Develop a premarital or marriage education program for a specific population of couples (incarcerated-partner or drug-rehabilitation-program couples). What would have to be done to alter the design? How would you incorporate and adapt the concepts that have proven to be the most successful in other programs?

2. Invite a leader couple trained in one of the marriage enrichment models to demonstrate their teaching technique in your class, using an interpersonal relationship topic. Your class can role-play the couples and small groups, or each class member can bring a friend to participate in this lesson with him or her. Using praxis, process the experience in the next class period.

eleven

Parent Education

I t's 3:00 AM. Your three-week-old son has been crying and fussing since 11:00 PM. You have fed him, changed him, and rocked him. You are out of ideas and patience. What is it that he needs?

Your day-care provider pulls you aside and informs you that your three-year-old has been biting the other children. Is this normal? Why is she doing it? What can you do to stop it?

Your 13-year-old has started to come home after his curfew. He has become sullen and uncommunicative. When he does talk to you, it is usually with disrespect or annoyance. The more you push him, the more he pulls away. What can you do to best deal with the situation?

How does a parent best respond to these situations? Is there one best way to respond? Are there books that have all the answers, or do parents just "know" what to do? Can you take a class to learn how to be a good parent?

Parent education as a profession and field of study is still in its adolescence. This chapter looks at the history of parent education, theories and disciplines influencing the field, and some popular programs and models. We discuss the competencies and qualifications needed to provide effective, quality parent education and support. Finally, we discuss and consider the future of this emerging profession.

THE HISTORY OF PARENT EDUCATION

Early psychological writing assumed that parenting came naturally and that women were biologically predetermined to raise children. It was assumed that parents just knew what to do when it came to discipline, nurturing, toilet training, and so forth. Or, they just modeled their parenting after their own childhood experiences. This perception is slowly changing. Today's parents are quicker to acknowledge that they don't always have the answers or that they may not want to raise their children as they were raised. In addition, as family size has become smaller, they are less likely to have had earlier experiences in caring for younger family members. Societal changes have made it more difficult to rely on parenting techniques from the past. The rapid pace at which these changes occur leave children facing issues their parents never dreamed of. They have little personal experience to fall back on.

Many parents are eager for sources of information and support that will help them perform in their role (Simpson, 2001). There is increased recognition that, among other things, knowledge of child development can be helpful in determining how to handle a specific behavior, as well as in identifying appropriate behavior and goals.

Early Influences and Organizations

Parent education in the United States has some of its earliest roots in the colonial period, when church and state shared the goal of influencing parents to raise their children according to religious mandates (Schlossman, 1976). It can be traced back to fields as diverse as medicine, social work, home economics, education, and psychology. G. Stanley Hall was perhaps the first psychologist to bring the study of children to a university setting, but Freud, Watson, Adler, Piaget, Gesell, and others had theories of their own. Hall focused on understanding the development of the child for the purpose of discovering how children learn. His methods were considered unconventional, and he eventually lost favor in the academic world, but his ideas were carried out among the women who gathered in 1897 at the first National Congress of Mothers, a nationwide parent-education organization known later as the Parent Teacher Association, or PTA (Schlossman, 1976). A lot has happened since then.

The PTA grew from that first meeting in 1897 to an organization of 60,000 members in 1915 to 6 million volunteers in 23,000 local units in 2006. The focus of the PTA shifted from early childhood to adolescence to an emphasis on helping children in trouble or at risk and on reeducating families in modern methods of child care. Eventually, its main objective centered on domestic science and the goal of preparing women in household management and child care, the goal presumably resulting in happier and more stable homes.

The PTA used a number of strategies in reaching families. One involved self-instruction and group discussion. A second included advocacy to the poor through home visiting and the formation of mothers' clubs. The PTA also took on political goals, including lobbying for child labor laws. "Thus to the PTA in the Progressive era, parent education was a lever for changing society by organizing mothers of the nation in common cause" (Schlossman, 1976, p. 451). Today the PTA has moved from the community mothers' club model into its current form as a school-based association of parents and teachers with the goal of optimum home-school collaboration.

A number of other organizations were involved in parent education in various capacities. The Child Study Association of America initiated the National Council of Parent Education in 1925 to coordinate lay and professional groups. This group contributed to the development of instructional materials and sponsored the first university course in parent education at Teachers College, Columbia, Missouri, in 1925. Likewise, the American Home Economics Association (AHEA) began to include parent education in its educational and lobbying interests, also in the mid-1920s. These initial efforts focused on poor families and those considered to be in need (Carter, 1996).

Benjamin Spock's *Baby and Child Care*, first published in 1946, brought the literature of child care and parenting to the middle class. Grassroots parenting groups began to appear and provided parents the opportunity to meet with each other to "compare notes." One grassroots mother-led organization was the La Leche League. Groups of women shared their experiences with breastfeeding via support groups and mentored new mothers with lactation consultation. With their efforts, breastfeeding was re-established as the preferred infant feeding method in an era when medical interventions were thought to be superior and more modern than nature's way. Despite the influence of the La Leche League, most parent education followed traditional educational designs, with an "expert" serving as the source of information and answers.

Slowly focus shifted away from experts and toward enhancing parents' own knowledge and experience. The federally-funded Head Start program, launched in the mid-1960s, acknowledged the value and impact of parents in the education of their children (Carter, 1996). By the 1980s community-based parent education programs were joined by state and federally funded programs and a growing number of nonprofit and for-profit organizations.

In 1995 parent educators began discussing the need to create an organization that could meet the needs of this growing field. The most notable discussions were held at Wheelock College in November 1995 and at the Family Support America (formerly Family Resource Coalition of America) conference in May 1996 (NPEN, 2006). The Parenting Education Network (PEN), later known as the National Parenting Education Network (NPEN), evolved from these discussions. The mission of NPEN is to advance the field of parent education. The development of NPEN represents an important step in the evolution of parent education as a profession. As discussed in chapter 2, one step in the development of a profession occurs when those trained in the field establish an association (East, 1980). NPEN's existence speaks to the recognition of the unique needs and goals of the field of parent education. The increased interest in this field no doubt comes in response to an increased need for parent education due to societal changes.

Societal Changes

Societal changes have caused modern-day parents to face challenges unparalleled in previous generations, increasing the need for both formal and informal parent education. A majority of American adults believe that it is harder to raise children today than it used to be (National Commission on Children, 1991b). The following, written over 25 years ago, is even truer today:

> The process of family nuclearization, erosion of community, role differentiation and specialization, geographical distancing of family generations, and the increased entry into the labor force—have created a new reality in which parents no longer benefit from traditional structure in their parenting roles. (Harmin & Brim, 1980, p. 14)

Families today are more likely to live away from extended family members, weakening their support network. Changes in health care require some mothers to return home as early as 24 hours after giving birth, sometimes to an environment that has little nursing or emotional support. A significant number of mothers work outside of the home, either by choice or necessity. In 2002, 16% of White children, 53% of African American children, and 25% of Hispanic children lived in single-parent families (Fields, 2003). Parents have less time to spend with their children and may rely on them to be more self-sufficient than is developmentally appropriate. "Expecting, indeed demanding, that children grow up fast was one way of avoiding the expenditure of energy that goes along with parenthood" (Elkind, 1987, p. xii).

Technology and retail design also play a role in increasing isolation. Individuals and families spend more time at computers and on the telephone and less time talking face-to-face. Neighborhood grocery and hardware stores have been

Families today are more likely to live away from extended family members, weakening their social support networks.

replaced with strip malls and warehouse retailers, leaving families more isolated and less connected. Neighbors are less likely to know each other and to share information "over the fence" (Carter, 1996).

There are greater influences on children originating from outside of the home as well. The media are filled with images of sex, violence, and consumer product advertising emphasizing beauty and materialism (National Research Council and Institute of Medicine, 2000). Drugs are more readily available. Changing demographics have revealed other needs. Increasing numbers of grandparents find themselves raising their grandchildren at a time when they thought they would be retired. And since 9/11, parents have sought guidance on explaining terrorism to children.

With fewer built-in support networks, parents are more receptive to outside help. Our profession has a challenge: to make high quality family research accessible to families, nationally and internationally. The field of parent education needs to continue to grow in response to the increased challenges and complexities of modern life.

DEFINITIONS AND ASSUMPTIONS

Definitions

The goals and targets of parent education are as varied as the approaches used. Some use the term "parent" education; others use "parenting" education to recognize that some people who are not biological or legal parents have a role in the care and rearing of children. Nick Carter (1996) defined parent education as "programs, support services and resources offered to parents and caregivers that are designed to support them or increase their capacity and confidence in raising healthy children" (p. 6). Brock et al. (1993) described parent education as "an organized, programmatic effort to change or enhance the child-rearing knowledge and skills of a family system or a child care system" (p. 88). The National Parenting Education Network defines parent education as:

> a process that involves the expansion of insights, understanding and attitudes and the acquisition of knowledge and skills about the development of both parents and of their children and the relationship between them. Education is most effective, parent educators recognize, if it occurs in an emotionally supportive environment. (www.npen.org)

Assumptions

The National Extension Parenting Education Model (Smith, Cudaback, Goddard, & Myers-Walls, 1994) does not define parent education specifically but includes nine key assumptions regarding parents and their relationships with their children:

- Parents are the primary socializers of their children
- Parenting attitudes, knowledge, skills, and behaviors can be positively influenced by parent education efforts
- Parenting is a learned skill that can be strengthened through study and experience
- Parent education is more effective when parents are active participants in and contributors to their parent education programs
- The parent-child relationship is nested within and influenced by multiple social and cultural systems
- Programs should be responsive to diversity among parents
- Effective parent education may be accomplished by a variety of methods
- Both the parent and the child have needs that should be met
- The goal of parent education is strengthening and educating the parent (or caregiver) so that he or she is better able to facilitate the development of caring, competent, and healthy children

Carter (1996) includes a similar list of assumptions regarding parent education. Wandersman (1987) states that "parent education can positively affect the satisfaction and functioning of families by communicating knowledge about human development and relationships that increases their understanding, providing alternative models of parenting that widen their choices, teaching new skills, and facilitating access to community resources" (p. 211).

Parent education programs therefore cover a number of subjects. Some of the more commonly covered include child development, discipline and limit setting, building self-esteem, health, communication skills, stages of parenthood, parent involvement in education, balancing work and family, family systems, family transitions, conflict resolution, advocacy and parent empowerment, parents with specialized needs and concerns, and collaboration and networking.

FORMATS, AUDIENCES, AND SETTINGS

Variations in goals and target audiences are reflected in the settings and approaches used to carry out parent education.

Formats

Parent education can be presented in a variety of settings and formats and to a number of different audiences. Harmin and Brim (1980) identify three modes of instruction for parent education: individual, group, and mass. The individual mode is often carried out under the guise of counseling or home visits and is typically focused on interventions for problems. The group mode is a more widely used approach through which instruction is delivered in traditional classroom settings, workshops, seminars, or more informal support groups. The mass mode refers to education carried out through the print media, that is, newsletters, books, and pamphlets, or radio and television programs. Contact through the mass mode is wider reaching but less personal.

Audiences

Parent education can be administered in one of two ways: for universal access by all parents, or targeted to specific groups with identified problems or risk factors (Smith, Perou, & Lesesne, 2002). Universal access programs are designed to inform and prepare parents regarding normative parenting responsibilities and experiences with the intention of preventing problems and promoting optimal development.

Targeted programs are those that focus on a specific audience that is at risk or is likely to face problems if some form of intervention is not introduced. Targeted programs might be focused on teenage mothers, low-income or low-education parents, or parents with children with disabilities and/or behavior problems. They might include efforts to prevent child abuse and neglect, juvenile delinquency, or youth violence. The varying situations and issues of each group influences the approaches used.

Settings

Parent education programs are offered in a number of different settings, including schools, cooperative extension programs, family service agencies, neighborhood resource centers, community education facilities, faith communities, and health care settings. In addition, for-profit businesses and corporations have begun to offer brown-bag lunchtime workshops for employees because they recognize the impact personal issues and concerns can have on company productivity. The government offers parent education through family support programs provided to family members serving in the armed forces. And parents who enter the state child protection system are often required to attend parenting classes by judicial mandate.

School programs.   Parent education programs are taught within schools to help elementary and secondary students know what is involved in parenting as well as learn how to care for others in general. These programs have been shown to be effective in preventing violence and pregnancy (Schiffer, 2002). One popular approach to parent education in junior high and high school classes involves giving students an egg or a sack of flour to serve as their "baby" for a set amount of time. The egg and flour have recently been replaced with a doll that cries unpredictably day or night and can only be quieted by a student with a nonremovable key that is attached to his or her wrist. The intention of these exercises is to give the students a more realistic view of the demands and constancy of parenting. These approaches could probably be considered an indirect form of sex education as well, by providing a glimpse into the possible consequences of sexual intercourse!

Faith communities.   Parent education in faith communities usually appears in the form of workshops and classes dealing with such topics as "Communicating with Your Adolescent" and "Setting Limits." These classes may or may not involve a religious perspective. Parents may sometimes just feel more comfortable attending parenting classes offered through their faith community rather than an outside organization and may find them to be more accessible.

Neighborhood and family resource centers.   Neighborhood and family resource centers often offer classes for first-time parents or parents with children of specific ages, such as "Wonderful Ones" or "Terrific Twos." Classes for parents of twins and other multiple births are becoming more common, especially in this time of increased use of fertility drugs. Neighborhood and family resource centers often have lending libraries that feature parenting information. In addition to offering information and support to parents, these classes strengthen communities by providing opportunities for neighbors to meet and support each other.

Corporations and businesses.   Corporations and businesses are increasingly recognizing that workers who face stress at home are less productive at work. Many employers offer lunchtime brown-bag seminars at which employees can learn communication tips, ways to balance work and family, and other ideas to strengthen family connections. Employers hope that attention to these personal issues will increase productivity and reduce absenteeism. The military incorporates parent education into their family support programs. Life within the military involves unique challenges for parents who must sometimes cope with not only spousal separation but also the added stress of living away from extended family and frequent relocation in unfamiliar cities and countries.

Health care.   Hospitals and clinics are also offering more parent education programs in the form of prenatal classes, childbirth education, lactation groups, women's health programs, and stress reduction classes. Waiting rooms are often equipped with closed-circuit televisions that carry special parent education information. As with some businesses, health care organizations recognize the impact of prevention and education on their bottom line.

Court-ordered programs. Parent education, although often offered as a preventive measure, can also be carried out in response to specific problems or issues. In some states, legislation mandates parent education for all divorcing parents to help them understand and minimize the effects of divorce on their children. In addition, perhaps the most challenging client for parent educators is the involuntary client: a court-ordered participant who is required to attend parenting classes as a component of a child protection case.

These types of programs, though more problem-focused, should not be confused with therapy. Parent education differs from therapy in its emphasis on (1) normative development and the prevention of family problems rather than individual personality and family dysfunction, (2) techniques that provide support rather than conflict and confrontation, and (3) goals that increase self-confidence and satisfaction rather than restructure personality or family dynamics (Wandersman, 1987).

The National Extension Parenting Education Model (Smith, Cudaback, Goddard, & Myers-Walls, 1994) identifies fifteen program delivery strategies for reaching out to parents, including parent education groups, radio programs, hospital programs, and newsletter articles (box 11.1). Many of these delivery strategies are carried out in the settings described above.

Box 11.1   Program Delivery Strategies for Parent Education

Parent education groups	Community forums
Parent education resource centers	Interagency support/collaborations
Newsletters	Support groups
Radio programs	Community coalitions/task forces
Home visits	Learn-at-home programs
Mentor mother/godparent programs	Parent advisory groups
Hospital programs	Social change groups: liberation pedagogy
Newspaper articles/tabletop messages	

Smith, C. A., Cudaback, D., Goddard, H. W., & Myers-Walls, J. A. (1994). *National extension parent education model.* Manhattan, KS: Kansas Cooperative Extension Service. Available: http://www.k-state.edu/wwparent/nepem/index.htm

---

COMMON THEORIES INFLUENCING PARENT EDUCATION

Numerous theories and approaches influence parent education programs. Volumes could be written on the many theories, so our discussion is limited to a summary of some of the main components of the most well-known and utilized human behavior theories and approaches. These include psychoanalytic theory, behaviorism, cognitive-developmental theory, social learning theory, moral development theory, psychosocial development theory, developmental systems theory, temperament theory, Adlerian theory, and humanism. In addition, we look at an approach that focuses on parenting styles. Although parent educators may operate predominantly within the context of one main theory—behaviorism or humanism, for example—they may incorporate a variety of approaches and may be open to implementing different theories, depending on the situation. Awareness of a number of theories can help parents and parent educators better understand children's abilities and behaviors. Theories also provide a framework on which to base responses, as well as a context in which to view the child.

The theories discussed in this chapter differ in the ways in which they view the following questions (Murray, 1992):

- Nature versus nurture: What is the influence of biology versus the environment? How much influence can the parent have on the child?
- Active versus passive development: Who is in control? Does the environment act on the child or the child on the environment?
- Discontinuous versus continuous development: Are stages of development sequential or independent of each other?
- Qualitative versus quantitative measurement: How easily can responses be measured?
- Developmental direction: Does learning occur in one direction or is it multidirectional?

The "nature versus nurture" argument has been debated for years, but it received increased attention in 1998 when *The Nurture Assumption* by Judith Harris (1998) was published. Harris argued that parents have almost no influence on their children's development and that peers play a much bigger role. This idea brought cries of protest from psychologists, child development experts, teachers, and parents. Most parent educators recognize the role of outside influences but would argue that parents play a key role in a child's development (Simpson, 2001).

Psychoanalytic/Psychosocial Theory

Psychological theories that have influenced parent education include Freud's psychoanalytic theory and Erikson's psychosocial theory. Freud applied his concepts of id, ego, and superego to the development of the child's psyche and viewed the parent as mainly responsible for the child's psychological development (Strong & DeVault, 1998).

Behaviorism

A number of learning theories have influenced parent education as well. John B. Watson's and B. F. Skinner's theories of behaviorism argued against genetic influence and emotional or internal drives as motivation for behavior. Instead, they argued that behaviors increase and decrease through reinforcement and rewards. They sought to explain behavior entirely on the basis of what can be observed.

Cognitive-Developmental Theory

One of the most commonly referenced theories in parent education is Jean Piaget's cognitive-developmental theory. Piaget determined that children's ability to reason and understand change as they grow older proceeded in a series of sequential stages: sensorimotor (birth to two years), preoperational (two to six years), concrete operational (seven to 11 years), and formal operational (12 years and older). Piaget also used the terms *assimilation* (making new concepts compatible with existing knowledge) and *accommodation* (adjusting cognition to incorporate new experiences) to describe a child's learning process.

Box 11.2   Erikson's Stages of Development

Trust vs. Mistrust (Birth to one year)
Babies learn to trust others to meet their needs.

Autonomy vs. Shame and Doubt (one to three years)
Children learn either to be self-sufficient or to doubt their own abilities.

Initiative vs. Guilt (three to six years)
Children want to learn and try new things, but if not encouraged, they can experience guilt.

Industry vs. Inferiority (seven to 11 years)
Children learn either to be competent and productive or to feel inferior and unable to do things.

Identity vs. Role Confusion (Adolescence)
Adolescents either establish an identity or are confused over what future roles to play.

Intimacy vs. Isolation (Adulthood)
Young adults seek companionship and love or become isolated from one another.

Generativity vs. Stagnation (Adulthood)
Adults are productive and have meaningful lives or become stagnant and inactive.

Integrity vs. Despair (Adulthood)
Adults make sense out of their lives or despair over goals never reached.

Social Learning Theory

Social learning theory, most often attributed to Albert Bandura, emphasizes the role of thinking or cognition in learning (Bandura, 1977). It considers the interactions of culture, society, and the family, as well as the inner qualities of the individual (Strong & DeVault, 1998). "Social learning theory accepts many of the tenets of behavioral psychology but adds to it the individual's innate ability to think and make choices to change his or her environment" (Schickendanz, Schickendanz, Hansen, & Forsyth, 1993).

Moral Development Theory

According to developmental psychologist Lawrence Kohlberg, humans progress through stages with regard to moral development. Kohlberg theorized that there are six possible levels of moral reasoning ability throughout the life span (Kohlberg, 1984). At stage one, obedience is an end in itself in order to avoid punishment. At stage two, people follow rules to obtain rewards for themselves.

Stage three is characterized by complying with norms as defined by others in the social circle. At stage four, Kohlberg theorizes that humans value "doing the right thing" by following what the larger society defines as "right." Human moral development at stage five is defined less by social convention and more by the person's internal sense of obligation and responsibilities to set an example. In the last stage, the individual's behavior is driven by conscience and by adhering to universal ethical principles, even if they violate the "law" and even in the face of personal disadvantage. Although frequently cited in the life span development literature, most researchers are careful to qualify Kohlberg's theory by noting that it may have limited applicability across individual differences, including age, gender, class and culture.

Psychosocial Development Theory

Theorist Erik Erikson also advanced a developmental stage theory to explain human life span development. While influenced by Freud, Erikson placed greater emphasis on the influence of society on the development of the child. Erikson described eight distinct stages through which humans pass from birth to the end of life. These stages focus on changes in emotional growth and development that have biological, as well as social, influences. Each stage specifies a "task" to be completed in order to progress to a higher level, and he also identified signs associated with each stage that indicate that an individual has not successfully negotiated a developmental task. The eight stages are identified as trust vs. mistrust, autonomy vs. shame, initiative vs. guilt, industry vs. inferiority, identity vs. role confusion, intimacy vs. isolation, generativity vs. stagnation, and ego-integrity vs. despair (Strong & DeVault, 1998; see box 11.2). Erikson's theory is important because it was the first to suggest that development does not end at adolescence, but occurs across the life span. However, like all developmental theories, family scientists are quick to add that his model may not hold true in non-Western cultures and may not correspond well with regard to gender and other individual differences.

Developmental Systems Theory

The developmental systems approach recognizes that children develop within the context of a family system and that influences between the child and the parent are reciprocal. The family in turn is influenced by larger systems that include friends, community, government, and so forth. Bronfenbrenner's ecological model (Bronfenbrenner, 1979) is perhaps the most widely known model that uses a developmental systems approach and is perhaps the first theory that suggests that family policy may influence optimal child development.

Temperament Theory

Stella Chess and Alexander Thomas introduced the first theory that ascribes the child's own inborn behavioral tendencies as a factor in the child's development. According to Chess and Thomas (1987) children are born with their own dispositional tendencies, which, when combined with environment, form a dynamic mix of "nature" and "nurture." Chess and Thomas's research revealed that babies exhibit behaviors that cluster around three categories of temperaments and the incidence in which the three temperaments occur across the population. "Easy" babies (40% of infants) are of cheerful dispositions and are adaptable, predictable, and easy to soothe. "Difficult" babies (10%) react intensely and negatively to change or discomfort, are difficult to soothe, and are often irritable and unpredictable. "Slow to warm up" babies (15%) are slow to adapt to new situations and can accept soothing, but require more time to adjust. The remaining 35% of babies are of mixed temperament. In assigning temperament, Chess and Thomas measured infant behavior across nine dimensions of temperament activity level: approach-withdrawal, adaptability, mood, attention span and persistence, distractibility, rhymiticity, intensity, and responsiveness.

Temperament theorists believe that humans are born with these varying innate tendencies and characteristics as infants and that these attributes persist into adulthood with common adult manifestations of the same traits (Kagan & Snidman, 1991). Unlike Chess and Thomas, Jerome Kagan argued that reaction to stimulus by 4-month-old babies could predict certain personality traits evident years later. Babies who responded to high levels of activity and stimulation with distress were more likely to be shy, whereas babies that reacted calmly or positively to the same stimuli were more likely to be outgoing. Kagan's research, however, shows that biology is not necessarily destiny. Although temperamental differences may be rooted in genetics, they can be reinforced through interactions with the environment. A baby who responds positively to lots of activity and stimulation probably encourages his parents to respond with more energy, whereas the parents of a baby who is shy and withdrawn probably respond to their baby's cues by remaining calm and low-key. Lerner and Lerner (cited in Brooks, 1994) stress the importance of "goodness of fit" between a child's temperament, those of the parents, and environmental factors. Parents who are aware of and sensitive to their child's temperament are better able to understand and react to their child's behavior. Thus, "goodness of fit" theory gave rise to the idea that the child-parent relationship is a dynamic one, affected by both child and parent temperament. More recent research supports this hypothesis even further, asserting that child behavior and temperament has an effect on parent well-being. This back-and-forth parent-child influence on each other is referred to as *bidirectionality* (Crouter & Booth, 2003).

Adlerian Theory

The theories of Alfred Adler and Rudolf Dreikurs combine social theory with behaviorism. They assert that child behavior is goal-directed and that environment can reinforce or discourage behaviors within a social context. Adlerian parent education helps parents understand the goal of the child's misbehavior. Adler argued that children have a strong need to belong and will implement mistaken goals in an attempt to be accepted. He identified these mistaken goals as attention, power, retaliation and revenge, and frustration and giving up (Dreikurs, 1964). Dreikurs built on this theory with the notion of natural and logical consequences.

Educators using an Adlerian or Dreikurs approach can encourage appropriate behavior by rewarding pro-social behavior and reduce negative behaviors by allowing children to experience the resultant natural and logical consequences. Natural consequences are those that are the logical results from a behavior—for example, going outside without a jacket may result in the child becoming cold. Logical consequences might require implementation by the parent but relate to the behavior. If a child leaves his or her toys out in the living room, the parent may put them away and not allow the child to play with them for a while. In colloquial terms, the punishment fits the crime in Adlerian/Dreikurs theory.

Adler, in particular, was also very interested in the atmosphere of the family, as well as birth order and position within the family. The Adler and Dreikurs methods of training and guidance have become common concepts in parent education today (see box 11.3).

Box 11.3   Concepts and Approaches in the Adlerian Approach to Parent Education

Adlerian Theory	Methods of Training and Guidance
Mistaken goals	Encouragement
Attention	Natural consequences
Power	Logical consequences
Retaliation and revenge	Maintain order
Frustration and giving up	Avoid conflict
	Avoid pampering and overprotection
	Family council

Humanism

Carl Rogers and Abraham Maslow ushered in humanistic psychology. Child rearing from a humanistic perspective involves the child's conception of self, or self-identity. It contends that development is holistic and moves toward the goal of self-actualization. In order to reach this goal, the child must have love, security, and acceptance. The parent's job is to accept the child as he or she is, trust in the child's ability to solve problems, and provide an environment of acceptance, or in the words of Carl Rogers, "unconditional positive regard."

Parenting Styles

Although it is not technically a theory of parent education, Diana Baumrind (1983) identified three basic parenting styles, permissive, authoritative, and authoritarian, which have been widely accepted as a basis for parent education approaches. These styles apply to the interaction and structuring of the relationship between parent and child and have influenced many of the parent education programs in place today (Brock, Oertwein, & Coufal, 1993).

Permissive style. (low demands–high response) According to Baumrind, permissive parents generally place few demands upon their children and are highly responsive to their children's needs. They treat their children as though the children's rights are greater than their own or others' and use low coercion. Children in permissive households have a lot of developmentally inappropriate power within the family.

Authoritative style. (high demand–high response) Parents with a more authoritative style attempt to balance their demands and the norms of society with the needs of the child. They promote individuality by encouraging the child to make his or her own decisions, yet they also set firm rules and enforce them. Authoritative parents tend to discuss behavior with their children rather than punish them, but they will use punishment if the child does not comply with clearly stated expectations.

Authoritarian style. (high demands–low response) Authoritarian parents set rigid rules and make strong demands for compliance. Obedience is highly valued. They have low responsiveness to the needs and wants of the child. Children in authoritarian families are seen as having very few rights and therefore have little power in the family.

A fourth parenting style, *indifferent*, was identified after Baumrind's initial work and is characterized by low demands and low responsiveness. This style is seen in cases of child neglect (Maccoby & Martin, 1983). Most parents use a variety of styles depending upon the situation. They may be authoritarian when it comes to a situation that they think could be dangerous for their child, such as insisting that he or she is supervised when crossing the street, but more lenient when it comes to allowing the child to decide when to do his or her homework, for example.

Baumrind has expanded her work on parenting styles to include a consideration of parenting styles over time. Relationships with adolescent children require more variation in parenting approaches regarding responsiveness and control (Baumrind, 1991). Baumrind's parenting styles provide a framework within which to consider the goals and processes of parenting.

Meta-Parenting

Current writing and research is exploring a new area of parenting theory and applied practice. The term *meta-parenting* has been coined to describe parent-child relationships from a family dynamics perspective. In a meta-parenting approach, parents are encouraged to analyze their own behavior as well as the child's and use these insights and awareness to improve their parenting skills and the home environment. This theory holds promise for the new concept of "parent development." Meta-parenting promotes that the adult's own development provides the basis for the best environment for child well-being. As the field of parent education develops, it will be interesting to watch further developments emerge in meta-parenting theory. A question yet to be answered is how useful or teachable these skills are across diverse populations. The meta-parenting process requires fairly advanced self-insight and critical thinking skills that may be more accessible to some parents than to others (Holden & Hawk, 2003).

PARENTING PROGRAMS AND MODELS

There are a number of widely used parent education programs and curricula available, including Parent Effectiveness Training (Gordon, 1975), Systematic Training for Effective Parenting (Dinkmeyer & McKay, 1976), and Active Parenting (Popkin, 1987). Many of these "packaged" programs provide training and certification opportunities for facilitators. While they can be effective in certain situations, it is important that parent educators possess a wide repertoire of approaches and strategies. The parent education professional must be prepared to match the needs of the parents and the children with appropriate programs. Increasingly, professionals in the field of parent education are recognizing that the needs of families vary depending upon family composition, ethnicity, culture, economic status, and so forth. Likewise, they recognize the limitations of any one program to meet such varying needs.

Brock et al. (1993) argue that an understanding of family systems theory must be integrated into parent education programs in order for lasting change to occur. Rather than simply teaching parents techniques to influence the child's behavior, the whole family might be better served if the child participated in the program as well. This allows both parent and child to practice new skills while also considering sibling and couple relationships. Most packaged parent education programs are geared specifically toward the parent, and few involve the children.

National Extension Parenting Education Model

The National Extension Parenting Education Model (NEPEM) (Smith et al., 1994) was developed to help stimulate and conceptualize parent education programs at the state and county levels. The model includes eight underlying guiding principles:

- What parents do to enhance the well-being of their children
- Priority parent practices that are significant across the full range of childhood and adolescence
- Core priorities
- Skills and practices as more important than the arrangement of practices
- Parent skills as having fluid, not rigid, boundaries
- NEPEM as dynamic, not static
- Parent strengths and empowerment
- Parent strengths as sufficiently broad and flexible to be useful in developing programs across the cultural spectrum

NEPEM identifies six categories of skills needed by parents for optimal parenting: care for self, understand (children, their developmental needs and uniqueness), guide, nurture, motivate, and advocate.

In 2000, a group of extension professionals met in order to outline the critical skills and practices of parent educators. Their efforts combined the NEPEM "priority practices for parents" with a set of "priority processes for parent educators" to create a new structure, the National Extension Parenting Education Framework

Figure 11.1   The National Extension Parenting Education Model

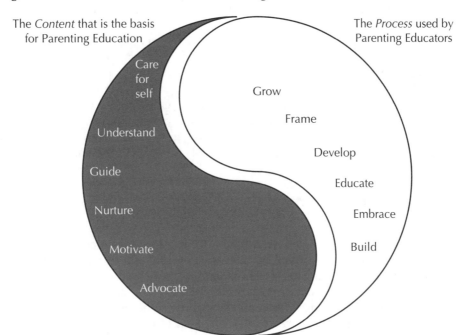

The *Content* that is the basis
for Parenting Education

The *Process* used by
Parenting Educators

Care
for
self

Understand

Guide

Nurture

Motivate

Advocate

Grow

Frame

Develop

Educate

Embrace

Build

(NEPEF) (DeBord et al., 2006). In NEPEF, the six content practices for parents are used along side six processes for parent educators (grow, frame, develop, educate, embrace, and build). NEPEF provides an excellent format in which to consider numerous aspects of parent education.

Other Programs and Models

A number of other approaches, models, and programs related to parent education exist throughout the country. Following are some of the more well known.

Parents as Teachers (PAT).   This is a program that promotes the development of children from birth to age 3. PAT began in Missouri and now operates at more than 2,000 sites across the country. In 2005, PAT merged with MELD (Minnesota Early Learning Design), an early parent education program founded in 1973.

Hawaii's Healthy Start.   This program serves families identified through screening at birth as highly stressed and/or at risk for child abuse.

Home Instruction Program for Preschool Youngsters (HIPPY).   This program seeks to prepare three- to five-year-olds for kindergarten and first grade.

STAGES OF PARENTAL DEVELOPMENT

An important concept to consider within parent education is that of parental development. Becoming and being a parent can have a profound impact on the development of both the mother and father. Theory and research on the stages of parental development includes consideration of parenthood as a developmental stage, the transition to parenthood, and stage theories of parenthood and the family life cycle. Demick considers the issue of stages of parenthood as "developmental changes in the experience and action of parents over the course of bearing and rearing children" (Demick, 2002). Additional research on this important area is needed but those involved in parent education would do well to include concepts relevant to parental development when planning and implementing parent education programs.

PARENT EDUCATION AS A PROFESSION

The notion of parent education as a profession and the parent educator as a professional has been evolving steadily over recent years. Historically, parent education has been carried out formally within the domains of a number of different disciplines, including medicine, social work, therapy, and education, and informally by parent-to-parent advising. For example, parents might ask a pediatrician how best to deal with their toddler's temper tantrums. Although this is not necessarily a medical question, the doctor may be inclined to offer advice. In some situations, parenting advice is given without the benefit of formal training in the area as parent educator is one of many roles played by these professionals. Seldom is parenting directly addressed in training programs for many of the helping professions.

Many national programs, such as PET or STEP, may use paraprofessionals to carry out their particular curriculum. Instructors may have no formal training in child development or parenting, but become certified upon completion of a prescribed training program that follows their particular approach or curriculum.

Other parenting programs involve the use of volunteers, usually experienced parents who offer support or facilitation. The Minnesota-based MELD (now merged with Parents as Teachers) is a good example. Experienced parents are trained in facilitation techniques and given supporting research-based material on child development and parenting issues. These trained parents then lead parenting groups with new parents. One of the strengths of the MELD model is that it includes parents from the community in leadership roles as group facilitators. These parents often share the same cultural and socioeconomic status as the parents in the rest of the group. This shared background gives the facilitators increased credibility and acceptance.

A relatively small but growing number of professionals have trained specifically in parent education and consider it to be their primary profession. Degree-granting programs in parent education are on the rise throughout the United States. There is a slowly emerging consensus on the parameters of parent education and the competencies needed for effective practice.

THE ROLE OF THE PARENT EDUCATOR

What exactly does a parent educator do? Does his or her role vary depending upon the group or the objective? Myers-Walls (1998) identified three possible role paradigms expected of parent educators. Understanding these varying expectations is necessary in order to identify needed competencies for parent educators.

The first role paradigm is that of the expert. Parent educators acting in this role are knowledgeable in certain information and facts and share that knowledge with parents, who see the parent educator as having answers they need and want.

The parent educator can also take a much less active role. In this situation, the parents are assumed to already have the information and knowledge they need, but the parent educator can provide a perspective or a setting for discussion and can access appropriate resources. In this role paradigm, the parent educator operates more as a facilitator to guide group process than as a leader—a "guide on the side" as opposed to a "sage on the stage." The parents establish the agenda and goals. This type of approach is especially effective with disadvantaged or oppressed populations, but it takes an especially competent parent educator who knows how to use evidence-based research and adapt it to diverse populations. "Liberation pedagogy" is one educational approach that has been used to nurture marginalized peoples. This approach seeks to empower learners and encourages them to challenge and change oppressive systems and hierarchical power structures (Shor & Freire, 1986).

A third role paradigm falls between the expert and the facilitator. In the collaborator approach, the educator and the parents work together to determine the goals and agenda of the program. The parents are valued for their knowledge, and the parent educator is recognized for his or her knowledge base, as well as his or her skills in group facilitation.

Because the role of the parent educator can vary depending upon the audience, the setting, and the goals of the group, a truly competent parent educator should be capable of moving into whatever role is needed in the particular situation. An educator offering a one-day workshop may need different skills than one facilitating an ongoing group or writing a newspaper column. Those currently working to define and establish the field of parent education are faced with the difficulty of trying to move the field forward by defining content and competencies while still supporting the broad diversity of the profession.

COMPETENCIES

Discussion about establishing parent education as a field and parent educators as professionals has led to consideration of competencies. What do parent educators need to know in order to effectively practice? What skills should they possess? Campbell and Palm (2004) identified three stages of growth and development (novice, intermediate, and master) for parent educators in five areas of development—knowledge, group facilitation skills, teaching skills, professional identity and boundaries, and understanding diversity. These levels of professional development provide insight into the competencies needed by parent educators as they increase their level of professionalism.

Minnesota was one of the first states to require parent and family educators to be licensed. Originally, in order to be licensed, parent and family educators had to have completed a specified number of credits in family structures and functions, family dynamics, child development, interpersonal relationships, parenting, and teaching methods (University of Minnesota, 1991). The criteria later were changed to focus on a competency-based model (Minnesota Department of Children, Families, & Learning, 2000).

The ability to adequately evaluate parent education materials and curricula is an important competency for the professional family life educator. Professional parent educators possess the knowledge and skills needed to determine what, if any, theory a program might be based upon and can assure that the information is based on solid research. The literature regarding the evaluation of parenting curricula and programs is increasing as the field becomes more firmly established.

There has been increased discussion among parent education professionals regarding the feasibility of certification or licensure of parent educators on a national basis. The CFLE certification program for family life educators requires knowledge in most of the areas deemed relevant for parent education. Some argue that professionals practicing in parent education should have preparation in the broad areas that make up the CFLE criteria. However, many parent educators who operate as facilitators, paraprofessionals, and volunteers, as well as many that consider themselves to be professional parent educators, may not be able to meet all of the requirements of the CFLE designation. The idea of licensure and/or certification of parent educators has been met with concern by those who support peer-facilitator models and other grassroots community-based programs. These programs are typically operated through community centers and utilize experienced parents from the surrounding neighborhood. These parents, often trained in facilitation skills but not formally in child development or parent education, can be especially effective because they often share experience, culture, and economic status with other parents. Establishment of specific academic criteria could prevent many of these parents from practicing as parent educators.

A multitiered or leveling certification process, one that identifies a career track for parent education, may address these concerns. The Center for Parent Education at the University of North Texas (http://www.cpe.unt.edu/) developed a leveling system for parent educators based on core knowledge and skills (Texas Registry of Parent Educator Resources, 2000). The North Carolina Parenting Education Network (www.ncpen.org) has created a certification program containing four levels of certification. Continued interest and discussion in this area will no doubt result in additional credentialing opportunities.

SUMMARY

In this chapter we've looked at the history of parent education and some of the societal changes that lead to increased interest and participation. In addition to considering varying definitions and assumptions and the settings in which parent education often takes place, we reviewed some common theories that have influenced the field. A brief review of some of the more widely used parent education programs and models was followed by a discussion of the current status of parent education as a profession, the role of the parent educator, and competencies needed for effective practice.

This is an exciting time for the field of parent education. The growing number of professionals who consider parent education to be their primary profession is actively discussing new ideas, approaches, theories, and criteria. Increased recognition of the value and impact of positive parenting on the well-being of individuals and society will no doubt result in continued discussion and growth in this important field.

Questions/Problems for Discussion and Review

Class Discussion

1. Can parent educators be effective if they have never had children themselves?

2. Discuss your thinking about whether parent education is a profession or a discipline within the profession of education.

3. Should parent educators be required to have at least a baccalaureate degree in order to practice?

4. Which term is better: parent educator or parenting educator? Why?

Research Problems/Activities

1. Where do the theories presented in this chapter (humanism, behaviorism, and so on) fall in relation to Murray's criteria (page 224)?

2. What would a community-based parenting program using an Adlerian approach look like if you were to design one for your neighborhood resource center?

3. Apply Doherty's levels of family involvement model (discussed in chapter 2) to Harmin and Brim's three modes of instruction for parent education: individual, group, and mass.

4. Investigate the availability of parent education programs in your community. In what settings are they held (health care, community education, extension)? From the descriptions, can you tell what theory of child development they are based on (behaviorism, Adlerian, temperament, and so on)?

Case Study Design

1. Julian and Marie are the parents of 13-year-old Ruby. Ruby refuses to clean her room, and it has become quite a mess. Describe how Julian and Marie would react if they parented using each of the styles described by Baumrind: permissive, authoritative, and authoritarian.

2. How would a parent educator following a behavioral approach suggest that Julian and Marie deal with Ruby and her room? One following an Adlerian approach?

twelve

Adapting Programs for Diverse Settings

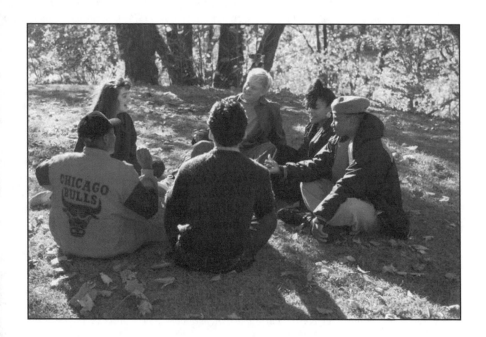

Anywhere in America, an upscale church is sponsoring a family life weekend. The family life minister has her hands full with this one: more than 500 people are registered, representing a wide variety of family types: newlyweds; intact families with children of all ages; stepfamilies with children of all ages and assorted in-laws and former spouses; singles with aging parents, singles with surrogate family, divorced singles, widows; new parents; parents of teens and/or young adults. The varieties and categories overlap and intertwine, and all have special needs. Affluent families are not immune to problems and crises either: divorce, drugs and alcohol abuse, violence, teen pregnancies—even sexual abuse (although no one will talk about it). Often programs about dealing with these stresses have to be presented in disguised form as a way to help those "outside the church," but they need to be dealt with nonetheless. Where to start? How to follow up this one-shot weekend? What will help families to truly learn new coping and communication skills? Can families really learn better ways of coping???

Aleza Brown hopes so. She teaches family life education in an elementary school as part of her job as school counselor. It's elementary, all right. . . . What can you do to help your family? How can you acceptably tell someone you're angry? Are all mothers the same? Are all fathers? It is sort of a ludicrous question when you look at the makeup of the school: 12 different language groups and untold cultural interests are represented. Some of the children are well dressed and well groomed—products of that privileged life in which Mother stays home "for the kids" and Dad may work 10 to 16 hours a day "for the kids." Other children haven't had it so lucky. Mary's parents have just divorced after an extended battle lasting more than two years, and now the custody issue is a battle. George is the oldest son of migrant workers who have spent their lives plucking up crops and themselves from California to Florida. George's father and mother are like many other migrant families. They speak enough English to get by, but they neither read nor write. They want better for George, but they have to keep moving if they are to earn a living the only way they know how. Now that George's father is injured, the fifth grader's chances of finishing high school look extremely dim. Aman's family fled an oppressive political regime in their native country. Although the parents have professional training, they are still struggling to get jobs, learn English, and maintain some of their own cultural heritage. The family has not been welcomed in every context of "melting pot" America. Aman's shyness is understandable.

From a high-rise office building, Sylvia Sanchez of Baker, Simon, and Sanchez, Attorneys at Law, looks down on the school where Aleza Brown teaches and where her daughter Esmeralda goes to school. Sylvia has just had another child. Her husband, Roberto, was from a large family, and they both wanted at least one sibling for Esmeralda. But it makes a law career so hard! She is looking forward to the brown-bag lunch discussions that start today on balancing work and family. A professor from the Department of Family Studies at the local university will be leading the sessions. Sylvia hopes to get some pointers on how to cope better with her schedule, her guilt, her stress, and her marriage. She also hopes that the professor won't just talk all the time. Sylvia wants to hear how others in the group have coped with similar situations. That would be so helpful!

The variety of settings in which family life education is offered poses both challenges and opportunities for family life educators. One thing all of the settings have in common is that they tend to relate to people where they live and spend their time, particularly the contexts of school, community, work, or religion. Each context has its own set of expectations and limitations. If the family life educator does not understand or honor these, he or she will not be successful in accessing and maintaining contact with that particular group. In this chapter, we discuss various contexts and how to work within their expectations and limitations to develop and maintain good programs and good relationships. The final section reviews promising paradigms for the future.

WHAT IS YOUR ROLE?

In any of the settings mentioned previously or in many of the other community settings that call for family life education, a first consideration is your role in the education process. Perhaps you are a staff member with responsibility for planning both short- and long-term family life programs for the agency or institution. Or you may be someone from outside the institution who is called upon to offer a time-limited program on a particular topic. Do you see yourself as the expert, the consultant, or the facilitator?

The *expert* tends to come loaded with material, handouts, and a very set agenda. She or he does most of the talking and offers strong decisive opinions about situations and skills. There is little acknowledgment of the participants' unique situation or culture. The expert has the answers and little personal involvement with the participants.

The *consultant* recognizes her or his expertise in an area and seeks to apply that knowledge to the particular situations of the participants. Prior planning and a review and assessment of the group's interests and expressed needs are often part of the consultant's preparation for working with the group. Presentation is usually in the form of a minilecture or brief report on results of assessment, followed by feedback and questions from the group. A consultant values the involvement of the participants and their ownership of the group process.

The *facilitator* focuses on group dynamics and participant involvement in the education process. He or she draws on the participants' strengths to enhance discussion and resolve issues that surface. Using open-ended questions, reflection, and review of comments made, the facilitator moves the group toward resolution of "problems." The facilitator's own opinions or input are kept to a minimum, although he or she may provide worksheets or case studies to encourage discussion. Although the facilitator is definitely the group "leader," leadership is shared through high levels of interaction with the participants.

One decision about your role may be the situation itself. Are you speaking to a large group in a time-limited format? Is this an ongoing workshop or seminar with a limited number of participants? Have you been specifically asked to serve as consultant or to assist a group in a carefully defined task? The age group you are working with is also a consideration. Adults are more likely to tolerate—and even appreciate—an "expert" approach. Adolescents and young adults respond much better to a facilitator-leader.

THE RELIGIOUS SETTING

Definition of Family Ministry

Garland and Yankeelov (1998) define family in a religious context as:

> those persons who commit themselves to God and then to one another to serve as family for one another for the rest of their lives. Family may include biologically and legally related relationships, such as parents and children, and spouses, but it is not necessarily limited to these culturally recognized relationships. (p. 14)

This highlights an important distinction: The members often serve as surrogate or extended family to each other. "It is exceedingly difficult in our culture to reach beyond the bonds of blood and marriage to embrace others as family, yet that is the first responsibility of congregational family ministry" (Garland & Yankeelov, 1998, p. 15). *Family ministry* is defined as "everything that a church and its representatives do which has an impact on the founding, development, and ministry of families" (p. 16).

A second distinction of religious family life education is the strong role of faith in the lives and decision making of the individual and families within the church. Specific beliefs are held as standards against which any education—or educator—is judged. This can be restricting at times, particularly when dealing with sex education or parenting principles such as acceptable discipline. The presenter should be prepared to answer challenges from audience members with acknowledgement and grace.

A third distinction is the general homogeneity of the congregation. Members tend to hold the same values and beliefs—whether conservative, moderate, or liberal—and to be of the same socioeconomic level. There is also usually a higher level of intact families than in the general population, and more families exhibit identified family strengths. The last 30 years have seen a vast number of church members divorcing and remarrying. Although this new reality has presented problems regarding the biblical intent of "oneness in marriage," most churches are now less judgmental and more inclusive and welcoming of stepfamilies and other nontraditional family forms (Jenks, 2002, as quoted in Strozdas, 2004). On the whole, church members are less willing to talk candidly about "problem areas" in their family life. They prefer an educational and more impersonal, rather than therapeutic, format for support.

Rarely does a congregation have much cultural diversity within its membership, although there are notable exceptions, particularly in urban settings. A comprehensive survey and statistical analysis of 16 congregations that represented diverse cultural, denominational, and racial perspectives revealed that family functioning and reported family stressors were similar in all groups (Yankeelov & Garland, 1998). Surprisingly, the stressor most often reported was "difficulty on the job for a family member," an area not usually addressed by family ministry programming. Other widely reported stressors were centered within family relationships: tasks and chores left undone, parent-child conflict, disagreement about friends or activities, financial strain, and conflict in another family relationship.

When Yankeelov and Garland looked at the reported stressors according to family type, single parents and single senior adults reported more marital conflicts (presumably with ex-spouses or in the marriages of children). Single parents in all samples also reported more financial strain and unsolved problems. The researchers concluded, "With respect to this dimension of family life, as well as others explored in previous sections of this article, denominations have much to gain by perceiving that their families are far more alike than they are different" (p. 45). Garland and Yankeelov (1998) propose a "perspective" approach to family ministry, in contrast to the conventional "programmatic" approach. Such an approach looks at each congregation as unique in its family makeup and challenges. It focuses on equipping rather than telling or directing.

General Characteristics

Understanding some of the general characteristics of religious institutions can lay a foundation for a perspective-taking approach and assist family life educators to relate more effectively to families in a spiritual context.

Congregations tend to be family-oriented but age-divided.   This characteristic parallels the educational assumption of our society that people should be taught in age-graded classes. However, a trend is beginning, particularly in religious organizations, toward sponsoring multiage programs. Such cross-generational groupings have never died out in many ethnic congregations and faith groups and in smaller congregations. I (Powell) recall being asked to speak at a

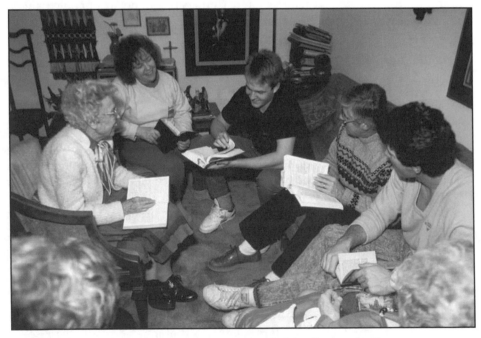

Church members often serve as surrogate or extended family to each other.

"mother-daughter" brunch in a rural church in Alabama. I worked hard at identifying parent-adolescent issues to address in my presentation and finding some interactive exercises. Much to my surprise, the brunch was attended by every woman in the church, most of whom weren't mother-teen daughter pairs. I had to do some creative scrambling to refocus my presentation. I should have checked out the composition of the audience more fully before going!

Values and beliefs are of prime importance and form the bond for the congregation.   If the family life educator has a religious orientation, this will help a trust relationship to develop quickly. Biblical grounding for your presentation and a personal sharing of faith experience, when appropriate, can also enhance an outsider's credibility. I have found this to be particularly helpful when presenting sexuality education seminars. The fact that I am a seminary graduate and the wife of a minister gives me credibility and trustworthiness with the parents and the ministerial staff. Sexuality education, as well as substance abuse prevention, are two areas in which congregations could potentially have a major impact on adolescent decision making and health promotion. Unfortunately, these are issues most congregations have not addressed in a consistent way. A 1995 survey of 527 religious youth workers determined that only 4% of congregations have regular programs to discuss sexuality or substance abuse prevention (Burrill, 1999). Opportunities for clarifying and sharing values and beliefs are crucial. People of faith need to establish their own beliefs about the meaning of sexual expression, then look for opportunities to share these beliefs with young people. "If we don't communicate what we believe about love—about the nature, role and purpose of humanity and how we understand God to be acting in our lives and in the world—who will do it?" (Burrill, 1999, p. 3).

Endorsement of your program by the congregation's minister, priest, or rabbi will influence many people to attend.   This has certainly been the case when marriage enrichment programs are church-sponsored. If the religious leader urges the membership to attend and, in the best case, plans to attend with his or her spouse, the membership will likely follow.

The religious family life education program can address values and moral decision making in ways that school programs cannot.   On the other hand, some congregations are very uncomfortable with too much candor about controversial issues. In developing sexuality programs for church youth, I ask the congregation's own ministers to address the controversial issues, while I provide a framework of information, a format, and a forum for discussion of the pros and cons of various issues. I have never had trouble with opposition from parents concerned about what I might teach their children, because the congregation's ministers and youth leaders were integrally involved in the program implementation from the start. This brings up another distinctive strength of congregational family life education.

Many adult role models are available to assist with small group discussions and interaction.   With the exception of community organizations such as the Scouts, this availability of adult mentors is a unique and valuable resource for family life education in the religious context.

"Families genuinely are a cornerstone of human existence, with the power to bless or curse us, as God told Abraham. And because people tend to replicate their family way of being in the workplace, the marketplace, school, or wherever they are, let us work for blessing" (Wigger, 1998, p. 25). The religious setting has many opportunities to promote and educate for "blessing" the family that will spill over into many other arenas of their lives. For more resources that focus on family ministry, see www.fmef.org. This Web site is nondenominational and provides information on new program emphases and research links to articles that will be especially helpful to family ministers and educators.

THE WORK SETTING

Composition of the workforce has changed drastically over the past 25 years. It is more racially and ethnically diverse and older (median age is 40) and comprises more women—nearly 50%. Yet two in five men still believe that a woman's place is in the home (Bond, Thompson, Glinsky, & Prottas, 2005). The great majority of workers, both male and female, have day-to-day family responsibilities at home. Some 46% have children under 18 who live with them at least half of the time. Dual earner families have increased over the past 25 years from 66% of the workforce in 1977 to 78% in 2002. Combined work hours for dual earner couples with children rose ten hours per week, from 81 hours in 1977 to 91 hours today. At the same time, parents report an increase in the daily time spent in children's activities after work: from 5.2 hours in 1977 to 6.2 hours today. The difference is squeezed out of time parents spend for themselves. Men report about 1.3 hours per day (down from 2.5 hours, in 1977) and women report .9 hours as compared with 1.6 hours in 1977 (Bond et al., 2005).

Single parents make up 20% of the parent population, with 27% of that group being single fathers. All employed fathers report more time spent with their children: 2.3 hours per day, an increase of 30 minutes over 20 years ago. This compares with the constant finding that employed mothers spend 3.2 hours daily with their children. This information is from the findings of a National Study of the Changing Workforce conducted in 1997 by the Families and Work Institute (see http://www.familiesandwork.org). The study also reported that workers are most likely to be satisfied with their jobs, committed to their employers, and productive at work when they have jobs that offer autonomy, meaning, learning opportunities, support from supervisors, and flexible work arrangements that are responsive to individual needs. A 2005 study by the Families and Work Institute studied work expectations in America and found that one in three employees consider themselves chronically overworked (Galinsky & Bond, 2005), with 54% reporting having felt overwhelmed by so much work in the last month.

So is there a place for family life education in the workplace? Stress is lessened by "effective" workplaces where employees ". . . continue to learn, whose supervisors support them in succeeding on the job, who have the flexibility they need to manage their job and their personal and family life, and who have input into management decision-making. . ." (Galinsky & Bond, 2005, p. 2). This confirms a 1998 study of young adult priorities regarding interest in family issues of

---

Box 12.1   When Work Works

WHEN WORK WORKS

Part I: Flexibility: A Critical Ingredient in Creating an Effective Workplace

Today's economy is far different than the economy of the past.

- It is increasingly knowledge- and service-based and technology-driven.
- It is global.
- It is fast-paced and fiercely competitive.
- It is 24/7.

Today's workforce is different than the U.S. workforce in the past.

- It is more ethnically diverse—21% are people of color today versus 12% in 1977.
- It includes almost equal numbers of men and women—51% men and 49% women.
- It has also aged as the Baby Boom generation has moved through the ranks—with fewer young employees (22% under 30 today versus 37% in 1977) and more older employees (56% are 40 or older today versus 38% in 1977).

This is not your father's workforce.

- In fact, far fewer fathers are the only ones bringing home the bacon—one in three (33%) today, compared with just more than one in two (51%) 25 years ago.
- The job-for-life has been replaced with growing job mobility and job insecurity—only 36% feel truly secure in their jobs (or report that it is not at all likely that they will lose their jobs in the next two years) versus 45% 25 years ago.
- Employees no longer work from 9 to 5—men now work 48.2 hours per week on average while women (including the 24% who work part-time) average 41.4 hours. And just more than one in four (26%) U.S. employees works at least one weekend day.

See www.whenworkworks.org: When Work Works: Research Highlights and Project Overview

---

those entering the workforce ("USA Snapshots," 1998). Comparing 1998 responses with those from a similar survey conducted in 1989, the researchers found that 83% of the respondents named a "close-knit family" as their number one priority, a 15% gain since 1989. The second-place priority, job and career, moved down 4 percentage points to 68%, with financial success placing third at 57%. Both studies indicate that employee satisfaction and productivity are more influenced by job quality and workplace support than by pay and benefits, which appear to be generally competitive for the workplace as a whole.

Marketing Your Program

Work-family seminars are one effective way to provide workplace support, but the family life educator will most likely have to "sell" his or her program to company managers. It shouldn't be hard to sell: A 1986 study found that 51% of the companies questioned favored work-family seminars, yet only 13% said they were providing such seminars (Friedman, 1986). On the other hand, it is important to be thoroughly prepared when you approach a business with your idea.

Apgar, Riley, Eaton, and Diskin (1982) give step-by-step assistance in designing programs for the work setting (see box 12.2). The authors emphasize that it is crucial that your program idea fit the mission of the organization and the goals of the particular department. The more familiar you are with the organization, the better chance you will have of selling your idea to administrators and line staff.

Box 12.2   Steps in Designing Family Life Education Programs for Business

1. Realistically appraise your ability to develop and provide services.
   - Why do you want to develop a FLE program for business?
   - What will this program offer the employees?
   - What resources do you have to support the start-up phase of the program?
   - Is your agency or sponsoring group willing to make a commitment to provide services?

2. Select your target organization.
   - Do you or your board have members who can assist in making contacts?
   - Which worksites do your clients come from?
   - Are there any potential buyer organizations that are known for their interest in human resources or that have a history of community involvement?
   - Have you or your agency had any previous formal or informal contacts with any organizations?

3. Research the organization.
   - What is the size of the organization?
   - What is the relationship between employees and management?
   - What are the workforce characteristics or specific workforce concerns (alcoholism rate or well-being of retirees, for example)?
   - Are there any related service programs in existence?

4. Schedule a meeting.
   - Identify the persons within the organization who are responsible for such programs.
   - Arrange a meeting, bringing a descriptive brochure that you can leave with them.
   - Help the organization's representatives to identify what some of the needs are that these programs might address.
   - Be clear about what you and your agency can and cannot provide.
   - Describe other existing agency programs so they can get a sense of where the seminar service fits in with the total service delivery of your agency.

5. Follow up on the contact.
   - Send a letter referring to the visit and suggesting what the next steps are.
   - Keep in touch personally.
   - Identify whether additional persons should be involved.

Note. From Apgar, K., Riley, D. P., Eaton, J. T., & Diskin, S. (1982). *Life education in the workplace.* New York: Alliance for Children and Families. Copyright 1982 by Alliance for Children and Families, reprinted by permission of Manticore Publishers.

Before approaching a business, it is also important to have your proposed seminars carefully designed, complete with learning objectives and methods and evaluation plan. Develop an attractive brochure or notebook with key points and ideas that you can discuss in your meeting and that you can leave with the employer. Present yourself as someone who is capable of providing a quality service. The presentation meeting must minimize the business's anxiety about sponsoring this service: Whom will I be dealing with . . . is it worth the money . . . will our problems be helped by this service?

Apgar et al. (1982) refer to the four "Ps" of marketing: program, promotion, price, and place. Regarding price, they advise that you price your services so that you make a profit. A business expects you to include a profit margin. The place, unless the services are out of the ordinary, would be the employer's premises, most often during the lunch hour.

Key Concepts

Apgar et al. (1982) condense the theoretical and practical heart of any adult education program to four key concepts:

1. *Participation.* High involvement by employees in articulating needs to be addressed and an interactive program design.

2. *Powerful ideas.* Address a few key concepts that you can communicate well.

3. *Parsimony.* Sessions should not be overloaded. Remember that you usually have less than an hour per session. Select the most important ideas, skills, or attitudes that you wish to convey in a participatory fashion.

4. *Practicality.* Adults enroll in programs that address issues of immediate, rather than future, concerns.

The Working Family Resource Center of St. Paul, Minnesota, a collaborative effort with the public school system, outlines some options for work-family seminars in a brochure that they present to company managers (Working Family Resource Center, 1999). Under the major headings of "Work/Family Balance," "Child Development," "Self-Esteem," "Personal Development," "Communication," and "Consumer," they list several appealing seminar titles. For example, under "Personal Development" are listed "Living Positively in a Negative World" and "Seven Habits of Happy and Effective People." The Resource Center also offers parent education, individual consultations, work/family specialist consultations, a resource library, and a newsletter that employer-subscribers can distribute to their employees. "The Center's role is to provide information, stimulate thought and facilitate discussion in order to encourage individuals to improve their personal and family life. Programming covers work/family issues throughout the life cycle" (Working Family Resource Center, 1999).

The growing interest of both employees and employers in quality-of-life issues and how they affect the work environment is good news to family life educators. Well-designed and well-presented programs should get a warm reception from businesses who want to be seen as family-friendly.

THE SCHOOL AND COMMUNITY SETTING

The Value of Relationship Skills Training

Schools also are increasingly interested in relationship issues. A course in relationship development is now required for all high school students in Minneapolis, Minnesota. Other cities and states are incorporating values education and conflict management courses as well. Probably the hardest thing we ever have to do in life is develop and maintain close relationships, yet we have the least formal education in how to do this successfully.

"With the increasing rate of violence between people, the high rate of divorce and family problems, we need to be more proactive and help prevent relationship problems," says David Olson, codeveloper and author, with John DeFrain and Amy K. Olson, of a new relationship development program for use in schools and community settings (Olson, 1999). "We need to add the *fourth* R for 'Relationships' to the three 'R's taught in schools. Relationship skills are something that people can use every day."

Family life educators who are employed by public schools have an opportunity to share new knowledge and skills training with more students and families than in any other setting. Additionally, community agencies and public schools are forming collaborations that address high-risk children and their families. One successful example is a program called Families and Schools Together (FAST), developed in 1990 by family scientist Lynn McDonald and the Family Service America organization (now Alliance for Children and Families). A school-based, collaborative, multi-family program, FAST is designed to "build protective factors for children ages 4–12 and empower parents to be the primary prevention agents for their own children" (Alliance for Families and Children, 2005). The program, now under FAST national supervision, involves a well-defined collaboration between parents, the school, a local mental health agency, and a local substance-abuse prevention provider.

Participation by the whole family in eight weeks of carefully orchestrated, research-based fun activities is the heart of the program. This is followed by two years of monthly family self-help support group meetings. The program has been highly successful, with programs in more than 45 states and five other countries (Canada, Germany, Australia, Austria, and Russia).

According to Laura Pinsoneault, the national training coordinator of FAST, family life educators can "plug in" through the mental health agency role, or other community partners can be added. The program can also be sponsored primarily by a domestic violence agency or a community resource center rather than by a school district.

Working with Schools

Pinsoneault (personal communication, 1999) offers suggestions on how to work with schools to establish collaborative programs of any kind. (1) Cooperation is greatest when the school decides that they want the program. They buy into it and don't have to be persuaded. Often, observing an effective program in action is the turning point. Linking with principals who are already involved is also helpful. (2) Exercise care in choosing a school partner. Make sure the principal fully understands the extent of the school's involvement and the needed time commitment. The principal and the teachers need to be fully committed to the concept. An in-service meeting that explains the program's goals and outcomes can be very helpful, because it gives the teachers opportunities to ask questions and hear and see firsthand what is being considered. (3) The family life educator must convey a spirit of cooperation and competency. This enhances the administration-teacher comfort level, and the school representatives become more supportive. (4) If there are resisters, get them involved as soon as possible. Encourage them to talk with students and parents who are "graduating" from the program to see what effect it had on their family life. (5) A final suggestion is to develop reasonable goals. Sexuality education—and indeed all family life education programs—is often held to much higher standards than other school programs. Few other school courses are expected to demonstrate behavior change (as opposed to knowledge increase) in order to be deemed successful.

> Many family life education programs embody the assumption that learning is equivalent to behavior change and knowledge acquisition. The "personally lived" nature of most family life education content suggests, however, that considerations of the learners' prior experiences should be central in program conceptualization. (Thomas, Schvaneveldt, & Young, 1993, p. 115)

All learners do not start at the same point nor do they assimilate or accommodate experiences and information in the same way. Family life educators must stress this point to program sponsors and funders who may expect universal, visible changes in behavior.

Gaining community support and involvement is also key to establishing comprehensive sexuality education programs in local schools. Many communities have developed community advisory committees, which may be appointed by the school board or may consist of interested citizens who convince the school board of the need for a sexuality education program. Such a committee is most effective when its members represent the broad spectrum of diversity and interests of the community. A community-wide educational forum can provide an opportunity to caution people about the risks of inaccurate information on sexual health issues. Experts in the fields of research, public health, and medicine (including doctors, family planning providers, nurses, professors, HIV/AIDS prevention educators, and teachers) can educate parents and school board members on the value of comprehensive sexual health education. SIECUS (1998a) also advises advocates to work in coalitions and to remember that the target audience is not the opposition minority. Although they are often more vocal, the opposition rarely reflects the majority opinion. SIECUS also advises considering help from national organizations, contacting other community leaders, and involving local religious leaders.

LOOKING TO THE FUTURE

Family support programs, another collaborative community approach, continue to gain momentum as a model paradigm for engaging the family and providing needed resources for successful family functioning. They began in the

1970s as spontaneous shoestring organizations of parents who wanted information, friendships, and support in raising their children. Currently, some family support programs have evolved into large complex systems funded by a variety of public sources, complete with target populations, eligibility standards, and outcome measures (Goetz, 1992, p. viii). The settings in which family support programs operate vary widely, as do the types of services and resources they offer to families. But all programs are geared toward a common goal: increasing the ability of families to successfully nurture their children. In addition, policy makers and other national groups such as the Boys' and Girls' Clubs of America have begun infusing family support principles into the services that they provide to children and families. Believing that families often struggle with multiple difficulties, the family resource center provides a variety of services under one roof, from literacy and GED classes to health clinics and child care.

The Center for Family Life (CFL) in Sunset Park, Brooklyn, New York, is an example of such an approach. Located in a low-income, ethnically diverse neighborhood in which 30% of the population is under 18, the center aims to sustain children and youth in their own homes by enhancing the capacity of parents in a variety of ways. The center is open 15 hours a day, and around-the-clock emergency service is available from the live-in project director and the director of clinical services.

> CFL's philosophy is that (1) child well-being and family strengths are closely interrelated and (2) are themselves outcomes of a large number of factors within the family and within the community; and therefore, that (3) social services—including personal social services to families and children—are important, particularly in economically depressed neighborhoods. (Goetz, 1992, p. 3)

Such a holistic approach in the context of a multiservice center is proving to be very effective. Goetz (1992) stresses the concept of parent empowerment as the key:

> A central challenge to the family resource field is to maintain and enhance this empowerment theme as the principles of family support are translated ever more widely into use in arenas which have not traditionally viewed parents as partners or even as worthy participants in their children's lives. Institutions such as schools or child welfare systems which are reaching out to involve parents in new ways are learning to alter their own expectations and assumptions about parents, and to create many avenues of communicating and facilitating the new partnership they hope to build. (p. x)

Resources for family life educators also continue to expand. Instant access to Web sites on life management topics opens up innumerable information channels. For those who want ready-to-use materials, Family Information Services, established in 1989, provides monthly professional resource materials to its subscribers. Now available online, FIS materials include information and updates on contemporary family issues, program designs, transparency and handout masters, and interviews with researchers and practitioners on their latest work. Increasingly, program designers utilize video productions to illustrate concepts and present case studies that form the basis for discussion by a local family life educator/facilitator. For a well-trained facilitator, the packaged program can be easily adapted to fit the needs of the particular audience and setting. Videoed subjects are frequently representative of the diversity in our society, and issues also vary by cultural context. Professional organizations and certification are also more available and responsive to community educators, yet this is still a challenging area. As family scientists and educators enter the new century, there is growing awareness that cooperation and collaboration with families and professionals at all levels of involvement are the keys to success. Family life educators are no longer seen as the "source of all knowledge," but as valuable resources and catalysts for family development and strength.

Family Support America (formerly Family Resource Coalition of America) articulated its organizational vision in 1995 in a way that can apply to all who work with families. We conclude our discussion with their bright hope:

> We envision an America in which:
>
> All children, youth and families can get the resources they need, right in their own neighborhoods, to be strong and healthy. Classes and support groups, after-school programs, emergency assistance, counseling, or job training: whatever families need, they find it.
>
> All communities reinforce the efforts of families to raise responsible, productive, confident, joyous children. Neighbors watch out for each other across racial, ethnic, religious, and economic lines. Diversity is a cause for celebration, not discrimination.
>
> All institutions that serve children and families (including schools, human services, health and mental health care providers, and private agencies) work together. They embrace family support principles and put those principles into practice.
>
> All levels of government make family and youth needs (including economic security, adequate housing, and the viability and safety of every community) a priority.
>
> All workplaces have family-friendly policies and practices. (www.familyserviceamerica.org)

For the good of all families in all circumstances, the future is full of promise.

Questions/Problems for Discussion and Review

Class Discussion

1. In program design, how do you determine which role to assume as a family life educator (expert, consultant, facilitator)? What are the advantages and disadvantages of each role in terms of teaching effectiveness?

2. Look at the general characteristics of religious congregations and compare them with your own experience for similarities and differences. What could account for the differences? If you do not have a strong religious background, how could you establish trust and validity with a congregational group?

3. Which institution do you think it would be harder to convince that a family life education program would be of benefit: church, business, or school? Give the reasons for your answer.

4. Future directions of family life education are moving toward more comprehensive services, more collaboration, and more input from target group participants. What additional preparation do you think family life educators need in order to be well equipped for their role(s) in this new paradigm?

Research Problems/Activities

Choose a specific example of one of the three areas (church, business, school). Interview the head of that organization about her or his interest in family life education programs and ask permission to conduct a survey of representative persons in the organization to ascertain their interest in family life education programs. Design the survey and review the results with your class. What characteristics of the particular group might have skewed the survey results? How would you change the survey so that you can get more specific results and more generalizable data?

Case Study Design

Design the presentation of a workplace program for a specific organization with which you are familiar. Perhaps it is the place where your parents work, or it could be the university you attend. Use the planning steps in box 12.2 to develop your plan.

‹ thirteen

International Perspectives on Family Life Education

Carol Anderson Darling

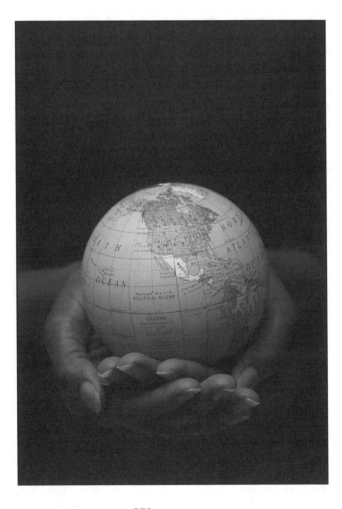

THE NEED FOR GLOBAL AWARENESS

We live in a complex world where understanding other individuals and cultures is critical. Global awareness is no longer a luxury, but a necessity as we extend our focus to families that are unlike our own. The need for students to become culturally competent and work with diverse populations is also becoming increasingly important, particularly in the family science field. By incorporating cross-cultural awareness and education into our classrooms, we can enhance a sense of understanding, appreciation, and acceptance of diverse family settings and cultures that can enrich both our own lives and the well-being of individuals and families worldwide.

More than ever, global issues are influencing the lives of families due to advances in communication, technology, science, and transportation. Information, goods, and services produced in one country quickly become available to others in various parts of the world. The clothes we wear, the foods we eat, the music we enjoy, the art we view, the technology we employ, and the natural resources we use all result from this global process. Consequently individuals and families around the world are more connected to each other. The trends of internationalization and the expanding interrelationships among nations and their peoples have resulted in global interdependence, as well as a growing diversification of the world's population racially, ethnically, economically, and culturally. Globalization has not only reduced distance and time, but has also linked countries at opposite ends of the Earth, resulting in a complex transition of many advanced countries into multi-ethnic and multicultural societies (Dini, 2000).

While international migration can be seen as facilitating global interdependence and unity, it also brings widening demographic, economic, political, and ecological disparities that greatly influence families (Brubaker, 2001). Therefore, viewing families from an international context is not only important to increase our understanding of those beyond our borders, but also to gain insights about those who have recently immigrated to new countries. Because international travel and migration are bringing people of the world together, migration is emerging as one of the major issues of our times. Mobility of families is also a concern, because family members no longer necessarily live in close proximity. When family members move, they often become disconnected from the unifying features of the extended family. While some families maintain communication with access to the Internet and cellular phones, quality time still may be lost. There may be circumstances due to geography, time, and finances that prevent families from joining together for important family occasions. Thus, family members may not be present for significant family transitions, times of joy and sorrow, or opportunities to resolve family issues and disagreements. Because of these challenges, younger generations may also not have opportunities to interact and bond with their relatives as they did when living in their countries of origin.

Although the functions and structures of families vary by culture, families are still societies' most important resource. They provide the buffer and protection that keep children and other members safe. However, some families are vulnerable in terms of health care and economics, as well as environment and social influences. At times, they cannot manage alone and government steps in to create policies and programs that could affect family structure, education, and financial well-being. While various professionals can help families, family life educators incorporate a preventive and educational approach to individual and family issues. They provide the skills and knowledge to enrich individual and family life.

An international perspective is needed when teaching about families. Since many students attending American universities have an ethnocentric view of culture, it is important to provide an alternative perspective that is not focused specifically on one's own culture, but provides an ethnorelative approach. Whether teaching about family relations, parenting, or marriage education, cultural differences and implications can enhance learning within our own society, as well as learning about others. Providing a cross-cultural approach to family life education is important because it allows us to go beyond a narrow focus of Western culture and concepts. We need to create a climate within family science classrooms that fosters thinking not only about family content, but also multicultural understanding. While some family science programs have specific courses in cultural diversity, cultural learning can also be infused into a variety of courses and topics in order to provide and enhance an international perspective to the study of families.

GLOBAL ISSUES OF CONCERN TO FAMILIES

In order to understand the context underlying the development of family life education programs, an awareness of issues of concern to families is critical. Some countries are facing the unchecked devastating effects of HIV and AIDS, along with SARS and concerns about the H5N1 avian flu virus. These health concerns add multiple stressors to the lives of children and their parents. Other countries see family planning and pregnancy as primary issues and are working on education regarding contraception, pregnancy prevention, prenatal care, and parenting. In some countries marriage education predominates, with legislation to assist couples with premarital education, whereas other countries are focusing on helping couples with their relationships as they make the transition to parenthood. Other communities face the ravages of war and terrorism that influence individuals and families as they deal with the physical and emotional pain of both the actual acts of terrorism and the fear that encompasses these acts.

While this myriad of issues confronts individuals and families worldwide, essentially, five trends impact families around the globe (United Nations Development Programme, 2003a; 2003b).

Globalization

Globalization and technological development will continue at a rapid pace that can result in anxiety, tension, and conflict for those cultures rooted in more traditional, agrarian, patriarchal value systems. While overall, Americans tend to view globalization as more positive than negative, that opinion is not held world-wide. Although Americans do not have any specific desire to spread their culture, it is widely known that American popular culture has a major impact on the world. Recent polls report that 71% of Americans agreed that cultural diversity was a "major reason" for America's success and 73% perceived themselves as citizens of the world, as well as the United States (Americans and the World, 2004). In contrast, countries ruled by fundamentalist religious leaders are frustrated by the dress and actions of teenagers who wear rebellious fashions in public that they have seen on popular Western television programs beamed down from satellites. As people are exposed to the more gender-equal and individualistic values of Western cultures, societal conflicts are erupting (Francoeur & Noonan, 2004a).

Increase in Migration

The number of countries concerned and involved in human mobility is steadily rising. None of the 190 sovereign states of the world is beyond the reach of migration, being either countries of origin, transit, or destination for migrants and often all three simultaneously. Whereas some migration is internal, the rising number of people crossing borders is the most reliable indicator of the intensity of globalization. As a result, the traditional boundaries between languages, cultures, ethnic groups, and nations are eroding. Migrants are only a small percentage of the world's population. Yet, if all international migrants lived in the same place, it would be the world's fifth largest country (International Organization for Migration, 2003). The annual number of migrants is estimated to be between five and ten million people. Demographers project an increase in the world population to nine billion by 2050, which will include approximately 230 million migrants. Those who migrate are often highly educated and qualified persons, resulting in a "brain drain" from the home economy. Some prefer to be "circular" rather than permanent migrants, and thus eventually return home to family and friends. About half the migrants are women, who either migrated as spouses or family members or moved independently of family to work abroad as primary breadwinners. Because opportunities for legal migration are limited, many women have resorted to unusual forms of migration involving smuggling and trafficking. As a result women are prone to experience gender-specific forms of abuse and exploitation (International Organization for Migration, 2003).

Changes in Family Structure

In the past many cultural groups assumed that couples would get married, stay married, have children, and deal with two sets of kin. However, in many societies things are changing. Increasing divorce, mobility, and migration have altered family structure and the notion of intergenerational relationships. Other developments, such as the use of contraception, increasing numbers of single parents, women joining the labor force, postponement of marriage, and improved education of women, have resulted in smaller families. These changes appear to have eroded some of the traditional values placed on childbearing, as well as altered the ages at which family traditions such as marriage and childbirth have commonly occurred within a culture. Moreover, poor economic conditions in some countries have resulted in greater maternal and child mortality. Not only have the composition and structure of families changed in many countries, but also migrants who carried with them the idea of family structure based on their home countries often find that changes in culture and context evolve into further alterations to their family structures (Manning, 2001; United Nations Development Programme, 2003b).

Demographic Aging

The current global rate of population aging is unprecedented and pervasive with increases in the proportion of older persons (60 years or older) being accompanied by declines in the proportion of the young (under age 15). The aging of the world population will be even more rapid in the twenty-first century than in the past. However, the pace of change is quite varied and countries are at very different stages in this process. Those countries that started the process later have less time to adjust. Because of decreasing fertility, we will not return to the young populations of our ancestors. The aging of the population will affect every man, woman, and child and will have a direct bearing on intergenerational and intragenerational relationships. Aging will not only influence economics, but also health and health care, family composition, living arrangements, housing, and migration. The world median age is currently 26, but by 2050, it is expected to be 36 years of age (United Nations Department of Economic and Social Affairs, 2001).

HIV/AIDS Pandemic

As of December 2005, a global summary of the AIDS epidemic indicated that 40.3 million people were living with HIV with 4.9 million newly infected and 3.1 million deaths that year (World Health Organization, 2005a). Women are increasingly being infected by HIV, especially in the Caribbean and sub-Saharan Africa. Nearly 70% of the word's HIV-infected people live in Africa, where HIV/AIDS is the leading cause of death and where most new victims are women. These women are infected by their husbands who have both a "home wife" and one or more traveling wives for company when they are away at work. Gender inequality makes it more difficult for African women to negotiate condom use. Moreover, sexual violence can also increase the widespread risk of HIV transmission. HIV is also increasing among women in Asia, including large epidemics in China and India, due to women's low economic and social position and poor health status. In Asia injected-drug use, in conjunction with sexual relations, influences the HIV epidemic. Women are often ignorant about the ways HIV can be spread and are prevented by cultural norms from insisting on prevention methods, such as condoms, when they have sexual relations with their husbands. As in Africa, gender inequalities and the cultural rules governing sexual relations for men and women are central to this health issue. Increases in the percentage of HIV-infected women are also occurring in North America, Oceania, Latin America, and Eastern Europe (World Health Organization, 2004a; 2005a).

MULTIPLE MEANINGS OF "FAMILY"

What Is a Family?

We live in a world of different meanings and contrasting perspectives of family life, so we cannot impose an arbitrary definition of what constitutes a family. Various government entities, employers, and religions as well as individual family members and family groups may view families differently (Adams & Trost, 2005). They may perceive the meaning of "family" as family of origin, family of procreation (biological family), or family of commitment or affiliation. These latter socially constructed families have been created to serve the nurturance and acceptance needs of the individual. In fact, some individuals define "family" as both their family of origin and their family of choice (Bor & du Plessis, 1997). Depending on one's culture, family can be perceived as a nuclear family or extended family with multiple generations. In fact, in some cultures, the deceased are still considered to exert a strong presence in the family. Family can also be defined legally as to who can be married or adopted by law, whereas some perceive taking in a child or nonfamily member as constituting a family without the need of legal documentation. Thus, if we impose a single definition of family upon others, we may be sending a message that their family values and structures are not important (Schmid, 1995).

While there is no consensus as to what constitutes a family, particularly across cultures, it could be meaningful to view the family as a bonded unit of interacting and interdependent individuals who have some common goals, resources, and values and may share living space at least for part of their life span (Darling, 1987). This non-exclusionary definition of the family embraces differing family forms, sizes, ages, and roles, whether we are discussing same-sex marriages and families, children who divorce their parents, or families who socially open their boundaries to a non-relative. Such a paradigm facilitates viewing the family as a collection of interdependent, yet independent, individuals whose corporate entity differs from the characteristics of its individual members. When the family is viewed as an interacting group of individuals who are emotionally, physically, and socially interdependent, the focus shifts from the attributes of the group or the individual to the relationships among the family members. In the complex world where we live, a flexible perspective of "family" is essential to facilitate the bonds that may have eroded through death, divorce, family separation, or circumstance (Darling, 2005). Recent natural disasters, wars, and terrorist activities have brought attention to the loss of family members and the need to create flexible boundaries to incorporate those in need of familial support.

Using Theory to Understand International Families

Theories contribute to our understanding of families by providing reasonable explanations of individual and family behaviors. Although no single theory is intended to explain everything in the universe, scientific theory utilizes a certain set of concepts to explain a particular set of phenomena (Klein & White, 2002). There are multiple theories from various disciplines that can be used to understand international family structures and functions. Since we are affected by our childhood, familial, gendered, and socialization experiences along with our cultural beliefs, the integration of multiple theories is warranted. For example, exchange theory can be incorporated to understand the rewards and costs of living in a particular location versus migrating to another country (Klein & White, 2002). Moreover, immigrants to various cultures may experience differing levels of adaptation to their new cultures due to stressors in their lives, resources for coping, and perception of these events. Thus, understanding stress theory and the ABC-X model as it applies to the normative and nonnormative stressors of immigrant families can provide

Through new technology and communication access, individuals and families around the world are more connected to each other.

insight into family adaptability and resilience (Boss, 2002). While families can be analyzed from numerous theoretical frameworks, a few need to be highlighted to illustrate how theory can be applied to facilitate greater understanding of international families.

Family systems theory.   Viewing the family as a system provides an important paradigm for analyzing human behavior (Klein & White, 2002). Understanding "intergenerational communications" about families, physical and psychological boundaries, and feedback in coupled relationships, as well as parent-child communications, can provide insight into interpreting the complex relationships between individuals and their families. Theoretical clarifications can evolve from discussions of boundaries and distance regulation along with cohesion and adaptability. What types of cultural boundaries exist for persons of varying ethnic, age, or gender backgrounds? What kinds of expectations for family togetherness and adaptability exist for different ethnic and religious groups? For example, cohesion and enmeshment can have different meanings in cultures that value familism rather than individuality. A discussion of family stories, rituals, and rules can also provide understanding and meaning about differing cultural groups.

Developmental theory.   Incorporating a developmental framework for both individuals and families can be helpful when trying to understand families across cultures within a perspective of change (Klein & White, 2002). Whereas change is an ever-present, gradual part of individual aging, families and society are changing even faster. Along with media influences, alternate lifestyles, and advances in biotechnology, family life has also evolved.

A way to understand the idea of developmental influences in one's life is an analogy of baking chocolate chip cookies (Maddock, personal communication, 2002). Some people use different kinds of shortening, sugar, salt, nuts, chocolate chips, and eggs and may mix, bake, and store the cookies in a variety of ways. Each person's chocolate chip cookies would be tasty, but there would be similarities and differences in appearance, texture, and flavor. The cookie analogy applies to cultural differences regarding prenatal development, early childhood experiences, adolescent changes, adult development, and family socialization experiences, all of which influence the development of individuals and families (Darling & Hollon, 2002). The cultural context can be incorporated by examining the role of different environments—accessibility of ingredients (raw materials), using different ovens (temperature, time, and altitude), or values placed on foods for sustenance versus pleasure. Just as all people develop differently based on various values and conditions in their cultures, so do our cookies. While some people and cookies may be quite different due to their development and culture, all have value.

Family as an ecosystem.   International families not only exhibit many different family customs, but also different social contexts for those customs. Some examples, which may seem different to Westerners, are widow inheritance in Kenya, "adultery hoots" in Ghana, *hijra* in India, living apart together (LAT) in Germany and Sweden, transgendered *kaneeths* in Bahrain, *kathoey* in Thailand, temporary marriage (*mut'a*) in Iran, hymen reconstruction in South Korea and Greek Cyprus, "try everything" (*faxendo tudo*) advice given to Brazilian boys and girls, and the subordinate roles of women in many cultures (Francoeur, 2004).

The family ecosystem approach can be quite useful to add context to family life education (Bubolz, Eicher, & Sontag, 1979; Bubolz & Sontag, 1993; Darling, 1987; Darling & Hollon, 2003; Klein & White, 2002). With individual, family, and world issues becoming increasingly complicated, we need a framework that can incorporate a holistic view of these complex issues. Since different cultures and ecosystems influence the actions and decisions related to these issues in different countries, a family ecosystem framework can guide our thinking. The reciprocal interactions between environmental influences and families differentiate each country's issues and the preferred mode to ameliorate these concerns. There is increasing awareness that human beings are interdependent creatures and not independent organisms. This is not only true in our relationships with each other, but also with the total environment in which we live. This holistic view of individuals and groups in their association with the physical, biological, and social conditions and events around them provides a frame of reference that has come to be generally known as "human or family ecology."

Several basic premises underlie an ecosystem model. The first and most basic is that individuals and families are viewed as interacting with their environment, which constitutes an ecosystem (Bubolz, Eicher, & Sontag, 1979; Bubolz & Sontag, 1993; Darling, 1987). In such an ecosystem, the parts and wholes are interrelated and interdependent. A second premise is that the family carries out certain essential physical, biological, economic, psychosocial, and nurturing functions for its members, for the family as a collective, and for the larger society. Thus, the unique and powerful value of an ecological perspective lies in its potential to examine these multilevel functions and systems in relation to each other over time.

The third premise consists of the interdependence of all persons worldwide along with their resources. The overall well-being and health of the planet and of all people cannot be viewed in isolation or outside the context of the whole ecosystem. The underlying moral value structure of an ecological framework is grounded in a balance between demands of the ecosystem for cooperation and integration and demands of the individual for autonomy and freedom. An ecosystem perspective takes seriously the complementary needs of the individual with the needs of the global ecosystem. Ideally, this complementarity facilitates the development and well-being of the individual and family, as well as the ecosystem.

One core value in an ecosystemic framework is that of survival, not just of humans, but of other living species as well. This also includes the survival and well-being of the nonliving environment, which is critical for sustaining all life. The goal of human amelioration becomes the central focus with virtues such as economic adequacy, justice, freedom, peace, education, health, work, and nurturing relationships contributing to the ultimate good and to quality of life. Most family life educators dealing with international family life education resonate with the perspective of Bubolz and Sontag (1993), who proposed that the grounding of family ecology theory in values places an important responsibility on scholars and practitioners. We must attend to special problems of groups and subcultures that lack power, self-determination, and access to resources and who experience discrimination and prejudice. These can include racial and ethnic minorities, the handicapped, women, the poor, and the old. Attention must be given not only to the "haves" but also to the "have nots." The scope of family ecology must be international and address the needs of people in developing nations, as well as the less privileged in more developed areas of the world. Because human betterment and the quality of the environment are interdependent, the value base of family ecology is grounded in this interdependence.

The family ecosystem model is built on three major concepts: the *organism or human environed unit*, the *environments* encompassing societies' families, and the *interrelationships* between the family system and its surrounding environments (Darling, 1987; see figure 13.1). The *organism or human environed unit* can be a single individual or plurality of individuals who have some feelings of unity; share some common resources, goals, values, and interests; and have some sense of identity. While many times the group of interest is the family, from the paradigm of international family life education, the focus of the human environed unit is on the population of family groups from different countries. The *environments* can be categorized into three types. Whereas the *natural environment* (NE) is formed by

Figure 13.1   Family Ecosystem Model

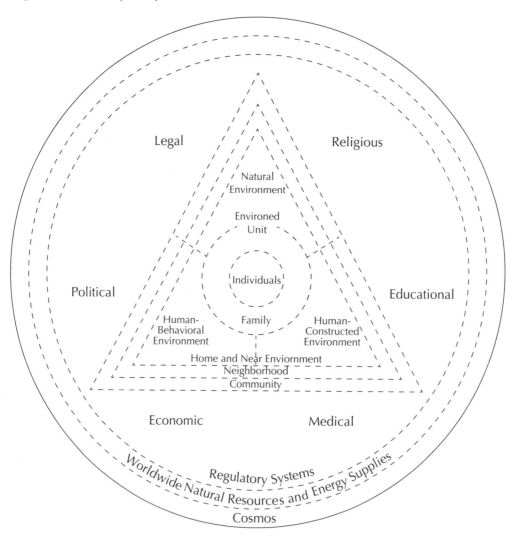

Source: "Family Life Education" by Carol Anderson Darling from *Handbook of Marriage and the Family*, M. Sussman & S. Steinmetz (eds.) 1987. Permission granted by Springer.

nature and the *human constructed environment* (HCE) is that which is altered or created by human beings, the *human-behavioral environment* (HBE) is socialized by human beings and their behaviors. Regulatory systems include the legal, political, economic, religious, educational, and medical systems. However, one should not forget the role of worldwide natural resources and energy supplies, as well as the cosmos. With our need for natural resources and energy along with the influence of global warming and weather systems, elements of the natural environment need to be examined in context of the ecosystems of families. *Interrelationships* can occur within the environed unit, between environments, and between the environed unit and the environments. By applying the ecosystem framework, students can examine global issues of family concern and their impact on individuals and family members. This approach can provide an ethnorelative approach to understanding cultural perspectives of families, public policies, and environmental conditions.

What Is Family Life Education?

Various countries beyond the United States have developed extensive programs in family life education (e.g., Singapore); passed new legislation to support family life education (e.g., Taiwan); proposed marriage/couples/parent education (e.g., Norway); focused on issues of concern to families, such as AIDS and HIV (e.g., China, India, and South Africa); and developed academic programs related to family life education (e.g., Taiwan and Canada). However, information and communication about the progress of these initiatives worldwide is varied and inconsistent. From an international perspective, family life education exists, but its definition, meaning, goals, and methods can be quite diverse. This is due, in part, to the breadth of the field and the different disciplines it encompasses, especially in the international arena. In fact, an Internet search on international family life education programs resulted in 275,000,000 entries. While all these entries may not be applicable to specific programs, family concerns in various countries are resulting in organized programs to assist those in need.

Although there is little consensus regarding the definition of family life education within Western culture, generally it is perceived to be any effort to strengthen family life through education or support (see chapter 1). Family life education can include anything from teaching about relationships in schools to providing premarital education or dealing with the developmental issues of aging. Knowledge about human development, interpersonal relations, and family life is not innate. Thus, there is a universal societal need to transmit knowledge about family living intergenerationally. While some of this learning is done informally, the complexities of society mandate that new methods be created to assist individuals preparing for family life and responsibilities. The objective of all family life education is to enrich and improve the quality of individual and family life. While family life education does not impose some arbitrary definition of what constitutes a family, it does emphasize processes that help people develop into healthy adults, work together in close relationships, and bring out the best in others (Cassidy, 2003; Darling, 1987; National Council on Family Relations, 2003).

To understand the role of culture in providing family life education, it might be helpful to learn about the experiences and insights of an American-born CFLE who resides part-time in Japan (Southwick, personal communication, 2006). For over 20 years Edward Southwick has periodically been providing counseling and self-improvement lessons for individuals, couples, and groups in Japan. While he has had considerable experience in Japanese culture, he comes with a cultural lens of both an "insider" and "outsider" in viewing families and family life education, and thus provides some unique insights. He has had considerable success in helping people, but it has been difficult to develop this professional pursuit in Japan. He reports that Japanese are very private people who consider receiving counseling or any assistance as a sign of weakness. Thus, they keep their problems secret and referrals are rare due to the potential stigma of being perceived as having a mental disorder. He has thus learned that it is best to disguise his sessions as "lessons for self-improvement."

Japan is not considered a family-friendly society because there is no family leave for childbirth and companies put business before families. Furthermore, companies do not like to hire women for higher-paying permanent positions. Because it is assumed that women will get married and leave the workforce, it can become a large sacrifice for the company to hire women. Child rearing is almost totally the woman's responsibility, and she is not seen as an equal or recognized partner. Japanese wives are still often referred to as a "company manager's" wife. In other words, the identity of women is tied to the status of their husbands and children.

Because business is considered a higher priority than family, it is quite unusual for a male, especially in a high-profile position, to leave work for a family illness or if his wife were having a baby. Males do not get time to see children participate in sports events and normally have to spend their after-work hours socializing with co-workers. They may often be forced to work in another city or country for periods of a year or longer without their families. When a Japanese man loses his job, he basically loses his identity, which accounts for a high rate of suicide among Japanese men. Once husbands enter a Japanese company and get immersed in that culture, they can no longer make their families and their needs a priority.

Members of the younger generations are beginning to question their priorities. Whereas some rare individuals put their families over their jobs and refuse company demands, others have rejected positions because of the resultant sacrifices to their families. Although the numbers are still small, more and more Japanese men are willing to focus primarily on their families. Concomitantly, a small number of companies are beginning to offer more understanding and flexibility.

Lack of communication is another issue in Japanese culture. In Japan a saying similar to "silence is golden" has been mistakenly applied to almost every aspect of family communications, as well as relationships with friends and business. As a result couples rarely talk about their love and many rely on a phrase that is roughly translated as "it goes without saying." In other words, Japanese couples supposedly know each other's needs without having to speak. Since there is so little communication within families, especially between fathers and children, children seldom develop good communication skills. Many individuals really would like to communicate more and are thrilled when they make a foreign friend or live abroad. They often become more open after their experience and do not necessarily want to return to Japan and live in a closed, non-communicative society.

It is quite difficult to get Japanese fathers to attend any FLE programs unless they have very deep and painful personal problems. The most one can expect is to help the wives/mothers better deal with their distant husbands in the ways that they interact with them. Since mothers are the primary caregivers to the children, it is easier to give them useful advice on how to better raise their children. However, it is very difficult to address the systemic nature of any family issue.

While Japanese families would not participate in family counseling or family life education because it would be considered embarrassing, studying "self improvement" while being a "normal" person without any real problems is acceptable. It is much easier for a Japanese to take a course to get some kind of certificate or qualification in counseling, child-rearing, or self-improvement education. Women who actually have the time to participate in this type of course seldom use it professionally or even to help others, but hopefully use the information to help themselves and their families. Courses such as parent effectiveness training offering lessons and certificates for completion are quite popular.

The case of Japan is helpful in revealing the role of culture in implementing family life education programs. Family life education has to develop in context of the ecosystem because one has to understand elements in the culture before offering guidance in an acceptable form within that context. Some Japanese counselors have a difficult time getting to the essence of their clients' problems and have to spend considerable time sorting out their clients' issues. However, by showing real concern and appreciation for clients and a nonjudgmental attitude coupled with openness and friendliness, Japanese people can open up their feelings and begin to communicate. To reduce the stigma of needing family assistance, marketing family life education through the media and television can make family life education courses more acceptable to potential clients. It can also encourage government and business leaders to develop more family-friendly policies and certificate-based courses that can assist with family problems while avoiding embarrassment.

STATUS OF FAMILY LIFE EDUCATION INTERNATIONALLY

There are numerous programs dealing with some aspect of family life education worldwide. However, we have little comparative data regarding the status of family life education in other countries. Conducting research internationally has several challenges involving communication, coordination, and interpretation. Nevertheless, it is important to collect data from other countries and develop a global network of colleagues to assist each other with issues of professional and social concern. An exploratory study was conducted to determine the status of family life education internationally by examining the involvement, interest, and available course work in family life education offered worldwide. While the sample, questions, and data collection procedures may limit interpretation and generalizability of conclusions, it is important to examine worldwide family issues of public concern and how family life education is related to these family concerns.

The participants in the study consisted of international (non-U.S.) members of four international organizations dealing with family issues through the coordination and support of the National Council on Family Relations and International Federation of Home Economics (IFHE). NCFR is an international multidisciplinary professional organization linking family research with family education, practice, and policy formation. IFHE is an international non-governmental organization concerned with home economics and consumer studies. Both organizations have consultative status with the United Nations.

After examining several United Nations documents to determine worldwide issues, a survey was developed with the assistance of international colleagues from Europe, Asia, and the United States (United Nations Development Programme, 2000;

2003a; 2003b; 2004). Since professionals in various countries have varying definitions and perceptions of "family" and "family life education," pertinent definitions were included in the survey as they applied to family life education, marriage education, and parent education. In addition, some questions included family issues of public concern, level of legislation/regulation regarding general family issues, and need for professional training and family programs. The survey was in English. While many family professionals speak English as a second language to facilitate professional communication and collaboration, English fluency was a limitation of this study.

The final sample consisted of 277 respondents from five continents and 50 countries. Seventy-eight percent of the respondents were female and 21.5% were male, with a majority (67.9%) reporting that they were married and 19.6% saying they were never married. In regard to race and ethnicity, the majority of the respondents were White (71.1%) followed by Asian (19.6%), Black (4.4%), Hispanic or Latino (1.1%), and other (3.7%). This sample was well educated with 85.3% having a graduate/doctoral degree and 14.6% completing their education with a baccalaureate college degree.

Because the field of family life education is still emerging in many countries, respondents were asked three separate questions about whether they were family life educators, marriage educators, and/or parent educators. Each question provided a definition of these three types of educators in order to operationally define these concepts across cultural perceptions. Involvement in family life education was reported by 32.5% of the respondents, whereas 16.8% were involved in parent education and 7.8% considered themselves to be marriage educators. Although the percentage of respondents who were family, marriage, or parent educators was low, interest in becoming a family life educator was expressed by 67.8% of the respondents with 25.9% indicating that they were "very interested." When asked a Likert-type question (1 = no interest to 5 = great interest) about the public interest in their countries regarding legislation for family life, marriage, and parent education, there was more interest for parent education (mean = 3.43), followed by family life education (mean = 3.08) and marriage education (mean = 2.87). The developing international interest in family life education is obvious. While the contexts of these data were not apparent, the case study of having to disguise family life education in Japan indicates that the perception of the name and what it means can be a problem in interpreting cross-cultural data.

Because of increasing international interest in NCFR's Certified Family Life Educator credential, its ten content areas were described and the respondents were asked to indicate the amount of university-level course offerings in their country that were applicable to these ten content areas. The responses were noted in a Likert-type scale of 1 = no course work to 5 = considerable course work. *Human growth and development* had the most course coverage (mean = 3.78), followed by *families in society* (mean = 3.74), *internal dynamics of families* (mean = 3.52), *interpersonal relationships* (mean = 3.41), *family and the law* (mean = 3.25), *human sexuality* (mean = 3.23), *ethics* (mean = 3.16), *family resource management* (mean = 3.15), *parent education and guidance* (mean = 2.94), and *family life education methodology* (mean = 2.77). The totals of the mean scores of involvement in each of these content areas by continent are shown in a stacked graph in figure 13.2. This graph is

Figure 13.2

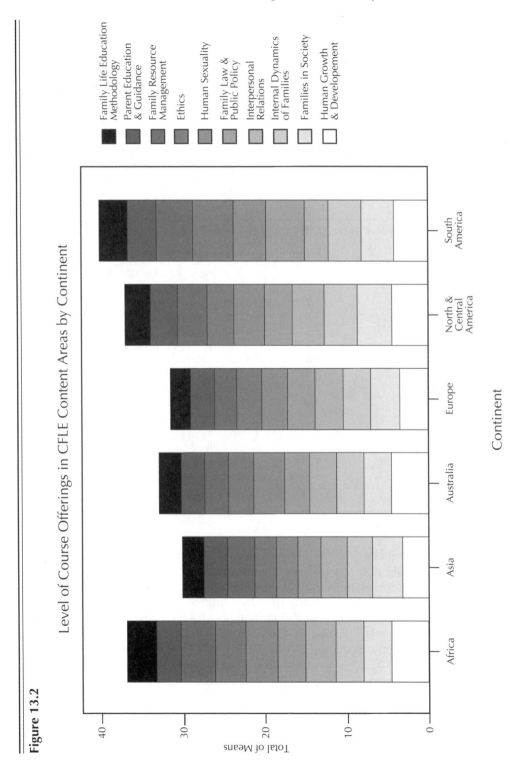

Level of Course Offerings in CFLE Content Areas by Continent organized from the bottom upward by rank order. It is gratifying to see that so many continents and countries have course work applicable in family life education, however, the need for family life education methodology is readily apparent.

The professionals noted that various family issues were of public concern to the people in their countries. For 30 issues related to family well-being, public concern was noted by a Likert-type scale of 1 = no interest to 5 = great interest. The five greatest issues of concern were drug and alcohol abuse, aging, family violence, adolescent health, and unemployment, whereas the issues of least concern were cohabitation, family structure, and homelessness (see table 13.1). Some of these issues, such as unemployment and aging, are related to previously reported world concerns, but a few are worth some special attention.

Table 13.1   Level of Interest in Family Issues of Public Concern

Public Issue	Mean*	Public Issue	Mean*
Drug and alcohol abuse	3.88	Universal primary education	3.25
Aging	3.82	Contraception	3.22
Family violence	3.70	Family well-being	3.21
Adolescent health	3.66	Legislative support of families	3.03
Unemployment	3.64	Family planning	3.01
Caregiving	3.53	Therapy and counseling	2.96
Gender equality	3.45	Marital stability	2.94
Health insurance	3.41	Reduction of child mortality	2.88
HIV/AIDS	3.40	Employer support of families	2.86
Divorce	3.40	Fatherhood	2.85
Adolescent pregnancy	3.38	Infertility	2.85
Cultural diversity	3.33	Adoption	2.85
Parenting issues	3.33	Homelessness	2.80
Maternal health care	3.26	Family structure	2.76
Poverty	3.25	Cohabitation	2.46

*Range: 1 = no interest to 5 = great interest

Alcohol and Drug Abuse.   Use of alcohol and other controlled substances is growing rapidly and contributing significantly to the global burden of disease, taking a major toll on both individuals and families (World Health Organization, 2004b). Worldwide data indicate that 76.3 million persons are diagnosed with alcohol-use disorders, whereas 15.3 million persons have problems with drug use. Injected-drug use is reported in 136 countries with 93 countries reporting HIV infection among this population (World Health Organization, 2003). There is often a misconception that the only problem with alcohol is dependence, but many public health problems arise from acute intoxication resulting from occasional high-risk drinking by normally light to moderate drinkers. Misuse of alcohol takes a disproportionate toll on the poor, who spend a greater percentage of their incomes on alcohol and, when problems occur, have less access to services, may lose their jobs, and bring difficulties to their families. Experience has shown that the most effective way of reducing consumption is by restricting availability (Sharman, 2005).

Domestic Violence.   A World Health Organization study on domestic abuse of 24,000 women from rural and urban areas in ten countries revealed that intimate partner violence is the most common form of violence in women's lives and surpasses assaults by strangers or acquaintances. Domestic violence is known to affect women's sexual and reproductive health, as well as increase the risk of receiving a sexually transmitted infection (STI). Although pregnancy is perceived as a time when women should be protected, between 4 to 12% of these women were beaten during pregnancy. More than 90% of these women had been abused by the father of the unborn child, and at least 20% had never told anyone about the abuse prior to being interviewed (World Health Organization, 2005b). The social and economic costs of family violence are considerable. The losses are not just financial, but involve the diminished productivity of individuals who are unable to function fully, have lost their psychic identity, or have died. Family violence is a human rights issue deeply rooted in cultural and religious gender bias and often supported by patriarchal societies (Bahá'í International Community, 1994).

Adolescent Health.   Adolescent health is a concern in both developed and developing countries, but the problems of youth are often ignored. While adolescence is a period of exploration and experimentation, young people lack the knowledge and ability to avoid some of the risks that confront them. Sexuality is a major challenge for healthy adolescent development with adolescents facing problems of early pregnancy, substance abuse, and violence that make them vulnerable to life-threatening diseases and conditions. Evidence shows that new HIV infections among adolescents are increasing along with other STIs, which often go undetected. Moreover, unwanted pregnancies are often resolved by unskilled practitioners, who perform unsafe abortions illegally. Tobacco use is another serious health issue for adolescents, who are often enticed to smoke by adult smokers or advertising. Very few adolescent smokers stop smoking as adults; however, those young people who do not use tobacco before age 20 are unlikely to start smoking as adults (International Clinical Epidemiology Network, 2001).

A further regression analysis of data from international colleagues indicated significant relationships between level of concern for family issues and the general level of interest in legislative support for families, legislation related to family life education, and the degree of family life education course work in their countries pertaining to the ten CFLE content areas. There were no relationships between family concerns for legislative interest in parent or marriage education. In other words, those people who perceived public concerns for family issues were also interested in legislation for families and family life education and perceived that their countries had a greater degree of course work pertaining to family life education. These education and policy variables explained 55% of the variance in public issues of family concern and suggest the emerging importance of public consciousness about family issues and family life education in various countries of the world. It is hoped that the data from this study will further a global understanding and education of professionals and students about families. By under-standing world families and international efforts in family life education, family professionals can promote multicultural understanding both at home and abroad.

EDUCATIONAL METHODS TO ENHANCE CROSS-CULTURAL AWARENESS

Opportunities for Current Professionals

Preparation of family professionals to work with culturally diverse popula-tions and increase their global awareness is becoming increasingly important. Current professionals can get involved in international conferences, meet with groups of international families within their own communities or universities, or become involved in international travel. The Fulbright Scholar Program is quite exceptional for providing cross-cultural understanding. As a Fulbright Scholar, one has an opportunity to be a cultural ambassador for the United States while undergoing a large array of experiences from which cross-cultural learning can be acquired. There are a number of Fulbright programs for both students and profes-sionals, although the more familiar one provides travel and living allowances for U.S. scholars to teach or conduct research abroad (see http://www.cies.org/). One should not be discouraged if you cannot find "family life educator" in the list of academic disciplines for potential exchange programs. Family life educators are welcomed in various other disciplines and professions, such as education, family and consumer sciences, or the social sciences. Whereas human develop-ment and family science departments are prominent in the U.S., the study of fam-ily is located within various other programs depending on the country of interest.

Opportunities for Future Professionals

Travel programs: Cross-cultural study courses.   Future family professionals have various opportunities to get involved in cross-cultural study courses to learn about international families (Hamon & Fernsler, 2006). These programs provide experiential opportunities to help students develop an appreciation for families and cultures that are different from their own. Rather then merely visit a country, students become immersed in the culture and have sustained contact with fami-lies in the host culture that can involve home stays, ethnographies, and/or service projects as a part of their course work. Students become involved in the activities of daily living, such as eating meals with the family, spending time with children, or becoming involved in family-related events. Students take an active part in these cross-cultural experiences by reading required books, writing papers, and sharing in planning their participation in field trips. In addition, students take part in organized "scavenger hunts" in the community by learning about local facts and attending lectures or presentations on family-related topics. Living in a different environment can be a life-changing experience when confronting living standards different from one's own, realizing the importance of language in understanding others, being aware of looking different, facing one's own ethno-centricity, and observing similarities and differences in family life. Cross-cultural courses related to families provide excellent opportunities for exposing students to some of the content areas for NCFR's CFLE program, such as families in society, internal dynamics of families, family resource management, parent education and guidance, interpersonal relationships, and human sexuality.

Classroom activities: Brief reports.   Since cross-cultural travel experiences are not feasible for some students, various activities can integrate cross-cultural learning into the classroom. These vary in complexity and depth of exposure. Individually or in small groups students can investigate a country by the use of international references on families (Adams & Trost, 2005; Francoeur & Noonan, 2004b). Through sharing with class members how families function in other countries and how culture has influenced the attitudes and behaviors of the people in that country, students become aware of the differences in families and family issues in diverse cultures.

Classroom activities: Electronic portfolios.   Classroom projects can be expanded by having students create electronic portfolios on various countries (Subramaiam, 2006). Students incorporate technology and research to prepare an in-depth examination of a country and its families. They can examine geography, lifestyles, political and economic systems, culture of families, economic data, and information on housing, health, consumption patterns, or financial management. As a group they prepare an electronic portfolio by developing a PowerPoint presentation using charts, tables, clipart, and video clips along with creating Web sites. Several Internet sources are useful, including *International Database; Population Reference Bureau; Demography and Population Studies; United Nations Population Fund; United Nations Educational, Scientific, and Cultural Organization;* and *Fact Monster.* Students are not only able to enhance their research skills on the Internet, but also have a meaningful in-depth learning experience about families in other cultures.

Classroom activities: Circular role-play.   In order to better understand and enhance a cross-cultural perspective in family science courses, a circular role-play teaching method can be implemented using any topic of interest, such as marital interaction, sibling relationships, or parent-child communication. By varying the focus, this activity can facilitate the infusion of cultural learning into a variety of courses and topics. While a family life educator can utilize any teaching method in different cultures for the purpose of comparison and cross-cultural sharing, Darling and Howard (2006) described a circular role-play technique applied to parent-youth communication about sexuality within three different cultural contexts (Finland, Costa Rica, and the United States). In this experience, students were asked to depict the roles of a parent and an adolescent daughter by listening to a read scenario and then thinking through how they might react or what they might say as the parent and as the adolescent in that situation. The following steps were involved in this activity.

- Students were asked to join others in a small circle.
- A paragraph was read to the class about a potential dilemma for parent-youth communication regarding sexuality.

- Student respondents were asked to write what they would say as a *parent* in this situation.
- The response was passed to the person on the right who, acting as a *teenager*, responded to the parental statement.
- The response of the teenager was passed back to the person role-playing his/her *parent* for a response to the adolescent statement.
- The second response of the parent was passed to the person on the right acting as a *teenager*, who again responded to this parent.

Thus, each individual simultaneously played the roles of a parent and adolescent in two different hypothetical family scenarios. The parent and adolescent characters each wrote two comments due to time limitations, although this exchange could occur several more times.

After the exchange of statements between pairs of students, the parent-youth communication patterns were discussed from the perspective of the culture in which the activity was being conducted. Reactions from other cultures to the same scenario were then shared with the students, who were amazed at the differences in responses. While this teaching method could be used with any topic, the statements from students in these three cultures can be shared with students to illustrate cross-cultural differences in parent-youth interactions related to sexuality (Darling & Howard, 2006). This learning experience, along with the discussion of the results from other cultures, stimulated cross-cultural learning and understanding about the purposes and processes underlying family behaviors. By looking at cultural evidence from three different countries, this teaching endeavor facilitated the exploration of the richness and diversity of parent-youth communication concerning sexuality issues from a cross-cultural perspective. Considering variations from others' experiences facilitates putting our own culture's parenting and sexual understandings in perspective.

FUTURE DIRECTIONS FOR INTERNATIONAL FAMILY LIFE EDUCATION

What does the future hold? Globalization and struggles with interdependence will continue along with inherent issues in family adaptations to the stress of migration and acculturation. While there are several challenges that our students will need to face, there is also hope as evidenced by some family life education initiatives.

- **Worldwide health issues and the accessibility of affordable diagnoses and treatment**. This is not just the obvious issue of HIV/AIDS, but illnesses such as SARS and the H5N1 avian flu virus. What can we do to protect persons from current and future pandemics? Family life educators need to work collaboratively with health professionals to provide relevant educational materials and determine what types of educational programs can provide the knowledge necessary to assist families with these problems.
- **Population growth, decline, and mobility**. While the world's population is multiplying, some countries will experience a decline in inhabitants due to

mobility. Migration will continue to be a major topic in the twenty-first century and will pose certain challenges in the future. What steps should family life educators take to help immigrants, who find themselves in a very different world from the one they left, with new traditions, attitudes, behaviors, and values? How can families manage their resources in crowded environments with a shortage of natural resources for sustenance?

- **Equality of rights**. In some countries, such as Nigeria and Pakistan, young women who have been raped and then courageously named their assailants have triggered international protests when they were tried and convicted of fornication and sentenced to death by stoning. Meanwhile, other countries, such as China, still have one-child-per-family policies, forced abortions, and female infanticide (Francoeur & Noonan, 2004a). What can family life educators do to promote equal legal rights for all regardless of their age, gender, race, ethnicity, religion, or sexual orientation?

- **Gender equity**. Women are perceived to be a huge untapped economic resource and are taking more of a public stance for gender equality. Moreover, women are also surpassing men in educational achievement and aspiration. Patriarchy will not disappear overnight, but a shift toward equality is occurring (Francoeur & Noonan, 2004a). Gender issues are evident in health, family structure, and violence. However, increasing the status of women does not necessarily decrease family violence, since often an increase in violence occurs when men feel threatened by a loss of power. Therefore, educators need to redesign curricula, texts, media presentations, and other activities to promote gender equality as part of cultural change. For example, one Caribbean community had an elective secondary school course on child development and parenting that was composed of more than 50% boys. Youth-oriented organizations also need to educate boys about developing nonviolent attitudes and behaviors along with new symbols and models for masculinity (Bahá'í International Community, 1994).

- **Public policies for family well-being**. There is an increasing need to incorporate a family lens when creating public policy. While progress is slow, family life educators should take notice of the passage of a "Family Education Law" in Taiwan in 2003. The Ministry of Education sought a legal means for promoting family education and the integration of work from all levels of governments, non-governmental organizations, and educational organizations to actively empower people of all ages to have better family life. This legislation promotes preventive education by improving family education knowledge, strengthening psychological and physical development, and improving family and social harmony. They define family education as all kinds of education activities for furthering family relations and functioning including parent education, filial education, sexuality education, marriage education, ethical education, education about family resources and management, and other family education matters. This legislation makes Taiwan the first country in the world that has passed a national bill regarding family life education. They have rewritten world history regarding family life education and are now working on implementing this bill (N. Huang, 2003; W. Huang, 2005).

Families have a profound impact on their members. However, when they cannot provide for the healthy nurturance of members, the effects reverberate across their lives and are ultimately felt by society (Public Education Committee on Family, 2001). As a result, there is a need for family life education aimed at strengthening family ties and relationships and preventing some of these problems. As the interest and need for family life education expand, we will also need to work on creating varied approaches that can be used by multiple countries, professions, and individuals.

As a call to action, data from the study to examine the international status of family life education indicated the level of interest in various professional issues concerned with the delivery of family life education. The top three issues with the greatest interest were increased attention to family issues in the workplace, increased research on issues critical to families, and increased assistance with family policy issues. Creatively targeting the workplace means that access to family life education is more readily available to all. In addition, the need for research-based curricula is also evident along with developing policies to aid families and family support services. The two lowest ranking issues dealt with increased international assistance and connections to colleagues. In other words, there is a higher priority on in-country assistance and progress compared to help from outsiders who may not understand the culture. Thus, multicultural understanding is paramount.

Table 13.2   Level of Interest in Professional Issues

Professional Issue	Mean*
Increased attention to family issues in the workplace	4.05
Increased research on issues critical to families	4.04
Increased assistance with family policy issues	3.79
Increased family programs—planning and implementing FLE programs	3.63
Increased training opportunities for family professionals	3.60
Strengthening existing family life education programs	3.57
Connection with international network of family colleagues for advice	3.47
Increased assistance from colleagues in other countries	3.18

*Range: 1 = low level of emphasis to 5 = high level of emphasis

Various family professionals may create opportunities to learn about other cultures from within their own community or university. The tenth anniversary of the International Year of the Family was designed to highlight the role of families and increase awareness of family issues among governments, as well as the private sector. Other objectives were to stimulate efforts to respond to family problems and improve collaboration among national and international non-governmental organizations in support of families (United Nations Programme on the Family, 2003). Some suggestions from international colleagues who reported on activities from their countries included the following:

- Meetings with families and students from other cultures and hearing their concerns
- Academic symposia on various topics such as wellness of families, child care and work, worldwide gender equality, national health insurance, family violence, parenting, HIV/AIDS and the teenage population, and the impact of war on family life
- Grants to organizations involved in family support services
- Media presentations on family issues and family programs
- National Family Day
- International Family Strengths Conference
- Development of fact sheets on family issues
- Provision of new support services for international families
- Cross-cultural entertainment presentations
- "Knowledge exists, but more action is needed"

These findings call attention to the need for developing innovative methods and materials that are culturally sensitive to the country of interest. One cannot use family life education methods that work in the United States and assume that they are universal. Here are a few suggestions for working with other cultures.

- Examine how different cultures perceive and value marriage, family, gender, aging, children, and parenting, as well as the roles of education, government, and religion. This knowledge can be gained from talking to individuals, families, and colleagues; attending seminars and classes; reading cross-cultural literature; conducting cross-cultural research; and studying public policies from other countries. We need to understand what is taught to whom and the differences in cultural perceptions of family structure, composition, and life stages.
- Understand your own assumptions, values, and biases regarding cultural diversity in general, and specifically to the cultural group whom you will be teaching. Then assist family life education students to further understand their beliefs about culture. Using Bennett's model of cultural competency can facilitate development of cultural sensitivity by moving from ethnocentrism to ethnorelativism (Bennett, 1993).
- Use current, culturally-relevant research to support the content of your program. If you have not conducted such research, make contact with researchers in the country of interest. By incorporating research from the country of interest, we display understanding of their world and a willingness to connect with their issues.
- Incorporate relevant theory into your teaching. Theory helps learners of all ages to understand the knowledge, attitudes, and behaviors being integrated into the course. However, some theories that are quite usable in Western culture may not work in other cultures or may have to be altered for different circumstances. For example, using developmental theory in

some cultures may be difficult unless you realize that different develop-mental transitions or milestones may vary in timing, definition, and impor-tance. Using attachment theory may also have cultural implications.

- Build rapport with your students by learning some phrases in their native language. Students appreciate your attempt to speak their language and thereby embrace their culture. Similarly, be aware that some verbal and nonverbal communications may have different meanings in various cultures. Touch, hand gestures, or eye contact that might be acceptable in one country could be offensive in another.

- Use culturally-appropriate metaphors that relate to the country of interest. If you are using sports to communicate a concept, use soccer, rugby, cricket, or cycling rather than baseball or football depending on the popularity of a sport in the country.

- Attempt to understand the family boundaries, rituals, cohesion, and adapt-ability of cultures and apply metaphors to assist with learning abstract concepts. One example relates to Asians, who appreciate metaphors when discussing love, anxiety, and boundary issues. Therefore, you might tell them that "healthy love is like Post-it notes—a little sticky, but not too sticky" (Huang, 2005, p. 171).

- Be sensitive to cultural norms since some content could put your learners at increased risk. In Asian countries women can be emotionally or physically harmed when they "speak their minds" (Huang, 2005). You also need to be aware of multiple contexts of culture. While some members of a culture may follow its traditional practices and views, others may be more modern in their approaches. Thus your integration of theory and research may vary depending on the target audience in your country of interest.

- Be patient. Finding simple answers to complex problems can take time. Americans do not always endure delays in progress, but cross-cultural rap-port building and learning require tolerance and persistence without appearing frustrated.

In order for future family life educators to have a place in the evolving inter-national importance of family life education as a profession, it is essential to develop an exchange of ideas and practices regarding the content and direction of global approaches to family life education. We need to be internationally aware of the needs and concerns that families experience and the environmental contexts of their ecosystems. If we cannot think globally, we will fail to connect with the context in which families live. Including research, learning experiences, and text-books from the United States is not a viable approach when teaching in other cultures. Culturally relative and sensitive methods and materials need to be incorporated for both classroom use and for professional development to assist teachers, leaders, and administrators in their work with families. It is also impor-tant to not only help individual families, but also to sensitize public opinion on family-related issues. Since we are dealing with complex issues, we need complex solutions to provide a preventive approach to assisting families. The global concerns that affect families affect us all no matter where we live. Thus, it will take a multinational, multicultural, and multidisciplinary network of family professionals working together to enhance family well being worldwide.

Questions/Problems for Discussion and Review

Class Discussion

1. Talk with students from other cultures or students who have been exchange students and find out about their experiences in different cultures. What did you learn about other cultures and what insights did you receive about your own culture? How do these cultural experiences influence families?

2. Select a country to which you might want to emigrate. How would your life be different in regard to various changes in family life, school, gender, dating, extracurricular activities, or employment?

3. What are some cultural traditions in which you and your family participate either from U.S. culture or another cultural group? What traditions might you take with you in into the next generation?

Research Problems/Activities

1. Using the ecosystem approach or any other theory mentioned in this chapter or text, analyze a global issue applying one or more theories.

2. Experience an environment unlike the one with which you are familiar. This could be a cultural celebration, restaurant with specialized cultural foods, or religious setting. How does it feel to be different in this setting? What feelings might you have if you were to become a permanent or semi-permanent resident within this culture? What did you learn about this culture?

Framework for Life Span Family Life Education

This framework expands on definitions of family life education by specifying major content for broad, life span family life education programs. It reflects current conceptual development and empirical knowledge in each topic area and gives attention to relevant knowledge, attitudes, and skills. Communicating, decision making, and problem solving have not been treated as separate concepts but should be incorporated into each topic area. It is assumed that this framework incorporates education that is multicultural, gender fair, and aware of special needs.

Areas Addressed in FLE Programs for Stages of
I. Childhood   II. Adolescence   III. Adulthood   IV. Later Adulthood

- A. Families in Society
- B. Internal Dynamics of Families
- C. Human Growth and Development
- D. Human Sexuality
- E. Interpersonal Relationships
- F. Family Resource Management
- G. Parent Education and Guidance
- H. Family Law and Public Policy
- I. Ethics

I. Childhood

A. Families in Society
- Jobs, money, and the family
- Programs that support individuals and families
- Importance of families, neighborhood, and the community
- Families and schools working together
- Differing spiritual beliefs and practices

B. Internal Dynamics of Families
- Family members as individuals
- Individuality and importance of all family members
- Getting along in the family
- Expressing feelings in families
- Personal family history
- Family similarities and differences
- Impact of change on families
- Responsibilities, rights, interdependence of family members
- Family rules
- Families as sources of protection, guidance, affection, support
- Families as possible sources of anger and violence
- Family problems

C. Human Growth and Development
- Emotional and social development
- Responsibility for keeping healthy—nutrition, personal hygiene
- Uniqueness of each person
- Similarities and differences in individual development
- Understanding people with special needs
- Perceptions about older people—adolescents, adults, elderly
- Social and environmental conditions affecting growth and development

D. Human Sexuality
- Physical and sexual development
- Body privacy and protection against sexual abuse
- Uniqueness of each person
- Similarities and differences in individual sexual development
- Aspects of human reproduction—prenatal development, birth, puberty
- Children's perceptions about sexuality
- Social and environmental conditions affecting sexuality

E. Interpersonal Relationships
- Respecting self and others
- Sharing feelings constructively
- Expressing emotions
- Developing, maintaining, and ending relationships
- Building self-esteem and self-confidence
- Identifying and enhancing personal strengths
- Communicating with others
- Learning from and teaching others
- Sharing friends, possessions, time
- Acting with consideration for self and others
- Handling problems with others

F. Family Resource Management
- Taking care of possessions
- Helping with family tasks
- Learning about time and schedules
- Learning to choose
- Earning, spending, and saving money
- Understanding space and privacy
- Developing talents and abilities
- Selecting and consuming—food, clothing, recreation
- Using and saving human and nonhuman resources
- Influences on consumer decisions—values, costs, media, peers

G. Parent Education and Guidance
- Safety for children
- Responsibilities of parents
- Different types of caregivers
- Parents who live away from children
- Rewards and demands of parenthood
- Meeting children's needs at different stages of development
- Differing parenting styles and behaviors
- Responsibilities of children
- Sources of help for parents—family, neighborhood, community
- Problems of family violence, abuse, neglect

H. Family Law and Public Policy
- Understanding and respecting the law
- Laws and policies affecting families

- Children's legal rights
- Public policy as it affects families with children, including taxes, civil rights, social security, economic support laws, regulations

I. Ethics
- Taking responsibility for actions
- Consequences of actions for self and others
- Discovering spirituality
- Respect for all persons
- Gaining new rights and responsibilities with age
- Rights of all persons

II. Adolescence

A. Families in Society
- Families and the workplace
- Reciprocal influences of the economy and families
- School as preparation for the future
- Education throughout the life span
- Functioning in the school system
- Individual and family responsibility in the community
- Influence of religion and spirituality on families
- Support for families with special needs and problems
- Reciprocal influences of technology and families
- Population issues and resource allocation
- Role of family in society
- Supportive networks—family, peers, religious institutions, community

B. Internal Dynamics of Families
- Becoming an adult within the family
- Changes in family composition—births, divorce, death
- Managing and expressing feelings in families
- Coping with internal change and stress in the family
- Interaction of friends and family
- Personal and family decision making
- Communicating in families
- Interaction between family members
- Different needs and expectations of family members
- Responsibilities, rights, and interdependence of family members
- Family rules—overt and covert
- Intergenerational relationships

- Influence of family background
- Family history, traditions, and celebrations
- Families as sources of protection, guidance, affection, support
- Families as possible sources of anger and violence
- Family differences—membership, economic level, role performance, values

C. Human Growth and Development

- Accepting individual differences in development
- Responsibility for personal health—nutrition, personal hygiene, exercise
- Effects of chemical substances on physical health and development
- Types of development—physical, cognitive, affective, moral, personality, social, sexual
- Interaction among types of development
- Patterns of development over the life span—conception to death
- Stereotypes and realities about adulthood and aging
- Developmental disabilities
- Social and environmental conditions affecting growth and development

D. Human Sexuality

- Physical and sexual development
- Interaction among types of development
- Body privacy and protection against sexual abuse
- Communicating about sexuality—personal values, beliefs, shared decision making
- Choices, consequences, responsibility of sexual behavior
- Prevention and transmission of sexually transmitted diseases
- Human reproduction and conception
- Normality of sexual feelings and sexual responses
- Stereotypes and realities about human sexuality
- Varying family and societal beliefs about sexuality

E. Interpersonal Relationships

- Respecting self and others
- Changing and developing one's thoughts, attitudes, values
- Dealing with success and failure
- Accepting responsibility for one's actions
- Assessing and developing personal abilities and talents
- Communicating information, thoughts, and feelings
- Managing and expressing emotions

- Initiating, maintaining, and ending friendships
- Building self-esteem and self-confidence in self and others
- Assessing compatibility in interpersonal relationships
- Acting with consideration for self and others
- Understanding the basis for choosing a family lifestyle—values, heritage, religious beliefs
- Understanding the needs and motivations involved in dating
- Factors influencing mate selection—social, cultural, personal
- Understanding the dimensions of love and commitment
- Exploring the responsibilities of marriage

F. Family Resource Management
- Allocating time for work, school, leisure
- Negotiating privacy and independence
- Selection of resources to meet personal needs—food, clothing, recreation
- Using personal resources
- Earning, spending, and saving money
- Responsibility for decisions
- Developing leisure interests
- Values as a basis for choices
- Choosing long- and short-term goals
- Exploring career choices
- Assessment of and changes in personal and family resources
- Influences on consumer decisions—values, costs, media, peers

G. Parent Education and Guidance
- Parent-child communication
- Meeting children's needs at different stages of development
- Responding to individual differences in children
- Rewards and demands of parenthood
- Understanding marital and parenting roles
- Factors to consider in deciding if and when to become a parent
- Child-rearing practices
- Teaching life skills to children—self-sufficiency, safety, decision making
- Family conflict and conflict resolution
- Problems of family violence, abuse, neglect
- Sources of help for parents—family, neighborhood, community
- Varied parenting situations—single parenting, stepparenting, adoption, caretaking of disabled children
- Influences on parenting styles—ethnic, racial, gender, social, cultural

H. Family Law and Public Policy
- Respecting civil rights of all people
- Understanding legal definitions and laws affecting families
- Individual and family legal protection, rights, and responsibilities
- Laws relating to marriage, divorce, family support, child custody, child protection and rights, family planning
- Family conflict and legal protection of family members
- Families and the justice system
- Impact of laws and policies on families
- Public policy as it affects families with adolescent children, including taxes, civil rights, social security, economic support laws, regulations

I. Ethics
- Developing a personal ethical code
- Exploring personal spirituality
- Personal autonomy and social responsibility
- Interrelationship of rights and responsibilities
- Ethical principles as one kind of value
- Ethical values as a guide to human social conduct
- Complexity and difficulty of ethical choices and decisions
- Ethical implications of social and technological change

III. Adulthood

A. Families in Society
- Family participation in the education of children
- Utilizing the education system
- Influence of religion and spirituality on families
- Supportive networks—family, peers, religious institutions, community
- Understanding and obtaining community support services
- Lifelong learning
- Population issues and resource allocation
- Reciprocal influences of technology and families
- Economic fluctuations and their impact on families
- Interrelationship of families, work, and society
- Individual and family responsibility in the community
- Role of the family in society

B. Internal Dynamics of Families
- Individual development in the family
- Individual and family roles

- Intimate relationships in the family
- Sources of stress and coping with stress
- Lifestyle choices
- Changing needs and expectations of family members
- Intergenerational dynamics throughout the life span
- Responsibilities, rights, interdependence of family members
- Family transitions—marriage, birth, divorce, remarriage, death
- Family history, traditions, and celebrations
- Factors affecting marital and family relationships
- Giving and receiving affection
- Power and authority in the family
- Effects of family on self-concepts of its members
- Family rules—overt and covert
- Families as sources of protection, guidance, affection, support
- Differences in families—membership, economic level, role performance, values
- Families as possible sources of anger and violence
- Varying influences on family interaction patterns—ethnic, racial, gender, social, cultural

C. Human Growth and Development

- Factors influencing individual differences in development
- Types of development: physical, cognitive, affective, moral, personality, social, sexual
- Interaction among types of development
- Responsibility for personal and family health
- Promoting development in self and others
- Patterns of development over the life span—conception to death
- Myths and realities of adulthood and aging
- Adjusting to disabilities
- Social and environmental conditions affecting growth and development

D. Human Sexuality

- Responsible sexual behavior—choices, consequences, shared decision making
- Normality of sexual feelings and sexual responses
- Communicating about sexuality—personal values, beliefs, shared decision making
- Prevention and transmission of sexually transmitted diseases
- Contraception, infertility, genetics

- Prevention of sexual abuse
- Varying societal beliefs about sexuality

E. Interpersonal Relationships
  - Establishing personal autonomy
  - Building self-esteem and self-confidence in self and others
  - Achieving constructive personal changes
  - Communicating effectively
  - Managing and expressing emotions
  - Developing, maintaining, and ending relationships
  - Exercising initiative in relationships
  - Recognizing factors associated with quality relationships
  - Taking responsibility and making commitments in relationships
  - Evaluating choices and alternatives in relationships
  - Acting in accordance with personal beliefs with consideration for others' best interest
  - Understanding the effects of self-perceptions on relationships
  - Varying influences on roles and relationships—ethnic, racial, gender, social, cultural
  - Types of intimate relationships
  - Creating and maintaining a family of one's own
  - Changes in the marital relationship over time
  - Dealing with crises

F. Family Resource Management
  - Expendability of human energy
  - Developing personal resources
  - Development of personal resources through career choices
  - Values as a basis for choices
  - Developing leisure interests
  - Varying needs of family members for privacy and independence
  - Using resources to meet basic needs of family—food, clothing, shelter
  - Differing views about uses of family resources
  - Establishing long- and short-term goals
  - Financial planning
  - Resource consumption and conservation—material and nonmaterial
  - Balancing work and family roles
  - Influences on consumer decisions—values, costs, media, peers
  - Retirement planning

G. Parent Education and Guidance

- Factors to consider in deciding if and when to become a parent
- Preparation for birth and parenthood
- Changing parental responsibilities as children become independent
- Parent-child communication
- Child-rearing practices, guidance, and parenting strategies
- Changing parent-child relationships over the life span
- Importance of parental communication regarding child-rearing practices
- Providing a safe environment for children
- Teaching life skills to children—self-sufficiency, safety, decision making
- Rewards and demands of parenthood
- Varied parenting situations—single parenting, stepparenting, adoption, caretaking of disabled child, elderly parent
- Sources of help for parents—family, neighborhood, community
- Problems of family violence, abuse, neglect
- Influences on parenting styles—ethnic, racial, gender, social, cultural

H. Family Law and Public Policy

- Transmitting values regarding education, justice, and the law
- Understanding and affecting laws and policies
- Laws relating to marriage, divorce, family support, child custody, child protection and rights, family planning
- Family conflict and legal protection of family members
- Public policy as it affects families, including taxes, civil rights, social security, economic support laws, regulations

I. Ethics

- Establishing an ethical philosophy of life
- Acting in accordance with personal beliefs with consideration for others
- Continued growth in personal spirituality
- Personal autonomy and social responsibility
- Interrelationship of rights and responsibilities
- Ethical principles as one kind of value
- Ethical values as a guide to human social conduct
- Complexity and difficulty of ethical choices and decisions
- Assisting in the formation of ethical concepts and behavior in others
- Ethical implications of social and technological change

IV. Later Adulthood

A. Families in Society

- Influence of religion and spirituality on families
- Supporting the education system
- Supportive networks—family, peers, religious institutions, community
- Understanding and obtaining community support services
- Lifelong learning
- Population issues and resource allocation—health care, transportation, housing
- Reciprocal influences of technology and aging families
- Social issues—age discrimination, elder abuse, caregiving
- Role of the family in society
- Economic fluctuations and their impact on aging families

B. Internal Dynamics of Families

- Individual development in the family
- Individual and family roles
- Intimate relationships in the family
- Sources of stress and coping with stress, diseases, disabilities
- Lifestyle choices and changes—retirement planning, retirement
- Changing needs and expectations of family members
- Intergenerational dynamics through the life span
- Responsibilities, rights, interdependence of family members and productivity
- Family transitions—marriage, divorce, remarriage, retirement of mate, death
- Family history, traditions, and celebrations
- Factors affecting marital and family relationships
- Giving and receiving affection
- Effects of family on self-concepts of its members
- Family rules—overt and covert
- Families as sources of protection, guidance, affection, support
- Differences in families—membership, economic level, role performance, values
- Families as possible sources of anger and violence
- Varying influences on family interaction patterns—ethnic, racial, gender, social, cultural
- Changes in power and authority in the family
- Understanding the effects of self-perceptions on relationships

C. Human Growth and Development
- Factors influencing individual differences in development
- Types of development: physical, cognitive, affective, moral, personality, social, sexual
- Interaction among types of development
- Patterns of development over the life span—conception to death
- Myths and realities of aging
- Adjusting to disabilities
- Social and environmental conditions affecting growth and development
- Adapting to and coping with physical changes in later adulthood
- Responsibility for personal health and safety
- Grieving and adjusting to loss

D. Human Sexuality
- Human sexual response and aging
- Normality of sexual feelings and sexual responses
- Communicating about sexuality—personal values, beliefs, shared decision making
- Body privacy and prevention of sexual abuse
- Sexuality education about later adulthood
- Sexual expression and intimacy in later adulthood
- Awareness of sexuality needs in adult living situations
- Varying societal beliefs, myths, and realities about sexuality and aging

E. Interpersonal Relationships
- Continuing personal autonomy
- Building self-esteem and self-confidence in self and others
- Communicating effectively
- Managing and expressing emotions
- Exercising initiative in relationships
- Recognizing factors associated with quality relationships
- Taking responsibility and making commitments in relationships
- Evaluating choices and alternatives in relationships
- Acting in accordance with personal beliefs with consideration for others' best interest
- Varying influences on roles and relationships—ethnic, racial, gender, social, cultural
- Maintaining relationships with one's own family
- Changes in the marital relationship over time
- Dealing with crisis and loss

F. Family Resource Management
- Values as a basis for choices
- Establishing a plan for the distribution of resources and management if incompetent—will, living will
- Using personal resources
- Expanding leisure interests
- Balancing life patterns of retirees with work roles of children
- Varying needs of family members for privacy and independence
- Using resources to meet basic needs of family—food, clothing, shelter
- Differing views about uses of family resources
- Establishing long- and short-term goals
- Managing financial resources in retirement
- Resource consumption and conservation—material and nonmaterial
- Influences on consumer decisions—values, costs, media, peers

G. Parent Education and Guidance
- Changing parent-child relationships in later life—negotiating adult relationships with adult children
- Demands and rewards of grandparenthood, including the possibility of rearing and caring for grandchildren
- Importance of parental communication regarding differences in parenting styles and values between parents and grandparents
- Grandparent-child communication
- Sources of help for grandparents—family, neighborhood, community
- Family conflict and conflict resolution
- Problems of family violence, elder abuse, neglect
- Adapting to the complexities of varied parenting situations—single parenting, stepparenting, caretaking of disabled children, return of adult children to the household

H. Family Law and Public Policy
- Transmitting values regarding education, justice, and the law
- Understanding and affecting laws and policies
- Protecting the civil rights of all people
- Laws relating to marriage, divorce, family support, protection and rights of vulnerable individuals, property, wills, estate planning, and living wills
- Family conflict and legal protection of family members
- Public policy as it affects families, including taxes, civil rights, Social Security, economic support laws, regulations

I. Ethics
- Acting in accordance with personal beliefs with consideration for others
- Continued growth in personal spirituality
- Personal autonomy and social responsibility
- Interrelationship of rights and responsibilities
- Ethical principles as one kind of value
- Ethical values as a guide to human social conduct
- Complexity and difficulty of ethical choices and decisions—quality-of-life issues, end-of-life issues
- Protection from exploitation
- Ethical implications of social and technological change
- Assisting in the formation of ethical concepts and behavior in others

From "Framework for Life-Span Family Life Education" (rev. ed.), by the National Council on Family Relations, 1997, Minneapolis, MN: Author. Copyrighted 1997 by the National Council on Family Relations, 3989 Central Ave. NE, Suite 550, Minneapolis, MN 55421. Reprinted by permission.

Family Life Education Content Areas for the Certified Family Life Educator Designation

1. FAMILIES IN SOCIETY

An understanding of families and their relationships to other institutions, such as the educational, governmental, religious, and occupational institutions in society.

Structures and functions; cultural variations (family heritage, social class, geography, ethnicity, race, and religion); dating, courtship, marital choice; kinship; cross-cultural and minority (understanding of lifestyles of minority families and the lifestyles of families in various societies around the world); changing gender roles (role expectations and behaviors of courtship partners, marital partners, parents and children, siblings, and extended kin); demographic trends; historical issues; work-family relationships; societal relations (reciprocal influence of the major social institutions and families).

2. INTERNAL DYNAMICS OF FAMILIES

An understanding of family strengths and weaknesses and how family members relate to each other.

Internal social processes (including cooperation and conflict); communication (patterns and problems in husband-wife relationships and in parent-child relationships, including stress and conflict management); conflict management; normal family stresses (transition periods in the family life cycle, three-generation households, caring for the elderly, and dual careers); family crises (divorce, remarriage, death, economic uncertainty and hardship, violence, substance abuse); special needs in families (including adoptive, foster, migrant, low income, military, and blended families, as well as those with disabled members).

3. HUMAN GROWTH AND DEVELOPMENT OVER THE LIFE SPAN

An understanding of the developmental changes of individuals in families throughout the life span. Based on knowledge of physical, emotional, cognitive, social, moral, and personality aspects.

Prenatal; infancy; early and middle childhood; adolescence; adulthood; aging.

4. HUMAN SEXUALITY

An understanding of the physiological, psychological, and social aspects of sexual development throughout the life span, so as to achieve healthy sexual adjustment.

Reproductive physiology; biological determinants; aspects of sexual involvement; sexual behaviors; sexual values and decision making; family planning; sexual response; sexual dysfunction; influence on relationships.

5. INTERPERSONAL RELATIONSHIPS

An understanding of the development and maintenance of interpersonal relationships.

Self and others; communication skills (listening, empathy, self-disclosure, decision making, problem solving, and conflict resolution); intimacy, love, romance; relating to others (respect, sincerity, and responsibility).

6. FAMILY RESOURCE MANAGEMENT

An understanding of the decisions individuals and families make about developing and allocating resources, including time, money, material assets, energy, friends, neighbors, and space, to meet their goals.

Goal setting and decision making; development and allocation of resources; social environment influences; life cycle and family structure influences; consumer issues and decisions.

7. PARENT EDUCATION AND GUIDANCE

An understanding of how parents teach, guide, and influence children and adolescents.

Parenting rights and responsibilities; parenting practices/processes; parent-child relationships; variation in parenting solutions; changing parenting roles over the life cycle.

8. Family Law and Public Policy

An understanding of the legal definition of the family and laws that affect the status of the family.

Family and the law (relating to marriage, divorce, family support, child custody, child protection and rights, and family planning); family and social services; family and education; family and the economy; family and religion; policy and the family (public policy as it affects the family, including taxes, civil rights, social security, economic support laws, and regulations.)

9. Ethics

An understanding of the character and quality of human social conduct, and the ability to critically examine ethical questions and issues.

Formation of values; diversity of values in pluralistic society; examining ideologies; social consequences of value choices; ethics and technological changes, ethics of professional practice.

10. Family Life Education Methodology

An understanding of the general philosophy and broad principles of family life education in conjunction with the ability to plan, implement, and evaluate such educational programs.

Planning and implementing; evaluation (materials, student progress, and program effectiveness); education techniques; sensitivity to others (to enhance educational effectiveness); sensitivity to community concerns and values (understanding of the public relations process).

Example of
Permission Form
to Do Needs Assessment

(Letterhead)

(Date)

Dear parents,

Smartkids Middle School has asked me to assist them in developing and conducting an "encouragement" program for girls in grades 6, 7, and 8. Many girls at this age struggle with their new identities as pubertal changes occur. Often academic scores in the sciences and math drop dramatically. Socially, many young women become vulnerable to peer—and boyfriend—pressures. Eating disorders and attempted suicides become an increasing problem. This program would encourage the development of positive and strong images for young women through the use of role models and peer support. It is designed as an after-school, optional program that will be held once a week for the coming school year.

I am a Certified Family Life Educator (CFLE) and a family support counselor at Community Services, Inc., where I have worked for the past three years. I have a master's degree in Human Development Counseling from the University of Ivytwine, and I have designed youth programs for school, community, and church organizations for more than 15 years.

In order to get to know the students better, and to design a program that truly meets their needs, I would like to meet with several "focus groups" of teens at Smartkids over the next two weeks. The permission slip below indicates that you agree for your daughter to participate in a focus group (if randomly selected). Participation is strictly voluntary and will be used anonymously. Please return the signed permission form by Friday to Ms. Joan Brown, Principal of Smartkids Middle School.

If you have other questions about the focus groups or the program, please feel free to call me at 222-2222. Thank you for your support of this new endeavor.

Sincerely,

Mary Jones, BA, MA, CFLE

Permission to Participate

My daughter _____ has my permission to participate in a focus group conducted by Ms. Mary Jones of Community Services, Inc., at Smartkids Middle School. I understand that all participation is voluntary and all information will be used anonymously.

Signed,

_____   _____
                                        (Relation—mother, father, guardian)

The National Coalition to Support Sexuality Education
Goals and Membership

The primary goal of sexuality education is to promote adult sexual health. It should assist young people in developing a positive view of sexuality, provide them with information they need to take care of their sexual health, and help them acquire skills to make decisions now and in the future. The *Guidelines* recognize that the goals of sexuality education fall into four areas:

- *Information:* Sexuality education seeks to provide accurate information about human sexuality, including growth and development, human reproduction, anatomy, physiology, masturbation, family life, pregnancy, childbirth, parenthood, sexual response, sexual orientation, gender identity, contraception, abortion, sexual abuse, HIV/AIDS, and other sexually transmitted diseases.

- *Attitudes, Values, and Insights:* Sexuality education seeks to provide an opportunity for young people to question, explore, and assess their own and their community's attitudes about society, gender, and sexuality. This can help young people understand their family's values, develop their own values, improve critical-thinking skills, increase self-esteem and self-efficacy, and develop insights concerning relationships with family members, individuals of all genders, sexual partners, and society at large. Sexuality education can help young people understand their obligations and responsibilities to their families and society.

- *Relationships and Interpersonal Skills:* Sexuality education seeks to help young people develop interpersonal skills, including communication, decision-making, assertiveness, and peer refusal skills, as well as the ability to create reciprocal and satisfying relationships. Sexuality education programs should prepare students to understand sexuality effectively and creatively in adult roles. This includes helping young people develop the capacity for caring, supportive, non-coercive, and mutually pleasurable intimate and sexual relationships.

- *Responsibility:* Sexuality education seeks to help young people exercise responsibility regarding sexual relationships by addressing such issues as abstinence, how to resist pressures to become involved in unwanted or early sexual intercourse, and the use of contraception and other sexual health measures.

Membership, as of 2006

Advocates for Youth
AIDS Action Council
AIDS Alliance for Children, Youth, and Families
Alan Guttmacher Institute
American Academy of Child and Adolescent Psychiatry
American Academy of Pediatrics
American Association for Health Education
American Association for Marriage and Family Therapy
American Association of Family and Consumer Sciences
American Association of School Administrators
American Association of Sex Educators, Counselors and Therapists
American Association of University Women
American Association on Mental Retardation
American College Health Association
American College of Nurses–Midwives
American College of Obstetricians and Gynecologists
American College of Sexologists
American Counseling Association
American Federation of Teachers
American Jewish Congress
American Library Association
American Medical Association
American Medical Students' Association
American Medical Women's Association
American Nurses Association
American Orthopsychiatric Association
American Psychiatric Association
American Psychological Association
American Public Health Association
American School Health Association
American Social Health Association
Association for Sexuality Education and Training
Association of Reproductive Health Professionals
Association of State and Territorial Directors of Public Health Education
Association of State and Territorial Health Officials
ASTRAEA National Lesbian Action Foundation
Balm in Gilead
Blacks Educating Blacks About Sexual Health Issues
Boston Women's Health Book Collective
Bridge for Adolescent Pregnancy, Parenting and Sexuality

Campaign for Access and Reproductive Equity
Catholics for a Free Choice
Center for Law and Social Policy
Center for Policy Alternatives
Center for Reproductive Health Policy Research
Center for Reproductive Rights
Center for Sexuality and Religion
Center for Women Policy Studies
Child Welfare League of America
Children's Defense Fund
Choice USA
Coalition on Sexuality and Disability, Inc.
Education Development Center, Inc.
Engender Health
Equal Partners in Faith
ETR Associates
Exodus Trust Archives of Erotology
Federation of Behavioral, Psychological and Cognitive Sciences
Feminist Majority Foundation
Gay and Lesbian Medical Association
Gay, Lesbian and Straight Education Network
Gay Men's Health Crisis
Gender Public Advocacy Coalition
Girls, Incorporated
Hetrick-Martin Institute
Human Rights Campaign
Institute for Advanced Study of Human Sexuality Alumni Association
International Center for Research on Women
Jewish Women International
Kinsey Institute for Research in Sex, Gender and Reproduction
Lambola Legal Defense and Education Fund, Inc.
Latina Roundtable on Health and Reproductive Rights
Mautner Project
Ms. Foundation
National Abortion Federation
NARAL Pro-Choice America
National Alliance of State and Territorial AIDS Directors
National Asian Women's Health Organization
National Assembly on School-Based Health Care
National Association for Equal Opportunity in Higher Education
National Association of Counties
National Association of County and City Health Officials
National Association of People with AIDS
National Association of School Psychologists
National Black Women's Health Project
National Center for Health Education
National Coalition of Abortion Providers
National Coalition Against Censorship
National Coalition of Advocates for Students
National Coalition of STD Directors
National Committee for Public Education and Religious Liberty
National Council of Jewish Women
National Council of La Raza
National Council of Negro Women

National Council of State Consultants for School Social Work Services
National Council on Family Relations
National Education Association Health Information Network
National Family Planning and Reproductive Health Association
National Gay and Lesbian Task Force
National Information Center for Children and Youth with Disabilities
National Latina Health Organization
National Latina/o Lesbian, Gay, Bisexual and Transgender Organization (LLEGO)
National Lesbian and Gay Health Association
National Medical Association
National Mental Health Association
National Minority AIDS Council
National Native American AIDS Prevention Center
National Network for Youth
National Organization on Adolescent Pregnancy, Parenting and Prevention
National Partnership for Women and Families
National Resource Center for Youth Services
National School Boards Association
National Urban League
National Women's Health Network
National Women's Law Center
National Youth Advocacy Coalition
Network for Family Life Education
New York State Department of Health: Bureau of STD Control
Office of Family Ministries and Human Sexuality, National Council of Churches
Parents, Families and Friends of Lesbians and Gays
People for the American Way
Physicians for Reproductive Choice and Health
Planned Parenthood Federation of America
Population Communications International
Population Connection
Presbyterians Affirming Reproductive Options
Religious Coalition for Reproductive Choice
Religious Institute for Sexual Morality, Justice, and Healing
Sexual Minority Youth Assistance League
Sexuality Information and Education Council of the United States
Shield Institute
Society for Adolescent Medicine
Society for Public Health Education
Society for the Scientific Study of Sexuality
Unitarian Universalist Association
United Church of Christ, Justice and Witness Ministries
United States Conference of Mayors
United States Student Association
Women of Reform Judaism
YAI/National Institute for People with Disabilities
Young Women's Project
YWCA of the U.S.A.

Selected Web Sites for Sexuality Information

Advocates for Youth:
  http://www.advocatesforyouth.org/factsfigures/suppsexed.htm
AIDS Virtual Library: wwwplanetq.com/aidsvi/index.html
Alan Guttmacher Institute: www.agi-usa.org
American Journal of Public Health: www.apha.org
Association of Voluntary and Safe Contraception: www.avsc.org./avsc
Body Health: A Multimedia AIDS and HIV Information Resource:
  www.thebody.com
CDC Division of STD Prevention: www.cdc.gov/hiv/pubs/facts.htm
CDC National AIDS Clearinghouse: www.cdcnac.org
Center for AIDS Prevention Studies: www.caps.ucs.edu/capsweb
Centers for Disease Control and Prevention: www.cdc.gov
Coalition for Positive Sexuality: www.positive.org
Contraceptive Contemplation:
  www.tripod. com/living/contraceptive/index.html
Does Sex Education Work?: www.caps.ucsf edu/sexedtext.html
Free Med-Line: National Library of Medicine:
  www.nlm.nih.gov/databases/freemedl.html
Menstruation Education (Planned Parenthood):
  www.ppfa.org/ppfa/period-main.html
National Abortion Rights League: www.naral.org
National Campaign to Prevent Teen Pregnancy: www.teenpregnancy.org
National Gay and Lesbian Task Force: www.ngltf org
National Right to Life: www.nric.org
Natural Family Planning: www.missionnet.com
Northeastern Centre Against Sexual Assault: www.northern.casa.org.au
Planned Parenthood Federation of America: www. plannedparenthood.org

Rape, Abuse, and Incest National Network (RAINN): feminist.com/rainn.htm
Ruth Westheimer's (Dr. Ruth's) Home Page: www.drruth.com
Sex Information and Education Council of the U.S.: http://www.siecus.org/
Sexual Health Advocate Peer Education:
   www.muhealth.org/~student health healthed.shtml
Sexuality in Later Life: www.nih.gov/nia/health/pubpub/sexual.htm
Sexually Transmitted Diseases: www.niaid.nih.gov/factsheets/stdinfo.htm
Teen Pregnancy: www.teenpregnancy.org
Teen Pregnancy Prevention Research:
   www.pserie.psu.edu/hss/psych/bibweb.htm
Women and AIDS: www.thebody.com/whatis/women.html

Program Evaluation
The Five-Tiered Approach

Level/Title	Purposes of Evaluation	Audiences	Tasks	Kinds of Data to Collect/Analyze
Tier One – Needs Assessment	1. To determine the size and nature of a public problem 2. To determine unmet need for services in a community 3. To propose program and policy options to meet needs 4. To set a data baseline from which later progress can be measured 5. To broaden the base of support for a proposed program	1. Policymakers 2. Funders 3. Community stakeholders	1. Review existing community, county, and state data 2. Determine additional data needed to describe problem and potential service users 3. Conduct "environmental scan" of available resources 4. Identify resource gaps and unmet needs 5. Set goals and objectives for intervention 6. Recommend one program model for range of options	1. Extant data on target population; services currently available 2. Interviews with community leaders 3. Interviews or survey data from prospective participants 4. Information about similar programs in other locations
Tier Two – Monitoring and Accountability	1. To monitor program performance 2. To meet demands for accountability 3. To build a constituency 4. To aid in program planning and decision-making 5. To provide a groundwork for later evaluation activities	1. Program staff and administrators 2. Policymakers 3. Funders 4. Community stakeholders 5. Media	1. Determine needs and capacities for data collection and management 2. Develop clear and consistent procedures for collecting essential data elements 3. Gather and analyze data to describe program along dimensions of clients, services, staff, and costs	1. MIS (management information system) data; collected at program, county, and/or state level 2. Case material; obtained through record reviews, program contact forms, etc.
Tier Three – Quality Review and Program Clarification	1. To develop a more detailed picture of the program as it is being implemented 2. To assess the quality and consistency of the intervention 3. To provide information to staff for program improvement	1. Program staff and administrators 2. Policymakers 3. Community stakeholders	1. Review monitoring data 2. Expand on program description using information about participants' views 3. Compare program with standards and expectations 4. Examine participants' perceptions about effects of program Clarify program goals and design	1. MIS monitoring data 2. Case material 3. Other qualitative and quantitative data on program operations, customer satisfaction, and perceived effects; obtained using questionnaires, interviews, observations, and focus groups

Level/Title	Purposes of Evaluation	Audiences	Tasks	Kinds of Data to Collect/Analyze
Tier Four – Achieving Outcomes	1. To determine changes, if any have occurred among beneficiaries 2. To attribute changes to the program 3. To provide information to staff for program improvement	1. Program staff and administrators 2. Policymakers 3. Community stakeholders 4. Funders 5. Other programs	1. Choose short-term objectives to be examined 2. Choose appropriate research design, given constraints and capacities 3. Determine measurable indicators of success for outcome objectives 4. Collect and analyze information about effects on beneficiaries	1. Client-specific data; obtained using questionnaires, interviews, goal attainment scaling, observations, and functional indicators 2. Client and community social indicators 3. MIS data
Tier Five – Establishing Impact	1. To contribute to knowledge development in the field 2. To produce evidence of differential effectiveness of treatments 3. To identify models worthy of replication	1. Academic and research communities 2. Policymakers 3. Funders 4. General public	1. Decide on impact objectives based on results of Tier Four evaluation efforts 2. Choose appropriately rigorous research design and comparison group 3. Identify techniques and tools to measure effects in treatment and comparison groups 4. Analyze information to identify program impacts	1. Client-specific data; obtained using questionnaires, interviews, goal attainment scaling, observations, and functional indicators 2. Client and community social indicators 3. MIS data 4. Comparable data for control group.

Source: Jacobs, F. H., and Kapuscik, J. L. (with Williams, P. H., and Kates, E.) (2000). *Making it count: Evaluating Family Preservation Services.* Medford, MA: Family Preservation Evaluation Project, Eliot-Pearson Department of Child Development, Tufts University.

References

Adams, B., & Trost, J. (2005). *Handbook of world families*. Thousand Oaks, CA: Sage.

Administration for Children and Families. (2006). *The Healthy Marriage Initiative mission statement*. Available: www.acf.hhs.gov/healthymarriage/about/mission.html

Advocates for Youth. (2000). *Americans support sexuality education including information on abstinence and contraception*. News report. Available: http://www.advocatesforyouth.org/factsfigures/suppsexed.htm

Advocates for Youth. (2006, March 24). *Advocates for Youth praises decision: Calls for moratorium on federal funding*. News report.

Ahlburg, D. A., & DeVita, C. J. (1992). New realities of the American family [Special issue]. *Population Bulletin, 47*(2).

Alan Guttmacher Institute. (1994). *Sex and America's teenagers*. New York: Author.

Alan Guttmacher Institute. (1996). *Facts in brief: Teen sex and pregnancy*. New York: Author.

Alan Guttmacher Institute. (1999). *Why is teenage pregnancy declining? The role of abstinence, sexual activity and contraceptive use*. New York: Author.

Alan Guttmacher Institute. (2001). *Teenage sexual and reproductive behavior in developed countries: Can more progress be made?* New York: Author.

Allen, K. R., & Baber, K. M. (1992). Starting a revolution in family life education: A feminist vision. *Family Relations, 41*(4), 378–384.

Allgeier, E. R. (1984). The personal perils of sex researchers: Vern Bullough and William Masters. *SIECUS Report, 12*(4), 16–19.

Alliance for Families and Children. (2005). Available: www.alliance1.org

American Guidance Service. (1991). *STEP research studies*. Circle Pines, MN: Author.

Americans and the World. (2004). *Globalization*. Retrieved March 11, 2006, from http://www.americans-world.org/digest/global_issues/globalization/

Andrews, M. P., Bubolz, M. M., & Paolucci, B. (1980). An ecological approach to the study of the family. *Marriage and Family Review, 3*(1–2), 29–49.

Annie E. Casey Foundation. (1998). When teens have sex: Issues and trends. *KIDS COUNT Special Report*. Baltimore: Author.

Apgar, K., Riley, D. P., Eaton, J. T., & Diskin, S. (1982). *Life education in the workplace*. New York: Family Service Association of America.

Arcus, M. E. (1986). Should family life education be required for high school students? An examination of the issues. *Family Relations, 35*, 347–356.

Arcus, M. E., Schvaneveldt, J. D., & Moss, J. J. (1993). The nature of family life education. In M. E. Arcus, J. D. Schvaneveldt, & J. J. Moss (Eds.), *Handbook of family life education* (Vol. 1, pp. 1–25). Newbury Park, CA: Sage.

309

Arcus, M. E., & Thomas, J. (1993). The nature and practice of family life education. In M. E. Arcus, J. D. Schvaneveldt, & J. J. Moss (Eds.), *Handbook of family life education* (Vol. 2, pp. 1–32). Newbury Park, CA: Sage.

Arlin, P. K. (1984). Adolescent and adult thought: A structural interpretation. In M. L. Commons, F. A. Richards, & C. Armon (Eds.), *Beyond formal operations: Late adolescent and adult cognitive development* (pp. 258–271). New York: Praeger.

Asay, S. M., Younes, M. N., Moore, T. J. (2006). The cultural transformation model: Promoting cultural competence through international study experiences. In R. Hamon (Ed.), *International family studies: Developing curricula and teaching tools* (p. 86). Binghamton, NY: Haworth Press.

Association for Couples in Marriage Enrichment. (1995). *Standards for the training and certification of leader couples for marriage enrichment.* Winston-Salem, NC: Author.

Aulette, J. R. (1994). *Changing families.* Belmont, CA: Wadsworth.

Avery, C. E. (1962). Inside family life education. *The Family Life Coordinator, 11*(2), 27–39.

Avery, C. E., & Lee, M. R. (1964). Family life education: Its philosophy and purpose. *The Family Life Coordinator, 13*(2), 27–37.

Bader, E., Microys, G., Sinclair, C., Wilett, E., & Conway, B. (1980). Do marriage preparation programs really work? A Canadian experiment. *Journal of Marital and Family Therapy, 6*, 171–179.

Bahá'í International Community. (1994). *Creating violence-free families.* Retrieved March 12, 2006, from http://www.bic-un.bahai.org/94-0526.htm

Bahr, K. S. (1990). Student responses to genogram and family chronology. *Family Relations, 39*(3), 243–249.

Bahrick, H. P. (1984). Semantic memory content in permastore: Fifty years of memory for Spanish learned in school. *Journal of Experimental Psychology: General, 113*, 1–35.

Baldwin, K. E. (1949). *The AREA saga.* Washington, DC: American Home Economics Association.

Bales, R., & Cohen, S. (1979). *SYMLOG: A system for multiple level observation of groups.* New York: The Free Press.

Bales, R. F. (1950). *Interaction process analysis: A method for the study of small groups.* Reading, MA: Addison-Wesley.

Bandura, A. (1977). *Social learning theory.* Englewood Cliffs, NJ: Prentice Hall.

Barbe, W. B. (1985). *Growing up learning.* Washington, DC: Acropolis Books.

Barozzi, R. L., & Engel, J. W. (1985). A survey of attitudes about family life education. *Social Casework, 66*, 106–110.

Bartley, P., & Loxton, C. (1991). *Plains women in the American West.* Cambridge, England: Cambridge University Press.

Baumrind, D. (1983). Rejoinder to Lewis's reinterpretation of parental firm control effects: Are authoritative families really harmonious? *Psychological Bulletin, 94*, 132–142.

Baumrind, D. (1991). Parenting styles and adolescent development. In R. M. Lerner, A. C. Petersen, & J. Brooks-Gunn (Eds.), *Encyclopedia of adolescence* (Vol. 2, pp. 746–758). New York: Garland.

Bearinger, L. H. (1990). Study group report on the impact of television on adolescent views of sexuality. *Journal of Adolescent Health Care, 11*(1), 71–75.

Bearman, P. S., & Bruckner, H. (2001). Promising the future: Virginity pledges and the transition to first intercourse. *American Journal of Sociology, 106*(4), 859–912.

Beebe, S. A., & Masterson, T. (1990). *Communicating in small groups: Principles and practices.* Glenview, IL: Scott, Foresman and Little, Brown.

Beecher, C. E. (1858). *A treatise on domestic economy* (3rd ed.). New York: Harper & Brothers.

Bennett, M. (1993). Toward ethnorelativism: A developmental model of intercultural sensitivity. In R. M. Paige (Ed.), *Education for the intercultural experiences* (pp. 21–71). Yarmouth, ME: Intercultural Press.

Berger, R., & DeMaria, R. (1999). Epilogue: The future of preventive interventions with couples. In R. Berger & M. T. Hannah (Eds.), *Preventive approaches in couples therapy* (pp. 391–428). Philadelphia: Brunner/Mazel.

Berger, R., & Hannah, M. T. (1999). Introduction. In R. Berger & M. T. Hannah (Eds.), *Preventive approaches in couples therapy* (pp. 1–24). Philadelphia: Brunner/Mazel.

Berne, E. (1963). *The structure and dynamics of organizations and groups.* New York: Grove Press.

Bertalanffy, L. V. (1950). An outline of general system theory. *British Journal of the Philosophy of Science, 1,* 134–165.

Bertcher, H. J., & Maple, F. F. (1996). *Creating groups* (2nd ed.). Thousand Oaks, CA: Sage.

Bion, W. R. (1961). *Experience in groups.* New York: Basic Books.

Bogenschneider, K. (1996). An ecological risk/protective theory for building prevention programs, policies, and community capacity to support youth. *Family Relations, 45,* 127–138.

Bond, J., Thompson, C., Galinsky, E., & Prottas, D. (2005). *Highlights of the national study of the changing workforce.* Executive summary, Families and Work Institute. Available: www.familiesandwork.org

Bor, R., & du Plessis, R. (1997). The impact of HIV/AIDS on families: An overview of recent research. *Families, Systems, and Health, 15,* 413–427.

Boss, P. (2002). *Family stress management: A contextual approach* (2nd ed.). Thousand Oaks, CA: Sage.

Botwinick, J. (1967). *Cognitive processes in maturity and old age.* New York: Springer.

Bowler, M. (1999). Women's earnings: An overview. *Monthly Labor Review, 122*(12).

Bowman, T. (1990a, September). Group methods for dealing with grief and loss. Reflections from a group leader's notebook (Material and Methods section, pp. 43–45). *Family Information Services Professional Resource Materials.* Minneapolis, MN: Family Information Services.

Bowman, T. (1990b, November). Striving for congruency: Matching intentions, words and methods. Reflections from a group leader's notebook (Material and Methods section, pp. 67–69). *Family Information Services Professional Resource Materials.* Minneapolis, MN: Family Information Services.

Bowman, T. (1991a, March). The importance of rituals and traditions for group life. Reflections from a group leader's notebook (Material and Methods section, pp. 15–17). *Family Information Services Professional Resource Materials.* Minneapolis, MN: Family Information Services.

Bowman, T. (1991b, November). Sharing the wisdom. Reflections from a group leader's notebook (Material and Methods section, pp. 58–59). *Family Information Services Professional Resource Materials.* Minneapolis, MN: Family Information Services.

Bowman, T. (1993, March). Encouraging full participation. Reflections from a group leader's notebook (Material and Methods section, pp. 58–59). *Family Information Services Professional Resource Materials.* Minneapolis, MN: Family Information Services.

Bowman, T. (1994a, January). Matchmaking: The variety of needs and learning styles. Reflections from a group leader's notebook (Material and Methods section, pp. 1–4). *Family Information Services Professional Resource Materials.* Minneapolis, MN: Family Information Services.

Bowman, T. (1994b, May). Bad hair days and the group leader. Reflections from a group leader's notebook (Material and Methods section, pp. 27–29). *Family Information Services Professional Resource Materials.* Minneapolis, MN: Family Information Services.

Bowman, T. (1995a, January). Dealing with surprises in groups: The pinch model. Reflections from a group leader's notebook (Material and Methods section, pp. 1–3). *Family Information Services Professional Resource Materials.* Minneapolis, MN: Family Information Services.

Bowman, T. (1995b, March). Dancing together: Experiential group processes. Reflections from a group leader's notebook (Material and Methods section, pp. 17–18). *Family Information Services Professional Resource Materials.* Minneapolis, MN: Family Information Services.

Bowman, T. (1995c, September). Bifocals: An asset for group leaders. Reflections from a group leader's notebook (Material and Methods section, pp. 44–46). *Family Information Services Professional Resource Materials.* Minneapolis, MN: Family Information Services.

Bowman, T. (1995d, November). Beginning and ending with effective closure. Reflections from a group leader's notebook (Material and Methods section, pp. 60–61). *Family Information Services Professional Resource Materials.* Minneapolis, MN: Family Information Services.

Bredehoft, D., & Cassidy, D. (Eds.). (1995). *College and university curriculum guidelines in Family Life Education Curriculum Guidelines* (2nd ed., pp. 12–14). Minneapolis, MN: National Council on Family Relations.

Bridgeman, R. P. (1930). Ten years' progress in parent education. *Annals of the American Academy of Political and Social Science, 151,* 32–45.

Brim, O. (1959). *Education for child rearing.* New York: Russell Sage Foundation.

Briscoe, D. (2000, February 10). Millions of Americans going hungry [Press release]. Washington, DC: Associated Press.

Brock, G. (1993). Ethical guidelines for the practice of family life education. *Family Relations, 42*(2), 124–127.

Brock, G. W., Oertwein, M., & Coufal, J. D. (1993). Parent education theory, research, and practice. In M. E. Arcus, J. D. Schvaneveldt, & J. J Moss (Eds.), *Handbook of family life education* (Vol. 2, pp. 87–114). Newbury Park, CA: Sage.

Bronfenbrenner, U. (1979). *The ecology of human development.* Cambridge, MA: Harvard University Press.

Brooks, J. (1994). *Parenting in the 90s.* Mountain View, CA: Mayfield.

Brown, J. (1995). *Sex and the mass media.* Menlo Park, CA: Henry J. Kaiser Family Foundation.

Brown, L. M., & Gilligan, C. (1992). *Meeting at the crossroads: Women's psychology and girls' development.* Cambridge, MA: Harvard University Press.

Brubaker, R. (2001). International migration: A challenge for humanity. *International Migration Review, 25,* 946–957.

Bubolz, M., Eicher, J., & Sontag, S. (1979). The human ecosystem: A model. *Journal of Home Economics, 71,* 28–30.

Bubolz, M., & Sontag, S. (1993). Human ecology theory. In P. G. Boss, W. J. Doherty, R. LaRossa, W. R. Schumm, & S. K. Steinmetz (Eds.), *Sourcebook of family theories and methods: A contextual approach* (pp. 419–448). New York: Plenum Press.

Burgess, E., Locke, H. J., & Thomas, M. M. (1971). *The family* (4th ed.). New York: Van Nostrand Reinhold.

Burgess, E. W. (1926). The family as a unit of interacting personalities. *The Family, 7,* 3–9.

Burr, W. R., Day, R. D., & Bahr, K. S. (1993). *Family science.* Belmont, CA: Brooks/Cole.

Burrill, M. (1999). *The role of religious congregations in fostering adolescent sexual health.* Religious Coalition for Reproductive Choice. Retrieved March 2000, from http://www.rcrc.org

Campbell, D., & Palm, G. F. (2004). *Group parent education: Promoting parent learning and support.* Thousand Oaks, CA: Sage.

Carrera, M. A. (1995). Preventing adolescent pregnancy: In hot pursuit. *SIECUS Report, 23*(6), 16–19.

Carter, N. (1996). *See how we grow: A report on the status of parenting education in the U.S.* Philadelphia: Pew Charitable Trusts.

Cassidy, D. (2003). The growing of a profession: Challenges in family life education. In D. Bredehoft & M. Walcheski, (Eds.), *Family life education: Integrating theory and practice* (pp. 44–55). Minneapolis, MN: National Council on Family Relations.

Centers for Disease Control and Prevention. (2001). *Tracking the hidden epidemics: Trends in STDs in the United States, 2000* (p. 4). Atlanta: Author.

Centers for Disease Control and Prevention. (2004, May 21). Surveillance summaries. *Morbidity and Mortality Weekly Report, 53*(SS-2).

Chess, S., & Thomas, A. (1987). Babies are different from the start: Temperament and its significance. *Know your child.* New York: Basic Books.

Child Trends. (1996). *Facts at a glance.* Washington, DC: Author.

Clark, J. E., Lanphear, A. K., & Riddick, C. C. (1987). The effects of videogame playing on the response selection processing of elderly adults. *Journal of Gerontology, 42,* 82–85.

Cohen, P. N., & Bianchi, S. M. (1999). Marriage, children and women's employment: What do we know? *Monthly Labor Review, 122*(12).

Cole, C. L. (2002). Toward a grounded theory of marriage potential: Conceptualization, measurement, and meaning. *NCFR Theory Construction and Research Methodology Workshop Proceedings, 31,* 298–324.

Cole, C. L., & Cole, A. L. (1999). Marriage enrichment and prevention really works: Interpersonal competence training to maintain and enhance relationships. *Family Relations, 48,* 273–275.

Cole, C. L., Cole, A. L., Fort, J., & Robertson, M. (in press). Marriage potential, intentionality, and relationship depth: An outcome study of ACME marriage enrichment.

Cole, S. (1979). Age and scientific performance. *American Journal of Sociology, 84,* 958–977.

Coles, R. (1997). *The moral intelligence of children.* New York: Random House.

Columbia School of Public Health. (1996). *One in four: America's youngest poor.* New York: Author.

Connelly, C. (2006). Unintended pregnancy linked to state funding cuts. *Washington Post,* March 1, 2000. Available: www.washingtonpost.com

Cooke, B. (1991, March). Family program evaluation basics. *Family Information Services Professional Resource Materials,* 10–14. Minneapolis, MN: Family Information Services.

Crain, W. (2000). *Theories of development: Concepts and applications* (4th ed.). Englewood Cliffs, NJ: Prentice Hall.

Crary, E. (1996). *Parenting education network.* Boston: Wheelock College.

Cromwell, B. E., & Thomas, V. L. (1976). Developing resources for family potential: A family action model. *The Family Coordinator, 25,* 13–20.

Crouter, A. C., & Booth, A. (Eds.). (2003). *Children's influence on family dynamics: The neglected side of family relationships.* Mahwah, NJ: Lawrence Erlbaum.

Czaplewski, M. J., & Jorgensen, S. R. (1993). The professionalization of family life education. In M. E. Arcus, J. D. Schvaneveldt, & J. J. Moss (Eds.), *Handbook of family life education* (Vol. 1, pp. 51–75). Newbury Park, CA: Sage.

Dail, P. W. (1984). Constructing a philosophy of family life education: Educating the educators. *Family Perspective, 18*(4), 145–149.

Daley, D. (1996). Fact sheet on sexuality education. *SIECUS Report, 24*(6).

Dallard, C. (2000, April). Fueled by campaign promises, drive intensifies to boost abstinence-only education funding. *The Guttmacher Report on Public Policy, 3*(2).

Dallard, C. (2002). Abstinence promotion and teen family planning: The misguided drive for equal funding. *The Guttmacher Report on Public Policy, 5*(1), 103.

Darling, C. A. (1987). Family life education. In M. B. Sussman & S. K. Steinmetz (Eds.), *Handbook of marriage and the family* (pp. 815–833). New York: Plenum.

Darling, C. A. (2005). Families in a diverse culture: Changes and challenges. *Journal of Family and Consumer Sciences, 97*, 8–13.

Darling, C. A., & Cassidy, D. (1998). Professional development of students: Understanding the process of becoming a Certified Family Life Educator. *Family Science Review, 11*, 106–118.

Darling, C. A., & Hollon, S. (2003). Human sexuality. In D. Bredehoft & M. Walcheski (Eds.), *Family life education: Integrating theory and practice* (pp. 82–91). Minneapolis, MN: National Council on Family Relations.

Darling, C. A., & Howard, S. (2006). Cultural lessons in sexuality: Comparison of parent-child communication styles in three cultures. In R. Hamon (Ed.), *International family studies: Developing curricula and teaching tools* (pp. 41–98). Binghamton, NY: Haworth Press.

Darroch, J. E., Landry, D. J., Singh, S. (2000). Changing emphasis in sexuality education in U.S. public secondary schools, 1988–99. *Family Planning Perspectives, 32*(5), 204–211, 265.

Datan, N., Rodeheaver, D., & Hughes, F. (1987). Adult development and aging. *Annual Review of Psychology, 38*, 153–180.

DeBord, K., Bower, D., Myers-Walls, J. A., Kirby, J. K., Goddard, H. W., Mulroy, M., & Ozretich, R. (2006). A professional guide for parenting educators. *The National Extension Parenting Educator's Framework, 44*(3). Available: www.joe.org

de la Vega, E. (1990). Considerations for reaching the Latino population with sexuality and HIV/AIDS information and education. *SIECUS Report, 18*(3), 1–8.

Demick, J. (2002). Stages of parental development. In M. H. Bornstein (Ed.), *Handbook of parenting: Vol. 3. Being and becoming a parent* (2nd ed.). Mahwah, NJ: Lawrence Erlbaum.

Derman-Sparks, L. (1989). *Anti-bias curriculum: Tools for empowering young children.* Washington, DC: National Association for the Education of Young Children, ABC Task Force.

Dickinson, H. E. (1950). *The origin and development of the aims of family life education in American secondary schools.* Unpublished doctoral dissertation, George Peabody College for Teachers, Nashville, TN.

Dini, L. (2000). An Italian statement on international migration. *Population and Development Review, 26*, 849–852.

Dinkmeyer, D., & McKay, G. (1976). *Systematic training for effective parenting: Parent's handbook.* Circle Pines, MN: American Guidance Service.

Doherty, W. J. (1995). Boundaries between parent and family education and family therapy: The levels of family involvement model. *Family Relations, 44*(4), 353–358.

Doyle, R. E. (1992). *Essential skills and strategies in the helping process.* Pacific Grove, CA: Brooks/Cole.

Dreikurs, R. (1964). *Children: The challenge.* New York: New York Books.

Duncan, S. F., & Goddard, H. W. (2005). *Family life education: Principles and practices for effective outreach.* Thousand Oaks, CA: Sage.

Duvall, E. M. (1950). *Family living.* New York: Macmillan.

Duvall, E. M. (1957). *Family development.* Philadelphia: Lippincott.

Duvall, E. M. (1977). *Marriage and family development* (5th ed.). New York: Lippincott.

Duvall, E. M., & Hill, R. (1945). *When you marry.* New York: Heath.

Duvall, E. M., & Miller, B. C. (1985). *Marriage and family development* (6th ed.). New York: Harper & Row.

Dyer, P. M., & Dyer, G. H. (1989). *Marriage enrichment process, methods, and techniques.* Winston-Salem, NC: Association for Couples in Marriage Enrichment.

Dyer, P. M., & Dyer, G. H. (1999). Marriage enrichment, A.C.M.E.-style. In R. Berger & M. T. Hannah (Eds.), *Preventive approaches in couples therapy.* Philadelphia: Brunner/Mazel.

Dyer, P. M., & Dyer, G. H. (2003). *Marriage enrichment process, methods and techniques.* Paper presented at the 2003 annual conference, National Council on Family Relations, Vancouver, BC, Canada.

Early Childhood Family Education Demonstration Site Coordinators. (1997). *Manual for implementing levels 3 and 4 family involvement in early childhood education.* St. Paul: Minnesota Department of Children, Families, and Learning.

East, M. (1980). *Home economics: Past, present and future.* Boston: Allyn & Bacon.

Elin, R. J. (1999). Marriage encounter: A positive preventive enrichment program. In R. Berger & M. T. Hannah (Eds.), *Preventive approaches in couples therapy* (pp. 55–71). Philadelphia: Brunner/Mazel.

Elkind, D. (1987). *Miseducation: Preschoolers at risk.* New York: Knopf.

Engel, J. W., Saracino, M., & Bergen, M. B. (1993). Sexuality education. In M. E. Arcus, J. D. Schvaneveldt, & J. J. Moss (Eds.), *Handbook of family life education* (Vol. 2). Newbury Park, CA: Sage.

Epstein, N. B., Bishop, D. S., & Baldwin, L. M. (1984). McMaster Model of family functioning. In D. H. Olson & P. M. Miller (Eds.), *Family studies review yearbook* (Vol. 2). Beverly Hills, CA: Sage.

Families and Schools Together (FAST). (1999). Supporting the natural strength of families: A proven approach to success with at-risk kids. In *Circles of support for stronger families* (pp. 1–2). Milwaukee, WI: Alliance for Children & Families.

Families and Schools Together (FAST). (2005). Available: www.fastnational.org

Family Information Services. (2005). Available: www.faminfoserv.com

Family Service Association of America. (1976). *Overview of findings of the FSAA Task Force on family life education, development, and enrichment.* New York: Author.

Felton, R. L. (1919). *Country life in Georgia in the days of my youth.* Atlanta: Index Printing.

Fields, J. (2001). *Living arrangements of children: Fall 1996* (U.S. Census Bureau Current Population Reports, 70-47). Washington, DC: Government Printing Office.

Fields, J. (2003). *Children's living arrangements and characteristics: March 2002.* (U.S. Census Bureau Current Population Reports, 20-547). Washington, DC: Government Printing Office.

Figueroa, D., & Hanock-Jasie, L. (1999, June 2). *Public support for sexuality education reaches highest level.* Retrieved June 24, 1999, from http://www.siecus.org/media/press/press0005.html

Finkelhor, D. (1984). The prevention of child sexual abuse: An overview of needs and problems. *SIECUS Report, 13*(1), 1–5.

Fisher, B. A. (1975). Communication study in systems perspective. In B. Rubin & J. Y. Kim (Eds.), *General systems theory and human communication.* Rochelle Park, NJ: Hayden Press.

Fisher, B. L., & Kerckhoff, R. K. (1981). Family life education: Generating cohesion out of chaos. *Family Relations, 30,* 505–509.

Fletcher, M. A. (1999, July 2). For better or worse, marriage hits a low. *The Washington Post,* p. A01.

Fohlin, M. B. (1971). Selection and training of teachers for life education programs. *The Family Coordinator, 20,* 231–240.

Forrest, J. D., & Silverman, J. (1989). What public school teachers teach about preventing pregnancy, AIDS and sexually transmitted diseases. *Family Planning Perspectives, 21*(2), 65–72.

Francoeur, R. (2004). Foreword. In R. Francoeur & R. Noonan (Eds.), *The Continuum complete international encyclopedia of sexuality* (pp. ix–x). London: Continuum International Publishing Group.

Francoeur, R., & Noonan, R. (2004a). Global trends: Some final impressions. In R. Francoeur & R. Noonan (Eds.), *The Continuum complete international encyclopedia of sexuality* (pp. 1373–1375). London: Continuum International Publishing Group.

Francoeur, R., & Noonan, R. (2004b). *The Continuum complete international encyclopedia of Sexuality.* London: Continuum International Publishing Group.

Frank, L. K. (1962). The beginnings of child development and family life education in the twentieth century. *Merrill-Palmer Quarterly of Behavior and Development, 8,* 207–227.

Franklin, B. (2000, February). America's poorest people have no place to go. *The Washington Spectator, 26*(3), 1–3.

Freeman, N. K. (1997, September). Using NAEYC's Code of Ethics: Mama and daddy taught me right from wrong. Isn't that enough? *Young Children, 52*(6), 64–67.

Freire, P. (1970). *Cultural action for freedom* (Monograph Series No. 1). Cambridge, MA: Harvard Educational Review.

Fresh look at population. (1998, December). *Kiplinger Washington Letter, 75*(52), 1–4.

Friedman, Z. P. (1986, January). Work-family seminars: Help for the home front. *American Way,* 30–33.

Fohlin, M. B. (1971). Selection and training of teachers for life education programs. *The Family Coordinator, 20,* 231–240.

Frost, J. J., & Forrest, J. D. (1995). Understanding the impact of effective teenage pregnancy prevention programs. *Family Planning Perspectives, 25*(5), 188–196.

Galinsky, E., & Bond, J. (2005). *Overwork in America: When the way we work becomes too much.* Executive summary, Families and Work Institute. Available: www.familiesandwork.org

Gambrell, A., & Haffner, D. (1993). *Unfinished business: A SIECUS assessment of state sexuality education programs.* New York: Sex Information and Education Council of the U.S.

Garland, D. R., & Yankeelov, P. A. (1998). The church census: A congregational assessment tool for family ministry. *Family Ministry, 12*(3), 11–22.

Gibb, J. R. (1961). Defensive communication. *Journal of Communication, 2,* 141–148.

Giblin, P., Sprenkle, D. H., & Sheehan, R. (1985). Enrichment outcome research: A meta-analysis of premarital, marital and family interventions. *Journal of Marital and Family Therapy, 11,* 257–271.

Gilgun, J. F., & Gordon, S. (1985). Sex education and the prevention of child sexual abuse. *Journal of Sex Education and Therapy, 11*(1), 46–52.

Gilligan, C., Taylor, J., & Ward, J. (Eds.). (1988). *Mapping the moral domain.* Cambridge, MA: Harvard University Press.

Gleason, J., & Prescott, M. (1977). Group techniques for premarital preparation. *Family Coordinator, 26,* 277–280.

Glenn, N. D. (1991). The recent trend in marital success in the United States. *Journal of Marriage and the Family, 53,* 261–270.

Goetz, K. (Ed.). (1992). *Programs to strengthen families: A resource guide.* Chicago: Family Resource Coalition.

Gordon, T. (1975). *Parent effectiveness training.* Bergenfield, NJ: Penguin.

Gottman, J. M. (2000). *Clinical manual for marital therapy: A research-based approach* (revised 2001). Seattle: Gottman Institute.

Gottman, J. M. (2001). *Clinical manual for marital therapy: A research-based approach* (Rev. ed.). Seattle: Gottman Institute.

Gottman, J. M., Coan, J., Carrere, S., & Swanson, C. (1998). Predicting marital happiness and stability from newlywed interactions. *Journal of Marriage and Family, 60,* 5–22.

Gottman, J. M., & Gottman, J. S. (1999). The Marriage Survival Kit: A research-based marital therapy. In R. Berger & M. T. Hannah (Eds.), *Preventive approaches in couples therapy* (pp. 304–330). Philadelphia: Brunner/Mazel.

Graham, L., & Harris-Hart, M. (1988). Meeting the challenge of child sexual abuse. *Journal of School Health, 58*(7), 292–294.

Graham, L., & Harris-Hart, M. (1989). *Child sexual abuse prevention programs.* Ottawa, Ontario, Canada: National Clearinghouse on Family Violence, Health and Welfare.

Gregorc, A. F. (1982). *An adult's guide to style.* Columbia, CT: Author. (Available from Learning Styles Unlimited, Inc., 1911 S.W. Campus Drive, Suite 370, Federal Way, WA 98023.)

Griggs, M. B. (1981). Criteria for the evaluation of family life education materials. *Family Relations, 30*(4), 549–555.

Gross, P. (1985). *On family life education: For family life educators* (2nd revised ed.). Montreal, Quebec, Canada: Concordia University Centre for Human Relations and Community Studies.

Gross, P. (1993). *On family life education: For family life educators* (3rd revised ed.). Montreal, Quebec, Canada: Concordia University Centre for Human Relations and Community Studies.

Groves, E. R., & Groves, G. H. (1947). *The contemporary American family.* Chicago: Lippincott.

Grunbaum, J. A., Kann, L., Kinchen, S. A., Williams, B., Ross, J. G., Lowry, R., & Kolbe, L. (2002, June 28). Youth risk behavior surveillance (YRBS)—United States, 2001. *Morbidity and Mortality Weekly Report, 51*(SS-4), 1–64.

Grunseit, A., & Kippax, S. (1993). Effects of sex education on young people's sexual behaviour. Unpublished manuscript, World Health Organization.

Guerney, B. G., Jr. (1977). *Relationship enhancement: Skill training programs for therapy, problem prevention, and enrichment.* San Francisco: Jossey-Bass.

Guerney, B. G., Jr., Brock, G., & Coufal, J. (1986). Integrating marital therapy and enrichment: The relationship enhancement approach. In N. S. Jacobson & A. S. Gurman (Eds.), *Clinical handbook of marital therapy* (pp. 151–172). New York: Guilford Press.

Guerney, B. G., & Maxson, P. (1990). Marital and family enrichment research: A decade review and look ahead. *Journal of Marriage and the Family, 52,* 1127–1137.

Haffner, D. (1990). Moving toward a healthy paradigm of teen development: Helping young people develop into sexually healthy adults. *SIECUS Report, 18*(4), 12–14.

Haffner, D. (1995). Facing facts: Sexual health for America's adolescents. The report of the National Commission on Adolescent Sexual Health. *SIECUS Report, 23*(6), 2–8.

Haffner, D. W., & Goldfarb, E. S. (1997). But does it work? Improving evaluations of sexuality education. *SIECUS Report, 25*(6), 2–15.

Haffner, D. W., & Kelly, M. (1987). Adolescent sexuality in the media. *SIECUS Report, 15*(4), 9–12.

Halford, W. K., Markman, H. J., Kline, G. H., & Stanley, S. M. (2003). Best practice in couple relationship education. *Journal of Marital and Family Therapy, 29,* 385–406.

Hamner, T. J., & Turner, P. H. (1990). *Parenting in contemporary society* (2nd ed.). Englewood Cliffs, NJ: Prentice Hall.

Hamon, R. R. (Ed.). (2006). *International family studies: Developing curricula and teaching tools.* Binghamton, NY: Haworth Press.

Hamon, R., & Fernsler, C. (2006). Using cross-cultural study courses to teach about international families. In R. Hamon (Ed.), *International family studies: Developing curricula and teaching tools* (pp. 347–364). Binghamton, NY: Haworth Press.

Hans, J. D. (Ed.). (2005). *Graduate and undergraduate study in marriage and family. A guide to bachelor's, master's, and doctoral programs in the United States and Canada.* Lexington, KY: Family Scholar Publications.

Harmin, D., & Brim, O. G., Jr. (1980). *Learning to be parents: Principles, programs, and methods.* Beverly Hills, CA: Sage.

Harris, J. R. (1998). *The nurture assumption: Why children turn out the way they do.* New York: Free Press.

Harris, L. (1986). *American teens speak.* New York: Planned Parenthood Federation of America.

Harris, L. (1988). *America speaks: Americans' opinion on teenage pregnancy, sex education and birth control.* New York: Planned Parenthood Federation of America.

Hauser, D. (2004). *Five years of abstinence-only-until marriage education: Assessing the impact.* Washington, DC: Advocates for Youth.

Heath, H. (1995, March 25). Defining parenting education. *National Parenting Educators Network Listserv.* Available: http://www.npen-1@postoffice.cso.uiuc.edu

Heighway, S. (1989). Promoting healthy sexual development for adolescents with developmental disabilities or chronic illnesses. *SIECUS Report, 18*(l), 4–5.

Henry J. Kaiser Family Foundation. (1998). *National survey of teens: Teens talk about dating, intimacy, and their sexual experiences.* Menlo Park, CA: Author.

Henry J. Kaiser Family Foundation. (2001). *Talking with kids about tough issues: A national survey of parents and kids, questionnaire and detailed results* (pp. 16–17). Menlo Park, CA: Author.

Henshaw, S. K. (2004). *U.S. teenage pregnancy statistics with comparative statistics for women aged 20–24.* New York: The Alan Guttmacher Institute.

Herold, E. S., Kopf, K. E., & deCarlo, M. (1974). Family life education: Student perspectives. *Canadian Journal of Public Health, 65,* 365–368.

HHS Poverty Guidelines, 64 Fed. Reg. 13,428 (1999).

Hickman-Brown Research. (1999). *Poll on America's attitudes toward sexuality education.* Washington. DC: Hickman-Brown.

Hildreth, G. J., & Sugawara, A. I. (1993). Ethnicity and diversity in family life education. In M. E. Arcus, J. D. Schvaneveldt, & J. J. Moss (Eds.), *Handbook of family life education* (Vol. 1, pp. 162–188). Newbury Park, CA: Sage.

Hill, R., & Rodgers, R. H. (1964). The developmental approach. In H. Christensen (Ed.), *Handbook of marriage and the family.* Chicago: Rand McNally.

Hof, L., & Miller, W. R. (1981). *Marriage enrichment: Philosophy, process, and program.* Bowie, MD: Robert J. Brady.

Hoff, T., Greene, L., & Davis, J. (2003). *National survey of adolescents and young adults: Sexual health knowledge, attitudes, and experiences* (p. 14). Menlo Park, CA: Henry J. Kaiser Family Foundation.

Holden, G. W., & Hawk, C. (2003). Meta-parenting in the journey of child-rearing: A mechanism for change. In L. Kuczynski (Ed.), *Handbook of dynamics of parent-child relations.* Thousand Oaks, CA: Sage.

Homans, G. (1958). Social behavior as exchange. *American Journal of Sociology, 63,* 597–606.

Homans, G. C. (1961). *Social behavior: Its elementary forms.* New York: Harcourt Brace.

Howard, R. (1981). *A social history of American sociology, 1865–1940.* Westport, CT: Greenwood.

Howe, R. L. (1963). *The miracle of dialogue.* New York: Seabury Press.

Huang, N. (2003). *Family education law in Taiwan.* Paper presented at the annual meeting of the National Council on Family Relations, Vancouver, BC, Canada.

Huang, W. (2005). An Asian perspective on relationship and marriage education. *Family Process, 44,* 161–173.

Hughes, R., Jr. (1999). Program clarification: What are we really trying to do? *Human Development and Family Life Bulletin, 5*(1), 6–7. Available: http://www.hec.ohiostate.edu/famlife/bulletin/volume.S/bull51xxhtml

International Clinical Epidemiology Network. (2001). *Adolescent health.* Retrieved March 12, 2006, from http://www.inclen.org/research/ah.html

International Organization for Migration (IOM). (2003). *World migration 2003: Managing migration—challenges and responses for people on the move* (Chapter 1). Retrieved March 11, 2006, from http://www.iom.int/DOCUMENTS/PUBLICATION/EN/chap01p1_24.pdf

Irwin, D. B., & Simons, J. A. (1994). *Lifespan developmental psychology.* Madison, WI: Brown & Benchmark.

Jacobs, F. H., & Kapuscik, J. L. (with Williams, P. H., & Kates, E.) (2000). *Making the count: Evaluating family preservation services.* Medford, MA: Family Preservation Evaluation Project, Tufts University.

Jaffeson, R. C. (1998, May). Continuing education credit. *Certification Communications, 53.*

Jemmott, J. B., III, Jemmott, L. S., & Fong, G. T. (1998). Abstinence and safer sex HIV risk-reduction interventions for African American adolescents: A randomized controlled trial. *Journal of the American Medical Association, 279,* 1529–1536.

Joint Committee on Standards for Educational Evaluation. (1981). *Standards for evaluation of educational programs, projects, and materials.* New York: McGraw-Hill.

Kagan, J., & Snidman, N. (1991). Temperamental factors in human development. *American Psychologist, 46*(8), 856–862.

Karoly, L. A., Kilburn, M. R., Cannon, J. S., Bigelow, J. H., & Christina, R. (2005, Fall). Many happy returns. Early childhood programs entail costs, but the paybacks could be substantial. *RAND Review.* Available: www.rand.org/publications/randreview/issues/fall2005/returns.html. Santa Monica, CA: RAND Corporation.

Kastenbaum, R. J. (1984). When aging begins: A lifespan developmental approach. *Research on Aging, 6,* 105–117.

Kelly, A. B., & Fincham, F. D. (1999). Preventing marital distress: What does research offer? In R. Berger & M. T. Hannah (Eds.), *Preventive approaches in couples therapy* (pp. 361–390). Philadelphia: Brunner/Mazel.

Kelly, C., Huston, T., & Cate, R. (1985). Premarital relationship correlates of the erosion of satisfaction in marriage. *Journal of Social and Personal Relationships, 2,* 167–178.

Kerckhoff, R. K. (1964). Family life education in America. In H. T. Christiansen (Ed.), *Handbook of marriage and the family* (pp. 881–911). Chicago: Rand McNally.

Kilpatrick, A. C., & Holland, T. P. (1995). *Working with families: An integrative model by level of functioning.* Boston: Allyn & Bacon.

Kirby, D. (1994). Sex education in the schools. In J. A. Garrison, M. D. Smith, & D. J. Besharov (Eds.), *Sexuality and American school policy.* Menlo Park, CA: Henry J. Kaiser Family Foundation.

Kirby, D. (1997). *No easy answers: Research findings on programs to reduce teen pregnancy* [Summary]. Washington, DC: National Campaign to Reduce Teen Pregnancy.

Kirby, D. (2001). *Emerging answers: Research findings on programs to reduce teen pregnancy.* Washington, DC: National Campaign to Prevent Teen Pregnancy.

Kirby, D. (2002). *Do abstinence-only programs delay the initiation of sex among young people and reduce teen pregnancy?* Washington, DC: National Campaign to Prevent Teen Pregnancy.

Kirby, D., Short, L., Collins, J., Rugg, D., Kolbe, L., Howard, M., Miller, B., Sonenstein, F., & Zabin, L. S. (1994). School-based programs to reduce sexual risk behaviors: A review of effectiveness. *Public Health Reports, 109*(3), 339–360.

Kirkendall, L. A. (1973). Education for marriage and family life. In A. Ellis & A. Abarbanel (Eds.), *The encyclopedia of sexual behavior* (2nd ed.). New York: Hawthorne.

Kirkendall, L. A. (1984). The journey toward SIECUS: 1964, a personal odyssey. *SIECUS Report, 12*(4), 1–4.

Klein, D., & White, J. (2002). *Family theories.* Thousand Oaks, CA: Sage.

Knapp, D. J., & Reynolds, D. H. (1996). Establishing credentialing policies and procedures. In A. H. Browning, A. C. Bugbee, & M. A. Mullins (Eds.), *Certification: A NOCA Handbook* (pp. 191–214). Washington, DC: National Organization for Competency Assurance.

Knowles, M. (1989). *The making of an adult educator.* San Francisco: Jossey-Bass.

Kohlberg, L. (1984). *Psychology of moral development.* New York: Harper & Row.

Kolb, D. A. (1984). *Experiential learning: Experience as the source of learning and development.* Englewood Cliffs, NJ: Prentice Hall.

Krivacska, J. J. (1991). Child sexual abuse prevention programs: The need for childhood sexuality education. *SIECUS Report, 19*(6), 1–7.

Krueger, M. M. (1991). The omnipresent need: Professional training for sexuality education teachers. *SIECUS Report, 19*(4), 1–5.

L'Abate, L. (1981). Skill training programs for couples and families. In A. S. Gurman & D. P. Kniskern (Eds.), *Handbook of family therapy* (pp. 631–661). New York: Brunner/Mazel.

L'Abate, L. (1983). Prevention as a profession: Toward a new conceptual frame of reference. In D. R. Mace (Ed.), *Prevention in family services: Approaches to family therapy and counseling* (pp. 46–52). Beverly Hills, CA: Sage.

L'Abate, L. (1986). *Systematic family therapy.* New York: Brunner/Mazel.

L'Abate, L. (1999). Structured enrichment and distance writing for couples. In R. Berger & M. T. Hannah (Eds.), *Preventive approaches in couples therapy* (pp. 106–124). Philadelphia: Brunner/Mazel.

Labouvie-Vief, G. (1986). Modes of knowledge and the organization of development. In M. L. Commons, L. Kohlberg, E. Richards, & J. Stinnott (Eds.), *Beyond formal operations: Models and methods in the study of adult and adolescent thought.* New York: Praeger.

Lapsley, D. G. (1989). Continuity and discontinuity in adolescent social cognitive development. In R. Montemayor, G. Adams, & T. Gullota (Eds.), *Advances in adolescence research* (Vol. 2). Orlando, FL: Academic Press.

LeBey, B. (2001, September). American families are drifting apart. *USA Today, 130*(2676), 20–22. Retrieved August 20, 2004, from http://wilsontxt.hwwilson.com/pdfhtml/00224/W4U98/8SB.htm

Lederer, W., & Jackson, D. (1968). *Mirages of marriage.* New York: Norton

Lee, D. A., & Fong, K. (1990). HIV/AIDS and the Asian and Pacific Islander community. *SIECUS Report, 18*(3), 16–19.

Lee, M. R. (1963). How do experts define "family life education"? *The Family Life Coordinator, 12*(3–4), 105–106.

Leiberman, M. E., Yalom, I. D., & Miles, M. B. (1973). *Encounter groups: First facts.* New York: Basic Books.

Leveat, R. F. (Ed.). (1986). *Psychoeducational approaches to family therapy and counseling.* New York: SpringerVerlag.

Levin, E. (1975). Development of a family life education program in a community social service agency. *The Family Coordinator, 24,* 343–349.

Lewin, K., Lippitt, R., & White, R. (1939). Patterns of aggressive behavior in experimentally created "social climates." *Journal of Social Psychology, 10,* 271–299.

Lewis, J. M., Beavers, W. R., Gossett, J. T., & Phillips, V. A. (1976). *No single thread: Psychological health in family systems.* New York: Brunner/Mazel.

Lewis-Rowley, M., Brasher, R. E., Moss, J. J., Duncan, S. F., & Stiles, R. J. (1993). The evolution of education for family life. In M. E. Arcus, J. D. Schvaneveldt, & J. J. Moss (Eds.), *Handbook of family life education* (Vol. 1, pp. 26–50). Newbury Park, CA: Sage.

Littell, J. H. (1986). *Building strong foundations: Evaluation strategies for family resource programs.* Chicago: Family Resource Coalition.

Maccoby, E. E., & Martin, J. A. (1983). Socialization in the context of the family: Parent child interaction. In P. H. Mussen & E. Hetherington (Eds.), *Handbook of child psychology: Vol. 4. Socialization, personality and social development* (4th ed., pp. 1–101). New York: Wiley.

Mace, D. (1970). *The Christian response to the sexual revolution.* Nashville, TN: Abingdon Press.

Mace, D. (1981). The long, long trail from information-giving to behavioral change. *Family Relations, 30,* 599–606.

Mace, D. (1982). *Close companions: The marriage enrichment handbook.* New York: Continuum Publishing.

Mace, D. R. (Ed.). (1983). *Prevention in family services: Approaches to family wellness.* Beverly Hills, CA: Sage.

Mace, D. R., & Mace, V. (1974). *We can have better marriages.* Nashville, TN: Abingdon.

Mace, D. R., & Mace, V. (1975). Marriage enrichment: Wave of the future? *The Family Coordinator, 24,* 171–173.

Mace, D. R., & Mace, V. (1976). Marriage enrichment: A preventive group approach for couples. In D. H. Olson (Ed.), *Treating relationships* (pp. 321–338). Lake Mills, IA: Graphic.

Mace, D. R., & Mace, V. (1978). Measure your marriage potential: A simple test that tells couples where they are. *The Family Coordinator, 27,* 63–67.

Manning, P. (2001). *Migration and family structure: Theses on the global history of families.* Paper presented at Interactions: Regional Studies, Global Processes, and Historical Analysis, Library of Congress, Washington, DC, February 28–March 3, 2001. Retrieved March 19, 2006, from http://www.historycooperative.org/proceedings/interactions/manning.html

Markey, B., & Micheletto, M. (1997). *FOCCUS facilitator manual* (2nd ed.). Omaha, NE: Archdiocese of Omaha, Family Life Office.

Markman, H. J. (1979). The application of a behavioral model of marriage in predicting relationship satisfaction of couples planning marriage. *Journal of Consulting and Clinical Psychology, 47,* 743–749.

Markman, H. J. (1981). Predicting marital distress: A 5-year follow-up. *Journal of Consulting and Clinical Psychology, 49,* 173–196.

Markman, H. J., Floyd, F. J., Stanley, S. M., & Lewis, H. (1986). Prevention. In H. Jacobson & A. Gruman (Eds.), *Clinical handbook of marital therapy* (pp. 173–196). New York: Guilford Press.

Markman, H. J., Floyd, F. J., Stanley, S. M., & Storaasli, R. D. (1988). Prevention of marital distress: A longitudinal investigation. *Journal of Consulting and Clinical Psychology, 56,* 210–217.

Markman, H., Stanley, S., & Blumberg, S. L. (1994). *Fighting for your marriage.* San Francisco: Jossey-Bass.

Maslow, A. (1959). Creativity in self-actualizing people. In H. H. Anderson (Ed.), *Creativity and its cultivation.* New York: Harper & Row.

Mattessich, P., & Hill, R. (1987). Life cycle and family development. In M. B. Sussman & S. K. Steinmetz (Eds.), *Handbook of marriage and the family.* New York: Plenum Press.

McAdoo, J. L. (1993). Decision making and marital satisfaction in African American families. In H. P. McAdoo (Ed.), *Family ethnicity: Strength in diversity.* Newbury Park, CA: Sage.

McConnell, E. (1970, September). The history of home economics. *Forecast for Home Economics, 86–87,* 134.

McGilly, K., & Siegler, R. S. (1989). How children choose among serial recall strategies. *Child Development, 60,* 172–182.

Mead, M. (1985). Is sex necessary? *SIECUS Report, 13*(3), 5–6. (Reprinted from *SIECUS Newsletter,* February 1969.)

Medina, C. (1987). Latino culture and sex education. *SIECUS Report, 15*(3), 1–4.

Merrill, C. D. (2002). *Workbook for family life education methods: CHFAM 4650.* Ogden, UT: Author.

Merrill, M. D. (1994). *Instructional design theory.* Englewood Cliffs, NJ: Educational Technology Publications.

Miles, M. B. (1981). *Learning to work in groups.* New York: Columbia University, Teacher's College Press.

Miller, B. C. (1998). *Families matter: A research synthesis of family influences on adolescent pregnancy.* Washington, DC: National Campaign to Prevent Teen Pregnancy.

Miller, J. P., & Seller, W. (1990). *Curriculum perspectives and practices.* New York: Longman.

Miller, S., & Sherrard, P. A. D. (1999). Couple communication: A system for equipping partners to talk, listen, and resolve conflicts effectively. In R. Berger & M. T. Hannah (Eds.), *Preventive approaches in couples therapy* (pp. 125–148). Philadelphia: Brunner/Mazel.

Miller, S. L., Miller, P. A., Nunnally, E. W., & Wackman, D. B. (1992). *Couple communication instructor manual.* Denver: Interpersonal Communication Programs.

Miller, S. L., Nunnally, E. W., & Wackman, D. B. (1975). *Alive and aware.* Minneapolis, MN: Interpersonal Communications.

Minnesota Council on Family Relations (MCFR). (1997). *Ethical thinking and practice for parent and family educators.* Minneapolis, MN: Ethics Committee, Parent and Family Education Section.

Minnesota Department of Children, Families, & Learning. (2000). *Minnesota State Board of Teaching adopted permanent rules relating to teaching licensing of parent and family educators.* Available: http://cfl.state.mn.us/teachbrd/8710 3100.html

Moore, K. A. (1995). *Adolescent pregnancy prevention programs: Interventions and evaluations.* Washington, DC: Child Trends.

Moreno, J. L. (1953). *Who shall survive?* (Rev. ed.). Beacon, NY: Beacon Press.

Morris, S. N., Dollahite, D. C., & Hawkins, A. J. (1999). Virtual family life education: A qualitative study of father education on the World Wide Web. *Family Relations, 48,* 23–30.

Moss, J. J., & King, K. F. (1970). Involving students for productive learning in marriage and family living classes. *The Family Coordinator, 19,* 78–82.

Mudd, E., Freeman, C., & Rose, E. (1941). Premarital counseling in the Philadelphia marriage counsel. *Mental Hygiene, 25*(1), 98–119.

Murray, T. R. (1992). *Comparing theories of child development* (3rd ed.). Belmont, CA: Wadsworth.

Myers-Walls, J. (1997, November 25). Competencies. *Talk About Parent Education.* Available: pareduc@extension.unm.edu

Myers-Walls, J. (1998). *What is your parent education approach?* Lafayette, IN: Purdue University Cooperative Extension Service.

Myers-Walls, J. (2000). Family diversity and family life education. In D. H. Demo, K. R. Allen, & M. A. Fine (Eds.), *Handbook of family diversity* (pp. 359–379). New York: Oxford University Press.

Napier, R. W., & Gershenfeld, M. K. (1983). *Making groups work: A guide for group leaders.* Boston: Houghton Mifflin.

National Campaign to Prevent Teen Pregnancy. (1998). *Snapshots from the front line II: Lessons from programs that involve parents and other adults in preventing teen pregnancy.* Washington, DC: Author.

National Campaign to Prevent Teen Pregnancy. (2001). *With one voice: America's adults and teens sound off about teen pregnancy.* Washington, DC: Author.

National Center for Health Statistics. (1996). *Advance report of final divorce statistics, 1989 and 1990.* Hyattsville, MD: Author.

National Center for Health Statistics. (1998). *Teen births in the United States: State trends, 1991–1996, an update.* Hyattsville, MD: Author.

National Center for Health Statistics. (2005). Executive summary. *Health, United States, 2005 with chartbook on trends in the health of Americans.* Hyattsville, MD: Author.

National Coalition to Support Sexuality Education. (1999). Available: http://www.siecus.org/pubs/fact/index.htm

National Commission on Children. (1991a). *Beyond rhetoric: A new American agenda for children and their families.* Washington, DC: Author.

National Commission on Children. (1991b). *Speaking of kids: A national survey of children and parents.* Washington, DC: Author.

National Commission on Family Life Education. (1968). Family life education programs: Principles, plans, procedures. A framework for family life educators. *The Family Coordinator, 17,* 211–214.

National Council on Family Relations (NCFR). (1994). *Standards and criteria for the certification of family life educators, college/university curriculum guidelines, and an overview of content in family life education: A framework for planning life span programs.* Minneapolis, MN: Author.

National Council on Family Relations (NCFR). (1995a). *Ethical principles and guidelines.* Minneapolis, MN: Author.

National Council on Family Relations (NCFR). (1995b). *Family life education curriculum guidelines.* Minneapolis, MN: Author.

National Council on Family Relations (NCFR). (1997a). *Framework for life-span family life education* (Rev. ed.). Minneapolis, MN: Author.

National Council on Family Relations (NCFR). (1997b). *Standards and criteria for the certification of family life educators, college/university curriculum guidelines, and content guidelines for family life education: A framework for planning programs over the life span* (Rev. ed.). St. Paul, MN: Author.

National Council on Family Relations (NCFR). (1999). *Tools for ethical thinking and practice in family life education.* Minneapolis, MN: Author.

National Council on Family Relations (NCFR). (2003). *Assessing the future: Family life education* (NCFR Fact Sheet). Minneapolis, MN: Author.

National Marriage Project. (1999). *The state of our unions, 1999.* New Brunswick, NJ: Author.

National Native American AIDS Prevention Center. (1990). *We owe it to ourselves and to our children.* Oakland, CA: Author.

National Parenting Education Network (NPEN). (2006). History of NPEN. Available: http://www.ces.ncsu.edu/depts/fcs/npen/work_hi.html

National Research Council and Institute of Medicine. (2000). *From neurons to neighborhoods: The science of early childhood development.* Committee on Integrating the Science of Early Childhood Development. Jack P. Shonkoff and Deborah A. Phillips, eds. Board on Children, Youth, and Families, Commission on Behavioral and Social Sciences and Education. Washington, DC: National Academy Press.

NCHS/CDC Public Affairs. (2002). *Cohabitation, divorce, and remarriage in the United States.* Series Report 23, Number 22. (PHS) 98-1998. Hyattsville, MD: National Center for Health Statistics.

Office of Technology Assessment. (1986). Indian health care (Publication No. OTA-H-290). Washington, DC: U.S. Government Printing Office.

Ohlemacher, S. (2006, January 18). *Study finds that marriage builds wealth—and divorce destroys it.* Available: http://www.abcnews.go.com/US/wireStory?id=1516617&CMP=OTC-RSSFeeds0312

Olson, D. (2006). *Marriage mentor program.* Life Innovations, Inc. Available: www.lifeinnovation.com

Olson, D. H. (Ed.). (1976). *Treating relationships.* Lake Mills, IA: Graphic.

Olson, D. H. (1983). How effective is marriage preparation? In D. R. Mace (Ed.), *Prevention in family services* (pp. 196–216). Beverly Hills, CA: Sage.

Olson, D. H. (1998). *PREPARE/ENRICH counselor's manual.* Minneapolis, MN: Life Innovations.

Olson, D. H. (1999). *Building relationships: Developing skills for life.* Available: http://www.lifeinnovation.com

Olson, D. H., Dyer, P. M., & Dyer, G. H. (1998). *Growing together: Leader's manual.* Minneapolis, MN: Life Innovations.

Olson, D. H., & Olson, A. K. (1999). PREPARE/ENRICH program: Version 2000. In R. Berger & M. T. Hannah (Eds.), *Preventive approaches in couples therapy.* Philadelphia: Brunner/Mazel.

Orlandi, M. A. (1992). The challenge of evaluating community-based prevention programs: A cross-cultural perspective. In M. A. Orlandi, R. Weston, & L. G. Epstein (Eds.), *Cultural competence for evaluators: A guide for alcohol and other drug abuse prevention practitioners working with ethnic/racial communities* (pp. 1–22). Rockville, MD: U.S. Department of Health and Human Services, Office for Substance Abuse Prevention.

Overton, W. E., & Byrnes, J. P. (1991). Cognitive development. In R. M. Lerner, A. C. Petersen, & J. Brooks-Gunn (Eds.), *Encyclopedia of adolescence* (Vol. 1). New York: Garland.

Palm, G. (1998, Spring). Ethical thinking and practice for family professionals. *Views,* 14–17.

Parker, F. J. (1980). *Home economics: An introduction to a dynamic profession.* New York: Macmillan.

Parrott, L., III, & Parrott, L. (1999). Preparing couples for marriage: The SYMBIS model. In R. Berger & M. T. Hannah (Eds.), *Preventive approaches in couples therapy* (pp. 237–254). Philadelphia: Brunner/Mazel.

Patton, M. Q. (1997). Utilization-focused evaluation: The new century text. Thousand Oaks, CA: Sage.

Peters, R. S. (1967). *The concept of education.* London: Routledge & Kegan Paul.

Peterson, D. A. (1985). A history of education for older learners. In D. B. Lumsden (Ed.), *The older adult as learner.* Washington, DC: Hemisphere.

Phinney, J. S. (1990). Ethnic identity in adolescents and adults: Review of research. *Psychological Bulletin, 108,* 499–514.

Popkin, M. (1987). *Active parenting: Teaching courage, cooperation, and responsibility.* New York: Harper Collins.

Powell, J. (1969). *Why am I afraid to tell you who I am?* Niles, IL: Argus Communications.

Powell, L., & Jorgensen, S. (1985). Evaluation of a sex-education program for church youth. *Family Relations, 34*(4), 475–482.

Powell, L., & Powell, S. (2003). *It's not what you say: Comparing communication styles of participants and non-participants in long-term marital support groups.* Paper presented at the 2003 annual conference, National Council on Family Relations, Vancouver, BC, Canada.

Powell, L., Powell, S., Dyer, P., Dyer, G., Cole, C., & Cole, A. (2004). The MEG: Examining how a marriage enrichment model can build and sustain positive interaction in relationships. *Vision 2004: What is the future of marriage?* Minneapolis, MN: National Council on Family Relations.

Public Education Committee on Family. (2001). *Family matters: Report of the Public Education Committee on Family.* Singapore: Ministry for Community Development and Sports.

Quigley, E. (1974). *Introduction to home economics* (2nd ed.). New York: Macmillan.

Quindlen, A. (1993). *Thinking out loud.* New York: Random House.

Rader, S., & Cooke, B. (2006). *A brief introduction to evaluation.* National Parenting Education Network. Available: http://www.ces.ncsu.edu/depts/fcs/npen/work_evl.html

Rasmussen, W. D. (1989). *Taking the university to the people.* Ames: Iowa University Press.

Remafedi, G. (1992). Demography of sexual orientation in adolescents. *Pediatrics, 89,* 714–721.

Rettig, K. D. (1988, November). *A framework for integrating family relations and family resource management.* Paper presented at the workshop on Theory Construction and Research Methodology, National Council on Family Relations, Philadelphia.

Rodgers, R. H., & White, J. M. (1993). Family development theory. In P. G. Boss, W. J. Doherty, R. LaRossa, W. R. Schumm, & S. K. Steinmetz (Eds.), *Sourcebook of family theories and methods: A contextual approach* (pp. 225–254). New York: Plenum Press.

Rodman, H. (1970). *Teaching about families: Textbook evaluations and recommendations for secondary schools.* Cambridge, MA: Doyle.

Rodriguez, M., Young, R., Renfro, S., Asencio, M., & Haffner, D. (1996). Teaching our teachers to teach: A SIECUS study on training and preparation for HIV/AIDS prevention and sexuality education. *SIECUS Report, 24*(2), 15–23.

Ross, S., & Kantor, L. M. (1995). Trends in opposition to comprehensive sexuality education in public schools: 1994–1995 school year. *SIECUS Report, 23*(6), 9–15.

Rowell, R. M. (1990). Native Americans, stereotypes, and HIV/AIDS: Our continuing struggle for survival. *SIECUS Report, 18*(3), 9–15.

Rudrauff, A. (1999). Student-centered sex education. *Human Development and Family Life Bulletin, 4*(4), 4.

Ryerson, E. (1984). Sexual abuse and self-protection education for developmentally disabled youth: A priority need. *SIECUS Report, 13*(1), 6–7.

Saluter, A. F. (1994). *Marital status and living arrangements: March 1993* (Bureau of Census Current Population Reports, Series P20-478). Washington, DC: Government Printing Office.

Samuels, H. (1995). Sexology, sexosophy, and African-American sexuality. *SIECUS Report, 23*(3), 3–5.

Santrock, J. W. (1992). *Life-span development* (4th ed., rev.). Dubuque, IA: Brown.

Satir, V. (1972). *Peoplemaking.* Palo Alto, CA: Science and Behavior Books.

Satir, V. (1988). *The new peoplemaking.* Mountain View, CA: Science and Behavior Books.

Schaie, K. W. (1977/1978). Toward a stage theory of adult cognitive development. *International Journal of Aging and Human Development, 8*(2), 129–138.

Schaie, K. W. (1991). Developmental designs revisited. In S. H. Cohen & H. W. Reese (Eds.), *Life-span developmental psychology: Methodological innovation.* Hillsdale, NJ: Erlbaum.

Schickendanz, J., Schickendanz, D., Hansen, K., & Forsyth, P. (1993). *Understanding children.* Mountain View, CA: Mayfield.

Schiffer, J. (2002). *Preparing tomorrow's parents today: How to bring parenting education for children and teens to your schools.* Boca Raton, FL: Parenting Project.

Schlossman, S. L. (1976, August). Before home start: Notes toward a history of parent education in America, 1897–1929. *Harvard Educational Review, 46*(3), 436–467.

Schmid, K. (1995). Multicultural family science. In R. Day, K. Gilbert, B. Settles, & W. Burr (Eds.), *Research and theory in family science* (pp. 54–70). Pacific Grove, CA: Brooks-Cole.

Schneider, D. M. (1980). *American kinship: A cultural account* (2nd ed.). Englewood Cliffs, NJ: Prentice Hall.

Schultz, B. G. (1989). *Communicating in the small group: Theory and practice.* New York: Harper & Row.

Schultz, J. B. (1994, Summer). Family life education: Implications for home economics teachers education. *Journal of Home Economics,* 30–36.

Scott-Jones, D., & Peebles-Wilson, W. (1986). Sex equity in parenting and parent education. *Theory into Practice, 25*(4), 235–242.

Selverstone, R. (1989). Where are we now in the sexual revolution? *SIECUS Report, 17*(4), 7–12.

Settles, M. (1998). *Sexuality education and a needs assessment.* Available: http://www.klingenstein. org/Additional Resources/projects/settles.htm

Sharman, C. (2005). The problem with drinking. *Perspectives in Health: Magazine of the Pan-American Health Organization.* Retrieved March 12, 2006, from http://www.paho.org/English/DD/PIN/Number21_article04.htm

Shaw, M. E. (1981). *Group dynamics: The psychology of small group behavior* (3rd ed.). New York: McGraw-Hill.

Sheek, B. W. (1984). *A nation for families.* Washington, DC: American Home Economics Association.

Sherwood, J. J., & Scherer, J. J. (1975). A model for couples: How two can grow together. In S. Miller (Ed.), *Marriages and families: Enrichment through communication.* Beverly Hills, CA: Sage.

Shor, L., & Freire, P. (1986). *A pedagogy for liberation: Dialogues on transforming education.* South Hadley, MA: Bergin & Garvey.

SIECUS. (1994). Teens talk about sex: Adolescent sexuality in the 90's. *SIECUS Report, 22*(5), 16–17.

SIECUS. (1997a). Fact sheet: Sexually transmitted diseases in the United States. *SIECUS Report, 25*(3).

SIECUS. (1997b). Fact sheet: The National Coalition to Support Sexuality Education. *SIECUS Report, 25*(4), 17–18.

SIECUS. (1997c). Fact sheet: Guidelines for comprehensive sexuality education, kindergarten–12th grade. *SIECUS Report, 25*(6).

SIECUS. (1998a). *SIECUS community action kit. Suggestions for community organizing.* Available: http://www.SIECUS.org/pubs/kits/kits/0001.html

SIECUS. (1998b). Fact sheet: Gay, lesbian, and bisexual adolescents. *SIECUS Report, 26*(4).

Silliman, B., & Schumm, W. R. (1995). Client interests in premarital counseling: A further analysis. *Journal of Sex and Marital Therapy, 21*(1), 43.

Simonton, D. K. (1977). Creativity, age and stress. *Journal of Personality and Social Psychology, 35,* 791–804.

Simpson, G., & Yinger, J. (1985). *Racial and cultural minorities.* New York: Plenum Press.

Simpson, R. (2001). *Raising teens: A synthesis of research and a foundation for action.* Boston: Center for Health Communication, Harvard School of Public Health.

Smith, C., Perou, R., & Lesesne, C. (2002). Parent education. In M. H. Bornstein (Ed.), *Handbook of parenting: Vol. 4. Social conditions and applied parenting* (2nd ed.). Mahwah, NJ: Lawrence Erlbaum.

Smith, C. A., Cudaback, D., Goddard, H. W., & Myers-Walls, J. A. (1994). *National extension parent education model.* Manhattan, KS: Kansas Cooperative Extension Service. Available: http://www.k-state.edu/wwparent/nepem/index.htm

Smith, I. (1999, September 13). Misjudged threat: The word about AIDS still needs to get out, especially among African Americans. *Time,* 88.

Smith, W. M., Jr. (1968). Family life education: Who needs it? *The Family Coordinator, 17,* 55–61.

Somerville, R. M. (1967). The relationship between family life education and sex education. *Journal of Marriage and the Family, 29,* 374–389.

Somerville, R. M. (1971). Family life education and sex education in the turbulent sixties. *Journal of Marriage and the Family, 33,* 11–35.

Special report: A conference stressing marital education over marital therapy. (1999, July). *Psychotherapy Finances, 1*(7), 6–10.

Sprafkin, J. N., & Silverman, L. T. (1981, Winter). Update: Physically intimate and sexual behavior on prime-time television, 1978–1979. *Journal of Communication.*

Stahmann, R., & Hiebert, W. (1987). *Premarital counseling: The professional's handbook* (2nd ed.). Lexington, MA: Lexington.

Stahmann, R., & Salts, C. (1993). Educating for marriage and intimate relationships. In M. E. Arcus, J. D. Schvaneveldt, & J. J. Moss (Eds.), *Handbook of family life education* (Vol. 2, pp. 33–61). Newbury Park, CA: Sage.

Stanley, S. M., Blumberg, S. L., & Markman, H. J. (1999). Helping couples fight for their marriages: The PREP approach. In R. Berger & M. T. Hannah (Eds.), *Preventive approaches in couples therapy* (pp. 279–303). Philadelphia: Brunner/Mazel.

Stern, E. E. (1969). Family life education: Some rationales and contents. *The Family Coordinator, 18,* 39–43.

Sternberg, R. J. (1988). Mental self-government: A theory of intellectual styles and their development. *Human Development, 31,* 197–224.

Strong, B., & DeVault, C. (1998). *The marriage and family experience: Intimate relationships in a changing society.* Belmont, CA: Wadsworth.

Strozdas, L. (2004, Summer). Double-take: A review of stepfamily ministry then and now. *Family Ministry, 19*(3).

Subramaiam, A. (2006). Creating an electronic portfolio to integrate multiculturalism in teaching family economics. In R. Hamon (Ed.), *International family studies: Developing curricula and teaching tools* (pp. 487–414). Binghamton, NY: Haworth Press.

Suskie, L. (2004). *Assessing student learning: A common sense guide.* Bolton, MA: Anker Publishing.

Taylor, R. (1994). Minority families in America: An introduction. In R. L. Taylor (Ed.), *Minority families in the United States: A multicultural perspective* (pp. 1–16). Englewood Cliffs, NJ: Prentice Hall.

Telljohann, S. K., & Price, J. H. (1993). A qualitative examination of adolescent homosexual's life experiences: Ramifications for secondary school personnel. *Journal of Homosexuality, 26*(1), 48.

Tennant, J. (1989). Family life education: Identity, objectives, and future directions. *McGill Journal of Education, 24*, 127–142.

Texas Registry of Parent Educator Resources. (2000). *Core knowledge for parents and professionals who work with families.* Denton: University of North Texas Center for Parent Education.

Thibaut, J. W., & Kelley, H. H. (1959). *The social psychology of groups.* New York: Wiley.

Thomas, A., Chess, S., & Birch, H. (1968). *Temperament and behavior disorders in children.* New York: New York University Press.

Thomas, J. (1988, November). *Theoretical perspectives of curriculum in family life education: Implications for practice.* Paper presented at the annual meeting of the National Council on Family Relations, Philadelphia.

Thomas, J., & Arcus, M. (1992). Family life education: An analysis of the concept. *Family Relations, 41*, 3–8.

Thomas, J., Schvaneveldt, J. D., & Young, M. H. (1993). Programs in family life education: Development, implementation, and evaluation. In M. E. Arcus, J. D. Schvaneveldt, & J. J. Moss (Eds.), *Handbook of family life education* (Vol. 1). Newbury Park, CA: Sage.

Torstendahl, R., & Burrage, M. (1990). *The formation of professions: Knowledge, state and strategy.* London: Sage.

Tuckman, B. W. (1965). Developmental sequences in small groups. *Psychological Bulletin, 63*, 384–399.

UNAIDS. (1997, October 22). Sexual health education does lead to safer sexual behavior. *UNAIDS Review.* Press release, Joint United Nations Programme on HIV/AIDS.

United Nations Department of Economic and Social Affairs, Population Division. (2001). *World population aging: 1950–2050.* Retrieved March 8, 2006, from http://www.un.org/esa/population/publications/worldageing19502050/

United Nations Development Programme. (2000). *Human development report 2000.* New York: Oxford University Press.

United Nations Development Programme. (2003a). *Major trends affecting families: A background document.* New York: United Nations.

United Nations Development Programme. (2003b). *Families in the process of development: Major trends affecting families worldwide.* Retrieved March 10, 2004, from http://www.un.org/esa/socedev/family/majortrends.htm

United Nations Development Programme. (2004). *Objectives of the follow-up to IYF.* Retrieved April 15, 2004, from http://www.un.org/esa/socedev/family/TenthAnv/10thanvrsry.htm

United Nations Programme on the Family. (2003). *International year of the family 1994–2004: 10th anniversary year.* Retrieved March 18, 2006, from http://iyfanniversary.org/mainNS.htm

United Way of America. (1996). *Measuring program outcomes: A practical approach.* Alexandria, VA: Author.

University of Minnesota. (1991). *Family education/parent education licensure.* St. Paul, MN: Department of Work, Family and Community Education.

U.S. Bureau of the Census. (1996). *Statistical abstract of the United States* (116th ed.). Washington, DC: U.S. Government Printing Office.

U.S. Bureau of the Census. (1999). *Selected characteristics of all persons.* Available: http://www.gov:80/population/socdemo/ancestry/ All-persons.txt

U.S. Census Bureau. (2000). *American fact finder,* Summary File 4. Available: http://factfinder.census.gov/home/en/datanotes/expsf4.htm

U.S. Census Bureau. (2003). *Statistical abstract of the United States* (123rd ed.). Washington, DC: Author. Available: www.census.gov/prod/www/statistical-abstract-2001_2003.html

U.S. Census Bureau. (2004a). *U.S. Interim Projections by Age, Sex, Race, and Hispanic Origin.* Available: http://www.census.gov/ipc/www/usinterimproj/

U.S. Census Bureau. (2004b). Press release, Public Information Office. July 19, 2004.

U.S. Census Bureau News. (2005, August 30). *Income stable, poverty up, numbers of Americans with and without health insurance rise.* Washington, DC: Author.

U.S. Department of Labor. Employment and Training Administration. (2006). *O*NET code connector. Step 2. Understanding the occupational code assignment (OCA) process.* Available: http://www.onetcodeconnector.org/oca/step2

USA snapshots: Young adult priorities. (1998, April 13). *USA Today.*

Vanier Institute of the Family. (1971). *Report of family life education survey: Part 2. Family life education in the schools.* Ottawa, Ontario, Canada: Author.

Vella, J. (1994). *Learning to listen, learning to teach: The power of dialogue in educating adults.* San Francisco: Jossey-Bass.

Vincent, C. E. (1973). *Sexual and marital health.* New York: McGraw-Hill.

Wandersman, L. P. (1987). New directions for parent education. In S. L. Kagan & E. F. Zigler (Eds.), *America's family support programs.* New Haven, CT: Yale University Press.

Weigley, E. S. (1976). The professionalization of home economics. *Home Economics Research Journal, 4*(4), 253–259.

Weiss, H. B., & Jacobs, F. H. (1988). *Evaluating family programs.* New York: Aldine DeGruyter.

Wertheimer, R., & Moore, K. (1998). Childbearing by teens: Links to welfare reform. *New federalism issues and options for states* (Series No. A-24). Washington, DC: The Urban Institute.

Whatley, A. E. (1973). Graduate students' perceptions of needed personal characteristics for family life educators. *The Family Coordinator, 22,* 193–198.

Whitehead, B. D., & Popenoe, D. (2005). *The state of our unions: The social health of marriage in America.* Available: http://marriage.rutgers.edu/Publications

Wigger, J. B. (1998). Entangled in mystery: History and hopes for the Center for Congregations and Family Ministries. *Journal of Family Ministry, 12*(2), 13–28.

Williams, J. (1707). *The redeemed captive returning to Zion.* Boston: The Brick Shop.

Winton, C. A. (1995). *Frameworks for studying families.* Guilford, CT: Dushkin.

Wood, J. T. (1977). Leading in purposive discussions: A study of adaptive behavior. *Communication Monographs, 44,* 152–165.

Working Family Resource Center. (1999). Available: http://www.spps.org/wfrc/wfrc.html

World Health Organization. (2003). *Management of substance abuse fact sheet.* Retrieved March 12, 2006, from http://www.who.int/substance_abuse/en/

World Health Organization. (2004a). *A global overview of the AIDS epidemic.* Retrieved March 11, 2006, from http://www.unaids.org/bangkok2004/GAR2004_html/GAR2004_00_en.htm

World Health Organization. (2004b). *Neuroscience of psychoactive substance use and dependence.* Retrieved March 12, 2006, from http://www.who.int/substance_abuse/publications/alcohol/en/

World Health Organization. (2005a). *AIDS epidemic update: December 2005*. Retrieved March 11, 2006, from http://www.who.int/hiv/pub/epidemiology/epiupdate2005/en/index.html

World Health Organization. (2005b). *WHO multi-country study on women's health and domestic violence against women*. Retrieved March 12, 2006, from http://www.who.int/gender/violence/who_multicountry_study/en/index.html

Yankeelov, P. A., & Garland, D. R. (1998). The families in our congregations: Initial research findings. *Family Ministry, 12*(3), 23–45.

Youcha, G. (1995). *Minding the children: Childcare in America from colonial times to the present.* New York: Scribner.

Ziglar, E. E., & Gilman, E. P. (1990). An agenda for the 1990's: Supporting families. In D. Blankenhorn, S. Bayme, & J. B. Elshtain (Eds.), *Rebuilding the nest: A new commitment to the American family* (pp. 237–250). Milwaukee, WI: Family Service America.

Zimmerman, S. L. (1995). *Understanding family policy: Theories and applications* (2nd ed.). Thousand Oaks, CA: Sage.

Index